MATTHEW, Volume 1

(Chapters 1-7)

THE

TEACHER'S

OUTLINE & STUDY

BIBLE

MATTHEW, Volume 1

(Chapters 1-7)

THE

TEACHER'S

OUTLINE & STUDY

BIBLE

NEW TESTAMENT

KING JAMES VERSION

Leadership Ministries Worldwide
PO Box 21310
Chattanooga, TN 37424-0310

The Teacher's Outline & Study Bible is written for God's people to use both in their personal lives and in their teaching. Leadership Ministries Worldwide wants God's people to use The Teacher's Outline & Study Bible. The purpose of the copyright is to prevent the reproduction, misuse, and abuse of the material.

May our Lord bless us all as we live, preach, teach, and write for Him, fulfilling His great commission to live righteous and godly lives and to make disciples of all nations.

Please address all requests for information or permission to:
Leadership Ministries Worldwide
PO Box 21310
Chattanooga TN 37424-0310
Ph.# (423) 855-2181   FAX (423) 855-8616   E-Mail outlinebible@compuserve.com
http://www.outlinebible.org

Library of Congress Catalog Card Number: 94-073070
International Standard Book Number: 1-57407-058-4

PRINTED IN THE U.S.A.

PUBLISHED BY LEADERSHIP MINISTRIES WORLDWIDE

H O W   T O   U S E

THE TEACHER'S OUTLINE AND STUDY BIBLE (TOSB)

To gain maximum benefit, here is all you do. Follow these easy steps, using the sample outline below.

1 STUDY TITLE

2 MAJOR POINTS

3 SUB-POINTS

4 COMMENTARY, QUESTIONS, APPLICATION, ILLUSTRATIONS
(Follows Scripture)

B. The Steps to Peace (Part II): Prayer & Positive Thinking, 4:6-9

1. **Peace comes through prayer**
   a. The charge: Do not worry or be anxious
   b. The remedy: Prayer
      1) About everything
      2) With requests
      3) With thanksgiving
   c. The promise: Peace
      1) Peace that passes all understanding
      2) Peace that keeps our hearts & minds
2. **Peace comes through positive thinking**
   a. The charge: Think & practice things that are...
      1) True
      2) Honest
      3) Just
      4) Pure

6 Be careful for nothing; but in every thing by prayer and supplication with thanksgiving let your requests be made known unto God.
7 And the peace of God, which passeth all understanding, shall keep your hearts and minds through Christ Jesus.
8 Finally, brethren, whatsoever things are true, whatsoever things are honest, whatsoever things are just, whatsoever things are pure, whatsoever things are lovely, what-

1. First: Read the **Study Title** two or three times so that the subject sinks in.
2. Then: Read the **Study Title** and the **Major Points** (Pts.1,2,3) together quickly. Do this several times and you will quickly grasp the overall subject.
3. Now: Read both the **Major Points** and **Sub-Points**. Do this slower than Step 2. Note how the points are beside the applicable verse, and simply state what the Scripture is saying—in Outline form.
4. Read the **Commentary**. As you read and re-read, pray that the Holy Spirit will bring to your attention exactly what you should study and teach. It's all there, outlined and fully developed, just waiting for you to study and teach.

<u>TEACHERS, PLEASE NOTE</u>:

⇒ Cover the **Scripture** and the **Major Points** with your students. Drive the **Scripture** and **Major Points** into their hearts and minds.

(Please continue on next page)

i

⇒ Cover *only some of the commentary* with your students, not all (unless of course you have plenty of time). Cover only as much commentary as is needed to get the major points across.
⇒ Do NOT feel that you must...
- cover all the commentary under each point
- share every illustration
- ask all the questions

An abundance of commentary is given so you can find just what you need for...
- your own style of teaching
- your own emphasis
- your own class needs

PLEASE NOTE: It is of utmost importance that you (and your study group) grasp the Scripture, the Study Title, and Major Points. It is this that the Holy Spirit will make alive to your heart and that you will more likely remember and use day by day.

<u>MAJOR POINTS</u> include:

APPLICATIONS:
Use these to show how the Scripture applies to everyday life.

ILLUSTRATIONS:
Simply a window that allows enough light in the lesson so a point can be more clearly seen. A suggestion: Do not just "read" through an illustration if the illustration is a story, but learn it and make it your own. Then give the illustration life by communicating it with *excitement & energy*.

QUESTIONS:
These are designed to stimulate thought and discussion.

A CLOSER LOOK:
In some of the studies, you will see a portion boxed in and entitled: "A Closer Look." This discussion will be a closer study on a particular point. It is sometimes too detailed for a Sunday School class session, but more adaptable for personal study or an indepth Bible Study class.

PERSONAL JOURNAL:
At the close of every lesson there is space for you to record brief thoughts regarding the impact of the lesson on your life. As you study through the Bible, you will find these comments invaluable as you look back upon them.

Now, may our wonderful Lord bless you mightily as you study and teach His Holy Word. And may our Lord grant you much fruit: many who will become greater servants and witnesses for Him.

REMEMBER!

The Teacher's Outline & Study Bible is the only study material that actually outlines the Bible verse by verse for you right beside the Scripture. As you accumulate the various books of The Teacher's Outline & Study Bible for your study and teaching, you will have the Bible outlined book by book, passage by passage, and verse by verse.

The outlines alone makes saving every book a must! (Also encourage your students, if you are teaching, to keep their student edition. They also have the unique verse by verse outline of Scripture in their version.)

Just think for a moment. Over the course of your life, you will have your very own personalized commentary of the Bible. No other book besides the Bible will mean as much to you because it will contain your insights, your struggles, your victories, and your recorded moments with the Lord.

> **"Study to show thyself approved unto God, a workman that needeth not to be ashamed, rightly dividing the word of truth" (2 Tim.2:15).**

> **"All scripture is given by inspiration of God, and is profitable for doctrine, for reproof, for correction, for instruction in righteousness: that the man of God may be perfect, throughly furnished unto all good works" (2 Tim.3:16-17).**

*** All direct quotes are followed by a Footnote number. The credit information for each Footnote is listed at the bottom of the page.

MISCELLANEOUS ABBREVIATIONS

&	=	And
Bckgrd.	=	Background
Bc.	=	Because
Circ.	=	Circumstance
Concl.	=	Conclusion
Cp.	=	Compare
Ct.	=	Contrast
Dif.	=	Different
e.g.	=	For example
Et.	=	Eternal
Govt.	=	Government
Id.	=	Identity or Identification
Illust.	=	Illustration
K.	=	Kingdom, K. of God, K. of Heaven
No.	=	Number
N.T.	=	New Testament
O.T.	=	Old Testament
Pt.	=	Point
Quest.	=	Question
Rel.	=	Religion
Resp.	=	Responsibility
Rev.	=	Revelation
Rgt.	=	Righteousness
Thru	=	Through
V.	=	Verse
Vs.	=	Verses

Publisher &
Distributor

DEDICATED:

To all the men and women of the world
who preach and teach the Gospel of our
Lord Jesus Christ
and
To the Mercy and Grace of God.

———————— *&* ————————

• Demonstrated to us in Christ Jesus our Lord.

"In whom we have redemption through His
blood, the forgiveness of sins, according to the
riches of His grace." (Eph. 1:7)

• Out of the mercy and grace of God His Word has
flowed. Let every person know that God will have
mercy upon him, forgiving and using him to fulfill
His glorious plan of salvation.

"For God so loved the world, that he gave his only
begotten Son, that whosoever believeth in him should
not perish, but have everlasting life. For God sent not
his Son into the world to condemn the world; but that
the world through him might be saved." (Jn 3:16-17)

"For this is good and acceptable in the sight of God
our Saviour; who will have all men to be saved, and to
come unto the knowledge of the truth." (I Tim. 2:3-4)

———————— *&* ————————

The Teacher's Outline and Study Bible™
is written for God's people to use
in their study and teaching of God's Holy Word.

LEADERSHIP MINISTRIES WORLDWIDE

OUR FIVEFOLD MISSION & PURPOSE:

- To share the Word of God with the world.
- To help the believer, both minister and layman alike, in his understanding, preaching, and teaching of God's Word.
- To do everything we possibly can to lead men, women, boys, and girls to give their hearts and lives to Jesus Christ and to secure the eternal life which He offers.
- To do all we can to minister to the needy of the world.
- To give Jesus Christ His proper place, the place which the Word gives Him. Therefore — No work of Leadership Ministries Worldwide will ever be personalized.

This material, like similar works, has come from imperfect man and is thus susceptible to human error. We are nevertheless grateful to God for both calling us and empowering us through His Holy Spirit to undertake this task. Because of His goodness and grace, *The Preacher's Outline & Sermon Bible*® - New Testament is complete in 14 volumes as well as the single volume of **The Minister's Handbook**.

God has given the strength and stamina to bring us this far. Our confidence is that, as we keep our eyes on Him and grounded in the undeniable truths of the Word, we will continue working through the Old Testament Volumes and introduce a new series known as *The Teacher's Outline & Study Bible.* Future materials will include CD-ROM, The Believer's *Outline* Bible, and similar *Outline* and **Handbook** materials.

To everyone, everywhere who preaches and teaches the Word, we offer this material firstly to Him in whose name we labor and serve, and for whose glory it has been produced.

Our daily prayer is that each volume will lead thousands, millions, yes even billions, into a better understanding of the Holy Scriptures and a fuller knowledge of Jesus Christ the incarnate Word, of whom the Scriptures so faithfully testify.

As you have purchased this volume, you will be pleased to know that a portion of the price you paid goes to underwrite providing similar volumes at affordable prices in other languages (Russian, Korean, Spanish and others yet to come) to a preacher, pastor, church leader, or Bible student somewhere around the world, who will present God's message with clarity, authority, and understanding beyond their own.
Amen.

- *Equipping God's Servants Worldwide with OUTLINE Bible Materials* -
— LMW is a 501(c)3 nonprofit, international nondenominational mission agency —   8/97

LEADERSHIP MINISTRIES WORLDWIDE

P.O. Box 21310, 515 Airport Road, Suite 107
Chattanooga, TN 37424-0310
(423) 855-2181 FAX (423) 855-87616
E-Mail - outlinebible@compuserve.com
www.outlinebible.org [Free download samples]

ACKNOWLEDGMENTS

Every child of God is precious to the Lord and deeply loved. And every child as a servant of the Lord touches the lives of those who come in contact with him or his ministry. The writing ministry of the following servants have touched this work, and we are grateful that God brought their writings our way. We hereby acknowledge their ministry to us, being fully aware that there are so many others down through the years whose writings have touched our lives and who deserve mention, but the weaknesses of our minds have caused them to fade from memory. May our wonderful Lord continue to bless the ministry of these dear servants, and the ministry of us all as we diligently labor to reach the world for Christ and to meet the desperate needs of those who suffer so much.

THE GREEK SOURCES

1   Expositor's Greek Testament, Edited by W. Robertson Nicoll. Grand Rapids, MI: Eerdmans Publishing Co., 1970

2.   Robertson, A.T. Word Pictures in the New Testament. Nashville, TN: Broadman Press, 1930.

3.   Thayer, Joseph Henry. Greek-English Lexicon of the New Testament. New York: American Book Co.

4.   Vincent, Marvin R. Word Studies in the New Testament. Grand Rapids, MI: Eerdmans Publishing Co., 1969.

5.   Vine, W.E. Expository Dictionary of New Testament Words. Old Tappan, NJ: Fleming H. Revell Co.

6.   Wuest, Kenneth S. Word Studies in the Greek New Testament. Grand Rapids, MI: Eerdmans Publishing Co., 1953.

THE REFERENCE WORKS

7.   Cruden's Complete Concordance of the Old & New Testament. Philadelphia, PA: The John C. Winston Co., 1930.

8.   Josephus' Complete Works. Grand Rapids, MI: Kregel Publications, 1981.

9.   Lockyer, Herbert, Series of Books, including his Books on All the Men, Women, Miracles, and Parables of the Bible. Grand Rapids, MI: Zondervan Publishing House.

10. Nave's Topical Bible. Nashville, TN: The Southewstern Co.

11. The Amplified New Testament. (Scripture Quotations are from the Amplified New Testament, Copyright 1954, 1958, 1987 by the Lockman Foundation. Used by permission.)

12.   The Four Translation New Testament (Including King James, New American Standard, Williams - New Testament In the Language of the People, Beck - New Testament In the Language of Today.) Minneapolis, MN: World Wide Publications.

13.   The New Compact Bible Dictionary, Edited by T. Alton Bryant. Grand Rapids, MI: Zondervan Publishing House, 1967.

14.   The New Thompson Chain Reference Bible. Indianapolis, IN: B.B. Kirkbride Bible Co., 1964,

THE COMMENTARIES

15.   Barclay, William. Daily Study Bible Series. Philadelphia, PA: Westminster Press.

16.   Bruce, F.F. The Epistle to the Colossians. Westwood, NJ: Fleming H. Revell Co., 1968.

17.   Bruce, F.F. Epistle to the Hebrews.Grand Rapids, MI: Eerdmans Publishing Co., 1964.

18.   Bruce, F.F. The Epistles of John. Old Tappan, NJ: Fleming H. Revell Co., 1970.

19.   Criswell, W.A. Expository Sermons on Revelation. Grand Rapids, MI: Zondervan Publishing House, 1962-66.

20.   Greene, Oliver. The Epistles of John. Greenville, SC: The Gospel Hour, Inc., 1966.

21.   Greene, Oliver. The Epistles of Paul the Apostle to the Hebrews. Greenville, SC: The Gospel Hour, Inc., 1965.

22.   Greene, Oliver. The Epistles of Paul the Apostle to Timothy & Titus. Greenville, SC: The Gospel Hour, Inc., 1964.

23.   Greene, Oliver. The Revelation Verse by Verse Study. Greenville, SC: The Gospel Hour, Inc., 1963.

24.   Henry, Matthew. Commentary on the Whole Bible. Old Tappan, NJ: Fleming H. Revell Co.

25.   Hodge, Charles. Exposition on Romans & on Corinthians. Grand Rapids, MI: Eerdmans Publishing Co., 1972-1973.

26.   Ladd, George Eldon. A Commentary On the Revelation of John. Grand Rapids, MI: Eerdmans Publishing Co., 1972-1973.

27.   Leupold, H.C. Exposition of Daniel. Grand Rapids, MI: Baker Book House, 1969.

28. Newell, William R. Hebrews, Verse by Verse. Chicago, IL: Moody Press.

29. Strauss, Lehman. Devotional Studies in Philippians. Neptune, NJ: Loizeaux Brothers.

30. Strauss, Lehman. Colossians & 1 Timothy. Neptune, NJ: Loizeaux Brothers.

31. Strauss, Lehman. The Book of the Revelation. Neptune, NJ: Loizeaux Brothers.

32. The New Testament & Wycliffe Bible Commentary, Edited by Charles F. Pfeiffer & Everett F. Harrison. New York: The Iverson Associates, 1971. Produced for Moody Monthly. Chicago Moody Press, 1962.

33. The Pulpit Commentary, Edited by H.D.M. Spence & Joseph S. Exell. Grand Rapids, MI: Eerdmans Publishing Co., 1950.

34. Thomas, W.H. Griffith. Hebrews, A Devotional Commentary. Grand Rapids, MI: Eerdmans Publishing Co., 1970.

35. Thomas, W.H. Griffith. Studies in Colossians & Philemon. Grand Rapids, MI: Baker Book House, 1973.

36. Tyndale New Testament Commentaries. Grand Rapids, MI: Eerdmans Publishing Co., Began in 1958.

37. Walker, Thomas. Acts of the Apostles. Chicago, IL: Moody Press, 1965.

38. Walvoord, John. The Thessalonian Epistles. Grand Rapids, MI: Zondervan Publishing House, 1973.

OTHER SOURCES

39. Chrnalogar, Mary Alice. Twisted Scriptures. Chattanooga, TN: Control Techniques, Inc., 1997.

40. Colson, Charles. The God of Stones and Spiders. Wheaton, IL: Crossway Books, 1990.

41. Farrar, Steve. Point Man. Portland, OR: Multnomah Press, 1990.

42. Farrar, Steve. Better Homes and Jungles. Portland, OR: Multnomah Press, 1991.

43. Green, Michael P. Illustrations for Biblical Preaching. Grand Rapids, MI: Baker Books, 1996.

44. Grounds, Vernon. Radical Commitment. Cited in Christianity Today. Carol Stream, IL: Christianity Today Inc., Vol. 30, #7.

45. Hendricks, Howard and William. Iron Sharpens Iron. Chicago, IL: Moody Press, 1995.

46. Hodgin, Michael. 1001 Humorous Illustrations for Public Speaking. Grand Rapids, MI: Zondervan, 1994.

47. INFOsearch Sermon Illustrations. Arlington, TX: The Computer Assistant, 1-888-868-9029, 1986-1996.

48. Knight, Walter B. Knight's Treasury of 2000 Illustrations. Grand Rapids, MI: Eerdmans Publishing Company, 1963.

49. Komp, M.D., Diane M. A Child Shall Lead Them. Grand Rapids, MI: Zondervan Publishing, 1993.

50. Larson, Craig B., Editor. Illustrations for Preaching and Teaching. Grand Rapids, MI: Baker Books, 1993.

51. Larson, Craig B.. Contemporary Illustrations for Preachers, Teachers, and Writers. Grand Rapids, MI: Baker Books, 1996.

52. Laurie, Greg. Life. Any Questions? Dallas, TX: Word Publishing, 1995.

53. Leadership Journal. Carol Stream, IL: Christianity Today, Inc.

54. Lucado, Max. A Gentle Thunder. Dallas, TX: Word Publishing, 1995.

55. Lucado, Max. In the Grip of Grace. Dallas, TX: Word Publishing, 1996.

56. Our Daily Bread. Grand Rapids, MI: RBC Ministries.

57. Samra, Cal & Rose. More Holy Humor. Nashville, TN: Thomas Nelson Publishers, 1997.

58. Samra, Cal and Rose. Holy Humor. Mastermedia Limited, 1996. Cited in INFOsearch Sermon Illustrations. Arlington, TX: The Computer Assistant, 1-888-868-9029, 1986-1996.

59. Smalley, Gary & McCartney, Bill. What Makes a Man. Colorado Springs, CO: The Navigators\NavPress, 1992.

60. Stanley, Charles. How to Handle Adversity. Nashville, TN: Oliver Nelson Books, 1989.

61. Strand, Robert. Moments for Pastors. New Leaf Press, 1994.

62. Swindoll, Charles. Improving Your Serve. Dallas, TX: Word Publishing, 1981.

63. Zodhiates, Th.D., Spiros. Illustrations of Bible Truths. Chattanooga, TN: AMG International Inc., 1995.

PUBLISHER & DISTRIBUTOR

Materials Published & Distributed by **LEADERSHIP MINISTRIES WORLDWIDE:**

- *THE PREACHER'S OUTLINE & SERMON BIBLE®* — DELUXE EDITION
  Volume 1 . . . . St. Matthew I (chapters 1-15)   3-Ring, looseleaf binder
  Volume 2 . . . . St. Matthew II (chapters 16-28)
  Volume 3 . . . . St. Mark
  Volume 4 . . . . St. Luke
  Volume 5 . . . . St. John
  Volume 6 . . . . Acts
  Volume 7 . . . . Romans
  Volume 8 . . . . 1, 2 Corinthians (1 volume)
  Volume 9 . . . . Galatians, Ephesians, Philippians, Colossians (1 volume)
  Volume 10 . . . . 1,2 Thessalonians, 1,2 Timothy, Titus, Philemon (1 volume)
  Volume 11 . . . . Hebrews -James (1 volume)
  Volume 12 . . . . 1,2 Peter, 1,2,3 John, Jude (1 volume)
  Volume 13 . . . . Revelation
  Volume 14 . . . . Master Outline & Subject Index
  FULL SET — 14 Volumes

- *THE PREACHER'S OUTLINE & SERMON BIBLE®* — OLD TESTAMENT
  Volume 1 . . . . Genesis I (chapters 1-11)
  Volume 2 . . . . Genesis II (chapters 12-50)
  Volume 3 . . . . Exodus I (chapters 1-18)
  Volume 4 . . . . Exodus II (chapters 19-40)   New volumes release periodically

- *THE PREACHER'S OUTLINE & SERMON BIBLE®* — SOFTBOUND EDITION
  Identical content as Deluxe above. Lightweight, compact, and affordable for overseas & traveling.

- The Minister's Personal Handbook - What the Bible Says...to the Minister
  12 Chapters — 127 Subjects — 400 Verses *OUTLINED* — Standard, Deluxe, 3-ring
  • More than 400 verses from OT and NT dealing with God's minister and servant; all assembled in
  the unique *Outline* style. Features God's Word for His chosen and called servants who minister the Word.

- Translations of N.T. Volumes and Minister's Handbook: <u>Limited Quantities</u>
  Russian — Spanish — Korean • *Future: Portuguese, Hindi, Chinese + others*
  — *Contact us for Specific Language and Prices* —

- THE TEACHER'S OUTLINE & STUDY BIBLE™ • New Testament Books •
  Average 17 lessons/book & 205 pages • Verse-by-Verse Study •• Also: Student Journal Guides

- CD-ROM New Testament - (Windows/STEP) - WORD*Search* 4™

All these great Volumes & Materials are also available at affordable prices in
quantity orders, particularly for overseas ministry, by contacting:

LEADERSHIP MINISTRIES WORLDWIDE   *Your OUTLINE Bookseller*
PO Box 21310
Chattanooga, TN 37424-0310
(423) 855-2181 (8:30 - 5:00 ET) • FAX (423) 855-8616 (24 hrs)
E•Mail - outlinebible@compuserve.com.
       → FREE Download Sample Pages — www.outlinebible.org

• *Equipping God's Servants Worldwide with OUTLINE Bible Materials* •
— LMW is a 501(c)3 nonprofit, international nondenominational mission agency — 8/97

Go ye therefore, and teach all nations

" "   *(Mt. 28:19)*

A SPECIAL NOTE FOR THE BIBLE STUDY LEADER

Dear Teacher:

The teaching material you hold in your hands gives your church the *maximum flexibility* in scheduling for the church year or for any Bible study program. The Teacher's Outline and Study Bible (TOSB) has been designed to help you in your teaching ministry. The wealth of material makes the TOSB the most unique Bible study material anywhere. The name says it all:

⇒ *The Teacher's* has been designed just for you, God's dear servant, the teacher of God's Holy Word.

⇒ *Outline* makes the material unique as every verse has been outlined--point by point--subject by subject--just for you.

⇒ *Study* allows you, the teacher, to study commentary that has been developed and has drawn upon over forty different sources. At your disposal are well thought out points that explain in simple language what the Scripture means. Suggestions for opening and closing each lesson assure that your students will be caught up from the beginning to the end. Practical points of application help you to bring the truth to whatever level of student you are teaching. Gripping illustrations have been interspersed through each lesson, illustrations guaranteed to hold the attention of your students as you drive the point home. Finally, well thought out discussion questions are a part of *every* major point in the lesson. Imagine-- all the benefits of the time spent collecting this study material are right in *your* hands, waiting for you to glean what *you need* for your next lesson.

⇒ *Bible* is the foundation of The Teacher's Outline and Study Bible. God's Holy Word, outlined for you--verse by verse, point by point, subject by subject--gives you, the teacher, the great advantage of having God's Word outlined, explained, made practical, and illustrated.

NOTE: As you have no doubt noticed, this particular book is a large one. Please do not let the size of the book overwhelm you or keep you from teaching the full counsel of God. We offer several different lessons plans to help you teach the Word. If you prefer not to follow a self-paced schedule, please note that the contents of this study (Matthew, Volume One) can be taught according to several different timetables using the following lesson plans:

A ONE QUARTER OR THIRTEEN WEEK LESSON PLAN

A SPECIAL NOTE FOR THE BIBLE STUDY LEADER

The teaching material you have before you gives your church the *maximum flexibility* in scheduling for the church year or for any Bible study program. If you prefer not to follow a self-paced schedule, please note the contents of this study (Matthew, Volume One) can be taught in **thirteen weeks** using the following lesson plan:

QUARTER #1
To Begin Your Exciting Study, Follow These Simple
LESSON PLANS FOR MATTHEW 1:1-7:29
13 weeks

I. THE BIRTH AND CHILDHOOD OF JESUS, THE MESSIAH, 1:1-2:3

WEEK #	LESSON TITLE	SCRIPTURE TEXT	PAGE NUMBER
1	*"Jesus: His Roots and Divine Birth"*	1:1-2:5	15
2	*"Jesus: Exciting Events of His Childhood"*	2:1-23	35
3	*The Preparation for the Messiah's Coming"*	3:1-4:11	50
4	*The Beginning of the Messiah's Ministry"*	4:12-25	78

IV. THE TEACHINGS OF THE MESSIAH TO HIS DISCIPLES:
THE GREAT SERMON ON THE MOUNT, 5:1-7:9

WEEK #	LESSON TITLE	SCRIPTURE TEXT	PAGE NUMBER
5	*"The True Disciple: Who He Is and His Reward (the Beatitudes)"*	5:1-12	100
6	*"The True Disciple: Serving and Being a Light for God"*	5:13-20	123
7	*"The Real Meaning of Personal Responsibility"*	5:21-48	147
8	*"Right Motives of People who are Right with God"*	6:1-6	196
9	*"Prayer and Fasting: The Believer's Essential Needs*	6:7-18	213
10	*"Three Great Warnings to the Believer"*	6:19-7:6	250
11	*"Persevering Prayer and the Golden Rule"*	7:7-14	285
12	*"The Warnings About False Prophets and False Pretenses*	7:15-23	301
13	*"Practical Wisdom for a Modern World"*	7:24-29	319

A TWO QUARTER OR TWENTY-SIX WEEK LESSON PLAN

A SPECIAL NOTE FOR THE BIBLE STUDY LEADER

The teaching material you have before you gives your church the *maximum flexibility* in scheduling for the church year or for any Bible study program. If you prefer not to follow a self-paced schedule, please note the contents of this study (Matthew, Volume One) can be taught in *twenty-six weeks* (six months) using the following lesson plan:

QUARTER #1
To Begin Your Exciting Study, Follow These Simple
LESSON PLANS FOR MATTHEW 1:1-7:29
13 Weeks

I. THE BIRTH AND CHILDHOOD OF JESUS, THE MESSIAH, 1:1-2:3

WEEK #	LESSON TITLE	SCRIPTURE TEXT	PAGE NUMBER
1	*"Jesus: His Roots and Divine Birth"*	1:1-2:5	15
2	*"Jesus: Exciting Events of His Childhood"*	2:1-23	35
3	*The Preparation for the Messiah's Coming: Jesus' Relationship with John the Baptist"*	3:1-17	50
4	*"Jesus' Temptation: Overcoming All"*	4:1-11	66
5	*The Beginning of the Messiah's Ministry"*	4:12-25	78

IV. THE TEACHINGS OF THE MESSIAH TO HIS DISCIPLES: THE GREAT SERMON ON THE MOUNT, 5:1-7:9

WEEK #	LESSON TITLE	SCRIPTURE TEXT	PAGE NUMBER
6	*"The True Disciple: Who He Is and His Reward (the Beatitudes)"*	5:1-12	100
7	*"The True Disciple: Serving and Being a Light for God"*	5:13-20	123
8	*"The Real Meaning of Murder"*	5:21-26	147
9	*"The Real Meaning of Adultery"*	5:27-30	155
10	*"The Real Meaning of Divorce"*	5:31-32	164
11	*"The Real Meaning of Oaths and Swearing"*	5:33-37	172
12	*The Real Meaning of the Law Governing Injury"*	5:38-42	179
13	*The Real Meaning of Human Relationships"*	5:43-48	187

QUARTER #2
LESSON PLANS FOR MATTHEW 1:1-7:29
13 Weeks

IV. THE TEACHINGS OF THE MESSIAH TO HIS DISCIPLES:
THE GREAT SERMON ON THE MOUNT, 5:1-7:9 (continued)

OUTLINE OF MATTHEW, Volume 1

(Chapters 1-7)

THE TEACHER'S OUTLINE & SERMON BIBLE is *unique*. It differs from all other Study Bibles & Sermon Resource Materials in that every Passage and Subject is outlined right beside the Scripture. When you choose any *Subject* below and turn to the reference, you have not only the Scripture, but you discover the Scripture and Subject *already outlined for you--verse by verse*.

For a quick example, choose one of the subjects below and turn over to the Scripture, and you will find this marvelous help for faster, easier, and more accurate use.

A suggestion: For the quickest overview of Matthew, first read *all the major titles* (I, II, III, etc.), then come back and read the sub-titles.

OUTLINE OF MATTHEW, Volume 1

(Chapters 1-7)

THE GOSPEL ACCORDING TO
MATTHEW

INTRODUCTION

AUTHOR: Matthew. The Bible in no place says that Matthew is the author; however, the evidence for Matthew's authorship is strong.

1. Early writers have always credited the Gospel to Matthew. William Barclay quotes one of the earliest church historians, a man named Papias (A.D. 100), as saying, "Matthew collected the sayings of Jesus in the Hebrew tongue" (*The Gospel of Matthew*, Vol.1. "The Daily Study Bible." Philadelphia, PA: The Westminster Press, 1956, p.xxi). Irenaeus (about A.D. 175), the saintly bishop of Lyons, wrote: "Matthew also issued a written Gospel among the Hebrews in their own dialect, while Peter and Paul were preaching at Rome and laying the foundations of the church" (Irenaeus, <u>Against Heresies</u>, 3.1.1).

2. Matthew was qualified to write the Gospel. He had been a tax collector which means that he was involved in large business transactions. A study of the Gospel shows that the author had an interest in figures, large numbers (Mt.18:24; 28:12), and statistics (Mt.1:17). The detailed messages of Jesus point to a man experienced with shorthand which he had apparently used in business transactions. Very little is given in the Scripture about Matthew.
   a. He was one of the twelve apostles (Mk.2:14).
   b. He left all to follow Christ (Lk.5:27-28).
   c. He introduced his friends to Christ by inviting them to a feast which he gave in honor of Christ (Lk.5:29).

DATE: Uncertain. A.D. 50-70. It was written some years after Jesus' ascension, but before A.D. 70.

1. The fall of Jerusalem, A.D. 70, is prophetic (Mt.24:1f).

2. The statements such as "unto this day" (Mt.27:8) and "until this day" (Mt.28:15) suggest a date sometime after Jesus' ascension, but not too far in the distant future.

3. The scattering of the Jerusalem Church due to persecution (Acts 8:4) suggests a date sometime after the ascension. A Gospel would not have been necessary so long as the church and apostles were together.

4. The quote by Irenaeus points to Matthew writing during Nero's reign, "while Paul and Peter were in Rome."

TO WHOM WRITTEN: The Gospel was written originally to the Jews. However, it breathes a message for all, a message proclaiming the Messianic hope of the world for the Great Deliverer.

PURPOSE: To show that Jesus is the Messiah, the Savior and King prophesied by the Hebrew prophets.

Matthew is a strong book, a book written to force belief in Jesus. Matthew sets out to prove that all the prophecies of the O.T. are fulfilled in Jesus, the carpenter from Nazareth. It has one recurring theme: "All this was done, that it might be fulfilled which was spoken by the prophets, saying...." This is repeated approximately sixteen times, and there are ninety-three O.T. quotations.

SPECIAL FEATURES:

1. Matthew is *The Ecclesiastical Gospel*. Down through the centuries, Matthew has been widely used by the church. Its material is arranged primarily by subjects, not by a strict chronological sequence. It is somewhat a topical arrangement of the ministry and teachings of Jesus. As such, it has been extremely useful to the church: as an apology to defend the faith, as a handbook of instructions for new believers, and as a book of worship to read in church services.

2. Matthew is *The Teaching Gospel*. Much of Jesus' teaching is arranged so that it can be easily taught and easily lived. This material is clearly seen in five sections.

    a. The Sermon on the Mount (Mt.5-7).

    b. The Messiah's messengers and their mission (Mt.9-10:42).

    c. The Messiah's parables (Mt.13).

    d. The Messiah's disciples and their behavior toward one another (Mt.18).

    e. The Messiah's prophecy of His return and the end of time: the great Olivet discourse (Mt.24-25).

3. Matthew is *The Royal Gospel* or *The Kingdom Gospel*. The heart of Matthew's Gospel is that Jesus is King. Jesus is the Son of David, the greatest of Israel's kings. He is the fulfillment of the Messianic prophecies that foretold the coming of a King like unto David.

    a. His genealogy shows Him to be David's son by birth (Mt.1:1-17).

    b. He was born King of the Jews (Mt.2:2).

    c. He was called the King of David time and time again (Mt. 9:27; 15:22; 20:30; 21:9, 15; 22:42).

    d. He personally claimed the power of a king by over-riding the law: "I say unto you...." (Mt.5:21-22, 27-28, 31-32, 33-34, 38-39, 43-44).

    e. He dramatically showed Himself to be King by His triumphal entry into Jerusalem (Mt.21:1-11).

    f. He deliberately accepted the title of King before Pilate (Mt.27:11).

    g. His cross bore the title, "King of the Jews" (Mt.27:11).

    h. He claimed the supreme power of the King of Kings, "All power is given unto me" (Mt.28:18).

    i. The word "Kingdom" is used fifty-four times and "Kingdom of Heaven" thirty-two times.

4. Matthew is *The Apocalyptic Gospel*. Among the Gospels, it has the most comprehensive account of the Lord's return and of the end time (Mt.24-25).

5. Matthew is *The Gospel of the Church*. It is the only Synoptic Gospel that mentions the church (Mt.16:13-23; 18:17; cp. Mk.8:27-33; Lk.9:18-22).

6. Matthew is *The Gospel of the Jew*. Matthew never failed to show that Jesus fulfills O.T. prophecy. He makes more than one hundred allusions or quotations from the O.T. He is determined to compel the Jew to believe that Jesus is the Messiah.

MATTHEW

CHAPTER 1

I. THE BIRTH & CHILDHOOD OF JESUS, THE MESSIAH, 1:1-2:23

A. Jesus' Genealogy: Interesting Roots,1:1-17 (cp. Lk. 3:23-28)

1. **It shows Jesus to be the legal heir**
   a. To the throne of David
   b. To the blessings of Abraham
2. **It encourages believers scattered abroad**
3. **It symbolizes God's glorious mercy**
   a. In the Gentile woman, Tamar

   b. In the Gentile woman, Rahab
   c. In the Gentile woman, Ruth

   d. In the sinful woman, Bathsheba

4. **It demonstrates that God's grace is not inherited; it is given as He wills**

The book of the generation of Jesus Christ, the son of David, the son of Abraham.
2 Abraham begat Isaac; and Isaac begat Jacob; and Jacob begat Judas and his brethren;
3 And Judas begat Phares and Zara of Thamar; and Phares begat Esrom; and Esrom begat Aram;
4 And Aram begat Aminadab; and Aminadab begat Naasson; and Naasson begat Salmon;
5 And Salmon begat Booz of Rachab; and Booz begat Obed of Ruth; and Obed begat Jesse;
6 And Jesse begat David the king; and David the king begat Solomon of her that had been the wife of Urias;
7 And Solomon begat Roboam; and Roboam begat Abia; and Abia begat Asa;
8 And Asa begat Josaphat; and Josaphat begat Joram; and Joram begat Ozias;
9 And Ozias begat Joatham; and Joatham begat Achaz; and Achaz begat Ezekias;
10 And Ezekias begat Manasses; and Manasses begat Amon; and Amon begat Josias;
11 And Josias begat Jechonias and his brethren, about the time they were carried away to Babylon:
12 And after they were brought to Babylon, Jechonias begat Salathiel; and Salathiel begat Zorobabel;
13 And Zorobabel begat Abiud; and Abiud begat Eliakim; and Eliakim begat Azor;
14 And Azor begat Sadoc; and Sadoc begat Achim; and Achim begat Eliud;
15 And Eliud begat Eleazar; and Eleazar begat Matthan; and Matthan begat Jacob;
16 And Jacob begat Joseph the husband of Mary, of whom was born Jesus, who is called Christ.
17 So all the generations from Abraham to David are fourteen generations; and from David until the carrying away into Babylon are fourteen generations; and from the carrying away into Babylon unto Christ are fourteen generations.

5. **It emphasizes the power of God to keep His promises**
   a. In delivering His people through terrible times (the Babylonian captivity)

   b. In sending forth the Christ, the Messiah

6. **It symbolizes generations of spiritual history**
   a. Abraham - David: Birth & growth
   b. David - Babylonian captivity: Regression & enslavement
   c. Babylon - Christ: Liberation & triumph

MATTHEW 1:1-17

Section I
THE BIRTH AND CHILDHOOD OF JESUS, THE MESSIAH,
Matthew 1:1-2:23

Study 1: **JESUS' GENEALOGY: INTERESTING ROOTS**

Text: Matthew 1:1-17

Aim: To grasp the great significance of our spiritual roots in Christ.

Memory Verse:
> "How great *are* his signs! and how mighty *are* his wonders! his kingdom *is* an everlasting kingdom, and his dominion *is* from generation to generation" (Dan.4:3).

INTRODUCTION:
What are three of the most significant questions people can ask today?
⇒ "Where did I come from?"
⇒ "Why am I here?"
⇒ "Where am I going?"

All three of these questions address a person's deepest need. The questions have eternal value. Every person needs to know his origin, where he has come from. Every person needs to know why he is here, what his purpose in life is. And every person needs to be concerned with his eternal state.

Matthew begins his book with the first question in mind: "Where did I come from?" He is concerned with facts, facts that add up. He pays close attention to the details of Jesus' genealogy. Matthew invites us to learn several major facts about the roots of Jesus Christ. The genealogy of Jesus Christ is not barren ground for teaching. It yields rich fruit for the person who will seek out Jesus' roots. (See Lk.3:23.)

OUTLINE:
1. Jesus' genealogy shows Jesus to be the legal heir (v.1-2).
2. Jesus' genealogy encourages believers scattered abroad (v.2).
3. Jesus' genealogy symbolizes God's glorious mercy (v.3-6).
4. Jesus' genealogy demonstrates that God's grace is not inherited; it is given as He wills (v.7-10).
5. Jesus' genealogy emphasizes the power of God to keep His promises (v.11-16).
6. Jesus' genealogy symbolizes generations of spiritual history (v.17).

1. JESUS' GENEALOGY SHOWS JESUS TO BE THE LEGAL HEIR (v.1-2).

The genealogy of Jesus Christ shows that Jesus is the legal heir to the throne of David. The genealogy is not given to satisfy man's curiosity about Jesus' roots nor to give His followers a reason to boast in His ancestors. Far from it. Matthew traces the roots of Jesus Christ in order to prove that Jesus Christ is the promised Messiah.

The Messiah was to be the son of Abraham and the son of David; that is, He was to be a descendant of both.

1. God gave to Abraham and his seed (the Messiah) *the promise of blessings* for the whole world (Gen.12:1-3; 22:18.)

2. God gave to David and his seed (the Messiah) *the promise of eternal government* (2 Sam.7:12; Ps.39:3f; 132:11.)

The Jews believed these promises of God. Therefore, Matthew sets out to prove that Jesus "who is called Christ" (Mt.1:16) is the promised son of Abraham and the promised son of David (Mt.1:1).

Note how often Jesus was called the son of David: Mt.12:23; 15:22; 20:30-31; 21:9, 15; Acts 2:29-36; Ro.1:3; 2 Tim.2:8; Rev.22:16. It was the common title and popular concept of the Messiah. Generation after generation of Jews longed and looked for the promised deliverer of Israel. The people expected Him to be a great general who would deliver and restore the nation to its greatness; in fact, they expected Him to make the nation the center of universal rule. He would, under God, conquer the world and center the glory and majesty of God Himself in Jerusalem. From His throne, the throne of David, He would execute "the Messianic fire of judgment" upon the nations and peoples of the world. If Matthew can prove that Jesus' roots go all the way back to David and Abraham, he will have shown how seriously man must take the claims of Jesus to be the Messiah.

APPLICATION 1:
Believers will share in the blessings of Abraham and in the eternal reign promised David.

> "And he [Abraham] received the sign of circumcision, a seal of the righteousness of the faith which he had yet being uncircumcised: that he might be the <u>father of all them that believe</u>, though they be not circumcised; that <u>righteousness</u> might be imputed unto them also" (Ro.4:11).
> "Therefore it is of faith, that it might be by grace; to the end the <u>promise</u> might be sure to all the seed [believers]; not to that only which is of the law, but to that also which is of the faith of Abraham; who is the <u>father of us all</u>" (Ro.4:16).

APPLICATION 2:
"Jesus, who is called Christ" (Mt.1:16) *actually came* through the line of Abraham and David. Everyone must sit up and take the claim seriously. Christ Himself has made the claim of Messiahship. Moreover, Christ has generations of people witnessing to the fact that they have experienced His presence and power as the Messiah. Matthew began the witness, and teeming thousands have followed. If Christ and His followers are telling the truth, then the world is making a fatal mistake in its rejection of Christ.

> "Jesus answered, My kingdom is not of this world: if my kingdom were of this world, then would my servants fight, that I should not be delivered to the Jews: but now is my kingdom not from hence. Pilate therefore said unto him, Art thou a king then? Jesus answered, Thou sayest that I am a king. To this end was I born, and for this cause came I into the world, that I should bear witness unto the truth. Every one that is of the truth heareth my voice" (Jn.18:36-37).

QUESTIONS:
1. What is the importance of being able to trace the roots of Jesus Christ to Abraham and David?
2. Have you ever used the genealogy of Jesus Christ as a witnessing tool? How could you do so?
3. As a believer, where do you fit into the family tree of Jesus Christ? Do you fully appreciate what you have inherited by your position?

2. JESUS' GENEALOGY ENCOURAGES BELIEVERS SCATTERED ABROAD (v.2).

Among Jacob's sons, only Judas was an ancestor of Christ. Why then are his eleven brothers, all the sons of Jacob, listed in the genealogy of Christ given in Genesis Chapter 46? There is probably one main reason. Every Jew knew he had come through the line of Jacob; every Jew was a descendant of one of Jacob's sons. During the time of Matthew's writing, Rome dominated the world. Rome, just like the Babylonians, had scattered the Jews all over the world. Matthew wished to encourage all Jews--encourage them by assuring them that they were descendants of Jacob's sons and as such they had a part in Christ, the true Messiah. They were all in line to receive the promises made to Abraham and his seed and to be gathered back together under the government of David's seed.

APPLICATION:

Believers sometimes feel scattered abroad: all alone, lonely, frustrated, depressed, without purpose, meaning, or significance in life. They feel as if they are in a rut--going no place. They feel God is far away, unapproachable. They wonder why God will not answer and meet their need. Matthew is saying to everyone: every believer is in line to receive the promise of God to Abraham and to David. God *meets* the believer's need in Christ and *will fulfill* His promises in Him.

"Whereby are given unto us exceeding great and precious promises: that by these ye might be partakers of the divine nature, having escaped the corruption that is in the world through lust" (2 Pt.1:4).

QUESTIONS:
1. What effect does...
   * your nationality have upon your salvation?
   * your race have upon your salvation?
   * your denomination have upon your salvation?
   * your economic or social status have upon your salvation?
2. Which of God's promises have meant the most to you personally? Why?
3. Which of God's promises have you failed to experience? Why?

3. JESUS' GENEALOGY SYMBOLIZES GOD'S GLORIOUS MERCY (v.3-6).

It is unusual to find the names of women in genealogies. They are listed in Jesus' lineage as a sign of God's mercy.
1. Tamar was a seducer and adulteress whom God reached (Gen.38:24f).
2. Rahab was a Gentile rejected by the Jews. She was a prostitute who was saved from judgment because she exercised faith in God and in Israel as *God's people* (Josh.2:1f).
3. Ruth was a citizen of a nation hated by the Jews, but she was a woman who chose to become associated with God and His people (Ruth 1f).
4. Bathsheba deliberately sinned with David, but she sought God's forgiveness along with David (2 Samuel Chapters 11-12).

APPLICATION:

There is a beautiful picture in the four women listed in Jesus' ancestry, a beautiful picture of the gospel of Christ: the sins of the women are forgiven and they are accepted by God as His own.

There are no barriers to God's mercy. He will have mercy upon anyone--no matter the sex, nationality, or sin. How marvelous is the mercy of God!

"Among whom [the disobedient] also we all had our conversation [behavior] in times past in the lusts of our flesh, fulfilling the desires of the flesh and of the mind; and were by nature the children of wrath, even as others. But God, who is rich in mercy, for his great love wherewith he loved us, even when we were dead in sins, hath quickened us together with Christ, (by grace ye are saved)" (Eph.2:3-5).

ILLUSTRATION:

The mercy of God never quits, is never depleted. No matter how terrible our sin against God, His mercy can reach down and lift us up into His eternal care.

"Naturalist Loren Eiseley tells a story about the time he was in the seaside town of Costabel. Plagued by insomnia, he spent the early morning hours walking the beach. Each day at sunrise, he found townspeople combing the sand for the starfish that had washed ashore during the night in order to kill them for commercial purposes. Eiseley thought this was a sign, however small, of all the ways the world says 'no' to life.

"One morning, however, Eiseley got up earlier than usual and discovered a solitary figure on the beach. This man, too, was gathering starfish, but each time he found one alive he would pick it up and throw it as far as he could out beyond the breaking surf, back to the nurturing ocean from which it came. As days went by, Eiseley found this man embarked on his mission of mercy each morning, seven days a week, no matter what the weather.

"Eiseley called this man 'the star thrower.' On the beach in Costabel, everything that Eiseley had been taught about evolution and the survival of the fittest was contradicted by one man. For this man, strong as he was, reached down to save the weak. There is a star thrower at work in the universe--a God who contradicts death, a God whose nature is mercy itself."[1]

QUESTIONS:
1. Which one of the following sins will not be forgiven by God:
   _____Leading others into sin?
   _____Adultery?
   _____Prostitution?
   _____Rejecting Jesus Christ?

   Explain your answer.
2. What practical lessons can you draw from the experiences of the four women mentioned in these verses?
3. Think carefully about this question: When does the mercy of God touch a sinner's life:
   _____Only when a person tries to live a good life?
   _____Only when a person does not commit a serious sin?
   _____Only when a person deserves mercy?
   _____Only when a person realizes that judgment is what he really deserves?

   How did you come to your conclusion?

---

[1] *The Carroller*, Mar. 1993, p.3-4. As cited in *INFOsearch Sermon Illustrations* (Arlington, TX: The Computer Assistant, 1-888-868-9029, 1986-1996).

4. JESUS' GENEALOGY DEMONSTRATES THAT GOD'S GRACE IS NOT INHERITED, IT IS GIVEN AS HE WILLS (v.7-10).

There are both good and bad kings in the ancestry of Christ. Just because a king was good did not mean that his goodness was inherited by the next king.
1. The good kings given in vs. 7-8 are:
   ⇒ Solomon (2 Ki.1:1-11:43).
   ⇒ Asa (1 Ki.15:9-24; 2 Chron. Chapters 14-16).
   ⇒ Josaphat (or Jehoshaphat, 2 Chron. Chapters 17-20).
2. The wicked kings are:
   ⇒ Roboam (or Rehoboam, 1 Ki.11:43f).
   ⇒ Abia (or Abijah, 2 Chron.12:16f).
   ⇒ Joram (or Jehoram, 2 Ki.8:21-24; 1 Chron.3:11).

APPLICATION:
   Godliness and righteousness are not inherited. Not a single king was able to pass his nature down to the next king. Every human being stands as an individual before God and is responsible for his own life and behavior (Jn.1:12-13). A person may have godly parents and a godly family, but godliness is not in the genes, is not passed from one person to another physically. A person has to confront Jesus Christ for himself.

   "Bring forth therefore fruits meet for repentance: and think not to say within yourselves, We have Abraham [a godly father] to our father: for I say unto you, that God is able of these stones to raise up children unto Abraham" (Mt.3:8-9).
   "But as many as received him, to them gave he power to become the sons of God, even to them that believe on his name: which were born, not of blood [heritage, godly family], nor of the will of the flesh, nor of the will of man, but of God" (Jn.1:12-13).

QUESTIONS:
1. Why can godliness and righteousness not be inherited? What if someone in your family or one of your best friends is a really strong Christian? Can he help you gain eternal life? Why or why not?
2. What must happen in order for every member of your family and every close friend to become a believer and go to heaven? What have you done personally in order to secure your place in heaven?

5. JESUS' GENEALOGY EMPHASIZES THE POWER OF GOD TO KEEP HIS PROMISES (v.11-16).

God's power is seen in particular events.
1. God's power is seen in His delivering His people through terrible times (for example, the Babylonian captivity). Why is the Babylonian captivity so prominent in the genealogy of Christ (v.11-12, 17)? Matthew wants to stress a great fact. God alone could save a nation of people through so great a trial. The Babylonians took the people of the nations they conquered and scattered them in mass all over the world. By such methods they destroyed the conquered nations. Succeeding generations forgot their identity and loyalty to the old land and attached themselves to their present country. But not so with Israel. Matthew is saying that God preserved the Jews through the impossible: an attempt to stamp them out as a nation. And God did it in order to preserve the line of the Messiah who had now come (cp. Is.45:8-9).

2. God's power is seen in His sending forth the Christ, the Messiah. Note these facts:
⇒ Evil men *could not* prevent God from sending Christ. Men like Pharaoh, Manassah, and Herod were powerless to hinder God's will.
⇒ Climatic world events *could not* stop God from sending Christ. Events like the fall in the garden, the great flood, and the glory of God leaving the Temple failed to stop God from sending Christ.
⇒ Satan and all his demons *could not* thwart God from sending Christ and keeping His sure promise to send the Messiah.

APPLICATION 1:

It is an historical fact that God has preserved the Jewish people through every mad attempt to stamp them out. By such power He has fulfilled His promise to send His Son through the line of Abraham and David. Every person should take note both as a warning and as a hope.

APPLICATION 2:

God preserved the Jews through the Babylonian captivity; He kept His promise to send the Messiah. The believer can rest assured in God's promises and power, for He will fulfill all His promises. The world can be overcome: despair, depression, discouragement, emptiness, loneliness, and lack of purpose can be conquered. There is assured victory in His promises.

> **"There hath no temptation [trial] taken you but such as is common to man: but God is faithful, who will not suffer you to be tempted above that ye are able; but will with the temptation also make a way to escape, that ye may be able to bear it" (1 Cor.10:13).**

APPLICATION 3:

It was centuries between the time of God's promise to send a Savior to the world and His fulfillment of the promise. Many had despaired; others had forsaken the belief. There were some who went so far as to mock and persecute those who still believed. But "when the fulness of the time was come, God sent forth His Son...." (Gal.4:4). There is application here for the second coming of Christ: "There shall come in the last days scoffers...saying, where is the promise of His coming...?" (Cp. 2 Pt.3:3-18.)

A CLOSER LOOK # 1

(1:16) **Jesus' Birth--Son of God**: note the changed expression from "who begat." Jesus was born of Mary but not of Joseph. Joseph was the husband of Mary, but Jesus was not born of Joseph. He was born of the Holy Spirit through Mary.

This stresses a vital fact: Jesus was not born of a man but of the Holy Spirit. He was Divine; yet He was human through His conception in Mary. He was God-Man, fully God--fully man. The real significance of this is that as God, He had the *capacity not to sin*. No other man since Adam has ever had this capacity, for all other men have had a human father and human mother, a father and mother contaminated with a sinful human nature. Therefore, the child of a man is born with the same nature, a nature that *cannot help but sin*. However Jesus Christ, as the only begotten Son of God born by the Holy Spirit, had the capacity to live a perfect and righteous life. He had the capacity never to sin.

Nonetheless, Jesus Christ as man did have the capacity to sin. He suffered the pull and strain and suffering of temptation as all men do. He could have *willed* to sin.

But there is this glorious difference. He utilized the capacity *not* to sin--never once. He learned obedience by the things that He suffered (Heb.5:8). He never gave in to temptation; He never sinned (2 Cor.5:21). Thereby He became the Perfect and Ideal Man in whom all men find their salvation.

---

6. JESUS' GENEALOGY SYMBOLIZES GENERATIONS OF SPIRITUAL HISTORY (v.17).

⇒ The first period of Israel's history can symbolize God giving *birth to Israel through Abraham* and *giving dominion and authority through David.*

⇒ The second period can symbolize Israel *losing its dominion* and being enslaved as a result of God's judgment upon sin.

⇒ The third period of Israel's history can symbolize Israel's *ultimate triumph* through the Messiah and His liberating power.

These historical periods can also symbolize the *spiritual pilgrimage* of any saved man.
   1. Man was born, designed, and purposed to rule as king.

> "And God said, Let us make man in our image, after our likeness: and <u>let them have dominion</u> over the fish of the sea, and over the fowl of the air, and over the cattle, and over all the earth, and over every creeping thing that creepeth upon the earth. So God created man in his own image, in the image of God created he him; male and female created he them" (Gen.1:26-27).
> "Thou madest him to have dominion over the works of thy hands; thou hast put all things under his feet" (Ps.8:6).

   2. Man, however, lost his right to dominion through enslavement to sin and the judgment of God.

> "Unto the woman he said, I will greatly multiply thy sorrow and thy conception; in sorrow thou shalt bring forth children; and thy desire shall be to thy husband, and he shall rule over thee. And unto Adam he said, Because thou hast hearkened unto the voice of thy wife, and hast eaten of the tree, of which I commanded thee, saying, Thou shalt not eat of it: cursed is the ground for thy sake; in sorrow shalt thou eat of it all the days of thy life; thorns also and thistles shall it bring forth to thee; and thou shalt eat the herb of the field; in the sweat of thy face shalt thou eat bread, till thou return unto the ground; for out of it wast thou taken: for dust thou art, and unto dust shalt thou return" (Gen.3:16-19).

   3. Man can now be liberated and restored to fulfill his original purpose through Jesus Christ, the Messiah.

"For God so loved the world, that he gave his only begotten Son, that whosoever believeth in him should not perish, but have everlasting life" (Jn.3:16).

ILLUSTRATION:

Every person is on a journey. Some are further along than others, but everyone is on the path of life with either heaven or hell as the eventual destination. Spiritual success is determined by how a person *finishes* the journey.

"A rehabilitation counselor took early retirement to spend the rest of his life preaching the gospel. Early in his career he found a young boy with several birth defects. He arranged financial and medical help. Skilled surgeons restored the child's facial appearance. Trained therapists taught him to speak and walk. By his teens, the boy was able to take part in all the activities of other young people.

"'What do you think has become of this young man?' the counselor asked. One guessed he was a great athlete; another, a skilled surgeon. 'No, none of these,' the retired counselor said sadly. 'The young man is a prisoner, serving a life sentence for murder. We were able to restore his physical features and his ability to walk and act, but we failed to teach him where to walk and how to act, I was successful in helping the boy physically, but I failed to help him spiritually.'"[2]

Has there been restoration in your life? Has it been external only--just physical changes? Or has God changed your heart?

QUESTIONS:

1. Where are you on your spiritual pilgrimage? Have you trusted Christ to save you?
2. How will history record your life; how will you be remembered? What will linger most in people's minds:
   - your physical characteristics?
   - your generosity?
   - your selfishness?
   - your bad attitude?
   - your spiritual strength?
   - your attitude of thankfulness?

SUMMARY:

The most important part of any story is the beginning. A careful study of our historical roots allows us to gain a better understanding of both the truth and relevance of modern-day Christian faith. Unlike mythical religious characters who have no historical record, Matthew gives the Christian believer a firm foundation on which to stand.

Knowing the origin of your faith is important to understanding where you are and where you need to go. As you look back over your life, are you a part of Jesus' genealogy? The person who is saved by Christ will understand the genealogy of Christ in a brand new way. Jesus' genealogy shows six different things:

1. It shows Jesus to be the legal heir.
2. It encourages believers scattered abroad.
3. It symbolizes God's glorious mercy.
4. It demonstrates that God's grace is not inherited; it is given as He wills.
5. It emphasizes the power of God to keep His promises.
6. It symbolizes generations of spiritual history.

---

[2] Ted Kyle & John Todd. *A Treasury of Bible Illustrations*. (Chattanooga, TN: AMG Publishers, 1995), p.124.

MATTHEW 1:1-17

PERSONAL JOURNAL NOTES:
(Reflection & Response)

1. The most important thing that I learned from this lesson was:

2. The thing that I need to work on the most is:

3. I can apply this lesson to my life by:

4. Closing Prayer of Commitment: (put your commitment down on paper).

	B. Jesus' Divine Birth: Unusual Events, 1:18-25 (Lk.1:26-28; 2:1-7)		
1. Jesus' birth was of the Spirit	18 Now the birth of Jesus Christ was on this wise: When as his mother Mary was espoused to Joseph, before they came together, she was found with child of the Holy Ghost.	ceived in her is of the Holy Ghost. 21 And she shall bring forth a son, and thou shalt call his name JESUS: for he shall save his people from their sins.	child is of the Spirit
2. Jesus' birth created a predicament			d. To reveal the child's destiny
a. Joseph's predicament: Mary was pregnant before marriage			1) His name: Jesus
			2) His mission: To save
b. Joseph's character & solution	19 Then Joseph her husband, being a just man, and not willing to make her a public example, was minded to put her away privily.	22 Now all this was done, that it might be fulfilled which was spoken of the Lord by the prophet, saying,	**4. Jesus' birth was a fulfillment of prophecy**
1) His character: A just man			
2) His solution: Not to expose Mary		23 Behold, a virgin shall be with child, and shall bring forth a son, and they shall call his name Emmanuel, which being interpreted is, God with us.	a. Predicting His virgin birth
3. Jesus' birth necessitated a special revelation to Joseph	20 But while he thought on these things, behold, the angel of the Lord appeared unto him in a dream, saying, Joseph, thou son of David, fear not to take unto thee Mary thy wife: for that which is con-	24 Then Joseph being raised from sleep did as the angel of the Lord had bidden him, and took unto him his wife:	b. Predicting His name: Emmanuel
a. To give assurance			**5. Jesus' birth brought about a great obedience**
1) He was chosen			
2) He was not to fear		25 And knew her not till she had brought forth her firstborn son: and he called his name JESUS.	
b. To guide: In taking Mary to be his wife			
c. To explain: The			

Section I
THE BIRTH AND CHILDHOOD OF JESUS, THE MESSIAH,
Matthew 1:1-2:23

Study 2:   JESUS' DIVINE BIRTH: UNUSUAL EVENTS

Text: Matthew 1:18-25

Aim: To understand in a fresh way the events that surrounded the birth of Christ.

Memory Verse:
> **"And she shall bring forth a son, and thou shalt call his name JESUS: for he shall save his people from their sins" (Matthew 1:21).**

INTRODUCTION:
When you think of the Christmas story, what is the first image that comes to your mind? For the more secular minded person, Christmas is a time for spending a lot of money on gifts that are quickly opened and sometimes just as quickly discarded or exchanged. For many people, Christmas is an excuse to take a vacation from work, to travel, to visit family, to party with friends. All of these examples can be part of the experience of Christmas, an experience that is celebrated over much of the world. But if this is all that is experienced, when

the music and the festivities of the season fade away, the only thing left is an empty feeling that never goes away. For the Christian believer, the story of Christmas should conjure up images of...
- a young couple trying to find a room in the inn
- a bright star and a host of angels singing
- a baby lying in a manger, surrounded by shepherds and livestock
- a magnificent promise fulfilled in the birth of Christ

The key to experiencing a truly joyful and meaningful Christmas is to focus in on what is really important. As a person studies about the birth of Christ, he will be struck with the perception that God worked in some very unusual ways. The coming of God's Son into the world was one of the most phenomenal events in all of history. It necessitated and caused some very unusual events.

OUTLINE:
1. Jesus' birth was of the Spirit (v.18).
2. Jesus' birth created a predicament (v.18-19).
3. Jesus' birth necessitated a special revelation to Joseph (v.20-21).
4. Jesus' birth was a fulfillment of prophecy (v.22-23).
5. Jesus' birth brought about a great obedience (v.24-25).

1. JESUS' BIRTH WAS OF THE SPIRIT (v.18).

Never before had a man been born "of the Holy Spirit," but Jesus was. A person either accepts the evidence of Scripture at this point or rejects it. The Scripture is clear in what it says: "Before they came together, she [Mary] was found with child of the Holy Spirit." It is a matter of faith and trust in the *God of love*
⇒ who is revealed in Scripture as caring for man with an eternal and perfect love
⇒ who set out to save man from his sins (v.21)
⇒ who caused the greatest event of human history: *God becoming one with man—"God with us"* (v.23)

QUESTIONS:
1. Why did Jesus Christ have to be born of the Spirit?
2. How would you explain this phenomenon to an unbeliever?

A CLOSER LOOK # 1
(1:18-25) **Jesus Christ, Birth**: Jesus' birth was one of the most convulsive and disturbing events in all history (cp. Lk.2:1-24).
1. There was Mary's pregnancy and the idea of her being an unwed mother (Mt.1:18; Lk.1:26f). Who of that day would ever believe her story? Required was a willingness to be available to God regardless of embarrassment and the opinions of family, friends, and neighbors.
2. There was Joseph's discovery of Mary's pregnancy (Mt.1:19). The shock of Mary's apparent broken trust and of personal embarrassment were more than Joseph could bear (Mt.1:20). Required was a willingness to forget self completely.
3. There was the child, the Son of God Himself, being born in a smelly manger (Mt.1:25; Lk.2:1f). Required was a willingness to be humble.
4. There was the family having to be uprooted and moved to a foreign nation, Egypt (Mt.2:13f). Required was a willingness to obey at any cost.
5. There was the slaughter of all children under two years of age (Mt.2:16f). The heavy weight of feeling some responsibility was bound to attack Joseph and Mary. Required was a willingness on their part to bear anything.

6. There was the visit of the wise men showing that the foreign relationships of nations were affected (Mt.2:1f). Required was a willingness to bear the pressure of responsibility and the demands of being in the limelight.

7. There was the uproar of Herod's household traumatically affecting the lives of both Joseph and Mary (Mt.2:7-8, 15-16, 22). Required was a willingness to stand against all odds.

QUESTIONS:

1. The life experiences of people cut across time and culture. How would you handle it if someone close to you...
   • became an unwed mother?
   • *appeared* to have betrayed your trust?
   • did not have the best housing accommodations?
   • had to move because of the threat of death?
   • had to bear the weight of tremendous emotional and mental stress?
   • had to stand up to the immoral acts of an evil leader?
2. How supportive would you be under any of the above circumstances? Could you be counted on?

A CLOSER LOOK # 2

(1:18) **Christ—Messiah**: the word for "Christ" and "Messiah" is the same word: *christos*. Messiah is the Hebrew word and Christ is the Greek word. Both words refer to the same Person and mean the same thing: *the Anointed One*. The Messiah is *the Anointed One* of God. Matthew says that Jesus "is called Christ" (Mt.1:16); that is, He is recognized as *the Anointed One* of God, the Messiah Himself.

In the day of Jesus Christ, people feverishly panted for the coming of the long promised Messiah. The weight of life was harsh, hard, and impoverished. Under the Romans, people felt that God could not wait much longer to fulfill His promise. Such longings for deliverance left the people gullible. Many arose who claimed to be the Messiah and led the gullible followers into rebellion against the Roman State. The insurrectionist, Barabbas, who was set free in the place of Jesus at Jesus' trial, is an example (Mk. 15:6f).

The Messiah was thought to be several things:

1. Nationally, He was to be the leader from David's line who would free the Jewish state and establish it as an independent nation, leading it to be the greatest nation the world had ever known.

2. Militarily, He was to be a great military leader who would lead Jewish armies victoriously over all the world.

3. Religiously, He was to be a supernatural figure straight from God who would bring righteousness over all the earth.

4. Personally, He was to be the One who would bring peace to the whole world.

Jesus Christ accepted the title of Messiah on three different occasions (Mt.16:17; Mk.14:61; Jn.4:26). The name *Jesus* shows Him to be man. The name *Christ* shows Him to be God's anointed, God's very own Son. *Christ* is Jesus' official title. It identifies Him officially as:

⇒ Prophet (Dt.18:15-19. See Lk.3:38 for fulfillment.)
⇒ Priest (Ps.110:4. See Lk.3:32-38 for fulfillment.)
⇒ King (2 Sam.7:12-13. See Lk.3:24-31 for fulfillment.)

These officials were always anointed with oil, a symbol of the Holy Spirit who was to perfectly anoint the Christ, the Messiah (Mt.3:16; Mk.1:10-11; Lk.3:21-22; Jn.1:32-33).

2. JESUS' BIRTH CREATED A PREDICAMENT (v.18-19).

Joseph faced the predicament of his life. The words "a just man and not willing to make her a public example" show a deeply troubled spirit. Joseph was literally torn between obeying the law (exposing Mary to the authorities, for the law said that a betrothed virgin who committed adultery was to be stoned to death [Dt.22:23-24]) and his love for her. He was perplexed and disappointed, struggling to keep his imagination from running wild. He felt deceived, experiencing jealousy and rage. He thought Mary had committed whoredom against him. Yet he cared for her and loved her deeply. He did not want Mary to be hurt. He wanted to divorce her quietly and secretly. But note: there were three steps involved in a Jewish marriage. (1) The engagement: the parents usually determined who a child was to marry—often at a very early age. (2) The betrothal: at a determined time the couple agreed or disagreed with the engagement. If they followed through, the betrothal was immediately binding. A legal divorce was thereafter required. The betrothal lasted one year. When Joseph discovered Mary's pregnancy, they were already betrothed to one another. (3) The marriage: the consummation of the couple took place. It should be noted that in Joseph's case consummation did not occur until after Jesus' birth.

APPLICATION 1:

Jesus' birth creates a predicament for every man. Imagine the emotions and the hurt Joseph felt when he discovered Mary, his fiancee, was pregnant. Imagine the thoughts that must have flooded his mind! What a predicament Jesus' birth created for Joseph! He had to make a decision whether to accept or reject Mary's claim and the claims of the angel about Christ. Jesus' birth also creates a predicament for every man in that every man is now forced to make a decision about Christ and *His claims*.

APPLICATION 2:

There is no room for gossip and censorious judgment among God's people. In Joseph's mind, Mary's sin was great: he felt she had committed whoredom against him. Yet he cared and truly loved her. It was just this love that helped him in his treatment of her: "Love shall cover a multitude of sins" (1 Pt.4:8). A person who truly loves will not be critical, judgmental, or censorious. The person who loves will not talk, gossip, or criticize. He will get alone with God and pray about the problem—just as Joseph did.

"Judge not, that ye be not judged. For with what judgment ye judge, ye shall be judged: and with what measure ye mete, it shall be measured to you again. And why beholdest thou the mote that is in thy brother's eye, but considerest not the beam that is in thine own eye? Or how wilt thou say to thy brother, let me pull out the mote out of thine eye; and behold, a beam is in thine own eye?" (Mt.7:1-4).

"Brethren, if a man be overtaken in a fault, ye which are spiritual, restore such an one in the spirit of meekness; considering thyself, lest thou also be tempted" (Gal.6:1).

APPLICATION 3:

Believers are not to be unequally yoked together. Joseph was a just man; Mary was a virtuous woman. Both were godly. Believers should be careful in selecting their companions for marriage:

"Be not unequally yoked together with unbelievers" (2 Cor.6:14).

There is real wisdom in taking time to confirm one's decision to marry. It is much better to delay and be sure than to rush and be sorry. It gives God time to melt and mold the couple into one being spiritually—much more time than in a quick marriage.

It also allows more time for a couple to grow together before being married. Having spent time growing together (not *living* together) prevents a multitude of heartaches and much pain.

QUESTIONS:
1. Joseph had to face some very serious circumstances. What were his choices? What lessons can you apply to your own life?
2. What advice would you give a couple who were planning a rushed marriage?
3. What are some practical advantages for a believer not to be yoked to an unbeliever? What are the pitfalls of such a relationship?
4. How would society be different if the law regarding adultery were enforced today (for both men and women)?
5. What was Jesus' response to the woman who committed adultery (see John 8:1-11)? How was this different from the custom of His culture? In what way can you apply His response to your own dealings with people who are trapped in a sinful lifestyle?

3. JESUS' BIRTH NECESSITATED A SPECIAL REVELATION TO JOSEPH (v.20-21).

Note the words, "while he thought on these things." Joseph did just what he should have done: he got alone with God to think and pray through the predicament. Because of his godly dependence and obedience, God met his need. God gave Joseph a special revelation. God's purpose was fourfold.

1. To give assurance to Joseph. When the angel called Joseph "Thou son of David," Joseph was shocked. He was awakened to a glorious call. He was chosen by God as a son of David to be the earthly father to "The Son of David," the Messiah! All Jews knew the prophecies that said the Messiah was to be of the line of David. Joseph knew them; but to hear himself addressed as "Joseph, thou son of David" quickened his attention and alerted him to an extremely important message. It indicated to some degree a divine call. Remember: Joseph was only a humble carpenter.

There is a right way to confront traumatic experiences. Joseph demonstrated the right way. He got alone and "thought on these things" (v.20). Being a just and godly man, he got alone with God; he shared his thoughts with God. He probably wept as a child pouring out his soul to God.

2. To guide Joseph.
3. To explain the predicament.
4. To reveal the destiny of the promised child (see A Closer Look #3—Mt.1:21).

APPLICATION 1:
The believer who gets alone with God and thinks through the trials confronting him will be met by God. He may weep when facing terrible trials, but God will give assurance and guide the believer (Mt.6:33; Ph.4:6-7; Jn.16:13; Ro.8:13; Heb.13:5).

> **"For we have not an high priest which cannot be touched with the feeling of our infirmities; but was in all points tempted like as we are, yet without sin. Let us therefore come boldly unto the throne of grace, that we may obtain mercy, and find grace to help in time of need" (Heb.4:15-16).**

ILLUSTRATION:
When a believer faces a difficult trial, the last thing he needs is a trite expression or a superficial cliché. What he needs are honest words and comforting thoughts that turn his heart toward God.

Ginger's husband committed suicide. Shock...disbelief...anger...sorrow... and unanswered questions--all swelled up within her heart. Chip was the last person you could imagine who would take his life. He had so much to live for--a loving wife, three precious children, and a fellowship of trusted friends. In a moment of deception, Chip surrendered to the enemy and threw his life away. The first night was the hardest night for Ginger. It would have been even more difficult were it not for a dear Christian friend, Christy. Christy put her faith in motion and made it a point to be there for her newly-widowed friend. God did not give Christy any profound words. God did not give her all the answers to the hard questions of life. What God did give Christy was the gift to be the hands of Christ, hands that held Ginger tenderly. God gave Christy the mind of Christ, a mind that felt the deep hurt inside Ginger's broken heart. What God gave to Ginger was a friend, a friend who directed her to the love and care of Christ.

That first night was a night of many tears as Ginger poured out her heart to God. The tears that night were a mixture of sorrow and grief, but also of hope and peace. They were the tears of a saint who trusts in God--even when the way is hard.

When you are faced with tragedy, to whom can you turn for assurance?

APPLICATION 2:

The vast majority of persons called by God are from humble stations in life--including Joseph and Christ. But a person is to say "yes" to God's call regardless of his station in life. When Joseph received the call of God, he accepted and was obedient. But most men reject God's call.

> **"Many are called, but few are chosen" (Mt.20:16).**
> **"For ye see your calling, brethren, how that not many wise men after the flesh, not many mighty, not many noble, are called...."**
> **(1 Cor.1:26-27).**

APPLICATION 3:

The baby's name was *Jesus*. God chose His name and instructed that He be called by that name. Every person should know and call upon the name "Jesus." Jesus' mission was to save. God gave Him His mission, His purpose for living. God will give a mission, a purpose for living, to every person who looks to God as Jesus looked.

> **"Even as the Son of man came not to be ministered unto, but to minister, and to give his life a ransom for many" (Mt.20:28).**
> **"For the Son of man is come to seek and to save that which was lost" (Lk.19:10).**

QUESTIONS:

1. When is the last time you needed a special revelation from God?
2. What lessons can you glean from Joseph's example?
3. What has God promised the believer who gets alone with Him?

A CLOSER LOOK # 3

(1:21) **Salvation—Jesus Christ, Mission**: Savior; He will save. The Hebrew form is *Joshua*, meaning Jehovah is salvation; He is the Savior. The idea is that of deliverance, of being saved from some terrible disaster that leads to perishing (cp. Jn.3:16; Ro.8:3; Gal.1:4; Heb.2:14-18; 7:25.)

The statement "He shall save his people from their sins" is full of meaning. (See Acts 2:37-40.)

1. The word *save* or *salvation* means to deliver. It is Jesus Christ, the promised Messiah, who saves.
2. The words "His people" are significant. It infers that all people are not "His people."

> **"Ye believe not, because ye are not of my sheep...My sheep hear my voice, and I know them, and they follow me: and I give unto them eternal life; and they shall never perish, neither shall any man [Greek: anyone, any being] pluck them out of my hand" (Jn.10:26-27).**

3. The words "from their sins" mean that Christ saves His people from:
   ⇒ the power of sin
   ⇒ the bondage of sin
   ⇒ the guilt of sin
   ⇒ the consequences of sin. (See Gal.1:4-5; 4:4-7; Heb.2:14-18; 7:25; Tit.2:14.)

Note Rev.14:4 where Christ is said to redeem believers "from among men [worldly men]." Note also Heb.7:26 where Christ is said to be "separate from sinners." The believer is called to separation: to live away from, above and over sin; to conquer sin; to live victoriously over sin. (Cp. 2 Cor.6:17-18; Ro.12:2; 1 Jn.2:15-16.)

ILLUSTRATION:
What does it really mean to be "saved from sin"? The believer who has trusted the shed blood of Christ can rest in the assurance that nothing can undo what Christ has done on the Cross.

> *"The great English preacher Charles Haddon Spurgeon told of a man who had been sentenced to death by a Spanish court. Because he was an American citizen and also of English birth, the consuls of both countries decided to intervene. They declared that the authorities of Spain had no right to take his life, but their protests went unheeded. Finally, they deliberately wrapped the prisoner in their flags--the Stars and Stripes and the Union Jack. Defying the executioner, they issued this warning: 'Fire if you dare! But if you do, you will bring the powers of two great nations upon you!' There stood the condemned. But the rifleman would not shoot. Protected by those flags and the governments they represented, the man was invulnerable [safe and secure]."*[1]

Even as Satan throws his fiery darts, are you protected by the blood of Christ?

QUESTIONS:
1. What has Jesus delivered you from this past week?
2. What has Jesus saved you from that was impossible for man to do?
3. Are you sure, absolutely sure, that you are saved? If not, what must you do to make it happen?

4. JESUS' BIRTH WAS A FULFILLMENT OF PROPHECY (v.22-23).

The basic elements of prophecy are threefold: (1) Prophecy is "the Word of the Lord." It is not the word of men. The future is revealed by God not by men. (2) The prophet is only a messenger—not the spokesman. (3) Prophecy must be fulfilled. It will always come to pass.

Matthew stresses two prophecies in particular. There was the prophecy predicting Jesus' virgin birth. There was the prophecy predicting His name: Emmanuel. The word

---

[1] *INFOsearch Sermon Illustrations* (Arlington, TX: The Computer Assistant, 1-888-868-9029, 1986-1996).

"Emmanuel" is not a name or a title. It is a descriptive term. It characterizes a person. Jesus is Emmanuel: God with us, God revealed in human flesh (cp. Is.1:26; 9:6; Jn.1:1, 14; 2 Cor.5:19; 1 Jn.1:2).

Notice four convincing things about the virgin birth of Christ.

1. Note the concern and great pains to which Matthew went in pointing out the supernatural birth of Jesus. He said very pointedly, "Now the birth of Jesus <u>Christ</u> [not just Jesus, but Jesus Christ, the Messiah] happened like this."

    a. "Mary...was found with child <u>of the Holy Ghost</u>" (v.18).
    b. "That which is conceived in her is <u>of the Holy Ghost</u>" (v.20).
    c. "Now all this was done, that it might be fulfilled....Behold, <u>a virgin</u>...shall bring forth a son" (v.22-23).
    d. "They shall call His name, Emmanuel...<u>God with us</u>" (v.23).

Matthew was not interested in giving a detailed account of Jesus' birth. His concern was simply to draw the reader's attention to two important facts.

   ⇒ The Old Testament prophecies of the Messiah's birth were fulfilled in Jesus Christ.

> **"For unto us a child is born, unto us a son is given: and the government shall be upon his shoulder: and his name shall be called Wonderful, Counselor, The mighty God, The everlasting Father, The Prince of Peace" (Is.9:6).**

   ⇒ The Jews needed to know that Jesus Christ was born of a virgin, especially those who misinterpreted the Old Testament prophecies and who were not expecting the Messiah to be virgin born. One of the slanderous reports facing the early Christian believers was that Jesus was born out of wedlock.

> **"Therefore the Lord himself shall give you a sign; Behold, a <u>virgin</u> shall conceive, and bear a son, and shall call his name Immanuel" (Is.7:14).**

2. Note the simple profession of Mary that shows shock and amazement: "How shall this be, seeing I know not a man?" (Lk.1:34).

3. Note the mystery of life about which man knows so little.

> **"Thou hast possessed my reins: Thou hast covered me in my mother's womb. I will praise thee; for I am fearfully and wonderfully made: marvelous are thy works...when I was made in secret, and curiously wrought" (Ps.139:13-15).**

4. Note the mystery of godliness.

> **"Without controversy [undoubtedly, it must be admitted] great is the mystery of godliness: God was manifest in the flesh" (1 Tim.3:16; cp. Gal.4:4; 1 Jn.1:1-3; Jn.1:14).**

<u>QUESTIONS:</u>
1. What makes prophecy different from the words of men?
2. How does prophecy prove the claims of Jesus Christ?
3. Why is the virgin birth of Jesus Christ such an important doctrine for the believer to claim?
4. When are you most aware of *God being with you*? Is this something you have control over? If so, should you be aware of it more often than you are?

5. JESUS' BIRTH BROUGHT ABOUT A GREAT OBEDIENCE (v.24-25).

Very simply, Joseph obeyed God. Despite the predicament—despite the appearance of things—Joseph obeyed. He did exactly what God said. Imagine how difficult it must have been! Mary was pregnant, yet they were not married. How much gossip was there? What did the neighbors think? What did Joseph and Mary tell them? Would people believe the story of angels and of a virgin birth from two people whom they knew so well? What a situation! Yet, Joseph did exactly as God said—despite all. What a lesson for great obedience on the part of every believer!

> "He that hath my commandments, and keepeth them, he it is that loveth me: and he that loveth me shall be loved of my Father, and I will love him, and will manifest myself to him" (Jn.14:21).
> "Though he were a Son, yet learned he obedience by the things which he suffered" (Heb.5:8).

APPLICATION:
Joseph acted as God would have every man to act.
1) He was merciful, gentle, and tender toward one whom he perceived had hurt him so much.
2) He forgave as one who had been forgiven. He had the attitude that is needed by believers when a loved one or a fellow believer is found in sin.

> "Brethren, if a man be overtaken in a fault, ye which are spiritual, restore such an one in the spirit of meekness; considering thyself, lest thou also be tempted" (Gal.6:1).

QUESTIONS:
1. Joseph obeyed God perfectly. What practical lesson can you learn from his example of obedience?
2. Obedience is necessary for the believer, even when we have been hurt or offended. Whom do you need to forgive in order to be obedient to Christ?

SUMMARY:

What images come to your mind when you think about the Christmas story? The greatest event in history took place when God sent His Son into the world. What took God so long? Why did Christ not come any sooner? The great Italian painter Leonardo da Vinci helps us see the answer to these questions a little more clearly:

> "Frank Zimmerman says that while Leonardo da Vinci was painting 'The Last Supper' on the wall of a monastery in Milan, Italy, 'the monks began to have many questions about his ability and his integrity.'
> "The picture was merely a copy of the dining hall in which it was being painted. The table, the linen, even the dishes used by the monks were all identical to those in the picture. Some of the monks thought da Vinci was taking advantage of his contract to paint this picture. They were resentful of da Vinci's long periods of inactivity, when he would stand for hours without touching his brush to the wall in front of him.
> "When they asked the painter about this apparent inactivity, he replied, 'After I pause the longest, I make my most telling strokes with my brush.'
> "No other event in the life of our Lord has been painted more often, but none can match the one painted by da Vinci nearly 500 years ago. In like manner, God paused, the world waited, 'but when the fullness of time was come, God sent forth His Son' (Gal. 4:4).

MATTHEW 1:18-25

"Christmas is the season when the world remembers the day when, after God had delayed and man had waited so long, that He accomplished His most wonderful work for mankind."[2]

1. Jesus' birth was of the Spirit.
2. Jesus' birth created a predicament.
3. Jesus' birth necessitated a special revelation to Joseph.
4. Jesus' birth was a fulfillment of prophecy.
5. Jesus' birth wrought a great obedience.

PERSONAL JOURNAL NOTES:
(Reflection & Response)

1. The most important thing that I learned from this lesson was:

2. The thing that I need to work on the most is:

3. I can apply this lesson to my life by:

4. Closing Prayer of Commitment: (put your commitment down on paper).

---

[2] *Pulpit Helps*, Dec. 1992, p.8. As cited in *INFOsearch Sermon Illustrations* (Arlington, TX: The Computer Assistant, 1-888-868-9029, 1986-1996).

CHAPTER 2

C. Jesus' Acknowledgment as King by Wise Men: An Unexpected Worship, 2:1-11

1. Jesus was born in Bethlehem
  a. In the days of Herod
  b. Wise men came seeking Him

2. Their unexpected question: Where is the newborn King?
  a. The unusual journey
  b. Their purpose: Worship

3. Their unexpected disturbance
  a. Disturbed all the people in Jerusalem
  b. Disturbed Herod: He misconceived a threat
  c. Disturbed the religionists
    1) Herod quizzed them
    2) They had ignored the Scripture (until now)

Now when Jesus was born in Bethlehem of Judaea in the days of Herod the king, behold, there came wise men from the east to Jerusalem,

2 Saying, Where is he that is born King of the Jews? for we have seen his star in the east, and are come to worship him.

3 When Herod the king had heard these things, he was troubled, and all Jerusalem with him.

4 And when he had gathered all the chief priests and scribes of the people together, he demanded of them where Christ should be born.

5 And they said unto him, in Bethlehem of Judaea: for thus it is written by the prophet,

6 And thou Bethlehem, in the land of Juda, art not the least among the princes of Juda: for out of thee shall come a Governor, that shall rule my people Israel.

7 Then Herod, when he had privily called the wise men, enquired of them diligently what time the star appeared.

8 And he sent them to Bethlehem, and said, Go and search diligently for the young child; and when ye have found him, bring me word again, that I may come and worship him also.

9 When they had heard the king, they departed; and, lo, the star, which they saw in the east, went before them, till it came and stood over where the young child was.

10 When they saw the star, they rejoiced with exceeding great joy.

11 And when they were come into the house, they saw the young child with Mary his mother, and fell down, and worshipped him: and when they had opened their treasures, they presented unto him gifts; gold, and frankincense, and myrrh.

4. Their unexpected commission: Having to search for the newborn King
  a. Their testimony: The star
  b. Their commission: To go, search, find

5. Their unexpected sign: The star guided them again

6. Their unexpected King: A humble child in humble surroundings
  a. They found Him in a house
  b. They gave Him worship
  c. They gave Him gifts

Section I
THE BIRTH AND CHILDHOOD OF JESUS, THE MESSIAH,
Matthew 1:1-2:23

Study 3: JESUS' ACKNOWLEDGMENT AS KING BY WISE MEN: AN UNEXPECTED WORSHIP

Text: Matthew 2:1-11

Aim: To allow no circumstance to hinder your worship of Christ.

35

MATTHEW 2:1-11

Memory Verse:
> "And they said unto him, In Bethlehem of Judaea: for thus it is written by the prophet, And thou Bethlehem, in the land of Juda, art not the least among the princes of Juda: for out of thee shall come a Governor, that shall rule my people Israel" (Matthew 2:5-6).

INTRODUCTION:
Can you remember a time when you were caught totally off guard, completely surprised by some event in your life? Unexpected events occur...
- in relationships with loved ones
- in relationships with strangers
- in the lives of believers
- in the lives of unbelievers

As you will soon discover, the wise men were led on a journey that was filled with the unexpected and full of surprises. But none of these interruptions hindered them from reaching their goal: to worship the King.

There was nothing usual or common about the birth and early childhood of Jesus Christ. Practically every event was unusual or uncommon, totally unexpected. There was the fact of His being God's very own Son, of the virgin birth, of the announcement by angels, of being born in a stable, and on and on. The unexpected continues right on through the experience of the wise men. The wise men are a picture of those who seek Jesus. As they sought Him, events totally unexpected happened time and again. This is usually the case with those who seek Jesus. But God is faithful. If a person is truly seeking Jesus, God takes the unexpected events and works them out for good (Ro.8:28). God leads the person to Jesus regardless of circumstances and events, expected or unexpected.

OUTLINE:
1. Jesus was born in Bethlehem (v.1).
2. Their unexpected question: Where is the newborn King (v.2)?
3. Their unexpected disturbance (v.3-6).
4. Their unexpected commission: having to search for the newborn King (v.7-8).
5. Their unexpected sign: the star guided them again (v.9-10).
6. Their unexpected King: a humble child in humble surroundings (v.11).

1. JESUS WAS BORN IN BETHLEHEM (v.1).

Three facts are worthy of note.

1. He was born in Bethlehem. The city was only six miles south of Jerusalem. Its fame was due to two facts: (1) It had been the home and city of David (1 Sam.16:1; 17:12; 20:6); and (2) it was prophesied to be the city of the Messiah's birth (Micah 5:2). All Jews knew this fact, and those who truly believed in a coming Messiah looked for the Messiah to come through David's line and to establish an eternal.

2. He was born during the reign of Herod the Great.

3. He was sought by wise men from the East. They were men from the East (probably Persia), emissaries from one or more foreign nations who were seeking truth. They were influential men of learning and authority, the skilled scientists of their day: skilled in philosophy, science, medicine, and astrology. It is thought that they were the priestly order of Persia, the ministers and advisors to the Persian rulers.

QUESTIONS:
1. Why is it important to be able to place Christ in certain geographical places and in certain historical events?
2. How can you use these facts to witness to unbelievers?

2. THEIR UNEXPECTED QUESTION: WHERE IS THE NEWBORN KING (v.2)?

How did the wise men know the King of the Jews had been born? The answer is not given, but two other significant facts are.

1. They had a most unusual journey: they were guided by "his" star. What is meant by "his star"? Again the answer is not given. However, v.9 seems to indicate that it was some astronomical light. This much is known: whatever it was, it was a miracle. It was a miracle at least in this sense: it appeared at the very time of Jesus' birth; it appeared to Gentile wise men far away in another nation; it guided them to Jerusalem where they were to worship Jesus; it appeared at the very time they were given knowledge of the newborn King; and it appeared again for the specific purpose of guiding them.

2. They had a most significant purpose: their purpose was to worship the newborn King. They had come to pay homage to a child whom they understood was to be King of the Jews. They expected what any foreigner would have expected: the child would be a son of the reigning king. Jesus, of course, was not. It was this fact that disturbed Herod so much. He concluded what any reigning monarch would: there was a movement to overthrow the throne (see note—Mt.2:3).

ILLUSTRATION:

The wise men displayed great faith as they followed the star to a foreign land. Even though they could not *see* God, they believed God would lead them to the Christ-child who was born to be King, to the child who was called *Immanuel, God with us*. God can be found--if we are looking for Him.

> *"An atheist and a Christian were engaged in an intense public debate. On the blackboard behind the podium the atheist printed in large capital letters, 'GOD IS NOWHERE.' When the Christian rose to offer his rebuttal, he added one small space. Then the statement read, 'GOD IS NOW HERE.'"*[1]

APPLICATION:

Where is He, Jesus Christ, the King of kings and Lord of lords? Every person needs to be asked the question, for Christ has already come and most are not aware of it. Why? Because they are preoccupied with self and worldly affairs, with ambition and material possessions, with the physical and the flesh.

⇒ "Where is He?" It is totally unexpected that the message would come from the Gentiles and heathen of the world.

⇒ "Where is He?" It is totally unexpected that His own people do not know.

⇒ "Where is He?" It is totally unexpected that the religionists do not know.

How far away from God and how lost the world has become—not to know that God has sent the true King, His own Son, into the world!

"For God so loved the world, that he gave his only begotten Son, that whosoever believeth in him should not perish, but have everlasting life" (Jn.3:16).

"He was in the world...and the world knew Him not" (Jn.1:10-11). How could God send His Son into the world and the world not know it? How clearly the wise men illustrate the world's blindness to eternal affairs. A wise man is a man who seeks after the King of the Jews.

---

[1]   Vernon Grounds. *Radical Commitment*. As cited in *Christianity Today*. (Carol Stream, IL: Christianity Today Inc.), Vol. 30, #7.

3. THEIR UNEXPECTED DISTURBANCE (v.3-6).

It was the wise men who affected the Jews, not the Jews who affected the wise men. Few Jews were even aware of their King's birth. Imagine the great anticipation of the wise men as they journeyed and approached Jerusalem. Picture the shock: no one knew about the newborn King—who He was, where He was, anything about Him.

Three groups in particular are mentioned as being disturbed. Why were they disturbed? They just did not know about Him—that He had already come.

1. *Some people* were disturbed because they had anticipated His coming, but He had not come as they expected. They had expected a king, not a humble child, not a self-giving Savior. Others just did not believe; they could care less. Still others did not want to know about a king who might upset and disturb their comfortable lives.

2. *The government* (represented in Herod) was disturbed because it did not want a king coming from God who might threaten the present line and form of authority.

3. *Some religionists* were disturbed because they did not want a king to come as He had come. He and His coming did not match their beliefs. Others did not want a king other than the one they had. They were comfortable in the material world and the humanistic religion of the world. Others were so wrapped up in their religious affairs and its *busyness* that they were not spiritually sensitive enough to be aware of His coming. However, some religionists did turn to Him later (Acts 6:7; 15:5; 18:8, 17).

Note that Matthew stressed a point that is too often true of our generation: the religionists, the very people who should have known about the newborn Messiah, had ignored the Scripture and its prophecy. The world (Herod) had to send them scurrying to pay attention to its message.

> **"For this people's heart is waxed gross, and their ears are dull of hearing, and their eyes they have closed; lest at any time they should see with their eyes, and hear with their ears, and should understand with their heart, and should be converted, and I should heal them"** (Mt.13:15).

A CLOSER LOOK # 1
(2:3-4) **Herod the Great**: a bloody tyrant. Secular history records that he murdered many of his own family including his favorite wife (he had ten), her grandfather, her brother, and some of his own children. On one occasion he had the whole Sanhedrin, the ruling body of Jewish government, assassinated. On another occasion he had every notable man in Jerusalem murdered. He was very capable of the crime reported here. Christ was born during the latter years of Herod's reign and his reign as king had been a long one (37 B.C.-4 A.D.).

This fact shows just how much of a bloody tyrant Herod really was. Just imagine! He would not even be around when a child king would inherit the throne, yet he felt threatened by the reports of a child king. He was a man possessed by evil. He was suspicious, savage, and warped. Note that Herod had all the children killed, not only in Bethlehem but "in all the coasts thereof" (v.16).

4. THEIR UNEXPECTED COMMISSION: HAVING TO SEARCH FOR THE NEW-BORN KING (v.7-8).

Note the wise men's testimony about the star. The wise men had unashamedly testified to the supernatural, the star that had led them to seek the newborn King. All the city had heard their testimony, even Herod. The wise men were now commissioned to go, search, and find the child. The *newborn King's* own people were not even aware of His coming. The wise men never expected they would have to search for Him.

APPLICATION:
What a shock! Some expect to find "the newborn king" *in the lives* of those who profess to be God's people, and they are unable to find Him! Too often they are forced to go elsewhere or to give up their search. But God used an evil man, Herod (without his knowing it), to help the wise men in their search. Any person who seeks *the newborn King* will be led by God to Him—no matter who God has to use to help the seeker (see Ro.2:14-15).

QUESTIONS:
1. How open are you in sharing supernatural experiences with believers and unbelievers? Why is it important for unbelievers to hear about God's supernatural work?
2. Unbelievers often attend church hoping to find the King but instead find great hypocrisy from professing believers. What would you tell a person who had this experience?

5. THEIR UNEXPECTED SIGN: THE STAR GUIDED THEM AGAIN (v.9-10).

Apparently the wise men did not expect the supernatural sign to appear again (v.10). They had searched faithfully and done all they could, and they were continuing on. God honors such effort. He met their need (Is. 64:5). But note: only the wise men went to search out the newborn King. And imagine—Bethlehem was only six miles south of Jerusalem!

APPLICATION:
God will meet the need of any man who faithfully searches and does all he can, the man who continues on and refuses to quit. Yet how few search Him out today (2 Cor.6:2).

"And ye shall seek me, and find me, when ye shall search for me with all your heart" (Jer.29:13).

QUESTION:
Note that the wise men did not give up their search when it became hard. What character traits kept them from giving up and returning home? Which of these traits do you need to work on today?

6. THEIR UNEXPECTED KING: A HUMBLE CHILD IN HUMBLE SURROUND-INGS (v.11).

They found the child King in a house. No doubt the wise men had *expected* the child to be the son of a reigning monarch with all the splendor, wealth, and royalty attached. They had expected Him to be known by all. How unlike what they found—a child with common parents in a humble house! Note: they gave the child King worship. Matthew records that they bowed down and worshipped the newborn king. He says nothing about their having worshipped Herod.

> "Give unto the LORD the glory due unto his name: bring an offer-ing, and come before him: worship the LORD in the beauty of holi-ness" (1 Chron.16:29).
> "O come, let us worship and bow down: let us kneel before the LORD our maker" (Ps.95:6).

ILLUSTRATION:
When the wise men found the King, they immediately fell down to their knees and worshipped Him. Their example is a lesson in humility for every believer.

> *"In 'Touch and Live,' George Vandeman wrote: 'A young stranger to the Alps was making his first climb, accompanied by two stalwart guides. It was a steep, hazardous ascent. But he felt secure with one guide ahead and one following. For hours they climbed. And now, breathless, they reached for those rocks protruding through the snow above them - the summit. The guide ahead wished to let the stranger have the first glorious view of heaven and earth, and moved aside to let him go first. Forgetting the gales that would blow across those summit rocks, the young man leaped to his feet. But the chief guide dragged him down. 'On your knees, sir!' he shouted. 'You are never safe here except on your knees.' That is also the appro-priate position when we agree upon God's grandeur."[2]*

QUESTIONS:
1. What thoughts or mental expectations did you have about Christ before you came to know Him? What adjustments or corrections did you have to make?
2. The wise men found Christ and worshipped Him. What does this say about their hearts? What must you change in your life in order to worship Christ more faith-fully?

APPLICATION:
God's ways are not man's way (cp. 1 Cor.1:26-31). The newborn King is not a hu-manistic Savior. He is *God's Savior* who has come in God's way.

> "For ye know the grace of our Lord Jesus Christ, that, though he was rich, yet for your sakes he became poor, that ye through his pov-erty might be rich" (2 Cor.8:9).
> "But [Christ] made himself of no reputation, and took upon him the form of a servant, and was made in the likeness of men: and being found in fashion as a man, he humbled himself, and became obedient unto death, even the death of the cross" (Ph.2:7-8).

---

[2] Vailo Weis in *Leadership Journal*. (Carol Stream, IL: Christianity Today Inc.), Vol. 11, #3.

SUMMARY:

Life is full of surprises for the Christian believer. What is most important is being able to keep your focus and respond to each surprise with one thing in mind: you must seek and follow the King of kings and Lord of lords in all you do. He may not do (or be) what you expect--but He will never disappoint you! You can learn this timeless example from the wise men.

1. Jesus was born in Bethlehem.
2. Their unexpected question: where is the newborn King?
3. Their unexpected disturbance.
4. Their unexpected commission: having to search for the newborn King.
5. Their unexpected sign: the star guided them again.
6. Their unexpected King: a humble child in humble surroundings.

PERSONAL JOURNAL NOTES:
(Reflection & Response)

1. The most important thing that I learned from this lesson was:

2. The thing that I need to work on the most is:

3. I can apply this lesson to my life by:

4. Closing Prayer of Commitment: (put your commitment down on paper).

D. Jesus' Childhood: Facing Danger after Danger, 2:12-23

1. The first danger: Herod plotted to find Jesus (see Mt.2:3-8, 12)
  a. The wise men were miraculously warned
  b. The wise men obeyed

2. The second danger: Herod attempted to destroy Jesus
  a. Joseph was miraculously warned to flee into Egypt

  b. Joseph obeyed

  c. Scripture was fulfilled: The family sojourned in Egypt

  d. Herod slaughtered the children

  e. Scripture was fulfilled: The prediction of the children's slaughter

3. The third danger: Archelaus reigned in Judea
  a. Joseph was miraculously instructed

  b. Joseph was again miraculously warned: Herod's son Archelaus was a threat

  c. Joseph obeyed

  d. Scripture was fulfilled: Jesus lived in Nazareth

12 And being warned of God in a dream that they should not return to Herod, they departed into their own country another way. 13 And when they were departed, behold, the angel of the Lord appeareth to Joseph in a dream, saying, Arise, and take the young child and his mother, and flee into Egypt, and be thou there until I bring thee word: for Herod will seek the young child to destroy him. 14 When he arose, he took the young child and his mother by night, and departed into Egypt: 15 And was there until the death of Herod: that it might be fulfilled which was spoken of the Lord by the prophet, saying, Out of Egypt have I called my son. 16 Then Herod, when he saw that he was mocked of the wise men, was exceeding wroth, and sent forth, and slew all the children that were in Bethlehem, and in all the coasts thereof, from two years old and under, according to the time which he had diligently enquired of the wise men. 17 Then was fulfilled that which was spoken by Jeremy the prophet, saying, 18 In Rama was there a voice heard, lamentation, and weeping, and great mourning, Rachel weeping for her children, and would not be comforted, because they are not. 19 But when Herod was dead, behold, an angel of the Lord appeareth in a dream to Joseph in Egypt, 20 Saying, Arise, and take the young child and his mother, and go into the land of Israel: for they are dead which sought the young child's life. 21 And he arose, and took the young child and his mother, and came into the land of Israel. 22 But when he heard that Archelaus did reign in Judaea in the room of his father Herod, he was afraid to go thither: notwithstanding, being warned of God in a dream, he turned aside into the parts of Galilee: 23 And he came and dwelt in a city called Nazareth: that it might be fulfilled which was spoken by the prophets, He shall be called a Nazarene.

Section I
THE BIRTH AND CHILDHOOD OF JESUS, THE MESSIAH,
Matthew 1:1-2:23

MATTHEW 2:12-23

Study 4: JESUS' CHILDHOOD: FACING DANGER AFTER DANGER

Text: Matthew 2:12-23

Aim: To place greater trust in God's ability to protect us.

Memory Verse:
"And he came and dwelt in a city called Nazareth: that it might be fulfilled which was spoken by the prophets, He shall be called a Nazarene" (Matthew 2:23).

INTRODUCTION:

What emotions run through your mind when you are in danger? Fear...anxiety...doubt...worry? We live in uncertain and dangerous times. The daily newspaper confirms that evil abounds all over the world. No person is immune from the reaches of evil people and evil things. The situation seems almost hopeless to some people. But we need to remember one important fact: God is God, and God is in complete control. We must learn how to trust Him as we walk in this dangerous world, and we must be prepared to deal with the dangers that come our way.

From the first, even as a child, Jesus Christ faced danger after danger. Time and again there were attempts to stamp out His life, yet God miraculously delivered and protected Him every step of the way. In confronting these dangers, the believer can learn much about the protection and care of God. God cares, and God will protect the person who places his life under God's care.

OUTLINE:

1. The first danger: Herod plotted to find Jesus (v.12).
2. The second danger: Herod attempted to destroy Jesus (v.13-18).
3. The third danger: Archelaus reigned in Judea (v.19-23).

1. THE FIRST DANGER: HEROD PLOTTED TO FIND JESUS (v.12).

Remember: Herod, a king and a bloody tyrant, became very upset when he heard about a child being born who was supposed to be a king; therefore, he sent the wise men to Bethlehem to search for the child king (cp. Mt.2:3-3, 12). It is difficult to imagine anyone harming a child, especially seeking to kill a child, yet it happens. (Note: this passage points out that two murderous attempts were made against the child Jesus.)

1. The wise men were miraculously warned by God. But note: God did not warn them of Herod's plot until they had followed through—actually found Jesus and worshipped Him.

APPLICATION:

There is an enormous drive in some men to worship God. The wise men had such a drive. They had a compelling drive to worship the newborn king, and they had been ever so faithful and diligent in seeking Him. Anyone who diligently seeks God's Son can expect to be met and directed by God. God met and warned the wise men of impending danger. He will meet and direct the path of any believer who diligently seeks Him.

"That they should seek the Lord, if haply they might feel after him, and find him, though he be not far from every one of us" (Acts 17:27).

43

2. The wise men obeyed God's warning. The wise men chose to obey God rather than Herod. They went God's way rather than return to Herod. Therefore, God directed and protected them.

ILLUSTRATION:

Just as the wise men had to choose between obeying God or obeying Herod, man still has to make a choice today: he either listens to God or listens to the world. God has given us fair warning. If we will obey, He will protect. His warning is briefly summed up in the following:

"A cartoon in Christianity Today portrayed Moses atop Mount Sinai holding the stone tablets containing the Ten Commandments. Looking heavenward, he says to God, 'They tend to lose interest rather quickly. Could I have a one-liner instead?'
"In a sense, God did give one-liners.' His ten laws are clear and pointed.
1. Love the only true God.
2. Don't make an image of God.
3. Hallow His name.
4. Keep His day holy.
5. Honor your parents.
6. Don't murder.
7. Don't commit adultery.
8. Don't steal.
9. Don't lie.
10. Don't covet.
"These laws express God's holy nature, and we function best as His image-bearers when we obey them."[1]

"But seek ye first the kingdom of God, and his righteousness; and all these things shall be added unto you" (Mt.6:33).

QUESTIONS:
1. How would you evaluate your desire to worship God?
____Cold
____Lukewarm
____Passionate
What has to take place in your heart for your worship of God to be passionate?
2. How are obedience *to* God and the protection *of* God linked together? How has this been illustrated in your life?

2. THE SECOND DANGER: HEROD ATTEMPTED TO DESTROY JESUS (v.13-18).

1. Joseph was miraculously warned to flee into Egypt. God knows all and He rules over all. God knew Herod's thoughts and heart, but apparently no one else did. Herod's act was to be so terrible and wicked that he shared it with no one else. But God knew, and He moved to protect the life of His Son.

It was not uncommon for Jews to flee into Egypt. From the beginning of Jewish history, many had sought refuge in Egypt from both the tyranny of nature (famine) and man (Gen.12:10f). Every large city in Egypt had a large pocket of Jewish refugees. The great Egyptian city, Alexandria, had over a million Jewish emigrants.

---

[1] *INFOsearch Sermon Illustrations* (Arlington, TX: The Computer Assistant, 1-888-868-9029, 1986-1996).

God's grace can be seen in the traumatic movement of Joseph and Mary into Egypt. He leads them to flee into a country where they could more easily settle down and find friends. It is thought that Jesus was in Egypt for six to seven years.

APPLICATION 1:

The believer can rest in God's knowledge and providence. God knows all: every danger, threat, and trial.

> **"Neither is there any creature that is not manifest in his sight: but all things are naked and opened unto the eyes of him with whom we have to do" (Heb.4:13).**

APPLICATION 2:

Believers are *in Egypt*, yet not *of Egypt*. Throughout Scripture Egypt is a type of the world and it symbolizes enslavement and bondage. There are several applications for the believer in this symbol of Egypt.

1) As Jesus Christ was sent into Egypt (the world) so believers are sent into the world (Jn.20:21; 2 Cor.5:20).
2) As Jesus Christ was "called out of Egypt" so believers are called out of the world.

⇒ Believers are called out of the world now.

> **"Wherefore come out from among them, and be ye separate, saith the Lord, and touch not the unclean thing; and I will receive you, and will be a Father unto you, and ye shall be my sons and daughters, saith the Lord Almighty" (2 Cor.6:17-18).**

⇒ Believers are called out of the world eternally.

> **"For I am now ready to be offered, and the time of my departure is at hand. I have fought a good fight, I have finished my course, I have kept the faith: henceforth there is laid up for me a crown of righteousness, which the Lord, the righteous judge, shall give me at that day: and not to me only, but unto all them also that love his appearing" (2 Tim.4:6-8).**

2. Joseph obeyed. Note that Joseph was totally unaware of the danger, but he had been obedient to God's call, a most difficult call that had created a traumatic predicament for him (Mt.1:24-25). Because of his obedience, God delivered him from a terrible danger. Note that God's expectation was twofold.

    a. God expected Joseph and Mary to be obedient without grumbling and murmuring. Joseph and Mary had two good reasons to be discouraged and to grumble.

    ⇒ This was God's child. Why was He having to flee anything?

    ⇒ They had been chosen to be very special servants of God. Why would God cause them to go through so much pain and trauma: being uprooted and having to move, being persecuted and threatened with death? Why did God not just take care of Herod?

    b. God expected Joseph and Mary to believe without questioning or doubting. And this they did. Joseph and Mary demonstrated great faith, great trust in God. They acted and obeyed without question.

> **"Commit thy way unto the LORD; trust also in him; and he shall bring it to pass" (Ps.37:5).**

APPLICATION:

God delivers His *obedient* servant. Far too often, we seek to negotiate terms with God when we are unsure of our circumstances. Scripture is filled with examples of believers who dared to obey God without questioning or doubting. These are just a few examples:

⇒ Noah obeyed the Lord and was delivered from the flood.

> **"Thus did Noah [make the ark]; according to all that God commanded him, so did he" (Gen.6:22).**

⇒ Abraham obeyed the Lord and was delivered from a corrupt culture.

> **"Now the LORD had said unto Abram, Get thee out of thy country, and from thy kindred, and from thy father's house, unto a land that I will show thee" (Gen.12:1).**

⇒ Elijah obeyed the Lord and was delivered from the prophets of Baal.

> **"And Elijah said unto them, Take the prophets of Baal; let not one of them escape. And they took them: and Elijah brought them down to the brook Kishon, and slew them there" (1 Ki.18:40).**

⇒ *Any believer* who obeys the Lord will be delivered from this world to an eternity with God.

> **"And the world passeth away, and the lust thereof: but he that doeth the will of God abideth for ever" (1 Jn.2:17).**

3. Scripture was fulfilled: Jesus sojourned into Egypt. His journey and life in Egypt was parallel to the sojourn of Israel (God's people) in Egypt. (See pt.1 of this note.)

4. Herod slaughtered the children. There are some very evil men in the world, men who are unreasonably wicked, cruel, savage, and bloody (Gal.5:19-21; Rev.21:8); men who cause unbearable pain (Mt.2:18); men who are *overly* wicked, excessively wicked (Eccl.7:17).

Their day of righteous judgment is coming. God will show His wrath against all evil men in the terrible day of judgment. Herod will be one of the men who will bear the righteous judgment of God.

> **"And as it is appointed unto men once to die, but after this the judgment" (Heb.9:27).**

5. Scripture was fulfilled regarding the prediction of the children's slaughter.

APPLICATION:

Believers should expect persecution. Jesus was persecuted from the very beginning. The attempts to stamp out Jesus and His claims upon human life have continued down through the centuries. Persecutors now strike out against His followers, those who live and teach His Word.

> **"For unto you it is given in the behalf of Christ, not only to believe on him, but also to suffer for his sake" (Ph.1:29).**

3. THE THIRD DANGER: ARCHELAUS REIGNED IN JUDEA (v.19-23).

1. Joseph was miraculously instructed. The family had been in Egypt for about six years. Joseph and Mary had probably asked God if they could return home (just as anyone would); however, they never attempted to return. They patiently waited for God's direction; and because they sat still, obeying God, God moved and directed them at the right time, miraculously.

APPLICATION 1:
Believers should wait upon God before acting. Waiting upon God is part of obedience, and God directs the obedient person time and again (cp. Mt.1:20-25; 2:13-14).

> **"Wait on the LORD: be of good courage, and he shall strengthen thine heart: wait, I say, on the LORD" (Ps.27:14).**

APPLICATION 2:
All men die. Herod died *despite* his fame, wealth, and power. Think of the difference stated in Scripture:

> **"The wages of sin is <u>death</u>; but the gift of God is <u>eternal life</u> through Jesus Christ our Lord" (Ro.6:23. cp. Heb.9:27).**

2. Joseph was again miraculously warned: Herod's son Archelaus was a threat. Archelaus was the son of Herod the Great who became king over Judea after Herod's death. He followed in the steps of his father: a cruel, bloody tyrant. Right after assuming the throne, Archelaus had over three thousand of the most influential Jewish people murdered.

Note that God led Joseph step by step. God did not tell Joseph where to go at first; He simply said "go into the land of Israel" (v.20). It was after he arrived back in Israel that God told him to go into Nazareth (v. 21-22).

APPLICATION 1:
Parents influence their children enormously. Look at the influence of Herod upon his son, Archelaus. Look at the influence of other fathers upon their children.

"He [Ahaziah, the son of Ahab] also walked in the ways of the house of Ahab: for his mother was his counselor to do wickedly" (2 Chron.22:3; cp. 1 Ki.22:52).

"But I said unto their children in the wilderness, Walk ye not in the statutes of your fathers, neither observe their judgments, nor defile yourselves with their idols: I am the LORD your God; walk in my statutes, and keep my judgments, and do them" (Ezk.20:18-19).

APPLICATION 2:
God leads the believer step by step. There are three reasons for this.
1) It keeps the believer close to God.
2) It strengthens the believer's faith.
3) It keeps the believer from becoming discouraged by seeing the trials lying out in the future.

"For this God is our God for ever and ever: he will be our guide even unto death" (Ps.48:14).

"Thou shalt guide me with thy counsel, and afterward receive me to glory" (Ps.73:24).

"Trust in the LORD with all thine heart; and lean not unto thine own understanding. In all thy ways acknowledge him, and he shall direct thy paths" (Pr.3:5-6).

3. Again Joseph obeyed. He was a man who walked in obedience—again and again (Mt.1:24-25; 2:14, 21, 22).

ILLUSTRATION:
The only way a person can walk in obedience to God is to spend quality time in the Word of God--studying it, meditating upon it, and living it. Obedience can never be a hit or miss methodology.

"Once a man who was seeking direction for his life took his Bible and blindly picked out a verse. He was startled by these words: 'Then Judas,...went and hanged himself.' Not telling the others of his unhappy choice, he closed his eyes and quickly pointed to a different portion. He was greatly distressed as he read, 'Go, and do thou likewise.' The Bible is much too sacred to be handled in this way. Its perfect leading cannot be gleaned in an unthinking manner. We are admonished to meditate upon the Word, study it, and rightly divide it if we expect the guiding light of God's truth to illumine our pathway."[2]

4. Again Scripture was fulfilled: Jesus lived in Nazareth. Nazareth was the hometown of Jesus' parents, Joseph and Mary, and of Jesus' childhood and early manhood. There were at least two advantages to Jesus being brought up in Nazareth.
   a. It was a small, quiet town, ready-made for a close community, neighborliness, and for quiet contemplation.
   b. It was also a town in touch with the modern life and world events of that day. Two of the major roads of the world passed within eyesight of the hills surrounding the city: the road that stretched between Rome and northern Africa (North and South) and the road that ran between the great cities of the East and West. Jesus can be imagined standing on the hills observing (perhaps even meeting) some of the travelers and caravans using the major routes as they crisscrossed the world. He had opportunity to observe and study the nature and dealings of all kinds of men and all

---

[2] *INFOsearch Sermon Illustrations* (Arlington, TX: The Computer Assistant, 1-888-868-9029, 1986-1996).

kinds of nationalities as they used the major routes. As a child, how often His heart must have ached and wept over a world lost and needing to be found.

The Jews were both the recipients and the trustees of God's Word (revelation) throughout the history of the Old Testament: "For the prophecy came not in old time by the will of man: but holy men of God spoke, as they were moved by the Holy Spirit" (2 Pt.1:21.) They were familiar with the prophecies predicting the coming of the Messiah. Thus Matthew stresses time and again that "Jesus, who is called Christ" fulfills the Old Testament prophecies.

APPLICATION:

It is no dishonor to come from a humble home or a small town. Everything about Jesus' family and childhood was humble: His parents (Lk.2:24); His home (Mt.2:11); His hometown of Nazareth (Jn.1:46). Despite all these factors--and because of all these factors--the believer can rest assured that Jesus is the true Messiah.

"He first findeth his own brother Simon, and saith unto him, We have found the Messias, which is, being interpreted, the Christ" (Jn.1:41).

QUESTIONS:
1. When are you most likely to wait for God's instructions before you act? In what circumstances are you likely to get ahead of God?
2. In what ways do parents influence children the most? What is the most important thing your parents taught you? Why?
3. What would have to happen in your community for it to have a strong Christian witness? What would have to happen in you?

SUMMARY:

What do you do when some danger confronts you? How you answer this question says a lot about your faith in God. It is important to remember that even in the midst of danger God is with you, and He will be with you as you face the danger--just as He was with His Son, the Lord Jesus!
1. The first danger: Herod plotted to find Jesus.
2. The second danger: Herod attempted to destroy Jesus.
3. The third danger: Archelaus reigned in Judea.

PERSONAL JOURNAL NOTES:
(Reflection & Response)

1. The most important thing that I learned from this lesson was:

2. The thing that I need to work on the most is:

3. I can apply this lesson to my life by:

4. Closing Prayer of Commitment: (put your commitment down on paper).

CHAPTER 3

**II. THE PREPARA-
TION FOR THE
MESSIAH'S
COMING, 3:1-
4:11**

**A. Jesus' Forerun-
ner, John the
Baptist: A Mes-
sage for All, 3:1-12**
(Mk.1:1-8; Lk.3:1-
20; Jn.1:6-8, 15-37)

1. John ministered in
the wilderness

2. His message to the
people: Repent, the
Kingdom of Heaven
is at hand
a. His message ful-
filled prophecy:
One crying, Pre-
pare"

b. His message was
the message of a
prophet: He
dressed & ate as a
prophet

c. His message bore
fruit
1) Crowds gathered

2) Crowds con-
fessed & were
baptized

In those days came
John the Baptist,
preaching in the wil-
derness of Judaea,
2 And saying, Repent
ye: for the kingdom of
heaven is at hand.
3 For this is he that
was spoken of by the
prophet Esaias, say-
ing, The voice of one
crying in the wilder-
ness, Prepare ye the
way of the Lord, make
his paths straight.
4 And the same John
had his raiment of
camel's hair, and a
leathern girdle about
his loins; and his meat
was locusts and wild
honey.
5 Then went out to
him Jerusalem, and all
Judaea, and all the
region round about
Jordan,
6 And were baptized
of him in Jordan, con-
fessing their sins.

7 But when he saw
many of the Pharisees
and Sadducees come
to his baptism, he said
unto them, O genera-
tion of vipers, who
hath warned you to
flee from the wrath to
come?
8 Bring forth there-
fore fruits meet for re-
pentance:
9 And think not to say
within yourselves, We
have Abraham to our
father: for I say unto
you, that God is able
of these stones to raise
up children unto
Abraham.
10 And now also the
axe is laid unto the
root of the trees: there-
fore every tree which
bringeth not forth
good fruit is hewn
down, and cast into
the fire.
11 I indeed baptize
you with water unto
repentance: but he that
cometh after me is
mightier than I, whose
shoes I am not worthy
to bear: he shall bap-
tize you with the Holy
Ghost, and with fire:
12 Whose fan is in his
hand, and he will
throughly purge his
floor, and gather his
wheat into the garner;
but he will burn up the
chaff with unquench-
able fire.

3. His message to the
religionists, the
Pharisees and Sad-
ducees
a. Point 1: Flee the
wrath to come

b. Point 2: Repent

c. Point 3: Heritage is
of no value

d. Point 4: Judgment
is at hand
1) Immediate: Now

2) Inevitable: Every
unfruitful tree is
cast into the fire
3) Basis: Fruit

4. His message to all:
Christ--Messianic
preaching
a. Christ is greater...

b. Christ shall bap-
tize...
c. Christ shall judge
& purge

1) Gather some

2) Burn some

**Section II
THE PREPARATION FOR THE MESSIAH'S COMING
Matthew 3:1-4:11**

Study 1:   JESUS' FORERUNNER, JOHN THE BAPTIST: A MESSAGE FOR ALL

Text: Matthew 3:1-12

MATTHEW 3:1-12

Aim: To capture the urgency of preparing for the Kingdom of Heaven.

Memory Verse:
> "And saying, Repent ye: for the kingdom of heaven is at hand" (Matthew 3:2).

INTRODUCTION:

What preparation did you undergo to become qualified in your profession or career? The key to success in anything is preparation. Before a soldier is sent out to fight, he must undergo a thorough period of basic training. Before a doctor is allowed to practice medicine, he or she must first undergo years of education and internship. A teacher must be taught before he or she can teach. There is one underlying principle to all these examples: To be successful, a person must **prepare**. This principle is also an essential element for every Christian believer. Too many believers are not prepared for the mission of sharing Christ with the world. As a result, the message of the gospel is muted, compromised, and watered down. In order to sharpen our focus, we need to study the example of a man whose very life is the embodiment of preparation.

John the Baptist set a blazing example for every minister and believer of the gospel. His message is a message for all; he speaks to the common person and to the religionist alike. The message preached by John stressed thirteen points.

1. Repentance (v.2).
2. The Kingdom of Heaven (v.2).
3. Prepare, for the Lord is coming (v.3).
4. Flee the wrath to come (v.7).
5. Bear fruit (v.8).
6. Do not be deceived over the merits of a godly heritage (v.9).
7. Acknowledge the power of God (v.10).
8. Judgment is at hand (v.10).
9. Fruit is demanded—now (v.10).
10. Everyone who bears bad fruit is condemned (v.10).
11. Repent - be baptized with water by man (v.11).
12. Repent - be baptized with the Holy Spirit and with fire (v.11).
13. The Messiah shall separate the wheat from the tares (v.12).

OUTLINE:

1. John ministered in the wilderness (v.1).
2. His message to the people: repent...the Kingdom of Heaven is at hand (v.2-6).
3. His message to the religionists, the Pharisees and Sadducees (v.7-10).
4. His message to all: Christ—Messianic preaching (v.11-12).

1. JOHN MINISTERED IN THE WILDERNESS (v.1).

This was a wilderness area, but not a desolate, desert-like area. It was a country area with at least six cities scattered about, probably small communities or villages. It was in this country area of Judaea that John emerged with the lightning cry for repentance: the long-awaited Messiah is at hand.

APPLICATION:

God often uses the wilderness (quiet places) to prepare and launch the ministry of men. The gospel began in a wilderness, not in a synagogue or temple or church (cp. Is.32:15; 35:1-2; 51:18-19). John's place was in the wilderness, but Christ's place was in the cities and synagogues as well as the countryside. Believers should witness and prophets should preach wherever they are—in the wilderness or in the city. God has the very place for every believer to serve. But in all cases, quietness is essential: "Be still and know that I am God" (Ps.46:10). Meditation is essential (Gen.24:63; Josh 1:8; Ps.1:2; 63:6; 77:12; 119:15, 78; 119:23, 48, 148; 143:5; 1 Tim.4:15). Yet believers are never alone. No matter how secluded they may be, God is there. He will reveal and manifest Himself in the place where believers are; He will use the believer in the place as a witness to His name.

ILLUSTRATION:

Sometimes believers find themselves cut off from the crowds, away from the *action*-- whether due to illness, job relocation, leaving home for school, rejection, etc. Instead of looking for a way to change their circumstances, believers should be looking for opportunities to serve God right where they are.

> *"During the reign of Oliver Cromwell, there was a shortage of currency in the British Empire. Representatives carefully searched the nation in hopes of finding silver to meet the emergency. After one month, the committee returned with its report. 'We have searched the Empire in vain seeking to find silver. To our dismay, we found none anywhere except in the cathedrals where the statues of the saints are made of choice silver.' To this, Oliver Cromwell eloquently answered, 'Let's melt down the saints and put them into circulation.'"*[1]

Remember: God knows exactly where you are. He has put you there for a reason. No matter where you are, God wants you serving Him, not gathering dust!

QUESTIONS:
1. Every believer needs a wilderness, a quiet place, in order to spend time with God. Where is your quiet place? If you do not have one, why not?
2. Where are you currently serving God? What lessons are you learning as you serve God? Why has God put you where you are?

2. HIS MESSAGE TO THE PEOPLE: REPENT, THE KINGDOM OF HEAVEN IS AT HAND (v.2-6).

1. John's message fulfilled prophecy. It had been four hundred years since a prophet had arisen in Israel. Malachi had been the last. John's appearance made a thunderous impact. (Cp. Is.40:3; 1 Ki.18:21; 2 Ki.1:8; Mal.3:1; 4:5.) John preached the gospel to all—to the general public and to the religionist alike. No one was excluded from the gospel (v.2-6; 7-10; 11-12). His message included three points.
   a. Repent: change your life; turn your life around.

> **"I tell you, Nay: but, except ye repent, ye shall all likewise perish" (Lk.13:3).**
> **"If my people, which are called by my name, shall humble themselves and pray, and seek my face, and turn from their wicked ways; then will I hear from heaven, and will forgive their sin, and will heal their land" (2 Chron.7:14).**

---

[1] *INFOsearch Sermon Illustrations* (Arlington, TX: The Computer Assistant, 1-888-868-9029, 1986-1996).

b. The Kingdom of Heaven is at hand. John meant two things.
1) The Kingdom *is the Lord's*. He is the sovereign Lord of the Kingdom of Heaven. His coming is now; it is immediately upon us. Therefore, His kingdom or sovereign rule is now. Repent and get ready for His sovereign rule.
2) The Kingdom is *of Heaven*. It is of another world, of another dimension of being. It is not of this earth. It is spiritual; it is not physical, not something which we see, look upon, and handle. Only the Lord can bring the kingdom to this earth. The kingdom is of God, not of man.

> **"Blessed are the poor in spirit: for theirs is the kingdom of heaven" (Mt.5:3; cp. Mt.25:34-35).**
>
> **"Jesus answered and said unto him, Verily, verily, I say unto thee, Except a man be born again, he cannot see the kingdom of God" (Jn.3:3).**
>
> **"For the kingdom of God is not meat and drink; but righteousness, and peace, and joy in the Holy Ghost" (Ro.14:17).**

c. Every man is to "prepare ye the way of the Lord" (v.3).

> **"The voice of him that crieth in the wilderness, Prepare ye the way of the LORD, make straight in the desert, a highway for our God" (Is.40:3).**

APPLICATION 1:
The cry of the prophet is:
1) Man has an inadequate righteousness; therefore, repentance is needed.
2) The present world is an inadequate world; therefore, the Kingdom of Heaven is needed.
3) Man has prepared an inadequate life for the Lord; therefore, he must prepare the way for the Lord.

APPLICATION 2:
God raises up His servant, His witness, His prophet in His own time (v.3). Every believer (witness and prophet) is chosen by God. God chose and ordained the believer before the foundation of the earth. He may not be predicted by name in the pages and prophecy of Scripture, but he is conceived (predestined) in the mind and foreknowledge of God. This glorious truth should instill both confidence and a sense of responsibility in the believer (v.3.)

APPLICATION 3:
Preaching is to be affirmative, authoritative, and positive not uncertain and negative. The gospel is not open for discussion; it is not just one of many possibilities; it is the truth of God (v.2-3, 6, 7-12).

> **"For God so loved the world, that he gave his only begotten Son, that whosoever believeth in him should not perish, but have everlasting life" (Jn.3:16).**

2. John's message was the message of *a prophet*: he dressed and ate as a prophet (v.4).

> **" And they answered him, He was a hairy man, and girt with a girdle of leather about his loins. And he said, It is Elijah the Tishbite" (2 Ki.1:8).**

APPLICATION:
The believer is to be disciplined and to live moderately.

> **"And he said to them all, If any man will come after me, let him deny himself, and take up his cross daily, and follow me" (Lk.9:23).**

The believer's dress and habits should be adapted to meet the needs of his people (v.4).

> **"And unto the Jews I became as a Jew, that I might gain the Jews; to them that are under the law, as under the law, that I might gain them that are under the law; to them that are without law, as without law, (being not without law to God, but under the law to Christ,) that I might gain them that are without law. To the weak became I as weak, that I might gain the weak: I am made all things to all men, that I might by all means save some" (1 Cor.9:20-22).**

3. John's message bore fruit. The crowds gathered and listened to his preaching. They *confessed their sins and were baptized* (v.5-6).

APPLICATION:
The world should hear, respect, and respond to the messenger of God (v.5-6). God forgives sin only when a person confesses and repents of his sin (v.6).

> **"Him hath God exalted with his right hand to be a Prince and a Saviour, for to give repentance to Israel, and forgiveness of sins" (Acts 5:31).**
> **"If we confess our sins, he is faithful and just to forgive us our sins, and to cleanse us from all unrighteousness" (1 Jn.1:9).**

If a person says he is innocent and refuses to believe and admit his sin, he is condemned already (v.6).

> **"He that believeth on him is not condemned: but he that believeth not is condemned already, because he hath not believed in the name of the only begotten Son of God" (Jn.3:18).**

QUESTIONS:
1. What does the word *repent* mean? Have you *repented* of all the sins you have *confessed*?
2. How is the Kingdom of Heaven different from the kingdoms of men? Which kingdom are you most faithful toward?
3. How do you "prepare ye the way of the Lord" at your workplace? School? Home? Church?

3. HIS MESSAGE IS TO THE RELIGIONISTS, THE PHARISEES AND THE SADDUCEES (v.7-10).

The religionists were a fact-finding committee sent from Jerusalem to investigate the phenomenal reports about John and his ministry: Could he honestly be a modern day prophet sent from God? When John confronted the religionists, he knew several dangers threatened to

deceive them. If they succumbed and were deceived by any of the dangers, they were doomed. Therefore, he warned them about...
- the danger of being a spectator only, of coming out to his meetings only to see what was happening.
- the danger of thinking that baptism protected them from the wrath to come.
- the danger of thinking that God's judgment was only for the heathen and the ungodly, not for them.
- the danger of verbal repentance only, thinking their conduct had no bearing on being accepted or rejected by God.
- the danger of thinking that the righteousness of their forefathers and families would cover and be sufficient for them.

John's message was fourfold.

1. Flee the wrath to come. The wrath of God was coming upon all who were only spectators. And baptism by itself was not enough, no matter how many baptisms a person went through.

> **"He that believeth on the Son hath everlasting life: and he that believeth not the Son shall not see life; but the <u>wrath</u> of God abideth on him" (Jn.3:36).**

2. Repent. Verbal repentance is not enough. Just being present in the midst of those who worship God is not enough. Repentance requires a change in conduct. The religionists rejected the message; they did not repent. Jesus informed us of their decision. What a warning (v.7-10)!

> **"And all the people that heard him, and the publicans, justified God, being baptized with the baptism of John. But the Pharisees and lawyers rejected the counsel of God against themselves, being not baptized of him" (Lk.7:29-30).**

APPLICATION:
Two persons often shut themselves off from God.
1) Persons of high estate (those of wealth and social standing).
2) Persons of religion (the self-righteous) (v.7-10).

> **"For where your treasure is, there will your heart be also" (Mt.6:21).**

3. Heritage is of no value. The righteousness of others cannot make a person acceptable to God. Each person has to stand before God as an individual.

APPLICATION:
Many persons rest in two deceptions:
1) the godliness of family or friends
2) the righteousness of some good behavior. They feel they have done enough good for God to accept them, that they are not bad enough for God to reject—not in the final analysis.

What is needed is to "wash thine heart from wickedness, that thou mayest be saved" (Jer.4:14).

> **"Bring forth therefore fruits worthy of repentance, and begin not to say within yourselves, We have Abraham to our father: for I say**

unto you, That God is able of these stones to raise up children unto Abraham" (Lk.3:8).

4. Judgment is at hand. Every tree that does not bear fruit shall be chopped down and destroyed. We must never forget that judgment is inclusive; it includes all. It does not matter how high (position) nor how green (appearance) the tree is. It must bear fruit or else be removed and destroyed (v.10).

> "Whosoever therefore shall be ashamed of me and of my words in this adulterous and sinful generation; of him also shall the Son of man be ashamed, when he cometh in the glory of his Father with the holy angels" (Mk.8:38).

APPLICATION:

Judgment should begin at the house of God, among the religious (v.10).

> "For if we would judge ourselves, we should not be judged" (1 Cor.11:31).
> "For the time is come that judgment must begin at the house of God: and if it first begin at us, what shall the end be of them that obey not the gospel of God?" (1 Pt.4:17).

Both John and Jesus called the Pharisees and Sadducees "vipers," meaning full of poison and venom (false doctrine) and malice and enmity (against the truth). (Cp. Mt.12:34; 23:33. Cp. Jn.8:44.)

QUESTIONS:
1. John the Baptist was a man who did not mince words. What qualities do you see in his life that you need in your own life? How can you make these qualities your own?
2. John's message was fourfold. How comfortable are you in presenting this message to a lost family member or friend? Do you know how to lead a lost person to Christ? What must you do to improve your presentation of the gospel?
3. Judgment is such a harsh word to use in today's "non-judgmental" society. How do you reconcile the judgment of God with the love of God? Who is under the judgment of God? Why?

4. HIS MESSAGE TO ALL: CHRIST--MESSIANIC PREACHING (v.11-12).

John's message had only one focus and one theme: the Messiah "cometh" (v.11); "this is he" (v.3); "prepare ye the way of the Lord" (v.3).
1. Christ is greater. Christ alone is to be exalted. John exalted Christ, not himself. The person whom God uses is the person who exalts Christ (v.11).

> "Whosoever therefore shall humble himself as this little child, the same is greatest in the kingdom of heaven" (Mt.18:4).
> "Humble yourselves in the sight of the Lord, and he shall lift you up" (Jas.4:10).

2. Christ shall baptize. The word baptism means to dip, to immerse, to submerge, to place into. John's baptism was with water, but Jesus' baptism was "in [en] the Spirit and fire."
   a. John's baptism was both a preparation and a symbol of the spiritual baptism that Jesus was to bring. John's water baptism meant two things.

1) It symbolized cleansing from all sin. A person was being prepared for the cleansing that Christ would provide.
2) It symbolized separation or dedication. A person was setting his life apart to God in a renewed spirit of dedication. He was committing himself to the Christ about whom John was preaching.
Note: John's baptism is called "the baptism of repentance"; that is, the person who repented was baptized. There could be no question; it was understood: if a person repented and actually turned to the Lord, he was baptized.
b. Jesus' spiritual baptism was a double baptism. (Only one preposition is used in the Greek for "the Spirit and fire," the preposition "in.")
1) Jesus baptizes the person *in the Spirit*. He dips, immerses, and places the person in the Spirit. Whereas the person was carnal and materialistic minded, he now becomes spiritual minded (Ro.8:5-7). The Jews had looked and longed for the day when the Spirit would come. The prophets had predicted His coming time and again. Therefore, the people knew exactly what John was predicting. The Spirit was expected to awaken and excite the people to such a degree that they would mobilize behind the Messiah and follow Him in the overthrow of all oppressors. The Spirit was to lead the people in freeing Israel and establishing it as one of the greatest nations on earth (cp. Ezk.36:26-27; 37:14; 39:29; Is.44:3; Joel 2:28).
2) Jesus baptizes the person *in fire*. Fire has several functions that graphically symbolize the work of Christ. It illuminates, warms, melts, burns, and utterly destroys. The difference between baptism with water and fire is the difference between an outward work and an inward work. Water only cleanses the outside; fire purifies within, that is, the heart. Jesus Christ separates a person from his former life and purifies him within by the fire of His Spirit. It should be noted that in John's mind the "baptism of fire" meant that the Messiah was to destroy the enemies of Israel. It was "the messianic fire of judgment" that was to come from the throne of David.

3. Christ shall judge and purge. His ministry was both to gather wheat, which is an act of love, and to separate and dispense with the chaff, which is an act of justice.
   a. There is a mixture of wheat and chaff right now: a mixture of true profession and false profession; true righteousness and false righteousness (v.12).
   b. There is a destiny for both the wheat and the chaff. The Kingdom of Heaven is the destiny of the wheat. The unquenchable fire is the destiny of the chaff (v.12).

ILLUSTRATION:
There will come a day when Jesus Christ will separate the wheat from the chaff, the sheep from the goats, the believers from the unbelievers. For unbelievers, a Christless eternity will be their tragic judgment. But for believers, for those who have been changed from unrighteousness to righteousness, they will be forever saved.
Max Lucado relates an amazing sight a friend of his saw at Disney World.

> "He was visiting Cinderella's castle. The place was filled with kids and parents. All of a sudden, all the children rushed over to one side of the big hall. Someone had come in. It was Cinderella herself!
> "The young lady in the costume was perfect for the part--beautiful features, long flowing blonde hair, radiant smile. The kids all crowded around her, each one wanting to touch her, to somehow get her attention.
> "Over on the other side of the room, however, stood a small boy of maybe six or seven. It was hard to tell how old he was because his little body was so deformed. He just stood there, looking longingly toward the lovely princess. You

could tell he wanted to go over and talk to her like all the other kids, but he remained transfixed, holding tightly to the hand of his older brother.

"It was fear that kept him there--fear of yet another rejection, of being mocked or rudely pushed aside. But above all the hubbub Cinderella noticed the boy and started walking toward him. Gently but firmly, she extricated herself from the clutching hands of the other children and made her way across the room. She dropped to her knees in front of him and placed a kiss on his forehead.

"Lucado likens this vignette to the story of God's love for us: Instead of a princess of Disney, we have the Prince of Peace. Rather than a handicapped boy, we are the thief on the cross. Both received a gift, but Jesus gave so much more than Cinderella. What if she'd taken upon herself the little boy's disfigurement and given him her beauty? That's what Jesus did for us!"[2]

And instead of being cast like chaff into the burning fires of a never-ending hell, Jesus Christ has gathered us up and given us the beauty of His righteousness.

QUESTIONS:

1. John had no personal agenda. He had no political point to make. John's task was simple: to prepare the way of the Lord. What can you do to make the Lord's agenda your own? How do some believers get off track?
2. Both wheat and chaff (believers and unbelievers) have certain destinies. What have you done to secure your eternal destiny?

SUMMARY:

If you knew Christ would return tomorrow, how prepared would you be? Have you prepared others for the return of Christ? Every day that Jesus Christ tarries is another day for you to prepare the way of the Lord. The successful believer is a person who is well prepared and spreading the gospel--just like John:

1. John ministered in the wilderness.
2. His message to the people: repent...the Kingdom of Heaven is at hand.
3. His message to the religionists, the Pharisees and Sadducees.
4. His message to all: Christ—Messianic preaching.

PERSONAL JOURNAL NOTES:
(Reflection & Response)

1. The most important thing that I learned from this lesson was:

2. The thing that I need to work on the most is:

3. I can apply this lesson to my life by:

4. Closing Prayer of Commitment: (put your commitment down on paper).

---

[2]   Max Lucado. *A Gentle Thunder.* (Dallas, TX: Word Publishing, 1995), p. 86-87.

	B. Jesus' Baptism: What Baptism is All About, 3:13-17 (Mk.1:9-11; Lk.3:21-22; Jn.1:28-34)	Suffer it to be so now: for thus it becometh us to fulfill all righteousness. Then he suffered him.	righteousness
		16 And Jesus, when he was baptized, went up straight way out of the water: and, lo, the	4. The unusual signs of Jesus' baptism
1. The startling request of Jesus: To be baptized	13 Then cometh Jesus from Galilee to Jordan unto John, to be baptized of him.	heavens were opened unto him, and he saw the Spirit of God de-	a. The heavens were opened
2. The humbling reaction of John: Humility & need	14 But John forbad him, saying, I have need to be baptized of thee, and comest thou to me?	scending like a dove, and lighting upon him: 17 And lo a voice from heaven, saying, This is my beloved	b. The Spirit descended c. The voice of God was heard
3. The godly purpose of Jesus: To fulfill all	15 And Jesus answering said unto him,	Son, in whom I am well pleased.	

Section II
THE PREPARATION FOR THE MESSIAH'S COMING
Matthew 3:1-4:11

Study 2: **JESUS' BAPTISM: WHAT BAPTISM IS ALL ABOUT**

Text: **Matthew 3:13-17**

Aim: To focus on the real purpose of Jesus' baptism.

Memory Verse:
> "And lo a voice from heaven, saying, This is my beloved Son, in whom I am well pleased" (Matthew 3:17).

INTRODUCTION:
We often find ourselves asking the wrong questions in search of the right answers. In the case of baptism, Scripture does not spell out the *how* but it is clear about *why* baptism is so important.

> "A Baptist pastor and a Lutheran pastor were overheard discussing the different ways their churches baptized people: total immersion and sprinkling on the head.
> "Lutheran pastor: 'Well, just how much water do you need? Up to their knees?'
> "Baptist pastor: 'More.'
> "Lutheran pastor: 'Up to their shoulders?'
> "Baptist pastor: 'More.'
> "Lutheran pastor: 'Over their head?'
> "Baptist pastor: 'That's right.'
> "Lutheran pastor: 'That's where we put it.'"[1]

One of the best known stories in the life of Christ is when He was baptized by John in the Jordan River. On the other hand, one of the least understood things in the Bible is *why* Jesus

---

[1] Cal & Rose Samra. *More Holy Humor.* (Nashville, TN: Thomas Nelson Publishers, 1997), p.3-4.

had to be baptized. What is baptism all about? The answer is found in studying Jesus' baptism and John's reaction to Jesus' baptism.

OUTLINE:
1. The startling request of Jesus: to be baptized (v.13).
2. The humbling reaction of John: humility and need (v.14).
3. The godly purpose of Jesus: to fulfill all righteousness (v.15).
4. The unusual signs of Jesus' baptism (v.16-17).

1. THE STARTLING REQUEST OF JESUS: TO BE BAPTIZED (v.13).

1. Note the words "to be baptized of Him [John]." Jesus came specifically to John to be baptized. Jesus was compelled to be baptized, but not *just* to be baptized. He was compelled to be baptized *by John*. He was to identify Himself with John's ministry. He was the Messiah, the Lamb of God, being proclaimed by John.
2. Note why Jesus would seek to be baptized. The very fact that the Son of God would be baptized is startling. He was the Author and Finisher of our faith, the Founder of the movement of Christianity. He was the One who was making baptism *possible and effectual* (working) for man. John's baptism was a call for men to take a stand and to become identified with a life of repentance and righteousness. Jesus needed no repentance; He was already perfectly righteous. He was the *Purchaser* of righteousness, the Ideal Man. His righteousness was the pattern, the very righteousness that could stand for and cover every man. Why then would Jesus be baptized? Very simply, in His own words, "to fulfill all righteousness."

QUESTIONS:
1. What was the significance of Jesus' being baptized by John and not someone else?
2. Does it matter who baptizes you or anyone else?

A CLOSER LOOK # 1
(3:13-17) **Galilee to Jordan**: Mark said that Jesus came "from Nazareth of Galilee" (Mk.1:9). Note several things.
1. The last recorded event of Jesus' childhood was His return to Israel from Egypt. He was only a "young child" at that time (Mt.2:19-21).
2. The only other event recorded about Jesus' childhood and early manhood was His sharing with the religious authorities in the temple at age twelve (Lk.2:42f).
3. Jesus' hometown was Nazareth. He apparently lived there between His return from Egypt until the launch of His ministry when He was about thirty years old.
4. The distance from Galilee to the Jordan river was a long journey on foot.
5. Jesus deliberately chose Jordan as the place to launch His ministry. It was in Jordan that His forerunner, John the Baptist, had been preparing the way for Him. Many were now waiting "for the consolation of Israel," that is, the coming of the Messiah.

---

2. THE HUMBLING REACTION OF JOHN: HUMILITY AND NEED (v.14).

John argued against Jesus coming to him for baptism. Why? John simply said, "I have need to be baptized of thee, and comest thou to me?" He was saying at least two things.
1. He was not worthy to baptize Christ. Christ's coming to him was too great an honor for him. He did not deserve the privilege of baptizing the Messiah, the Lamb of God (Jn.1:29).
John's humility was most unusual, for John was the *great one* in the eyes of the people at this time. Multitudes of people were flocking to him (Lk.3:7): the general public (Lk.3:10), tax collectors (Lk.3:12), soldiers (Lk.3:14), and religionists (Mt.3:7f). He had reached the summit in the public's eye. He was honored above all by vast numbers of people despite be-

ing opposed by religionists and traditionalists (Lk.7:28). Yet when Christ approached him, he lowered himself and acknowledged that he was nothing in comparison.

ILLUSTRATION:
The person who is truly humble knows one clear truth: anything good in him is because of God's grace. Human accolades and the praises of other people fall onto deaf ears. Why? Because the humble person *knows* the truth about himself.

> *"A man who had a high opinion of himself stepped on the scales in a penny arcade and was delighted with the statement on the card he received from the weighing device. Handing it to his wife, he said with much personal satisfaction, 'Here, look at this!' She took it and read aloud, 'You are dynamic, a born leader, handsome, and much admired by women for your personality.' Giving it a second look, she added, 'Hmmm, I see it's got your weight wrong too!' We may smile at that crestfallen egotist; yet he portrays the carnal man who is always pleased to think more highly of himself than he ought."[2]*

2. He personally needed the baptism of Christ. He needed what Christ had. Christ was to baptize with the Holy Spirit and fire, and John was confessing his need to receive the Holy Spirit and fire from Christ.
  ⇒ Jesus baptizes the person *in the Spirit*. He dips, immerses, and places the person in the Spirit.
  ⇒ Jesus baptizes the person *in fire*. Fire has several functions that graphically symbolize the work of Christ. It illuminates, warms, melts, burns, and utterly destroys. The difference between baptism with water and fire is the difference between an outward work and an inward work. Water only cleanses the outside; fire purifies within, that is, the heart. Jesus Christ separates a person from his former life and purifies him within by the fire of His Spirit.

APPLICATION 1:
No one is worthy of God's call; no one is worthy to minister to Christ. The fact that God allows any kind of relationship with Himself is beyond comprehension. Yet He has. He calls man to be with Him and to serve Him. This fact is too much for the human heart to contain.

> **"The centurion answered and said, Lord, I am not worthy that thou shouldest come under my roof: but speak the word only, and my servant shall be healed" (Mt.8:8).**
> **"Whosoever therefore shall humble himself as this little child, the same is greatest in the kingdom of heaven" (Mt.18:4).**

APPLICATION 2:
Everyone needs the humility that John had. It is no disgrace to confess one's need for Christ and for what He offers. John so confessed. How can a person be disgraced by confessing what everyone else already knows?
1) Man dies and desperately needs God to give him life—eternal life.
2) Man misbehaves and desperately needs the fulness of the Holy Spirit, that is, love, joy, peace.... (Gal.5:22-23).

Everyone needs the Holy Spirit and fire that Jesus had. The great (famous, powerful, wealthy) as well as the lowly need what only Christ can give. The believer always needs more and more of the infilling of the Holy Spirit. John had been "filled with the

---

[2] *INFOsearch Sermon Illustrations* (Arlington, TX: The Computer Assistant, 1-888-868-9029, 1986-1996).

Holy Spirit, even from his mother's womb" (Lk.1:15). Now with Christ confronting him face to face, he confessed his need for more of the Spirit of God and of the Lord's fire.

"Be filled with the Spirit" (Eph.5:18).

The closer a person lives to Jesus Christ, the *clearer* he sees his need for more humility and more of God's Spirit. John was already close to God; in fact, he had been "sent from God" (Jn.1:6). But he saw his need for what Christ had to give.

QUESTIONS:
1. John is a good example of a person marked by humility. Why do you think John grew to be a humble man? What characteristics in John do you need to gain in your life?
2. Do you have what John had (humility) and what Jesus had (the Holy Spirit and fire)? What is the only way a person can possess these things?
3. What is your relationship with the Holy Spirit?
    _____The Holy Spirit is an abstract, impersonal force
    _____The Holy Spirit comes and goes with the wind
    _____The Holy Spirit has filled me and continues to fill me daily

3. THE GODLY PURPOSE OF JESUS: TO FULFILL ALL RIGHTEOUSNESS (v.15).

Jesus was baptized primarily "to fulfill all righteousness." He was symbolically predicting what He was going to do for sinful man.

1. He was going to fulfill every law of God for man. Baptism was one of those laws. Therefore, he had to be baptized. (Cp. Ex.29:4-7.)

2. He was going to pay man's penalty for having broken the law—the penalty of death. His immersion was a symbol of His coming immersion into death.

3. He was demonstrating to the fullest extent His humiliation in becoming a man. He had emptied Himself and "made himself of no reputation and took upon him the form of a servant, and was made in the likeness of men" (Ph.2:6-7).

4. He was identifying with those He came to save, and He was insisting that all who follow Him become so identified.

5. He was pioneering the movement of repentance and righteousness which John was proclaiming. In founding the movement, that is, the life of righteousness, Jesus had to set the Ideal and the Pattern for every man. Every man was to be baptized; so the Son of God pioneered and established the ordinance of baptism.

6. He was initiating His ministry. John shows this (Jn.1:31-34). The High Priest had always entered his ministry in such a special ceremony (cp. Ex.29:4-7).

APPLICATION 1:
There are several lessons to learn from Christ's request to be baptized.
1) Righteousness. Every man must determine to "fulfill all righteousness" just as Christ did. Every commandment of God must be fulfilled in the believer's life.

"And this is his commandment, That we should believe on the name of his Son Jesus Christ, and love one another" (1 Jn.3:23).

2) Sacrifice. Every man should be *so willing* to give of himself that he would die in order to live for God.

"And he said to them all, If any man will come after me, let him deny himself, and take up his cross daily, and follow me" (Lk.9:23).

3) Humility. Every man should demonstrate to the fullest extent his willingness to serve others. He should become one with others and set the example of such before all.

> **"Likewise, ye younger, submit yourselves unto the elder. Yea, all of you be subject one to another, and be clothed with humility: for God resisteth the proud, and giveth grace to the humble" (1 Pt.5:5).**

4) Identifying with others. Every man should become one with all others, excluding no one from his life or service.

> **"We then that are strong ought to bear the infirmities of the weak, and not to please ourselves" (Ro.15:1).**

5) Pioneering the life of repentance and righteousness. Every man should repent and live the life of righteousness, and every man should pioneer and proclaim such a life to all other men.

> **"Repent therefore of this thy wickedness, and pray God, if perhaps the thought of thine heart may be forgiven thee" (Acts 8:22).**

6) Ministry. Every man should minister to others; he should let his willingness to minister be known.

> **"If I then, your Lord and Master, have washed your feet; ye also ought to wash one another's feet" (Jn.13:14).**

APPLICATION 2:

Christ calls and insists that a person accept His call, and Christ does not back down. Note four facts.
1) A person may feel unworthy and lacking in ability, but Christ has both the power and gifts to enable the person to accept His call.
2) A sense of unworthiness and inability is understood by God, but *refusal is not.*
3) Christ accepts only one answer to His call: "Yes, Lord—here am I" (1 Sam.3:4-6, 8; Is.6:8).
4) Humility does two puzzling things: on one hand it confesses unworthiness and inability, yet on the other hand it yields and accepts the task or gift.

QUESTIONS:
1. When you consider that Christ was baptized, what excuse is acceptable for any person not to be baptized?
2. Why is humility a necessary element in responding to God's call upon your life? How does pride quench the call of God?

4. THE UNUSUAL SIGNS OF JESUS' BAPTISM (v.16-17).

Three signs in particular are mentioned by Matthew.
1. The heavens were opened. This may be a scene of the clouds being rolled back and the dove descending from the heavens (clouds and sky). Or it may be some special vision given to Jesus and John, revealing that God was opening up heaven for the full approval and manifestation of God's power upon His Son. (Cp. Eph.1:1; Acts 7:56.)

> **"Blessed be the God and Father of our Lord Jesus Christ, who hath blessed us with all spiritual blessings in heavenly places in Christ" (Eph.1:3).**

2. The Spirit descended like a dove. The dove was given to John as a special sign that Jesus was the Son of God (Jn.1:33-34). This is the first time the Trinity, the three persons of the Godhead, is clearly seen in the New Testament. The Son, Jesus Christ, was being baptized; the Holy Spirit descended upon the Son; and God the Father voiced His approval.

APPLICATION:

Signs in Jesus' ministry were given to stir belief (Jn.5:36; 10:38). Most believers can point to very special signs and circumstances that were given by God to stir their faith and give direction to their lives. There are very special signs that prove a person has received the Holy Spirit.

> "But the **fruit of the Spirit** is love, joy, peace, longsuffering, gentleness, goodness, faith, meekness, temperance: against such there is no law" (Gal.5:22-23).

3. The voice of God was heard. Three significant things are said here.
   ⇒ *My Son*: this points to the deity of Christ (Mt.14:33; 27:43; 27:54; Mk.1:1; Jn.1:34; 3:18; 10:36; 11:4; 20:31; Acts 8:37; Ro.1:4; Heb.4:14; 1 Jn.3:8; 4:15; 5:5, 10, 13, 20).
   ⇒ *Beloved Son*: this points to the love within the Godhead (Trinity) (Jn.3:35; 10:17; Col.1:13; cp. Is.42:1).
   ⇒ *Well pleased*: this points to the perfect life Jesus lived. He was "yet without sin" (Heb.4:15; 7:26; cp. 2 Cor.5:21).

APPLICATION:

God saw the life and behavior of Christ, and He judged Christ as *well pleasing*. God sees every man, and shall judge the life and works of every man. Nothing is hidden from His eyes.

The one thing a believer should want to hear is what Jesus heard: "This is my beloved Son, in whom I am well pleased."

1) Believers are adopted as children of God (Ro.8:15; Gal.4:4-6).

2) Believers can have their lives and service approved by God.

> "Well done, thou good and faithful servant" (Mt.25:21).
>
> "For there is nothing covered, that shall not be revealed; neither hid, that shall not be known" (Lk.12:2).

ILLUSTRATION:

The record of a person's life is what God will use to render eternal judgment that will determine a person's fate. The cry of every human heart must be *"will God be pleased with me?"* God will be pleased with you if you allow the Holy Spirit to fill you with His presence.

> *"Max Lucado likens the role of the Holy Spirit in our lives to a guy who wants to learn to dance. This fellow is a rational, intelligent sort, so he goes to the bookstore and buys a how-to book. He takes it home and starts reading. He carefully does everything it says. When the instructions say sway, he sways. When the instructions say lean, he leans. When the instructions say spin, he spins. He even cuts out paper footprints and arranges them on the family room floor so he will know exactly where to step.*
>
> *"At last, he thinks he's got it down pat. He calls his wife in and says, 'Honey, watch!' With book in hand and reading aloud so she'll know he's done his homework, he follows the instructions step by step. It says, 'Take one step with your right foot.' So he takes one step with his right foot. Then it says, 'Turn slowly to the*

left.' He turns slowly to the left.' He keeps it up, reading and then dancing, reading and dancing, through the whole thing.

"Then he collapses exhausted on the sofa and says to his wife, 'What do you think? I executed it perfectly!' To which she replies, 'You executed it all right. You killed it!'

"The bumfuzzled husband says, 'But I followed the rules, I laid out the pattern, I did everything the book said.'

"'But,' she sighs, 'you forgot the most important part--the music!'

"She pops a tape into the stereo. 'Try it again. Quit worrying about the steps and just follow the music.' She holds out her hand, and he gets up and takes it. The music starts, and the next thing the guy knows he's dancing--without the book!

"Lucado observes: 'We Christians are prone to follow the book while ignoring the music. We master the doctrine, outline the chapters, memorize the dispensations, debate the rules, and stiffly step down the dance floor of life with no music in our hearts. Dancing with no music is tough stuff. Jesus knew that. For that reason, on the night before His death He introduced the disciples to the song maker of the Trinity, the Holy Spirit.'[3]

QUESTIONS:
1. What signs has God given you that stirred your faith? Is it ever wrong to base your faith in God on outward signs only? Why or why not?
2. What signs are in your life that show others that God is active in your life?
3. Are there things is in your life that do not have God's approval? What do you need to do to gain God's approval in those things that are displeasing to Him?
4. The doctrine of the Trinity is one of the essential foundations of the Christian faith. Why is it important to understand and explain this doctrine to other people?

SUMMARY:

The baptism of Jesus Christ is one of the foundational truths of the gospel. It is the responsibility of every believer to understand *why* Christ had to be baptized. Matthew gives each one of us an eye-witness account of one of the most dramatic accounts of the Bible. There was...
1. The startling request of Jesus: to be baptized.
2. The humbling reaction of John: humility and need.
3. The godly purpose of Jesus: to fulfill all righteousness.
4. The unusual signs of Jesus' baptism.

PERSONAL JOURNAL NOTES:
(Reflection & Response)

1. The most important thing that I learned from this lesson was:

2. The thing that I need to work on the most is:

3. I can apply this lesson to my life by:

4. Closing Prayer of Commitment: (put your commitment down on paper).

---

[3]   Max Lucado. *A Gentle Thunder*, p. 67-68.

CHAPTER 4

C. Jesus' Temptation: Overcoming All, 4:1-11,
(Mk.1:12-13; Lk.4:1-13)

1. Jesus' temptation
a. Led by the Spirit
b. Tempted by the devil

2. Tempt. 1: To prove His deity by using His power for personal reasons
a. The temptation
1) To secure by His own power
2) To trust Himself & His own ability instead of God
b. Jesus' answer: From Scripture
1) Man needs more than bread
2) Man needs God's life—spiritual

3. Tempt. 2: To prove His deity by the spectacular

a. The temptation
1) To test God

Then was Jesus led up of the Spirit into the wilderness to be tempted of the devil. 2 And when he had fasted forty days and forty nights, he was afterward an hungred. 3 And when the tempter came to him, he said, If thou be the Son of God, command that these stones be made bread. 4 But he answered and said, It is written, Man shall not live by bread alone, but by every word that proceedeth out of the mouth of God. 5 Then the devil taketh him up into the holy city, and setteth him on a pinnacle of the temple, 6 And saith unto him, If thou be the Son of

God, cast thyself down: for it is written, He shall give his angels charge concerning thee: and in their hands they shall bear thee up, lest at any time thou dash thy foot against a stone. 7 Jesus said unto him, It is written again, Thou shalt not tempt the Lord thy God. 8 Again, the devil taketh him up into an exceeding high mountain, and showeth him all the kingdoms of the world, and the glory of them; 9 And saith unto him, All these things will I give thee, if thou wilt fall down and worship me. 10 Then saith Jesus unto him, Get thee hence, Satan: for it is written, Thou shalt worship the Lord thy God, and him only shalt thou serve. 11 Then the devil leaveth him, and, behold, angels came and ministered unto him.

2) To attract attention by the spectacular
b. Jesus' answer: From Scripture
1) God is not to be tested

2) God is to be trusted, not the spectacular

4. Tempt. 3: To prove His deity by compromise
a. The temptation
1) To achieve His purpose by another route
2) To switch loyalties or to take a *shortcut*

b. Jesus' answer: From Scripture
1) A decisive choice
2) A worship of God alone

5. Conclusion: The triumphant victory

Section II
THE PREPARATION FOR THE MESSIAH'S COMING
Matthew 3:1-4:11

Study 3:   JESUS' TEMPTATION: OVERCOMING ALL

Text: Matthew 4:1-11

Aim: To have a plan of attack: To gain a practical strategy for overcoming even the strongest temptation.

Memory Verse:
"There hath no temptation taken you but such as is common to man: but God *is* faithful, who will not suffer you to be tempted above that ye are able; but will with the temptation also make a way to escape, that ye may be able to bear *it*" (1 Corinthians. 10:13).

MATTHEW 4:1-11

INTRODUCTION:

What does the devil have to do in order to "hook" you? Using language that is familiar to those who fish, it has been said that Satan has a vast collection of lures in his personal bait and tackle box. Every good fisherman knows that each kind of fish has different tastes. What might appeal to one fish will not necessarily appeal to another. He knows by experience which one of his lures will most likely tempt the fish he wants to catch. What kinds of lures does the devil have at his disposal? It does not require much imagination to guess some of his tempting enticements:

⇒ Sexual temptation, immorality
⇒ Ego
⇒ Materialism
⇒ Overeating
⇒ Pride
⇒ Intelligence
⇒ Physical strength

⇒ Power
⇒ Wealth
⇒ Fame
⇒ Idolatry towards sports heroes and other celebrities (including religious ones too)

If there is nothing in this list that appeals to you, do not be over-confident. Rest assured, the devil has one especially designed for you.

When are you at your weakest? When temptation comes your way, what kind of plan do you have to protect yourself from being hooked? There are far too many believers who have allowed themselves to become Satan's "catch of the day." Satan's collection can even include you--hook, line, and sinker--unless you can learn from Jesus' example.

Why was Jesus being tempted now, right after His baptism (a mountaintop experience) and right before the launch of His ministry? There is one primary reason.

Jesus Christ was about to launch His ministry--an unbelievable ministry that was to determine the eternal fate of every person who had ever lived or ever would live. The weight of its importance, the necessity of personal preparation, and the need for having the *right plan* pressed in upon Him. He had to be prepared--prepared mentally, prepared spiritually, prepared physically. How could He prepare Himself? There was only one way: He had to get alone with God and subject Himself; to gain complete control over His body and Spirit. He had to get completely apart from the world.

This Jesus did. He was "led by the Spirit" to separate Himself from food and from everything else. He got alone for forty days and nights in order to be with God. He was in earnest, ever so intense over His ministry that was about to be launched. He prayed; He thought; He meditated on the Scripture. And He planned. He bore so heavy a responsibility, and all the strain pressed in ever so heavily upon Him. Just imagine the pressure and weight pressing against His body. He prayed; He asked; He pleaded; He broke; He wept--He begged for strength and endurance to stand up under all that was to face Him in the upcoming years. The preparation went on for forty days and nights.

Once Jesus had worked out the plan necessary to launch His ministry, and once He had received the necessary strength to go forth, His personal preparation lacked only one more thing: confronting the temptations that would face Him in the upcoming years. Conquering the onslaught of temptations that lay ahead would complete His preparation. Thus "was Jesus led up of the Spirit into the wilderness to be tempted...And when He had fasted forty days and forty nights...the tempter came to Him" (Mt.4:1-2).

"Though He were a Son, yet learned He obedience by the things which He suffered" (Heb.5:8).

OUTLINE:

1. Jesus' temptation (v.1).
2. Temptation 1: to prove His deity by using His power for personal reasons (v.2-4).

3. Temptation 2: to prove His deity by the spectacular (v.5-7).
4. Temptation 3: to prove His deity by compromise (v.8-10).
5. Conclusion: the triumphant victory (v.11).

1. JESUS' TEMPTATION (v.1).

Three facts need to be noted about Jesus' temptation.
1. Jesus was tempted immediately after His baptism. The word "then" shows this. All three gospels stress this fact. He had just had a mountaintop experience, a very special experience with God. Then immediately Satan attacked Him.
2. Jesus was the *only person* who knew about the temptations. He was the only person there. What the gospel writers recorded was what He had shared with them.
3. Jesus was led by the Spirit to be tempted by the devil. Jesus was tempted for three reasons.

    a. To learn obedience--the control of His body, mind, and spirit.

> **"Though he were a Son, yet learned he obedience by the things which he suffered" (Heb.5:8).**

    b. To secure righteousness--the ideal perfection and sinlessness for man.

> **"For he hath made him to be sin for us, who <u>knew no sin</u>; that we might be made the righteousness of God in him" (2 Co.5:21).**

    c. To experience all the infirmities of human life so He would be able to help and support man.

> **"For we have not an high priest which cannot be touched with the feeling of our infirmities; but was in all points tempted like as we are, yet <u>without sin</u>. Let us therefore come boldly unto the throne of grace, that we may obtain mercy, and find grace to help in time of need" (Heb.4:15-16).**

In discussing temptation it is important to remember that God does not tempt man (Jas.1:13). God allows man to be tempted for the same reasons He led Christ to be tempted. God allows man to be tempted...
- to prove and demonstrate his faith
- to strengthen and prepare him for heavier responsibility
- to demonstrate the mercy, grace, and power of God in a human life

APPLICATION 1:
There are special times when communion with God is absolutely essential: (1) after a mountaintop experience (salvation, baptism, revival, youth camp, etc.); (2) before a great trial or time of temptation (loss of job, illness, death of a loved one, out of town business trip, chance meeting with old friends, etc.). Note that Jesus spent forty days alone with God *before* the tempter came to Him; (3) periods of great service for God. It is a great mistake to go before the public or to return from the public without spending a long time alone with God. The public, at least some of the public, will lay accolades at the feet of God's servant. Temptation lies just ahead. Preparation is essential.

APPLICATION 2:
Note three facts about the person who really knows God and is set on serving God.

1) The more a person seeks to serve God, the more he can expect to be tempted. Note how heavy and intense the temptation was against Christ.
2) The more a person seeks to serve God, the more he needs communion with God. Time alone with God is essential. A quiet time in God's Word--meditating, communing, and worshipping--is an absolute essential for the believer.
3) Spiritual strength and maturity do not exempt a person from temptation. Everyone is tempted, even the Son of God Himself. No one is exempt (1 Cor.10:13). Christ met temptation by doing three things.
> ⇒ He spent time alone with God.
> ⇒ He made sure He was led by the Spirit.
> ⇒ He relied upon the Scripture.

APPLICATION 3:

What should the believer learn about fasting from the Lord's experience? Jesus fasted for forty days. He was facing an important and critical moment in His life; the weight was pressing in upon Him. He needed special preparation. Therefore, He separated Himself from the world; He got alone with God. He was so sincere and intense that He even separated Himself from food.

How often do believers *miss out* because they are not sincere and intense enough to put time with God before all else, even before food? How much more could be done if believers sought God with the same intensity? How much more growth and ministry could be gained?

QUESTIONS:

1. Jesus was led into the wilderness by the Holy Spirit. What does this tell you about Christ's purpose in the wilderness?
2. God allows you to be tempted. What is His great purpose for doing this?
3. No one, neither the most carnal nor the most spiritual, is exempt from temptation. Everyone has to wrestle with the struggles that temptation brings. What one thing has helped you the most in overcoming temptation?

A CLOSER LOOK # 1
(4:1-11) **Jesus Christ, Temptation**: this was not the only time Jesus was tempted.
1. Satan tempted Jesus through Peter when Peter tried to divert Him from the cross. Jesus revealed what really was behind Peter's apparent concern: "Get thee behind me, Satan" (Mt.16:23).
2. Jesus commended His disciples by saying: "Ye are they which have <u>continued with me</u> in my temptations" (Lk.22:28).
3. Jesus faced the severest temptation of His life in the Garden of Gethsemane. It was there that Satan made a last ditch effort to divert Christ from the cross.
In referring to Christ's experience in Gethsemane, Scripture says to all believers: "Ye have not yet resisted unto blood, striving against sin" (Heb.12:4; cp. Lk.22:44).

APPLICATION:

The devil knows just where to tempt a person.
1) *In the wilderness*: when a person is without bread, when he really has need. This is the temptation that appeals to the lust of the flesh.
2) *On the pinnacle*: when a person is before multitudes. This is the temptation that appeals to pride--the pride of life (fame).
3) *On a high mountain*: when a person sees what is available--sometimes rightfully his, sometimes just desired. This is the temptation that appeals to the lust of the eyes.

1. Think of a time when you were in a wilderness--doing without something you needed. What was the strongest temptation you experienced? What was the outcome of your experience? Would you do anything differently today? Why or why not?
2. For many believers, gaining recognition and fame is a risky thing. Do you agree or disagree with this statement? Why?
3. What do you really want in life? How close are you to obtaining what you want? What is God's role in helping you get what you want?

A CLOSER LOOK # 2

(4:1-11) **Temptation**: the word temptation is used here in both a good and a bad sense. In the good sense it means to test, to try, to prove. It does not mean to seduce into sin. Its purpose is not to defeat or to destroy. The idea is not that one is tempted, seduced, enticed, and pulled into sin by the Holy Spirit (cp. Jas.1:13); but one is tested, proved, strengthened, reinforced, and purified through the trials of temptation.

In the bad sense, it means to tempt, to seduce, to entice, and to pull someone away from God into the way of sin, of self, and of Satan (Mt.4:1; 1 Cor.7:5; 1 Th.3:5; Gal.6:1; Jas.1:13-14).

Jesus was led into the wilderness by the Spirit *to be tested*. The Spirit did not seduce or entice Jesus to do evil, but He led Jesus into circumstances whereby He could learn obedience and discipline. Through such trials Jesus was to be perfected and enabled to succor all those who suffer trials (Heb.4:15-16; 5:8).

Six things need to be said about overcoming temptation.

1. Temptation has its deepest roots in passion and appetite (Mk.7:20-23; Jas.1:14). It comes directly from within, from man's heart, not from without. And it does not come from God. "God cannot be tempted with evil; neither tempteth he any man" (Jas.1:3). God does not tempt any man in a bad sense. What He does is look upon His people as they endure temptation, and He strengthens them to bear the temptation. By such He teaches them discipline and obedience for a greater work (Ro.8:28; 2 Cor.1:3-4; Heb.5:8; 1 Pt.1:6-7).

2. No man confronts any temptation that is not common to all men (1 Cor.10:13).

3. God does not allow the believer to be tempted beyond what he is able to bear. There is always a way to escape (1 Cor.10:13).

4. Jesus Christ understands temptation. He was tempted in all points just as all men are tempted, yet He never sinned (Heb.2:18; 4:15).

5. Jesus Christ is a sympathetic High Priest in helping the believer through temptation (Heb.2:17-18; 4:15).

6. Temptation is overcome...
- by submitting to God and resisting the devil (Jas.4:7-8; 1 Pt.5:8-9)
- by using and obeying Scripture to combat temptation (Lk.4:4; cp. Dt.4:8; 4:12; 6:13, 16; 8:3; 10:20).

---

1. What things are most likely to tempt you? What can you do to protect yourself when these temptations occur?
2. Jesus was led into the wilderness by the Spirit to be tested. What should you do when being led into a period of testing by God?
3. Before temptation comes your way, can you prepare?

A CLOSER LOOK # 3

(4:1-11) **Faith--Proof--Evidence--Corruption**: Jesus Christ was tempted three times by the devil. He was tempted to prove that He was the Son of God. What was wrong with proving His deity?

Proof is not God's way; faith is God's way. Proof is not what God wants; faith *is* what God wants. God wants to be trusted and loved. He wants to be freely loved, not loved because of force--because some person is constrained by irrefutable proof. There are facts, plenty of proofs that He is the Son of God; but in the final analysis, an act of faith has to be taken. No one has seen God. God cannot be known by the physical senses. To know God a person has to leap by faith, reach out for God in an act of belief, believing that God will reward his faith.

> **"Without faith it is impossible to please Him [God]; for he that cometh to God must believe that He is, and that He is a rewarder of them that diligently seek Him" (Heb.11:6).**

Jesus Christ had come to establish and construct the way of faith. Therefore, Jesus Christ had to reject anything that led men away from the life of faith. Note that all three temptations had to do with man's senses and the physical world. If Christ had given in and secured the loyalty of men by feeding bread to the whole world, or by performing a spectacular miracle, or by taking over the kingdoms of this world, life would end and end soon. Why? Because everything dies. Everything wastes away. The world is physical and material, corruptible and dying, deteriorating and decaying. It does not last. That is just the way of the physical world and all within it. This is the very reason Jesus Christ has come--to conquer the physical world of decay and death, and to usher in the eternal world of the spirit--by the way of faith.

Therefore, Jesus Christ had to live the life of faith Himself. He had to walk the way of faith, of trusting and believing God Himself. He had to reject the devil's *proofs* and show and lead men by faith.

2. TEMPTATION 1: TO PROVE HIS DEITY BY USING HIS POWER FOR PERSONAL REASONS (v.2-4).

The devil tempted Christ to prove that He was the Son of God, that is, to secure the loyalty of men by two acts.

1. Christ was tempted to use His own power to meet both a personal and a world-wide need: hunger. He was hungry and His hunger was critical. He had not eaten for forty days. The devil tempted Him to create bread and feed Himself, and in this suggestion was the hidden idea that He could feed the world and prove Himself to be the Son of God. By such He could secure what He was after: the loyalty and worship of men. Men would rush to serve any Messiah or man who could meet their physical and material needs.

2. Christ was tempted to trust Himself, not God, and to choose another way other than God's way. God's way was the way of faith which included both time--time to suffer the trials of life--and the cross. The devil was saying "trust yourself, take a shorter route. Feed yourself and the world. Your needs can be met, and you can have the loyalty of men immediately."

There are two things wrong with the reasoning of this temptation.

1. Man needs more than bread. He needs more than physical life and physical needs being met.

2. Man needs God's life. He needs eternal life and he needs his spiritual needs met.

Bread is a necessity of life. Jesus could have proven that He was the Son of God by using His supernatural power to create bread; He could have secured the loyalty of men by feeding them, that is, by meeting their physical needs. But He would have failed in at least two points.

⇒ He would have failed in meeting the spiritual needs of man.
⇒ He would have failed by teaching error--the error that the physical is more important than the spiritual, and that receiving is more important than giving.

There is a spiritual hunger that is just not met by bread. Man's responsibility is the same as Christ's was: to trust God and to seek the things of God as he walks day by day throughout life.

> "Seek ye first the kingdom of God, and His righteousness; and [then] all these things shall be added unto you" (Mt.6:33).
> "And Jesus said unto them, I am the bread of life: he that cometh to me shall never hunger; and he that believeth on me shall never thirst" (Jn.6:35).

APPLICATION 1:
Believers often face the very same temptation (cp. 1 Cor.10:13).
1) They are tempted to prove who they are and to act in their own strength and their own ability.
2) They are tempted to meet a real need (personal or community) in a wrong and illegitimate way: misusing one's position and abilities.
3) They are tempted to stress physical needs over the spiritual needs of men--to feed them bread only, never bringing them to the cross (see Lk.9:23).
4) They are tempted to trust self, not God, trusting one's own strength and abilities.

APPLICATION 2:
Four clear lessons are seen in this temptation.
1) Temptation often attacks an area of desperate need such as hunger. There is a right and a wrong way to meet any need. It is often felt that if a real need can be met, then how it is met is immaterial, excusable. That is, the end justifies the means.
2) Man must learn that he does not live by bread alone. The physical alone will not satisfy. Man is spirit; therefore, he needs God and is dependent upon God. He cannot live without God. "Thou shalt eat, but not be satisfied" (Micah 6:14 cp. Haggai 1:6, 9; Mt.6:24-34).
3) Temptation is to be resisted by using the Word of God. The believer must study and learn the Word of God in order to withstand temptation (Ps.119:9, 11; Col.3:16; 2 Tim.2:15; 3:16; 1 Pt.2:2-3).
4) When *needs arise*, a person must always strengthen himself against temptation. The greater the need, the greater the attack of temptation.

QUESTIONS:
1. When are you most likely to trust in your own power to overcome temptation?
2. How can the Word of God help you when temptation attacks you? What are your favorite verses to read when temptation comes?

3. TEMPTATION 2: TO PROVE HIS DEITY BY THE SPECTACULAR (v.5-7).

The devil tempted Christ to prove that He was the Son of God by doing two more acts.

1. Christ was tempted to test God. He was tempted to do the spectacular. He was to jump off the towering pinnacle of the temple and let God send His angels to catch Him in mid-air and lift Him gently to the ground. Since He was God's only Son, God would certainly bear Him up (so the devil reasoned).

2. Christ was tempted to attract attention by the spectacular. The worshippers at the temple, seeing such a spectacular event, would accept and proclaim Him to be the Son of God.

There are two things wrong with the reasoning behind this temptation.
⇒ God is not to be tested. His will, His power, His protection, His promises are not to be presumed upon, taken advantage of, or misused. God is not to be tested or tried; God is to be trusted. His will and His Word are to be trusted and obeyed just as they are laid down; all things are to be done exactly as He says.
⇒ God is to be trusted, not the spectacular. God wants men to believe Him because they love Him as their Father, not because of events and happenings, whether they be spectacular or commonplace (Is.43:10).

Christ would have failed in at least two points if He had given in to this temptation.
1. He would have tempted God to misuse His power. Christ would have placed Himself in a threatening position and risked His life, expecting God to save Him. This act would have abused God's will and misused what God had promised. This act would have ignored what God really wanted and had really said.
2. He would have centered people's attention on the spectacular. The mission of Christ was to focus people's attention on faith in God--in particular, their desperate need for God and His eternal kingdom.

> **"And Jesus answering saith unto them, Have faith in God"** (Mk.11:22).

APPLICATION 1:
Believers are often tempted the same as Christ was (cp. 1 Cor.10:13).
1) They are tempted to test God, to lay hold of some Biblical promise and take it out of context, to misuse and misapply it. The motive is sometimes good, for the believer wishes to do great things for God. What happens is that he lays hold of some great promise of God and launches out, but the promise is misused and misapplied. The *great things* were not God's will for the believer. We must always remember that God does give us great promises. But we must stay close to God (meditation and prayer) and stay in His Word in order to rightly understand His promises. This alone will keep us from misusing and misapplying His promises.
2) They are tempted to center people's attention upon the spectacular, not upon God and faith in God. God is to be trusted, not the spectacular. God is to be the focus and center of *all that is said and done*, not the spectacular.

APPLICATION 2:
Three things are absolutely essential in order to conquer this temptation.
1) Living with God moment by moment--genuinely living in constant communion with Him.
2) Living in God's Word--really knowing His promises in order to use them as they were meant to be used (cp. 2 Cor.2:12; 2 Tim.2:15; 3:16; cp. Acts 17:11; cp. Ps.1:2f).
3) Know that the power of Satan is a limited power. He can only tempt; he cannot force a person to sin. He could not push Christ off the pinnacle. He cannot push man into sin. The lust or desire is from within man. Satan's temptation can only stir and arouse the desire and lust. Satan cannot cause a man to lust. Therefore, if a person is living in communion with God and living in God's Word, he will be stirred to obey God more than he is stirred to yield to the temptation.

But remember: Satan knew Scripture and knew it well. It is possible to know the Scripture and not know God. It is even possible to know the Scripture and to stand against God, abusing and misusing His Word.

ILLUSTRATION:

Many believers are tempted to test God to try determine His perfect will in a particular area. History is full of people who have missed God's best because they put God to a foolish test.

> *"When John Wesley was a 32-year-old missionary in Georgia, he fell in love with a beautiful Christian young woman. He wanted to marry her, but some of his friends tried to convince him that remaining single would be more pleasing to the Lord. One of them suggested that they draw lots to discern God's will on the matter. Wesley agreed with the idea. The friend prepared three small slips of paper, writing on one, 'Marry'; on another, 'Think not of it this year'; and on the third, 'Think of it no more.' After he placed them in a container, Wesley closed his eyes and drew one out. It read: 'Think of it no more.' Wesley was heartbroken, but he ended the courtship. Fifteen years later he married a wealthy widow who turned out to be a poor companion and a hindrance to his ministry. After 20 years of mutual misery, she left him. Apparently he should have married the Georgia peach!"*[1]

QUESTIONS:

1. We live in a society where the spectacular is often the expected. What motivates people to pursue the supernatural instead of focusing upon God's will, God's movement, God's timing?
2. Have you ever claimed a verse of Scripture that was taken out of context? If so, what verse was it and what did you learn from your experience?
3. Even Satan knows the Bible. How is it possible to know so much about the Bible but never know the Lord? Do you know anyone like this? What can you share with this person who is so deceived?

4. TEMPTATION 3: TO PROVE HIS DEITY BY COMPROMISE (v.8-10).

The devil tempted Christ to prove that He was the Son of God by compromising.

1. Christ was tempted to compromise His ministry and His mission. He was tempted to secure the world without the cross, without paying the price. He was tempted to choose another way instead of God's way--to achieve His purpose by another route. He was attracted to use the wrong means for reaching a desired end. If He bowed down and worshipped the devil, the kingdoms of the world and the loyalty of men were to be His.

2. Christ was tempted to compromise His life and His loyalty. He was tempted to switch loyalties. He was offered the world and the sovereign leadership of the world if He would do just one thing: worship the devil. What does this mean? It means that Christ was tempted to allow the world (including man) to remain corruptible and dying with no hope of life eternal with God. It was a temptation to allow the world to continue as it is, and to allow the devil to continue his work within the world in order to frustrate God's eternal plan for the world.

There are two things wrong with the reasoning behind this temptation.
⇒ Compromise with the devil and the world is not God's way. God's way is to conquer the corruption and death of this world.
⇒ God alone is to be worshipped, not the devil nor the world and its power.

---

[1] *INFOsearch Sermon Illustrations* (Arlington, TX: The Computer Assistant, 1-888-868-9029, 1986-1996).

If Christ had given in to this temptation, He would have failed in at least two points.

⇒ He would have secured the kingdoms of this world through compromise, not by God's hands. God had promised Him the world and the loyalty of its citizens, but it was to come by way of the cross. The way of God was far better, for the kingdoms promised by God were to be eternal.

⇒ He would have switched His loyalty from God to the devil. He would have forsaken God for this world and its prince, Satan (Eph.2:2).

> **"For what is a man profited, if he shall gain the whole world, and lose his own soul? or what shall a man give in exchange for his soul?" (Mt.16:26).**

APPLICATION 1:

Note four significant lessons in this point.

1) A believer is often tempted to compromise both his life and his work or ministry. The tempter, Satan, wants a person to live for the world *only*, to ignore his spirit that is destined to live forever. He wants a person's attention and energy and effort. He wants a person given over to this world and to this life *only*.

2) Satan deceives and lies. The kingdoms of this world are only temporary--for a few short years. The life of a person and the life of the world itself is short, ever so short. It all ends.

3) Believers cannot receive from Satan what God has promised them, that is, eternal life (cp. 2 Pt.1:4; 3:8-15).

4) Temptation must be resisted immediately. Jesus did not hesitate a moment in resisting temptation.

APPLICATION 2:

When a believer is tempted time after time, he faces two critical dangers.

1) Discouragement. The sheer number and force of extreme temptations can discourage a person. But succumbing to temptation and sin can discourage a person even more! In fact, the greater the fall of a person, the more unworthy and self-accusing he becomes. Self-pity, shame, guilt, and failure always discourage to some degree. (Cp. 1 Pt.4:12-13.)

2) Over-confidence. When a believer overcomes temptation, he grows and becomes stronger and more mature, gaining more confidence. However, there is danger in this. He can begin to feel strong and mature enough to conquer temptation on his own. He can feel above temptation, begin to think everything he does is right, feeling so mature and strong that he can conquer any temptation.

QUESTIONS:

1. Think for a moment. When you are tempted and get pushed into a corner, what are you most likely to compromise?

    _____Your word   _____Your relationships with other people

    _____Your ethics   _____Your relationship with the Lord

    _____Your behavior before others _____None of the above

2. Everyday, people get their own way--by hook or by crook--and later come to regret it. What have you ever gotten that you later realized was not worth the cost?

3. A believer faces two very real dangers when tempted time and again: discouragement and over-confidence. Which one of these terms best describe where you are right now? What do you need to do in order to better deal with your particular situation?

5. CONCLUSION: THE TRIUMPHANT VICTORY (v.11).

Christ resisted the temptation the only way He could: by doing exactly what the Word of God said. He simply obeyed God; therefore, He never got out of the will of God. The devil was defeated and temptation and sin were conquered. Note that the devil left Jesus alone for awhile and some angels came and ministered to Him.

<u>**APPLICATION:**</u>
⇒ The devil is a conquered enemy.

> **"And having spoiled principalities and powers, he made a show of them openly, triumphing over them in it" (Col.2:15).**

⇒ There is always an escape from temptation. God knows how to deliver the godly out of temptation.

> **"The Lord knoweth how to deliver the godly out of temptations, and to reserve the unjust unto the day of judgment to be punished" (2 Pt.2:9).**

⇒ When temptation is resisted, the devil flees and the believer is relieved for a while.

> **"Submit yourselves therefore to God. Resist the devil, and he will flee from you" (Jas.4:7; cp. v.11).**

<u>**ILLUSTRATION:**</u>
If you are seeking to walk with the Lord, Satan takes the initiative and tempts you to fall away. Satan's attacks are a good sign that you are on the right track.

> *"A young Christian who worked for a rich man was always telling his employer that Satan was constantly battling with him, but he always won over Satan. The master made fun of him, telling him that Satan never bothered him. How was that? The young Christian could not answer him. One day, however, they went hunting together. The employer shot at some wild ducks. Some he killed, and some he just wounded. 'Run,' the employer said, 'and catch the wounded ones first before they run away.' The young Christian came back laughing. He had the answer to the big question. 'You know sir,' he said, 'why Satan does not tempt you? Because you are spiritually dead, just like those ducks. He goes after the live ones, ones like me.'"*[2]

Satan *is* after you if you are trying to walk with the Lord--but God is faithful--there *is* a means of escape.

<u>**QUESTIONS:**</u>
1. There is an end to every temptation. What can you do to help maintain your focus on God as you walk through a temptation?
2. What is the only way a person can escape from the harm of a temptation?
3. The devil is a defeated foe, a conquered enemy. If he is defeated why does he win so many battles in the lives of believers?
4. What guarantee do you have that once you have overcome one temptation, another one will not follow right behind?

---

[2] Spiros Zodhiates, Th.D. *Illustrations of Bible Truths*. (Chattanooga, TN: AMG International Inc., 1995), p.223-224.

SUMMARY:

What will it take to hook you and cause you to fall into temptation? Remember that God does not tempt you, but He does allow you to be tempted. Temptation should not be feared, but faced in the power of God: an opportunity to once again prove your love for God. In order to say no to temptation and yes to God, you must learn from Jesus' example.
1. Jesus' temptation: He was led by the Spirit but tempted by Satan.
2. Temptation 1: to prove His deity by using His power for personal reasons.
3. Temptation 2: to prove His deity by the spectacular.
4. Temptation 3: to prove His deity by compromise.
5. Conclusion: the triumphant victory.

PERSONAL JOURNAL NOTES:
(Reflection & Response)

1. The most important thing that I learned from this lesson was:

2. The thing that I need to work on the most is:

3. I can apply this lesson to my life by:

4. Closing Prayer of Commitment: (put your commitment down on paper).

	III. THE BEGIN- NING OF THE MESSIAH'S MINISTRY, 4:12-25 A. Jesus' Ministry: Going Forth with Purpose, 4:12-17	14 That it might be fulfilled which was spoken by Esaias the prophet, saying, 15 The land of Zabu- lon, and the land of Nephthalim, by the way of the sea, be- yond Jordan, Galilee of the Gentiles;	3. There was the delib- erate decision to fulfill Scripture 4. There was the mis- sion a. To go to needy lands
1. There was the sign to begin: John's im- prisonment 2. There was the chosen headquarters: Galilee a. Jesus left Nazareth b. Jesus headquar- tered in Capernaum	12 Now when Jesus had heard that John was cast into prison, he departed into Gali- lee; 13 And leaving Naz- areth, he came and dwelt in Capernaum, which is upon the sea coast, in the borders of Zabulon and Neph- thalim:	16 The people which sat in darkness saw great light; and to them which sat in the region and shadow of death light is sprung up. 17 From that time Je- sus began to preach, and to say, Repent: for the kingdom of heaven is at hand,	b. To take people in darkness & show them great light c. To take people in death & give them light 5. There was the mes- sage a. Repentance b. Reason: the K. of Heaven is at hand

Section III
THE BEGINNING OF THE MESSIAH'S MINISTRY
Matthew 4:12-25

Study 1: JESUS' MINISTRY: GOING FORTH WITH PURPOSE

Text: Matthew 4:12-17

Aim: To strive to be like Jesus: to learn how to block out all distractions and focus upon your God-ordained purpose.

Memory Verse:
"From that time Jesus began to preach, and to say, Repent: for the kingdom of heaven is at hand" (Matthew 4:17).

INTRODUCTION:
Life has often been described as a race. Imagine if you will, several expensive thorough-bred race horses. These striking animals have been bred from the purest lines. Years of preparation and training have been invested with the hope that the horses will do the obvious--run fast and win the race. More than one investor's dream has been dashed when the prized steed remains in the gate while the other horses responded to the starter's pistol and raced toward the prize.

The distracted horse is a lot like some believers: the starter's gun has cracked, but many of us are distracted and stuck in the gate. Why is this so? There are many who live day to day with no focus, no goal, no vision for the future, and consequently, with no impact upon the world for the cause of Christ. God has called each believer to make a difference in our world. The only way this is possible is to learn how to block out other distractions and focus upon our God-given purpose.

The time had now come for Jesus to go forth to His great purpose. There is much in this passage for every believer, layman and minister alike. Every believer is called of God, actually sent into the world for a specific purpose. The sad fact is that too many believers are not aware of their purpose. They do not know why God sent them into the world. They have not sought God to discover His purpose for their lives; therefore, they are just walking through life doing the same tasks and activities which occupied their time before they were saved. But for the believer who knows God's purpose for his life, the day comes when he is to go forth to that purpose. He is to go forth as Christ went forth, to carry on the great task which God has given him to do.

OUTLINE:
1. There was the sign to begin: John's imprisonment (v.12).
2. There was the chosen headquarters: Galilee (v.12-13).
3. There was the deliberate decision to fulfill Scripture (v.14).
4. There was the mission (v.15-16).
5. There was the message (v.17).

1. THERE WAS THE SIGN TO BEGIN: JOHN'S IMPRISONMENT (v.12).

God showed Christ when to begin His ministry. The imprisonment of John was His sign to launch out in full force. He had been ministering in Judea (Jn.4:1) but not as publicly or as extensively as He was now to do. He could now go forth and tackle His task to the fullest. Why now? Why not earlier?

Jesus could not give the appearance of competing with John. If He had begun His ministry in full force before John's ministry had been completed, the loyalty of the people would have been divided. John was sent to prepare the way, and the way was not fully prepared until John was removed from the scene.

APPLICATION 1:
The believer who lives and walks in Christ will be *directed* by God.
1) He will know God's purpose for his life, as will be pointed out throughout this lesson.
2) He will know when to go forth to his task, when to carry out God's purpose for his life—just as Christ knew.

> **"Howbeit when he, the Spirit of truth, is come, he will guide you into all truth: for he shall not speak of himself; but whatsoever he shall hear, that shall he speak: and he will show you things to come" (Jn.16:13).**

APPLICATION 2:
The overshadowing or overtaking of John by Jesus holds a significant lesson for believers of every generation. The believer is to be serving the Lord from day one of his conversion, and when the day comes for him to launch out in full force to carry out God's purpose for his life, he must go forth. Within every generation, God raises up witnesses to follow other witnesses in order to carry on the work of the ministry (Eph.4:11-12). Believers are not rivals. They are joint servants of the Lord who work together in their respective ministries. They are not to compete against one another. And when the time comes, when a servant's ministry is completed, he is to willingly step aside. In fact, a believer should prepare to have his ministry overtaken, to move aside while God raises up others to carry on after he is gone. God cannot wait until a generation is gone to raise up others. There would not be time for the new generation to take over and effect a smooth transition. God has to raise up new servants and thrust

them into the forefront as the older generation fades into the background. Such overtaking should be accepted willingly and graciously.

> "For I say, through the grace given unto me, to every man that is among you, not to think of himself more highly than he ought to think; but to think soberly, according as God hath dealt to every man the measure of faith. For as we have many members in one body, and all members have not the same office: so we, being many, are one body in Christ, and every one members one of another. Having then gifts differing according to the grace that is given to us" (Ro.12:3-6).

QUESTIONS:
1. God's timing is perfect and therefore should be considered most important to the believer. Can you think of a time when you got ahead of God and later regretted doing so? What should you have done differently?
2. You can take comfort in the fact that God will reveal His purpose for your life--if you are faithful to seek it. How can you go about seeking His purpose, seeking with assurance of an answer?

2. THERE WAS THE CHOSEN HEADQUARTERS: GALILEE (v.12-13).

Christ left Nazareth. Why? Nazareth was His hometown. Why did He not make His hometown His headquarters? The reason is clear: the city had rejected Christ. "No prophet is accepted in His own country" (Lk.4:24). They had thrown Him out and had attempted to kill Him (Lk.4:29). Therefore, Christ set up headquarters in the city of Capernaum, in the province of Galilee. Capernaum lay in the northernmost point of Palestine. It was deliberately chosen by Christ as "His own city" (Mt.9:1; Is.9:1-7).

God had prepared Galilee down through history for the coming of His Son's ministry. Several facts show this (cp. Gal.4:4).
1. Throughout history Galilee had been invaded and repopulated again and again with different people and cultures from all over the world. Over the years such an influx of differing people had created an atmosphere susceptible to new personalities and ideas.
2. Galilee was strategically located. The world's leading roads passed right through its borders. Merchants from all over the world passed through and boarded in its cities.
3. Galilee was heavily populated. It was also surrounded by the Samaritans, Phoenicians, and Syrians, making it an open door for world evangelization. It was one of the most fertile lands in that part of the world. This fact, plus the traveling trade, led numbers to settle within its borders. There were within the district over two hundred cities with a population of fifteen thousand or more.[1] There were multitudes for Jesus to reach.
4. Galilee was open to new and fresh ideas. Its people, having come from all over the world, were liberal minded, always looking for new and fresh ideas to stimulate and challenge their thinking.
It was for these reasons that Christ chose Galilee to begin His ministry. The area was an open door for people to spread the news that the Messiah had come and the Kingdom of Heaven was being ushered in.

APPLICATION:
People can reject the gospel and the Savior. Just imagine! The Lord's own hometown rejected Him (cp. Mt.9:1). Therefore, a person's place of ministry should be de-

---

[1] *Josephus.* Quoted by William Barclay. *The Gospel of Matthew,* Vol.1. "Daily Study Bible Series." (Philadelphia, PA: Westminster Press, Began in 1953), p.66.

liberately chosen. He should consider strategic locations and as many factors as possible.

> "Go ye therefore, and teach all nations, baptizing them in the name of the Father, and of the Son, and of the Holy Ghost: teaching them to observe all things whatsoever I have commanded you: and, lo, I am with you alway, even unto the end of the world" (Mt.28:19-20).

QUESTIONS:
1. How would you describe the openness of your community to the gospel:
   ⇒   a Nazareth which has rejected Christ?
   ⇒   a Capernaum which is open to the message of the gospel?
   What facts led you to make your decision?
2. God plants us where we can best serve Him. Where has He strategically placed you to share God's love? How have you made a difference?
3. Even Christ's closest neighbors rejected Him. When people reject you because of your love for Christ, what can you learn from Christ's experience?

3. THERE WAS THE DELIBERATE DECISION TO FULFILL SCRIPTURE (v.14).

This stresses the critical importance of the Scripture (Is.9:1-2; 42:6-7). A believer should heed the Scripture—all of it (see 2 Tim.3:16; 2 Pt.1:19-21).

> "Now ye are clean through the word which I have spoken unto you" (Jn.15:3).
> "All scripture is given by inspiration of God, and is profitable for doctrine, for reproof, for correction, for instruction in righteousness" (2 Tim.3:16).

ILLUSTRATION:
Somewhere along the way, many believers have concluded that obedience to God is based upon a mind filled with spiritual information and trivia. The line of reasoning is: "If I can quote a few verses of Scripture and I obey God most of the time, then I'm doing pretty good." It is this kind of thinking that leads to wrong conclusions, as illustrated by this example.

> "Howard Hendricks says we often make the mistake of equating Bible knowledge with spirituality. During his college days, Hendricks was a church youth director. One boy in the group had memorized over 600 verses and could recite them word-perfect! This kid was amazing--just give him a reference and he would reel off the verse.
> "One day Hendricks became aware that money was missing from the Sunday school offering. After a bit of investigation, he found the culprit. You guessed it! It was the Bible-memory expert!
> "Catching him red-handed, Hendricks escorted the boy to his office for a little talk. When he used a Scripture verse to drive home the point that stealing was wrong, the boy told him he had misquoted the verse. Finally, Hendricks asked, 'Do you see any connection between that verse and your stealing from the offering?'
> "At first, the boy said no. Then he said, 'Well, maybe.'
> "'What's the connection?'
> "'I got caught!'

"From God's perspective, says Hendricks, the name of the game isn't knowledge--it's active obedience."[2]

There are a lot of people like this boy who misquote the Bible and only believe what they like about God's Word. God's Word is true and must be obeyed--all of it, all of the time.

QUESTIONS:
1. Some believers are prone to "pick and choose" certain Scriptures while ignoring the more demanding commandments from God's Word. How can you guard against this happening to you?
2. All of Scripture is to be obeyed. What is the importance of this fact? What is the Scriptural basis for this fact?

4. THERE WAS THE MISSION (v.15-16).

Christ's mission was people; He focused on people.
   1. Note what is said about the mission of Christ.
      a. Christ went to people in needy lands.

> **"Even as the Son of man came not to be ministered unto, but to minister, and to give his life a ransom for many" (Mt.20:28).**
> **"For the Son of man is come to seek and to save that which was lost" (Lk.19:10).**

      b. Christ took people in darkness and showed them light.

> **"In him was life; and the life was the light of men" (Jn.1:4).**

      c. Christ took people in death and gave them light.

> **"Verily, verily, I say unto you, He that heareth my word, and believeth on him that sent me, hath everlasting life, and shall not come into condemnation; but is passed from death unto life" (Jn.5:24).**

APPLICATION:
The ultimate mission of *every* believer--through God's individual purpose for him or her--is people: to do what Christ did, that is, reach people. Since Christ came, two wonderful things are now present.
1) Light is now present. Man no longer has to seek light because God sent the light into the world.
2) Choice is now present. Man can now choose light; he does not have to remain in darkness.

   2. Note what is said about the people of the world.
      a. People are in darkness.

> **"But if thine eye be evil, thy whole body shall be full of darkness. If therefore the light that is in thee be darkness, how great is that darkness!" (Mt.6:23).**

---

[2] Howard and William Hendricks. *Iron Sharpens Iron*. (Chicago, IL: Moody Press, 1995), p. 123. Cited in *INFOsearch Sermon Illustrations* (Arlington, TX: The Computer Assistant, 1-888-868-9029, 1986-1996).

b. People sit in darkness. They accept and are comfortable in darkness, pleased with their lives. Scripture says men love darkness rather than light (Jn.3:19-21).

> "And this is the condemnation, that light is come into the world, and men loved darkness rather than light, because their deeds were evil. For every one that doeth evil hateth the light, neither cometh to the light, lest his deeds should be reproved. But he that doeth truth cometh to the light, that his deeds may be made manifest, that they are wrought in God" (Jn.3:19-21).

c. People sit in the region and shadow of death. Note: they are in the region (territory, country, area) of death; but right now, while living on the earth, death is only a shadow. There is hope for man: man has the opportunity to be saved from death, from doom, and from condemnation.

> "Forasmuch then as the children are partakers of flesh and blood, he also himself likewise took part of the same; that through death he might destroy him that had the power of death, that is, the devil; and deliver them who through fear of death were all their lifetime subject to bondage" (Heb.2:14-15).

d. People now see a *great* light, the greatest of lights: Christ Himself.

> "Then spake Jesus again unto them, saying, I am the light of the world: he that followeth me shall not walk in darkness, but shall have the light of life" (Jn.8:12).

e. People now have a light that is "sprung up." They have a light that grows and continues on. There is a growing opportunity to walk out of the darkness into the light and to live forever, conquering death (cp. Heb.2:14-15).

> "Verily, verily, I say unto you, He that heareth my word, and believeth on him that sent me, hath everlasting life, and shall not come into condemnation; but is passed from death unto life" (Jn.5:24).

QUESTIONS:
1. The most important task for any ministry is to meet the spiritual, physical, and emotional needs of people. What are some of the ways your church ministers to people? What needs are going unmet that you are aware of? What is your role, if any, in meeting the needs of other people through your church?
2. The lost people of the world, despite what they might claim, live in darkness. What is the only way to remove the darkness from their lives?
3. Do you ever struggle with a desire to return to the dark, to the shadows of sin? What spiritual tools has God given you to keep you walking in the light?

5. THERE WAS THE MESSAGE (v.17).

The words "from that time" are extremely significant. They indicate *urgency, persistence, perseverance*: three excellent words describing the obsession of Christ with His mission and message. It had two major points.

1. Christ preached repentance. Repentance means to change; to turn; to change one's mind; to turn one's life. It is a turning away from sin and turning toward God. It is a change

of mind, a forsaking of sin. It is putting sin out of one's thoughts and behavior. It is resolving never to think or do a thing again. (Cp. Mt.3:2; Lk.13:2-3; Acts 2:38; 3:19; 8:22; 26:20.) The change is turning away from lying, stealing, cheating, immorality, cursing, drunkenness, and the other so-called glaring *sins of the flesh*. But the change is also turning away from *the silent sins of the spirit* such as self-centeredness, selfishness, envy, bitterness, pride, covetousness, anger, evil thoughts, hopelessness, laziness, jealousy, lust.

    a. Repentance involves two turns. There is a turning *away* from sin and a turning *toward* God. It is a turning *to* God *away* from sin, whether sins of thought or deed. (Cp. 1 Th.1:9; Acts 14:15.)

    b. Repentance is more than sorrow. Sorrow may or may not be involved in repentance. A person may repent simply because he wills to change, or a person may repent because he senses an agonizing sorrow within. But the sense or feeling of sorrow is not repentance. Repentance is both the change of mind and the actual turning of one's life *away* from sin and *toward* God.

> **"I tell you, Nay: but, except ye repent, ye shall all likewise perish" (Lk.13:3).**
>
> **"Repent ye therefore, and be converted, that your sins may be blotted out, when the times of refreshing shall come from the presence of the Lord" (Acts 3:19; cp. Acts 2:38).**

ILLUSTRATION:

What is real repentance? Repentance is not some trite cliché or popular trend. Repentance changes a person's life. It is the only message that will fix a sinful heart.

> *"Noah's message from the steps going up to the Ark was not, 'Something good is going to happen to you!'*
>
> *"Amos was not confronted by the high priest of Israel for proclaiming, 'Confession is possession!'*
>
> *"Jeremiah was not put into the pit for preaching, 'I'm O.K., you're O.K.!'*
>
> *"Daniel was not put into the lion's den for telling people, 'Possibility thinking will move mountains!'*
>
> *"John the Baptist was not forced to preach in the wilderness and eventually beheaded because he preached, 'Smile, God loves you!'*
>
> *"The two prophets of the tribulation will not be killed for preaching, 'God is in his heaven and all is right with the world!'*
>
> *"Instead, what was the message of all these men of God? Simple, one word: 'Repent!'"*[3]

2. Christ preached the Kingdom of Heaven is at hand.

> **"Blessed are the poor in spirit: for theirs is the kingdom of heaven" (Mt.5:3).**

APPLICATION:

Four challenging lessons are seen in this point.

1) Believers should become obsessed with the mission of the Lord. They should be gripped and enslaved by the obsession of Christ! Here is why. Man no longer has to seek light. The Light of the world has come, but so many are still in darkness. They have not heard. Believers, in their lethargy and lack of urgency, have hoarded the mes-

---

[3]   Michael P. Green. *Illustrations for Biblical Preaching.* (Grand Rapids, MI: Baker Books, 1996), p.301.

sage and failed to go forth as God's messengers of light (2 Cor.5:19-20; cp. Jn.20:21; Lk.19:10).

2) The ministry of believers is the same as Christ's: to preach. All other work and ministries are important, but the primary ministry of all believers is to preach, to proclaim the gospel to a world crying for help (Acts 8:1).

3) The message of believers is the same as Christ's: (1) repent; (2) the Kingdom of Heaven is at hand. All other subjects are important, but the primary message must be these two points.

4) Believers are given the highest honor in the world: they are sent into the world on the same mission as God's very own Son!

QUESTIONS:

1. What does repentance involve? Why is repentance such an important experience for the person who has sinned?

2. If your passion to proclaim the gospel could be read by a thermometer, how would it read:

_____Sub-freezing (I'm as cold as ice)

_____Lukewarm (I've just gotten comfortable. Please don't ask me to get up.)

_____A heat wave (I've got to tell the lost that the heat they are feeling now is nothing compared to the eternal fires of hell.)

SUMMARY:

Are your spiritual eyes focused upon God's purpose for your life? There are a million things to distract you from doing what God wants you to do when He wants you to do it. God is more than willing and perfectly able to put you and every other believer on the right path at the right time. There will be no greater joy in your life than when God's purpose is fulfilled in your life. The way to this joy is best learned from the life and example of Jesus Christ.

1. There was the sign to begin: John's imprisonment.
2. There was the chosen headquarters: Galilee.
3. There was the deliberate decision to fulfill Scripture.
4. There was the mission.
5. There was the message.

PERSONAL JOURNAL NOTES:
(Reflection & Response)

1. The most important thing that I learned from this lesson was:

2. The thing that I need to work on the most is:

3. I can apply this lesson to my life by:

4. Closing Prayer of Commitment: (put your commitment down on paper).

1. The first men called a. Were brothers who worked together b. Were industrious workers c. Were called to follow Jesus-- at once	B. Jesus' Disciples: The Kind of Person Called, 4:18-22 (Mk. 1:16-20; cp. Lk.5:1-11; Jn. 1:35-51) 18 And Jesus, walking by the sea of Galilee, saw two brethren, Simon called Peter, and Andrew his brother, casting a net into the sea: for they were fishers. 19 And he saith unto them, Follow me, and	I will make you fishers of men. 20 And they straightway left their nets, and followed him. 21 And going on from thence, he saw other two brethren, James the son of Zebedee, and John his brother, in a ship with Zebedee their father, mending their nets; and he called them. 22 And they immediately left the ship and their father, and followed him.	d. Were called to another work e. Were responsive 2. The second men called a. Were obedient sons working with their father--closely knit b. Were industrious, frugal c. Were simply called d. Were responsive: Left their livelihood & family

Section III
THE BEGINNING OF THE MESSIAH'S MINISTRY
Matthew 4:12-25

Study 2: JESUS' DISCIPLES: THE KIND OF PERSON CALLED

Text: Matthew 4:18-22

Aim: To gain a true understanding of what it means to be called by God.

Memory Verse:
> "And he saith unto them, Follow me, and I will make you fishers of men" (Matthew 4:19).

INTRODUCTION:

If someone wants to give you a message, what is the best way you can be reached? Should the messenger call you on your phone? Should he page you? Does a letter to your mailbox get your attention faster? Is it better for the messenger to come personally to your home? How about where you work? Is that the best place for you to be reached? We live in a modern culture where the modes of communication are various and many. We also live in a society where nearly everyone stays busy, often too busy to listen to anyone else. Most persons are even too busy to listen to God; too busy to respond to the call of God. If God is trying to call you, are you listening?

What kind of person does Christ call? This passage shows that Christ calls ordinary people who will simply make themselves available to Him.

Note *where* Jesus called His first disciples. They were not in a religious center or a learning center. Neither were they in a position of authority or power; nor did they possess wealth or financial security. They were out in the work-a-day world. This is not to de-emphasize the importance of religion or of learning, but it does teach at least two things.

First, position and power, wealth and security, religion and learning can hurt and keep a person away from God. Such things can make a person so self-confident and assured that he becomes useless to God. God is unable to work His power through him. The man's own abilities and energy block God's gifts and power from flowing through him.

Second, God can use and call anyone who is really available, whether religious or nonreligious, learned or unlearned, ordinary or extraordinary. The main ingredient is to be available and willing to respond.

OUTLINE:
1. The first men called (v.18-20).
   a. Were brothers who worked together.
   b. Were industrious workers.
   c. Were called to follow Jesus—at once.
   d. Were called to another work.
   e. Were responsive.
2. The second men called (v.21-22).
   a. Were obedient sons working with their father—closely knit.
   b. Were industrious, frugal.
   c. Were simply called.
   d. Were responsive: left their livelihood and family.

1. THE FIRST MEN CALLED (v.18-20).

Five traits are seen in these men, traits that show what kind of person is called by Christ.

1. The men called by Christ were brothers who worked together. The fact that they were working together points strongly to at least three things.
   a. They had good parents who had taught them to love and care for one another.
   b. They came from a closely knit family, a family that worked together.
   c. They followed and obeyed the teaching of their parents and maintained a brotherly spirit throughout life.

APPLICATION 1:

There is one essential for serving Christ that must be stressed among God's people: cooperation—a nature and willingness to serve together. The disciples' friendly and cooperative spirit shows us three things.

1) The need for a brotherly spirit—the kind of spirit Christ desires of His followers. The kind of kingdom Christ is building is a kingdom of followers with a loving and cooperative spirit.

> **"Thou shalt love thy neighbor as thyself" (Mt.22:39).**
> **"By this shall all men know that ye are my disciples, if ye have love one to another" (Jn.13:35).**

2) The need for reaching families for Christ: brothers and sisters reaching one another.

> **"He first findeth his own brother Simon, and saith unto him, We have found the Messias, which is, being interpreted, the Christ. And he brought him to Jesus. And when Jesus beheld him, he said, Thou art Simon the son of Jona: thou shalt be called Cephas, which is by interpretations, A stone" (Jn.1:41-42).**

3) The need for parents to properly train their children in a godly and Scriptural manner.

> **"And thou shalt teach them [God's words] diligently unto thy children, and shalt talk of them when thou sittest in thine house, and when thou walkest by the way, and when thou liest down, and when thou risest up" (Dt.6:7).**

"Then departed Barnabas to Tarsus, for to seek Saul: and when he had found him, he brought him unto Antioch. And it came to pass, that a whole year they assembled themselves with the church, and taught much people. And the disciples were called Christians first in Antioch" (Acts 11:25-26).

2. The men called by Christ were industrious workers. Note how Peter and Andrew were busy at work when Christ called them. This is a second essential for serving Christ that must be stressed: energy, industry, a willingness to work and to work hard. When Christ calls a person, the person is working, not sitting. God does not choose the lazy and inactive but the energetic and industrious. Too many believers are sitting and are inactive. Therefore, they miss out on the higher calling of God.

"Then answered Amos, and said to Amaziah, I was no prophet, neither was I a prophet's son; but I was a *herdman*, and a *gatherer* of sycamore fruit: and the Lord took me as I followed the flock, and the Lord said unto me, Go, prophesy unto my people Israel" (Amos 7:14-15).

3. The men called by Christ were called to follow Him and they were to follow Him *immediately*. The point is this: the disciple is called to follow Christ personally, to attach himself to Christ before he does anything else. Personal discipleship, that is, personal attachment, is essential. A person must first *learn* Christ before he can *serve* Christ.

APPLICATION:
The Lord's call is to a personal relationship, to become attached to Him.

"Ye are my witnesses, saith the Lord, and my servant whom I have chosen: that ye may know and believe me, and understand that I am he: before me there was no God formed, neither shall there be after me" (Is.43:10).

The disciples, although unlearned, were given about three years of the best and most extensive training in the world. They were taught by Christ Himself, God's own Son. Every believer needs to get alone with Christ and to do it often, to study and meditate upon Him and His Word.

"Study to show thyself approved unto God, a workman that needeth not to be ashamed, rightly dividing the word of truth" (2 Tim.2:15).

4. The men called by Christ were called to another work. This was a call to a different kind of employment, to another work and profession. It was a drastic, traumatic change. Note several facts.
   a. The call to a personal relationship had already been issued. John tells us this (Jn.1:35-42). A personal relationship must always be stressed before service.
   b. This call, the call to "fish for men," was a call to service. It was a call to care for men, to help and minister to them. No greater call can come to a man, for helping another human being is the greatest act in all of life. Imagine a person who gives himself to nothing but ministering and helping people. What greater call is there? (Cp. Mt.20:26; Mk.10:43; Lk.9:48.)

ILLUSTRATION:

God has given each one of us a call to fish for men, to serve people in the name of Christ. There is no greater joy than to do what God has called us to do. We often fail when we forget our purpose: to fish!

> *The large bass mounted on Granddad's mantle had always fascinated Elizabeth. Her fantasy was to one day catch a fish and put it over her fireplace too. When she was eight, that opportunity finally came. Heading to the lake, Elizabeth and Granddad carried their cane poles and fish bait. After she baited her hook for what seemed the hundredth time, she sighed to herself, "This is taking all day long and I've haven't caught a fish yet."*
>
> *A lot of impatient fishermen would have packed up and called it a day, but not Elizabeth. She was bound and determined to catch her fish. Finally a strike came. She saw her bobber dive under the water and pulled up her pole with all her might. Out of the water came the catch of the day! Her prized catch was no more than the length of her tiny hand. In a high-pitched voice she said, "Granddaddy, how much will it cost to mount this thing?!"*

The size of the fish you catch for Christ does not matter. What does matter is that you are fishing!

c. The call was to *immediate and total detachment* from all else and to *immediate attachment* to Jesus and His mission.

"And he saith unto them, Follow me, and I will make you fishers of men" (Mt.4:19).

APPLICATION:

The Lord's call is twofold.
1) To follow Him, the Messiah. Before doing anything else, a disciple must first come to know Christ personally.
2) To become a fisher of men.

Christ adapts a person's call to the knowledge and experience of the person. These fishermen were called "to fish for men." This fact stirs some confidence and prevents some apprehension and fear in accepting the call of Christ. It means that Christ always considers a person's knowledge and experience when He calls him. This fact also enables a person to serve more efficiently and effectively—to accomplish much more for God.

5. The men called by Christ were responsive. They responded immediately.

APPLICATION:

The call of God is critical and demands a decision.
1) It is immediate—right now! A person is to get up now not tomorrow.
2) It is absolute. It demands a positive response—not a *no* or even a *maybe*. How tragic that many are called but few are chosen.

"So the last shall be first, and the first last: for many be called, but few chosen" (Mt.20:16).

QUESTIONS:
1. The believer needs to have a good witness, especially at work. How would the people who work closely with you describe you?
>   A loner, does his own thing.
>   A real team player, cooperative and friendly.
2. In what ways can your hard work be a witness for Christ?
3. The men whom Jesus Christ called to follow Him did so *immediately*. Why was this important? What might happen if a person hesitates when Christ calls?
4. How would your life be different if you were given three years of the best and most extensive spiritual training in the world?
5. Often, we tend to get busy for the Lord before we get to know the Lord. The key to anything we do is based upon our relationship with the Lord. What can you do today in order to know Him better?
6. Christ has called every believer to be a fisher of men, women, boys, and girls. How would you honestly evaluate your fishing skills:
>   A novice. I don't even know where to begin!
>   A weekend fisherman. I catch one every now and then.
>   An real angler. I'm always looking for an opportunity to fish!
>   What would make you a better fisherman?
7. God will not call you to do something He does not *equip* you to do. What comfort does this bring you? What challenges do you face in light of this fact?

A CLOSER LOOK # 1
(4:19) **Discipleship—Call**: this was a call to service. Peter and Andrew had already been called as disciples (Jn.1:35-42). The thought is *immediate and total detachment* from everything. Matthew emphasizes the call to the Lord's *official mission or work*. Mark stresses the call to a *changed life*: "To become fishers of men" (Mk.1:17). Luke stresses the call to a *different profession* (Lk.5:10). John stresses the call to a *personal relationship* (Jn.1:40-42).

QUESTIONS:
1. How does being a fisher of men change a person's life?
2. Has fishing for men produced spiritual fruit in your own life?

2. THE SECOND MEN CALLED (v.21-22).

Four traits are seen in these men, traits that also show what kind of person is called by Christ.

1. They were obedient sons working with their father. They were from a closely knit family, and a closely knit family has an important influence upon the lives of its children. The point is that obedience is essential, both as a child and as a servant.

> **"Children, obey your parents in the Lord: for this is right. Honour thy father and mother; (which is the first commandment with promise)" (Eph.6:1-2).**

2. They were industrious and frugal. Note how they were mending their nets, making use of what they had instead of running out to secure new nets. The point is that God does not care for wastefulness. The person God calls is frugal and thrifty, not wasteful.

"When they were filled, he said unto his disciples, Gather up the fragments that remain, that nothing be lost" (Jn.6:12).
"The slothful man roasteth not that which he took in hunting: but the substance of a diligent man is precious" (Pr.12:27).

3. They were simply called. There was nothing dramatic or spectacular about their call. A dramatic experience was not necessary to reach them.

<u>APPLICATION:</u>
Some persons receive very simple calls, but they are as equally called as those who receive more dramatic and spectacular calls. God's call matches the nature and needs of a person and the situation. God's call considers a person's emotional, mental, physical, and spiritual needs.

"And the Spirit and the bride say, Come. And let him that heareth say, Come. And let him that is athirst come. And whosoever will, let him take the water of life freely" (Rev.22:17).

4. They were responsive; they left their livelihood and family.

<u>APPLICATION:</u>
Some persons are called to leave more behind than others. Some leave not only businesses but fathers and mothers. In some cases, the call involves persecution and even the threat of death.

"And the brother shall deliver up the brother to death, and the father the child: and the children shall rise up against their parents, and cause them to be put to death" (Mt.10:21).

In most cases, God's call involves a drastic change. It involves both a change of life and a change of one's primary profession.

<u>ILLUSTRATION:</u>
One of life's greatest challenges for the believer is to change careers. Leaving behind what is known and launching out into the unknown can produce the emotions of fear, uncertainty, and anxiety. And yet when God calls us to leave our place of security and follow Him, we find ourselves in the safest place of all--in His perfect will.

Joe always wanted to be a medical doctor and make a lot of money. As a young person, Joe spent all his energy on one single goal--to zip through school and practice medicine in an affluent suburb. Joe got what he wanted and his practice took off. Judged successful by most men, Joe could not shake the feeling that there was more to life than grasping the proverbial brass ring of money and possessions. For as long as Joe could remember, he had always sensed that God wanted to use him to help people. Justifying this urging, Joe took the more lucrative path and became a physician.
The fork in the road came when Joe accepted an invitation to go with a team of other Christians on a mission trip to the Amazon Jungle. The impact of Joe's trip affected every fiber of his being. In his heart, he sensed the Lord speaking to him, "Joe, these are the people who need your help. They need someone to teach them the gospel and they need someone to care for their physical needs. You can do both of these things for Me." After returning home, Joe sold his practice and used the funds to support his ministry, his brand new profession--missionary doctor.

How far are you willing to go for God?

"Then Peter began to say unto him, Lo, we have left all, and have followed thee" (Mk.10:28).

QUESTIONS:
1. How would you describe your family life? Is it closely knit? Is Christ the head of your home? What needs to happen to bring your family into an even more obedient relationship with Christ?
2. How do you normally respond when God calls you to share your faith with an unbeliever?
3. What sacrifices have you made in order to respond to God's call?

SUMMARY:

Have you been listening for God's call? What has He called you to do for Him? You will sense no greater satisfaction than to follow Christ. The person whom God calls has the opportunity to respond and work along side the One who gave everything He had for the work of God. Will you do the same?

1. The first men called.
   a. Were brothers who worked together.
   b. Were industrious workers.
   c. Were called to follow Jesus—at once.
   d. Were called to another work.
   e. Were responsive.
2. The second men called.
   a. Were obedient sons working with their father—closely knit.
   b. Were industrious, frugal.
   c. Were simply called.
   d. Were responsive: left their livelihood and family.

PERSONAL JOURNAL NOTES:
(Reflection & Response)

1. The most important thing that I learned from this lesson was:

2. The thing that I need to work on the most is:

3. I can apply this lesson to my life by:

4. Closing Prayer of Commitment: (put your commitment down on paper).

	C. Jesus' Dramatic Fame: A Successful Ministry, 4:23-25	him all sick people that were taken with divers diseases and torments, and those which were possessed with devils, and those which were lunatic, and those that had the palsy; and he healed them.	4. Jesus' power a. Over the spiritual b. Over the mental c. Over the physical
1. Jesus' sphere of activity a. Through all Galilee b. In the synagogue 2. Jesus' daily activities a. Teaching b. Preaching the gospel c. Healing 3. Jesus' fame spread throughout all Syria	23 And Jesus went about all Galilee, teaching in their synagogues, and preaching the gospel of the kingdom, and healing all manner of sickness and all manner of disease among the people. 24 And his fame went throughout all Syria: and they brought unto		
		25 And there followed him great multitudes of people from Galilee, and from Decapolis, and from Jerusalem, and from Judaea, and from beyond Jordan.	5. Jesus' following a. Great multitudes followed b. From everywhere: Both Jew & Gentile

Section III
THE BEGINNING OF THE MESSIAH'S MINISTRY
Matthew 4:12-25

Study 3: JESUS' DRAMATIC FAME: A SUCCESSFUL MINISTRY

Text: Matthew 4:23-25

Aim: To formulate a personal plan of ministry as you walk with the Lord.

Memory Verse:
> "And Jesus went about all Galilee, teaching in their synagogues, and preaching the gospel of the kingdom, and healing all manner of sickness and all manner of disease among the people" (Matthew 4:23).

INTRODUCTION:
How do you gauge success? Is success...
- Making a lot of money?
- Living in a bigger house?
- Having many friends?
- Possessing physical strength or beauty?
- Driving an expensive car?
- Living in a wealthy neighborhood?
- Attaining a promotion or a prominent position of leadership?

The world would answer *yes!* to all these questions. But what is success to the Christian believer? When does God consider you to be successful? As you will soon see, God has elevated the meaning of success to a higher standard that reaches past the logic of fallen men.

A successful ministry is a ministry that follows in the footsteps of the Lord. This passage shows both what the Lord did and the results of what He did. His activities set a pattern for every believer, minister and layman alike.

OUTLINE:
1. Jesus' sphere of activity (v.23).
2. Jesus' daily activities (v.23).
3. Jesus' fame spread through Syria (v.24).
4. Jesus' power (v.24).
5. Jesus' following (v.25).

1. JESUS' SPHERE OF ACTIVITY (v.23).

Three things can be said about where Jesus ministered.

1. He went throughout *all* Galilee. He went throughout the *whole* area which He had set out to reach, the area (so to speak) which had been assigned to Him. *Once committed* to an area, He was responsible and faithful to it. (What a lesson for believers on commitment, assignments, and responsibilities.)

2. He went where there was a ready audience. He went where people would receive and hear Him, that is, in the synagogue.

3. He went where teaching and preaching were expected, in the synagogue. (He did not teach exclusively in the synagogue, but it was one of the primary places of His ministry.)

A CLOSER LOOK # 1

(4:23) **Synagogue**: the synagogue was the most important institution in the life of a Jew. It was the center of worship for the Jew, yet it was also the center of learning and education. Services and discussions were conducted daily in most synagogues. Wherever Jews were scattered over the world, every colony, no matter how small, had its synagogue.

Some cities had many synagogues. Jerusalem is an example: it has been estimated that there were hundreds of synagogues within the city. Five are mentioned in Acts 6:9. A synagogue service included prayers, Scripture reading, and a lecture or discussion. Distinguished persons, local or foreign, were invited to take part in the service; therefore, the door of the synagogue was wide open to Christ (cp. Lk.4:16f). Using the synagogue was part of His strategy (cp. Gal.4:4.) It was also the strategy of Paul when the synagogues were open to him (cp. Acts 9:20; 13:5, 14; 14:1; 17:1, 10; 18:4, 19; 19:8).

APPLICATION:
Every believer should have the same thing said about him that is said about Jesus: that he went forth just as God commanded Him.

"Even as the Son of man came not to be ministered unto, but to minister, and to give his life a ransom for many" (Mt.20:28).

Note a significant point: Jesus followed the form of service already established. He did not try to change the establishment, not organizationally. He was on a mission and He had to have a receptive hearing. He refused to be sidetracked by secondary matters that might cause change and disturb the people. Secondary matters would only detract from His preaching and ministering.

QUESTIONS:
1. What is your sphere of influence with regard to your Christian witness? School? Work? Church? Sporting events? Other? What can you do to strengthen your witness in these areas?
2. Why was Christ so careful not to be sidetracked by secondary matters when He preached? What lesson do you need to embrace from Christ's example?

2. JESUS' DAILY ACTIVITIES (v.23).

The three daily activities of Jesus were teaching, preaching, and healing. The three activities are simply stated but profound in their meaning.

Note there is a concentration of activity in this passage, a bombardment of ministry. Jesus is pictured moving rapidly about, as active as He could be, serving and meeting the needs of people in a committed and tireless spirit. People's needs were being met with very special care, and they were being met rapidly in a concentrated effort.

The great needs of men are threefold: (1) to hear the gospel; (2) to be taught the gospel; and (3) to be healed personally. Jesus Christ knew man's innermost being, what his being lacked and needed, what made man tick. Therefore, His activities were geared to man's innermost being, to that which would meet his need.

⇒ Jesus Christ proclaimed the gospel. There is hope—hope for an eternal kingdom, an eternal heaven, a whole new dimension of being that is eternal.

⇒ Jesus Christ taught the glorious truths of the gospel. Man can hope in the gospel and be healed; that is, he can be delivered from all the enslavement's of this life (Ro.8:1f; Heb.2:14-15).

APPLICATION 1:

God's servants ought to be engaged in the same daily activities as the Lord: teaching, preaching, and healing. That is their call and mission. In practical terms, this means the believer is to be...

• telling people about the gospel, the good news
• helping people to understand the gospel
• helping people to accept the gospel, to accept the healing it brings--the emotional, physical, and spiritual healing

"And as ye go, preach, saying, The kingdom of heaven is at hand. Heal the sick, cleanse the lepers, raise the dead, cast out devils: freely ye have received, freely give" (Mt.10:7-8).

"Go ye therefore, and teach all nations, baptizing them in the name of the Father, and of the Son, and of the Holy Ghost: teaching them to observe all things whatsoever I have commanded you: and, lo, I am with you alway, even unto the end of the world" (Mt.28:19-20; cp. Mk.16:15).

APPLICATION 2:

The mercy of God is being poured out in this passage—poured out upon people through preaching, teaching, and healing. Believers are now God's instruments of mercy. They are to pour out God's mercy upon all men who will receive it—through preaching, teaching, and ministry.

"To wit, that God was in Christ, reconciling the world unto himself, not imputing their trespasses unto them; and hath committed unto us the word of reconciliation. Now then we are ambassadors for Christ, as though God did beseech you by us: we pray you in Christ's stead, be ye reconciled to God" (2 Cor.5:19-20).

APPLICATION 3:

The works of Christ were His credentials, proof that He was God's Son. The believer's works are his credentials. Profession only, profession without works, is empty. A servant must serve.

"But I have greater witness than that of John: for the works which the Father hath given me to finish, the same works that I do, bear witness of me, that the Father hath sent me" (Jn.5:36).

A CLOSER LOOK # 2
(4:23) **Gospel—Kingdom of Heaven**: the gospel, the good news, *is* the Kingdom of Heaven; and the news of the Kingdom is the greatest news to ever come to earth. The Kingdom of Heaven surpasses the kingdoms of this world in two ways.

1. The Kingdom of Heaven is eternal. It is not physical and corruptible, lasting just for a season. It is a world in another dimension of being, a dimension entirely different from the physical world. It lasts forever and ever. What this means for man is that life is eternal. It is life that goes on forever and ever, but in a permanent, incorruptible, eternal dimension.

2. The Kingdom of Heaven brings wealth and assurance to the human soul forever. Man can be blessed by God Himself and live forever in those blessings.

QUESTIONS:
1. Where does God's call to preach, teach, and heal fit into your life, your schedule? Is it a priority or just something you do if an opportunity is staring you in the face?
2. You are God's instrument of mercy. Have you shared what you have with others lately or have you been keeping it to yourself?
3. Where could you go and what could you do to be better used of God in these areas?
4. Why is the Kingdom of Heaven superior to the kingdoms of this world?

3. JESUS' FAME SPREAD THROUGHOUT ALL SYRIA (v.24).

People everywhere needed Christ. There was *no person* who did *not* need Him, so God in His providence saw to it that the news of His Son spread everywhere, as will be seen in the next note.

> **"For all have sinned, and come short of the glory of God"**
> **(Ro.3:23; cp. Ro.6:23).**

APPLICATION:
Believers are now to carry the message of Christ everywhere. The world (so to speak) flocked to Christ, but believers are told to scatter all over the world and carry the gospel of the kingdom with them.

> **"But ye shall receive power, after that the Holy Ghost is come**
> **upon you: and ye shall be witnesses unto me both in Jerusalem, and in**
> **all Judaea, and in Samaria, and unto the uttermost part of the earth"**
> **(Acts 1:8).**

ILLUSTRATION:
Why is it so important to spread the gospel to those who have never heard? Because the gospel of Jesus Christ is the only thing that can take a man out of death and into eternal life. People need the Lord.

> *"The only way to make bad people good is to expose them to the Gospel. Even Charles Darwin, the man who contributed so much to evolutionistic thinking, admitted this. He wrote to a minister: 'Your services have done more for our village in a few months than all our efforts for many years. We have never been able to reclaim a single drunkard, but through your services I do not know that there is a drunkard left in the village!' Later Darwin visited the island of Tierra del Fuego at the southern tip of South America. What he found among the people was horrifying--savagery and bestiality almost beyond description. But when he returned after a missionary*

had worked among the people, he was amazed at the change in them. He acknowl-edged that the Gospel does transform lives. In fact, he was so moved by what he saw that he contributed money to the mission until his death.[1]

We are to carry the gospel to the world because it alone has the power to change the hearts of men.

QUESTIONS:
1. The news of God's love is spreading across the world. But today, there are still people who have yet to hear the Good News. What is your role in helping these people?
2. If you were given the choice, which would you prefer:
   To live in a land where the gospel was unheard of.
   To live in a land where the gospel had saturated the culture so much that many of the people were callous toward its message.
3. Can you think of any advantages or disadvantages toward either response concerning world missions?

A CLOSER LOOK # 3

(4:24) **Syria**: this was a great Roman province of which Palestine was a part. People from all over Syria were coming to see Jesus. Its chief cities were Damascus, Antioch, Byblos, Aleppo, Palmyra, and Carchemish. Beginning with the people flocking to hear Christ, Syria became prominent in the early history of the church. Paul was converted on the road to Damascus, and the first great Gentile church was founded at Antioch. It was the church at Antioch which sent out the first missionaries in Christian history and gave the name Christian to believers for the first time (cp. Acts 11:26).

QUESTIONS:
1. The church at Antioch sent out the first missionaries. What role does your church have in world missions? What role do you personally play in world missions?
2. Christianity had a great impact upon the Roman province of Syria. Do you believe God can move upon your country also? Why or why not?

4. JESUS' POWER (v.24).

Jesus' power was a great and glorious power. Jesus is said to have healed "all manner of sickness and...disease" (v.23) and "divers [many] diseases and torments" (v.24). However, only three specific healings are listed. These particular three symbolize the power of Christ over the whole man and over the physical universe.
⇒ There was spiritual healing: "Those possessed with devils."
⇒ There was mental healing: "Those which were lunatic."
⇒ There was physical healing: "Those that had the palsy."

The point is this: Jesus Christ has power over the whole physical universe. He has power over all the conceivable problems that can grip man: all the spiritual, mental, and physical problems.

---

[1] *INFOsearch Sermon Illustrations* (Arlington, TX: The Computer Assistant, 1-888-868-9029, 1986-1996).

APPLICATION:

This passage is a beautiful picture of Christ, the Great Physician. All believers must be physicians, and all must be about the ministry of healing the souls, minds, and bodies of men.

> "But when Jesus heard that, he said unto them, They that be whole need not a physician, but they that are sick. But go ye and learn what that meaneth, I will have mercy, and not sacrifice: for I am not come to call the righteous, but sinners to repentance" (Mt.9:12-13).

QUESTIONS:

1. Can you think of any problem that does not fall within the areas of spiritual, mental, or physical? Is there any problem God cannot handle?
2. How can Christ use you (man, woman, child, rich, poor, educated, uneducated, etc.) to minister to the needs of people?

5. JESUS' FOLLOWING (v.25).

Jesus' following was great. This verse is emphasizing two points: (1) great multitudes of all sorts of people began to follow Jesus, and (2) they came from everywhere—from the farthest reaches of the great province, Syria.

> "But when Jesus knew it, he withdrew himself from thence: and great multitudes followed him, and he healed them all" (Mt.12:15; cp. Mt.8:1).
> "And great multitudes were gathered together unto him, so that he went into a ship, and sat; and the whole multitude stood on the shore" (Mt.13:2).

APPLICATION:

Where are the multitudes today? After two thousand years why are the nations not as aroused as Israel was by the presence of Christ?

1) Are people no longer hungry for God? Are the fields no longer white unto harvest?

> "Behold, I say unto you, Lift up your eyes, and look on the fields; for they are white already to harvest" (Jn.4:35).

2) Do believers not seek God as much as Christ did?

> "And in the morning, rising up a great while before day, he went out, and departed into a solitary place, and there prayed" (Mk.1:35).
> "And when he had sent them away, he departed into a mountain to pray" (Mk.6:46).
> "And he withdrew himself into the wilderness, and prayed" (Lk.5:16; cp. Lk.9:18).

3) Are believers not as compassionate and concerned as Christ was?

> "But when he saw the multitudes, he was moved with compassion on them, because they fainted, and were scattered abroad, as sheep having no shepherd" (Mt.9:36).

ILLUSTRATION:

People who genuinely follow Christ show compassion and love just as He did. Opportunities come our way everyday to follow Christ and minister to hurting people.

"The story is told of two men riding on a sleigh during a blizzard. Almost frozen and afraid that they would not reach warmth and safety, they came upon another traveler who had fallen in the snow and was near death from the terrific cold. One suggested that they stop and help. The other refused, saying that to stop might keep them from reaching safety. He insisted on going on.

"However, the first man decided to stay and help. He set himself to the task of massaging the man's body to restore circulation. After long hard work, the man responded and was saved. The traveler's work in helping another helped keep himself warm and alive. The one who refused to stay and help was found some distance ahead, frozen to death." [2]

This timeless principle is true: Believers make the difference between life and death when they minister in Jesus' name.

QUESTIONS:

1. Jesus Christ attracts people from all over the world. People of different races, tribes, nations, social status, and political views know and love Christ. What does this tell you about the power and truth of the message of Jesus Christ?
2. Are you aware of any signs of revival in other nations of the world? What nations need your special intercession today?

SUMMARY:

Are you walking on the path of success? There are many roads a person can choose, but only one path leads to true success. The person who wants to have a successful ministry must follow in the footsteps of Jesus Christ. Note His example for success:

1. Jesus' sphere of activity.
2. Jesus' daily activities.
3. Jesus' fame spread through Syria.
4. Jesus' power.
5. Jesus' following.

PERSONAL JOURNAL NOTES:
(Reflection & Response)

1. The most important thing that I learned from this lesson was:

2. The thing that I need to work on the most is:

3. I can apply this lesson to my life by:

4. Closing Prayer of Commitment: (put your commitment down on paper).

---

[2]   Ted Kyle & John Todd. *A Treasury of Bible Illustrations*, p.53.

	CHAPTER 5	a mountain: and when he was set, his disciples came unto him:	a. Setting: Mountain
			b. Posture: Set--ready
	IV. THE TEACHINGS OF THE MESSIAH TO HIS DISCIPLES: THE GREAT SERMON ON THE MOUNT, 5:1-7:29 (Lk.6:20-49)	2 And he opened his mouth, and taught them, saying,	c. Audience: Disciples
			d. Purpose: To teach & prepare
		3 Blessed are the poor in spirit: for theirs is the kingdom of heaven.	e. Blessed
			2. The poor in spirit: Will be given the Kingdom of Heaven
	A. The True Disciple (Part 1): Who He Is & His Reward (the Beatitudes, 1-4), 5:1-6 (cp. Lk.6:20-23)	4 Blessed are they that mourn: for they shall be comforted.	3. Those who mourn: Will be comforted
		5 Blessed are the meek: for they shall inherit the earth.	4. The meek: Will inherit the earth
		6 Blessed are they which do hunger and thirst after righteousness: for they shall be filled.	5. Those who hunger & thirst after righteousness: Will be filled
1. Jesus saw multitudes		And seeing the multitudes, he went up into	

Section IV
THE TEACHINGS OF THE MESSIAH TO HIS DISCIPLES:
THE GREAT SERMON ON THE MOUNT
Matthew 5:1-7:29

Study 1: The True Disciple (Part I): Who He is and His Reward (the Beatitudes, 1-4)

Text: Matthew 5:1-6

Aim: To live a strong Christian life consistent with the great Beatitudes.

Memory Verses: (Note: The eight Beatitudes are verses every believer should memorize).
"Blessed *are* the poor in spirit: for theirs is the kingdom of heaven" (Mt.5:3).
"Blessed *are* they that mourn: for they shall be comforted" (Mt.5:4).
"Blessed *are* the meek: for they shall inherit the earth" (Mt.5:5).
"Blessed *are* they which do hunger and thirst after righteousness: for they shall be filled" (Mt.5:6).
"Blessed *are* the merciful: for they shall obtain mercy" (Mt.5:7).
"Blessed *are* the pure in heart: for they shall see God" (Mt.5:8).
"Blessed *are* the peacemakers: for they shall be called the children of God" (Mt.5:9).
"Blessed *are* they which are persecuted for righteousness' sake: for theirs is the kingdom of heaven" (Mt.5:10).

INTRODUCTION:
It is highly recommended that everyone have a regular physical checkup to make sure all is well inside the body. In the same sense, it is also important that a believer entrust himself on a regular basis to the Great Physician for a spiritual checkup. Why? Because we can suf-

fer from spiritual sickness just as quickly (if not more so) than physical sickness. And we must be honest enough to look inside and evaluate our true condition.

If your spiritual life could be x-rayed, what kinds of things would be seen?
⇒ Would your heart be pure?
⇒ Would your heart be broken because of the suffering of others?
⇒ Would your mind be programmed to be meek and gentle?
⇒ Would your backbone be strong enough to endure persecution?
⇒ Would your lungs be filled with heaven's air as you prayed?
⇒ Would your stomach be filled with righteousness?
⇒ Would your eyes look only toward godliness?
⇒ Would your ears be able to hear the voice of God and the desperate cries of needy people?
⇒ Would your mouth speak peace and comfort to those who need mercy?

His words concerning the Beatitudes are just as forceful today as they were when He shared them with His first disciples. Seldom in history have so few words been spoken with so much meaning. The Beatitudes of our Lord are powerful, holding before the world a descriptive picture of the true disciple of God. The Beatitudes cover the glorious hope and reward the believer can expect, now as well as in eternity.

OUTLINE:
1. Jesus saw multitudes (v.1-2).
2. The poor in spirit: shall be given the Kingdom of Heaven (v.3).
3. Those who mourn: shall be comforted (v.4).
4. The meek: shall inherit the earth (v.5).
5. Those who hunger and thirst after righteousness: shall be filled (v.6).

1. JESUS SAW THE MULTITUDES (v.1-2).

It is to be noted that the Sermon on the Mount was given to *the disciples* not to *the multitudes*. "Seeing the multitudes," Jesus was moved with compassion over their desperate plight and need. He knew that He could not reach them by Himself, so He was driven to get alone with His disciples. He had to begin preparing them for their ministry to the multitudes.

How long was He with His disciples on the mountain? A day? A week? Several weeks? It simply says that "when He had come down from the mountain, multitudes followed Him" (Mt.8:1).

APPLICATION 1:
Preaching and teaching are not to be done only in the church, but wherever people are found--on mountains, by the seashore, in homes, on the streets--*any* place and *every* place. There are two basic ingredients for reaching the multitudes.
1) Compassion: seeing the multitudes; keeping one's eyes open so people and their needs can be seen.

> **"But when he saw the multitudes, he was moved with compassion on them, because they fainted, and were scattered abroad, as sheep having no shepherd" (Mt.9:36).**

2) Discipleship: realizing that one cannot accomplish the task alone. Others must be taught to help in the great commission.

"Go ye therefore, and teach all nations, baptizing them in the name of the Father, and of the Son, and of the Holy Ghost: teaching them to observe all things whatsoever I have commanded you: and, lo, I am with you alway, even unto the end of the world" (Mt.28:19-20).

APPLICATION 2:

Crowds are important, but a small band of disciples is critical to accomplish the great commission. The mission of the Lord is reaching people, but the *method* of the Lord is to make disciples. It is giving intensive training to a small group so they can help in the ministry to the multitudes. Making disciples was also the method of Paul.

"Go ye therefore, and teach all nations, baptizing them in the name of the Father, and of the Son, and of the Holy Ghost: teaching them to observe all things whatsoever I have commanded you: and, lo, I am with you alway, even unto the end of the world" (Mt.28:19-20).

"Then came he to Derbe and Lystra: and, behold, a certain disciple was there, named Timotheus, the son of a certain woman, which was a Jewess, and believed; but his father was a Greek....Him would Paul have to go forth with him" (Acts 16:1, 3).

Christian leaders are to call together small bands of disciples for special training and preparation. Matthew says without any explanation that "His disciples came to Him" (v.1), but Mark and Luke say that Christ called the disciples together for training and preparation (Mk.3:13; Lk.6:13).

Three things are needed for training and preparation: a place, a time, and a message. The words "He went up...and when He was set" seem to be saying that Jesus had deliberately chosen this place and time for this training. All had been planned; Jesus was personally prepared. (What a lesson too often neglected!)

ILLUSTRATION:

The only way to make a difference in the world is to accept the challenge to be personally discipled and then disciple others. Have you been equipped for the Lord's service? Are you equipping others?

"Three military recruiters accepted an invitation to address the senior class of a local high school. Graduation was only a few months away, and the principal wanted his young men to hear of the options available in the military.

"The assembly was to be 45 minutes in length. It was agreed that each recruiter would have 15 minutes to make his pitch and then another 20 minutes in the cafeteria to meet with interested boys. The Army recruiter went first and got so excited about his speech that he talked for over 20 minutes. The Navy recruiter, not to be outdone, stood and also spoke for 20 minutes.

"The Marine Corps recruiter, realizing that his speaking time had been cut to five minutes, walked up to the podium and spent the first 60 seconds in silence. Wordlessly, he gazed over the group of high school seniors. They knew he was sizing them up. After what seemed to be an eternity, the recruiter said, 'I doubt whether there are two or three of you in this room who could cut it as Marines. I want to see those three men as soon as this assembly is dismissed.' He then turned on his heel and sat down. Predictably, he was mobbed by a herd of young men when he arrived in the cafeteria.

"The Marine Corps is always on the lookout for a few good men. So is the Lord. As a matter of fact, He wants you. And with His help, you can make a difference in this war."[1]

God is calling men and women to help serve the multitudes. How will you respond to His call?

QUESTIONS:
1. Jesus Christ is always looking for a few good men. Are you ready to respond? To be one of the few?
2. What is the main reason Christ shared the Sermon on the Mount with His disciples?
3. What does it mean to disciple someone? Are you open to being discipled? To discipling someone else? If not you, who?
4. Think for a moment. If you had to disciple someone or be discipled, how would you prepare yourself mentally? Physically? Spiritually?

A CLOSER LOOK # 1
(5:3) **Blessed**: spiritual joy and satisfaction that lasts regardless of conditions, that carries one through pain, sorrow, loss, and grief.

APPLICATION 1:
To be *blessed* is what men seek. The problem is that they seek it in the things of this earth: position, money, fame, power, and sensual pleasure.

> **"Lay not up for yourselves treasures upon earth, where moth and rust doth corrupt, and where thieves break through and steal: but lay up for yourselves treasures in heaven, where neither moth nor rust doth corrupt, and where thieves do not break through nor steal: for where your treasure is, there will your heart be also" (Mt.6:19-21).**

Man seeks to be blessed only in this world. This says several things about his nature.
1) Man is carnal and corruptible, sinful and dying.

> **"For they that are after the flesh do mind the things of the flesh; but they that are after the Spirit the things of the Spirit. For to be carnally minded is death; but to be spiritually minded is life and peace. Because the carnal mind is enmity against God: for it is not subject to the law of God, neither indeed can be. So then they that are in the flesh cannot please God" (Ro.8:5-8).**

2) Man is deceived and blinded to his real need, that of a renewed spirit.

> **"Jesus answered and said unto him, Verily, verily, I say unto thee, Except a man be born again, he cannot see the kingdom of God" (Jn.3:3).**

---

[1]   Steve Farrar. *Point Man.* (Portland, OR: Multnomah Press, 1990), p. 46-47. As cited in *INFOsearch Sermon Illustrations* (Arlington, TX: The Computer Assistant, 1-888-868-9029, 1986-1996).

3) Man is ignorant of the Kingdom of Heaven.
- ⇒ He is misguided and deceived about it
- ⇒ He is unbelieving about it.
- ⇒ He prefers something else to it.
- ⇒ He is hardened to it.`
- ⇒ He is neglectful of it.
- ⇒ He is unconcerned about it.

QUESTIONS:
1. Looking back over the last year, what has been your greatest blessing, that which has brought you the most true joy and satisfaction?
2. Why does the natural man have such a perverted view of true blessings? How have you struggled with these issues? What is key to gaining the right perspective of blessings?

2. THE POOR IN SPIRIT: SHALL BE GIVEN THE KINGDOM OF GOD (v.3).

Note several significant facts about the *"poor in spirit."*

1. Being *poor in spirit* does not mean that a man must be poverty-stricken and financially poor. Hunger, nakedness, and slums are not pleasing to God, especially in a world of plenty. Christ is not talking about material poverty. He means what He says: poor in *spirit*. Being "poor in spirit" means several things.

   a. To acknowledge our utter helplessness before God, our spiritual poverty, our spiritual need. We are solely dependent upon God to meet our need.
   b. To acknowledge our utter lack in facing life and eternity apart from God. To acknowledge that the real blessings of life and eternity come only from a right relationship with God.
   c. To acknowledge our utter lack of superiority before all others and our spiritual deadness before God. To acknowledge that we are no better, no richer, no more superior than the next person--no matter what we have achieved in this world (fame, fortune, power). Our attitude toward others is not to be proud or haughty, not superior or overbearing. To be "poor in spirit" means acknowledging that every human being has a significant contribution to make to society and to the world. The person "poor in spirit" approaches life in humility and appreciation, not as though life owes him, but as though he owes life. He has been given the privilege of living; therefore, he journeys through life with a humble attitude and he contributes all he can to a needy world out of a spirit of appreciation.

2. The opposite of being *"poor in spirit"* is having a spirit that is *full of self*. There is a world of difference between these two spirits. There is the difference of thinking that we are righteous versus acknowledging that we need the righteousness of Christ. There is the difference of being self-righteous versus being given the righteousness of Christ. Self-righteousness goes no further than self; that is, it goes no further than death. Self dies and everything with self including our self-righteousness. But the righteousness that is of Christ lives forever.

> **"But now the righteousness of God without the law is manifested, being witnessed by the law and the prophets; even the righteousness of God which is by faith of Jesus Christ unto all and upon all them that believe: for there is no difference" (Ro.3:21-22).**

3. Two critical steps are taken by the person who truly acknowledges his spiritual poverty.
   a. He turns his primary attention away from the things of this world. He knows material things can never make him rich in spirit.

b. He turns his primary attention to God and His kingdom. He knows God alone can make him rich in spirit.

4. The "poor in spirit" are weary and burdened for the world. They know the truth of this world and of eternity. Therefore, they have set their faces to do their part for both.

a. They are weary of the deceptive appearances and enticements of this world. They have learned that "all is vanity [empty]" and all is corruptible. All waste away, even human life itself. Therefore, they feel weary and burdened for those who are still lost in the world.

b. They are weary from having labored so much to reach their generation. They have labored to serve and make their contribution as God has called them. They have toiled so laboriously for one reason only: the love of Christ constrained them to reach their generation (2 Cor.5:14).

5. The "poor in spirit" are those who approach the world as a child (Mt.18:1-6). All children are very, very precious to God and are given angels to look over them (Mt.18:10 cp. Ps.91:11).

6. The "poor in spirit" are blessed with the Kingdom of Heaven, inheriting three significant things.

a. The poor in spirit receive forgiveness of sin and God's continued remembrance: the assurance that God will never forget.

> "For I will be merciful to their unrighteousness, and their sins and their iniquities will I remember no more" (Heb.8:12).

b. The poor in spirit receive a fellowship with other believers who walk as they walk.

> "And they continued stedfastly in the apostles' doctrine and fellowship, and in breaking of bread, and in prayers" (Acts 2:42).

c. The poor in spirit receive the gift of life that is forever: the eternal fellowship with both God and the congregation of those who are poor in spirit.

> "Verily, verily, I say unto you, He that heareth my word, and believeth on him that sent me, hath everlasting life, and shall not come into condemnation; but is passed from death unto life" (Jn.5:24).

QUESTIONS:
1. In practical terms, what does it really mean to be poor in spirit? Is this a negative or positive trait in the eyes of the world? In God's eyes? In what ways do you fall short of being poor in spirit?
2. Contrast being poor in spirit with being full of self. Have you experienced both characteristics in your life? Are you ever as poor in spirit as you could be? Should be?

3. THOSE WHO MOURN: SHALL BE COMFORTED (v.4).

To have a broken heart is the strongest description possible for mourning. It is like the deep mourning and wailing that occurs over the death of a loved one. It is sorrow--a desperate, helpless sorrow. It is a sorrow for sin, a broken heart over evil and suffering. It is a brokenness of self that comes from seeing Christ on the cross and realizing that our sins put Him there (cp. Jas.4:9). Note several significant facts.

1. Who is it that mourns? Who is it so full of grief that he cries and weeps and utters groanings deep from within? There are three persons who mourn and utter such groanings.

a. The person who is *desperately sorry* for his sins and unworthiness before God. He has such a sense of sin that his heart is just broken.

"And the publican, standing afar off, would not lift up so much as his eyes unto heaven, but smote upon his breast, saying, God be merciful to me a sinner" (Lk.18:13).

b. The person who *really feels* the desperate plight and terrible suffering of others. The tragedies, the problems, the sinful behavior of others, the state, the condition, the lostness of the world all weigh ever so heavily upon the heart of the mourner.

"But when he saw the multitudes, he was moved with compassion on them, because they fainted, and were scattered abroad, as sheep having no shepherd" (Mt.9:36).

c. The person who experiences personal tragedy and intense trauma.

APPLICATION:
Men are to mourn over their sins. This leads to confession and humility before God and results in being lifted up (Jas.4:8-10). The person who mourns is comforted by Christ Himself. Christ was called the "man of sorrows" and was acquainted with grief (Is.53:3). He is able to succor and to draw a person ever so close, to comfort and strengthen him beyond imagination (Heb.2:18; 4:15-16).

However, note: there is a godly sorrow, but there is also a worldly sorrow. There is also a self-centered sorrow. A person who suffers often becomes self-centered and begins to feel sorry for himself. He sometimes begins to feel self-pity and apathy and to want special attention. He may even become bitter. A believer must never let this happen.

2. They who mourn *shall be* comforted (2 Cor.1:3).
   a. There is a present comfort.

   ⇒ A settled peace: a relief, a solace, a consolation within.

   "Peace I leave with you, my peace I give unto you: not as the world giveth, give I unto you. Let not your heart be troubled, neither let it be afraid" (Jn.14:27).

   ⇒ An assurance of forgiveness and acceptance by God.

   "Blessed be the God and Father of our Lord Jesus Christ, who hath blessed us with all spiritual blessings in heavenly places in Christ" (Eph.1:3).

   ⇒ A fullness of joy: a sense of God's presence, care and guidance (Jn.14:26); a sense of His sovereignty; a sense of His working all things out for good to those who love Him.

   "And we know that all things work together for good to them that love God, to them who are the called according to his purpose" (Ro.8:28).

   b. There is an eternal comfort.

⇒ A passing from death to life.

"For God so loved the world, that he gave his only begotten Son, that whosoever believeth in him should not perish, but have everlasting life" (Jn.3:16).

⇒ A wiping away of all tears.

"And God shall wipe away all tears from their eyes; and there shall be no more death, neither sorrow, nor crying, neither shall there be any more pain: for the former things are passed away" (Rev.21:4).

QUESTIONS:
1. In what ways have you personally experienced mourning? How would you evaluate its impact upon your life?
2. What are the basic differences between a godly sorrow, a worldly sorrow, and a self-centered sorrow? Is there anything wrong with experiencing them all?
3. When have you received the kind of comfort described in this verse? What difference did it make in your life?

4. THE MEEK: SHALL INHERIT THE EARTH (v.5).

To be meek is to have a strong but *tender and humble* life, to have a strong *yet teachable* spirit. It is not being weak, bowing, or spineless. It is possessing all the emotions and ability to take and conquer, but being able to control it. It is discipline in action because God is in control. The opposite of meekness is arrogance or pride. In too many persons there is an air of self-sufficiency and superiority. A meek person knows that he has needs and does not have all the answers.
1. Who are the meek?
   a. The person who is *controlled not undisciplined*. The mind and body are disciplined, never let loose. Passion and urges, speech and behavior, sight and touch are always controlled.

   "Let not sin therefore reign in your mortal body, that ye should obey it in the lusts thereof" (Ro.6:12).

   b. The person who is *humble not prideful*.
      1) He is humble before God. He knows his need for God and for God's hand upon his life, his need to be saved and controlled by God.
      2) He is humble before men. He knows he is not the epitome of mankind nor the summit of knowledge among men. He does not have it all nor does he know it all.

   "For I say, through the grace given unto me, to every man that is among you, not to think of himself more highly than he ought to think; but to think soberly, according as God hath dealt to every man the measure of faith" (Ro.12:3).

   c. The person who is *gentle not easily provoked*. He is always in control when dealing with people: cool, even-tempered, able to show displeasure without reacting impulsively, able to answer softly. (Cp. Christ, Mt.11:29; 1 Pt.2:23; cp. Moses, Num. 12:3.)

"And the servant of the Lord must not strive; but be gentle unto all men, apt to teach, patient" (2 Tim.2:24).

d. The person who is *forgiving not revengeful*.

"For if ye forgive men their trespasses, your heavenly Father will also forgive you" (Mt.6:14).

2. The meek person is a *quiet* person. He studies to be quiet.

"Stand in awe, and sin not: commune with your own heart upon your bed, and be still" (Ps.4:4).

a. He is quiet before God. He quietly surrenders to God, acknowledging his need without show or pomp, and he quietly goes before God daily, depending upon God for guidance and care.

"Be still, and know that I am God: I will be exalted among the heathen, I will be exalted in the earth" (Ps.46:10).

b. He is quiet before men. He walks quietly before men, controlled in all things, in both speech and behavior.

"And that ye study to be quiet, and to do your own business, and to work with your own hands, as we commanded you" (1 Th.4:11).

QUESTIONS:
1. What is the world's view of a meek or gentle person? What does it really mean to be meek?
2. Describe the meekest person you know. What traits do you admire? What do you need to learn from this person and apply to your own life?

3. There are two points to be stressed in the reward to the meek (cp. Ps.27:11).
   a. The meek inherit the earth *now*; that is, they presently enjoy and experience the good things of the earth.

   ⇒ The meek are comfortable with themselves. They know who they are; therefore, they are strong and confident yet tender and humble.

   "Being confident of this very thing, that he which hath begun a good work in you will perform it until the day of Jesus Christ" (Ph.1:6).

   ⇒ The meek know where they are going; they are teachable. They have nothing to prove. They have purpose, meaning, and significance in life.

   "Henceforth there is laid up for me a crown of righteousness, which the Lord, the righteous judge, shall give me at that day: and not to me only, but unto all them also that love his appearing" (2 Tim.4:8).

⇒ The meek are assured of victory, conquest, triumph over whatever confronts them. They are controlled; therefore, they control circumstances instead of letting circumstances control them.

> "There hath no temptation taken you but such as is common to man: but God is faithful, who will not suffer you to be tempted above that ye are able; but will with the temptation also make a way to escape, that ye may be able to bear it" (1 Cor.10:13).

⇒ The meek have peaceful souls. They carry whatever pressure and tension comes their way to Christ and He relieves it all.

> "Come unto me, all ye that labour and are heavy laden, and I will give you rest. Take my yoke upon you, and learn of me; for I am meek and lowly in heart: and ye shall find rest unto your souls. For my yoke is easy, and my burden is light" (Mt.11:28-30).

b. The meek inherit the earth eternally, that is, the new heavens and earth. An inheritance of eternal life and dominion is promised them, for they are joint-heirs with Christ.

> "The Spirit itself beareth witness with our spirit, that we are the children of God: and if children, then heirs; heirs of God, and joint-heirs with Christ; if so be that we suffer with him, that we may be also glorified together" (Ro.8:16-17).

QUESTIONS:
1. What blessings does a meek person enjoy now, on this earth?
2. Are these blessings something you can claim for yourself? Are they worth making an effort to attain them?

5. THOSE WHO HUNGER AND THIRST AFTER RIGHTEOUSNESS: SHALL BE FILLED (v.6).

To hunger and thirst after righteousness is to have a starving spirit. It is real hunger and starvation of soul. It is a parched and dying thirst. It is a starving spirit and a parched soul that craves after *all righteousness*. It means a hunger and a thirst for the *whole thing*--for all righteousness, not for little tidbits. This is significant: it means that the promise of a *filled life* is conditional. A person must starve and thirst for *all righteousness* if he wishes to be filled with the fulness of life. Note several significant points.

1. Who is blessed? The person who hungers and thirsts *to be* righteous and *to do* righteousness. To do righteousness is not enough. To be righteous is not enough. Both are essential in order to be blessed.

2. There are those who *stress being righteous* and *neglect doing righteousness*. This leads to two serious errors.

a. The error of false security. It causes a person to stress that he is saved and acceptable to God because he has believed in Jesus Christ. But he neglects doing good. He does not live as he should, obeying God and serving man.

b. The error of loose living. It allows a person to go out and do what he desires. He feels secure and comfortable in his faith in Christ. He knows that wrong behavior may affect his fellowship with God and other believers, but he thinks his behavior does not affect his salvation and acceptance with God.

The problem with this stress is that it is a false righteousness. Righteousness in the Bible means *being righteous* and *doing righteousness,* not one without the other.

3. There are those who *stress doing righteousness* and *neglect being righteous.* This also leads to two serious errors.

    a. The error of self-righteousness and legalism. It causes a person to stress that he is saved and acceptable to God because he does good. He works, behaves morally, keeps certain rules and regulations, does the things a Christian should do, and obeys the main laws of God. But he neglects the basic law: the law of love and acceptance--that God loves him and accepts him not because he does good, but because he loves and trusts the righteousness of Christ.

    b. The error of being judgmental and censorious. A person who stresses that he is righteous (acceptable to God) because he keeps certain laws often judges and censors others. He feels that rules and regulations can be kept because he keeps them. Therefore, anyone who fails to keep them is judged, criticized, and censored.

The problem with this stress is that it, too, is a false righteousness. Again, righteousness in the Bible is both *being righteous* and *doing righteousness,* not one without the other.

4. The answer to attaining righteousness is not what most men think. When most men think of righteousness, they think of doing good--doing good deeds, good works, and helping their fellow man. As man walks through life, he faces appeal after appeal for help, and he helps. And he feels comfortable with himself because he has helped. He feels his *good deeds* make him acceptable and righteous before God. But the Bible is not saying that men never do good; it is saying that men are not righteous--not perfectly righteous within their hearts.

5. Christ does not say, "Blessed are the righteous," for no one is righteous (Ro.3:10). What is being said is that God alone is righteous; He alone is perfectly good. He says, "Blessed are they who hunger and thirst <u>after</u> righteousness." Man is not now and never can be perfectly righteous. His chance to be righteous is gone. He has already come short and missed the mark. He is already imperfect. Man has but one hope: that God will love him so much that He will somehow *count* him righteous. That is just what God does. God takes a man's "hunger and thirst after righteousness" and counts that hunger and thirst as righteousness. God does this because He loves man (Ro.5:6, 8-9).

APPLICATION:

The question each person needs to ask is this: How much am I seeking after righteousness? Am I seeking at all--seeking a little--seeking some--seeking much--seeking more and more? What Christ says is this: a person has to crave, starve, and thirst after righteousness. A person must seek righteousness more and more if he wishes to be saved and filled. Filled with what?

1) He is "full of goodness, filled with all knowledge" (Ro.15:14).
2) He is "filled with all the fullness of God" (Eph.3:19).
3) He is "filled with the Spirit" (Eph.5:18).
4) He is "filled with the fruits of righteousness" (Ph.1:11).
5) He is "filled with the knowledge of His [God's] will" (Col.1:9).
6) He is "filled with joy and with the Holy Spirit" (Gal.5:22-23; Acts 13:52).

6. Every person has some pull and some influence that urges him to do good. The pull and influence need to be nourished. In fact, they have to be nurtured or else they weaken, and they can be subdued and weakened so much that they are killed completely. They are just hardened against doing anything except what self wants to do (Heb.3:13 cp. Pr.21:29; 28:14; 29:1).

7. Righteousness is the only thing that will fill and satisfy man's innermost need. Food and drink will not. Any honest and thinking man knows there is nothing anywhere on this earth that can meet his deep need for life (permanent life, life that never ends). Only God can fill a life and satisfy the deep needs of man. This is the reason Christ says to *hunger* and *thirst* after righteousness.

ILLUSTRATION:

How hungry and thirsty are you? The person who really believes God and seeks Him diligently will yearn for more and more of God and His Word.

> *"A boy living in New Jersey waits expectantly every year for the mailman to deliver a special letter to him on his birthday. When his father was dying of a terminal disease, he knew the youngster would not have the benefit of his personal guidance and help as he grew into manhood. So he wrote him a letter for each year, and left instructions for them to be sent so that they would arrive annually on the proper date. A final envelope containing words of fatherly direction and advice will also be given to the son on his wedding day."*[2]

Do you regularly go to the Written Word with the hope and anticipation of hearing from your heavenly Father?

QUESTIONS:

1. How hungry are you for the things of God?
   _____I'm too full of the world's pleasures to want anything from God.
   _____Sometimes I spoil my spiritual appetite by snacking on worldly things.
   _____I've committed to a diet that feeds me with God's righteousness.
2. What does it really mean to hunger and thirst after righteousness?
3. What happens to a person when the righteousness of God governs his life?
4. If a person does not fill his life with righteousness, he fills it with other things. What kinds of things do people fill their lives with in the place of righteousness? How do these things affect a person's spiritual life?

SUMMARY:

The depth of your commitment to Christ is nowhere more apparent than in your character. The true disciple of Christ lives by the Beatitudes and is a powerful testimony to the world. Be sure these same qualities are what people see in you!
1. Jesus saw multitudes.
2. The poor in spirit: shall be given the Kingdom of Heaven.
3. Those who mourn: shall be comforted.
4. The meek: shall inherit the earth.
5. Those who hunger and thirst after righteousness: shall be filled.

PERSONAL JOURNAL NOTES:
(Reflection & Response)

1. The most important thing that I learned from this lesson was:

2. The thing that I need to work on the most is:

3. I can apply this lesson to my life by:

4. Closing Prayer of Commitment: (put your commitment down on paper).

---

[2] *INFOsearch Sermon Illustrations* (Arlington, TX: The Computer Assistant, 1-888-868-9029, 1986-1996).

		B. The True Disciple (Part 1): Who He Is & His Reward (the Beatitudes, 5-8), 5:7-12 (cp. Lk.6:20-23)	which are persecuted for righteousness' sake: for theirs is the kingdom of heaven.	be given the Kingdom of Heaven
1. The merciful: Will obtain mercy		7 Blessed are the merciful for they shall obtain mercy.	11 Blessed are ye, when men shall revile you, and persecute you, and shall say all manner of evil against you falsely, for my sake.	a. The persecution 1) Reviled & insulted 2) Slandered & lied against 3) Persecuted & hurt
2. The pure in heart: Will see God		8 Blessed are the pure in heart: for they shall see God.		b. The behavior expected: Joy
3. The peacemakers: Will be called the children of God		9 Blessed are the peacemakers: for they shall be called the children of God.	12 Rejoice, and be exceeding glad: for great is your reward in heaven: for so persecuted they the prophets which were before	c. The reason for joy 1) Great reward 2) Great examples: The prophets
4. The persecuted: Will		10 Blessed are they	you.	

Section IV
THE TEACHINGS OF THE MESSIAH TO HIS DISCIPLES:
THE GREAT SERMON ON THE MOUNT
Matthew 5:1-7:29

Study 2: The True Disciple (Part I): Who He is and His Reward (the Beatitudes, 5-8)

Text: Matthew 5:7-12

Aim: To make the Beatitudes a part of your day to day living: To have the maximum impact on the world for Christ.

Memory Verses: (Note: The eight Beatitudes are verses every believer should memorize).
"Blessed *are* the poor in spirit: for theirs is the kingdom of heaven" (Mt.5:3).
"Blessed *are* they that mourn: for they shall be comforted" (Mt.5:4).
"Blessed *are* the meek: for they shall inherit the earth" (Mt.5:5).
"Blessed *are* they which do hunger and thirst after righteousness: for they shall be filled" (Mt.5:6).
"Blessed *are* the merciful: for they shall obtain mercy" (Mt.5:7).
"Blessed *are* the pure in heart: for they shall see God" (Mt.5:8).
"Blessed *are* the peacemakers: for they shall be called the children of God" (Mt.5:9).
"Blessed *are* they which are persecuted for righteousness' sake: for theirs is the kingdom of heaven" (Mt.5:10).

INTRODUCTION:
Can God trust you to obey His Word and follow Him--even during the heat of battle? Many people find it easy to be a Christian when everything around is peaceful and serene. But it does not take long for life to become complicated when people begin to take other positions or disagree with us. We tend to quickly defend our own position and vow to gain the

advantage. Whether the opposition comes from friend or foe, our natural man wants to trust in the power of the flesh. God has a much better plan of *response* when we are threatened or opposed.

Our study of the Beatitudes continues with four more examples of how the believer is to live in the world. Instead of becoming a stumbling block to others, the believer who applies God's Word to his life and decides to follow Christ will be found trustworthy and will be given the opportunity to be God's vessel of blessing to the nations. More than ever before, the world needs men and women who are merciful, pure, peaceful, and willing to suffer for the cause of Christ and His gospel. These people God will trust.

OUTLINE:
  1. The merciful: will obtain mercy (v.7).
  2. The pure in heart: will see God (v.8).
  3. The peacemakers: will be called the children of God (v.9).
  4. The persecuted: will be given the Kingdom of Heaven (v.10-12).

1. THE MERCIFUL: SHALL OBTAIN MERCY (v.7).

To be merciful is to have a forgiving spirit and a compassionate heart. It is showing mercy and being kindhearted. It is forgiving those who are wrong, yet it is much more.
  ⇒ It is a desire to succor, to tenderly draw unto oneself and to care for.
  ⇒ It is empathy; it is getting right inside the person and feeling right along with him.
  ⇒ It is a deliberate effort, an act of the will to understand the person and to meet his need by forgiving and showing mercy.
  ⇒ It is the opposite of being hard, unforgiving, and unfeeling. God forgives only those who forgive others. A person receives mercy only if he is merciful (cp. Mt.6:12; Jas.2:13).

Two things are essential in order to have mercy: seeing a need and being able to meet that need. God sees our need and feels for us (Eph.2:1-3). Therefore, He acts; He has mercy upon us:
  ⇒ God withholds His judgment.
  ⇒ God provides a way for us to be saved.

> **"But God, who is rich in mercy, for his great love wherewith he loved us, Even when we were dead in sins, hath quickened us together with Christ, (by grace ye are saved;)" (Eph.2:4-5).**

Several significant facts need to be noted about mercy.
  1. The person who is merciful has a tender heart--a heart that cares for all who have need, seen or unseen. If he sees the needful, he feels for them and reaches out to do all he can. If he does not see them, he feels and reaches out through prayer and giving as opportunity arises. The merciful just do not hoard or hold back any kind of help, no matter the cost.
    a. They have the love of God dwelling in them.

> **"But whoso hath this world's good, and seeth his brother have need, and shutteth up his bowels of compassion from him, how dwelleth the love of God in him?" (1 Jn.3:17).**

    b. They know that it is "more blessed to give than to receive."

> **"I have showed you all things, how that so labouring ye ought to support the weak, and to remember the words of the Lord Jesus, how he said, It is more blessed to give than to receive" (Acts 20:35).**

2. Every believer can be merciful. Some may not have money or other means to help, but they can be tender and compassionate and demonstrate mercy through expression and prayer. In fact, God instructs the believer to be merciful. He charges the believer to do some very practical things:
    a. "Deal [share]...bread to the hungry" (Is.58:7; Jas.2:15).
    b. "Bring the poor that are cast out to thy house" (Is. 58:7).
    c. "Cover him [the naked]" (Is.58:7; Jas.2:15).
    d. Strengthen and comfort the broken and grieving soul (Job 16:5).
    e. Pity the afflicted (Job 6:14).
    f. Bear the burdens of others--even to the point of restoring them when they sin. But reach out to them in a spirit of meekness (Gal.6:2 cp. 6:1).
    g. Support the weak (Acts 20:35).
3. The results of being merciful are numerous.
    a. A person is given the mercy of God--forgiveness of sins (Ps.18:25; cp. 2 Sam. 22:26).
    b. A person does good to his own soul (Pr.19:17).
    c. A person is paid back what he gives--by God Himself (Pr.19:17).
    d. A person behaves like God Himself (Lk.6:36; cp. Ps.103:8; Joel 2:15).
    e. A person is blessed (Ps.51:1).
    f. A person is assured of finding "mercy in that day" (2 Tim.1:18).
    g. A person shall inherit the Kingdom of God--forever (Mt.25:34-35).
4. The unmerciful are warned by God.
    a. They shall face "judgment without mercy" (Jas.2:13).
    b. They shall face the anger and wrath of God (Mt.18:34-35).
    c. They are not forgiven their sins (Mt.6:12, 14-15).
5. Two opposite attitudes of mercy are shown.
    a. The attitude of shutting up one's compassion from those in need (1 Jn.3:17; cp. Jas.2:15-16).
    b. The attitude of putting on a heart of mercy (Col.3:12).

ILLUSTRATION:
    Is mercy a part of your life? At times we tend to be like a bull in a china shop--knocking over people and things without giving it a second thought. God has called every believer to have a heart of mercy, and to dispense mercy generously.

The day of the big dove hunt was coming to a close. The hunters gathered up their supplies in the corn field, feeling the day had been a complete waste. Every bird that flew overhead was well out of range. A few impatient hunters shot at the birds anyway, but to no avail. As the sun began to set, two hunters marched by a small pond surrounded by tall grass. One of the hunters peered through the grass and saw to his amazement a flock of ducks leisurely floating on the peaceful surface of the pond. Unseen by the ducks, the hunter smiled with pleasure. "Finally, a chance to get a good shot at something that's not moving" he said to himself as he raised his gun and peered into the sight. Fixing a large duck in the cross-hairs of his gun, the hunter's sweaty finger felt the trigger. But at the last second, he changed his mind, lifted his gun, and fired into the empty sky. The ducks flapped their wings and made a rapid escape toward the eastern sky. "Ha! You can't even hit a sitting duck" joked the other hunter. The hunter who fired his gun looked his friend in the eye and said, "No I can't hit a sitting duck. I'm a better hunter than that."

Every day we have the opportunity to put people into our sights and pull the trigger of anger, revenge, condemnation, criticism, conflict, combat. Mercy, though, causes us to fire into the air and not to go after sitting ducks. The person who is merciful can't hit a sitting duck. He is a much better believer than that.

Are there any targets in your sights who need your mercy?

2. THE PURE IN HEART: SHALL SEE GOD (v.8).

To be pure in heart is to have a clean heart; to be unsoiled and uncompromised; to be cleansed and forgiven; to have a single purpose, that of God's glory. There are several significant points to note about the "pure in heart."
1. The person who is "pure in heart" lives a clean life.
   a. He keeps himself from being soiled and tainted by the world.

   > "Pure religion and undefiled before God and the Father is this, To visit the fatherless and widows in their affliction, and to keep himself unspotted from the world" (Jas.1:27).

   b. He cleanses his heart from wickedness so that he may be saved.

   > "Wash thine heart from wickedness, that thou mayest be saved. How long shall thy vain thoughts lodge within thee?" (Jer.4:14).

   c. He obeys the truth with the help of the Holy Spirit.

   > "Seeing ye have purified your souls in obeying the truth through the Spirit unto unfeigned love of the brethren, see that ye love one another with a pure heart fervently" (1 Pt.1:22).

   d. He keeps his hands clean; that is, he has nothing to do with the filthy things of this world.

   > "He that hath clean hands, and a pure heart; who hath not lifted up his soul unto vanity, nor sworn deceitfully. He shall receive the blessing from the LORD, and righteousness from the God of his salvation" (Ps.24:4-5).

   e. He makes every effort to be without reproach.

   > "Wherefore, beloved, seeing that ye look for such things, be diligent that ye may be found of him in peace, without spot, and blameless" (2 Pt.3:14).

2. A person's very best behavior is seldom (if ever) free from some mixture of self. It is questionable if a sinful creature can ever act perfectly--perfectly free from mixed motives. As the Bible says, "there is none that doeth good, no, not one" (Ro.3:12). The believer is constantly to search his heart and cleanse it of impure motives. Motives involving self are sly and deceptive.

a. Is a person employed primarily for self, or to serve Christ and to earn enough to help others who have a need (Col.3:24; Eph.4:28)?
b. Is a person ministering to help the needful, or to have a sense of self-satisfaction (cp. Mt.5:7)?
c. Is a person worshipping to honor God, or to satisfy a feeling of obligation?
d. Is a person praying daily to fellowship with God, or to gain comfortable feelings that he pleases God through praying?

Impure motives enter the believer's heart so quietly, so deceptively. The believer is often unaware of their presence. He needs to pray often: **"Create in me a clean heart, O God" (Ps.51:10)!**

3. The "pure in heart" minister in many ways, among them two very practical areas:
   ⇒ They visit the fatherless.
   ⇒ They visit widows in their affliction.

> **"Pure religion and undefiled before God and the Father is this, To visit the fatherless and widows in their affliction, and to keep himself unspotted from the world" (Jas.1:27).**

4. There are two wonderful promises made to the "pure in heart." The pure in heart "shall see God" (Mt.5:8).
   a. Presently, on this earth, the pure in heart shall see God by faith, "through a glass darkly" (1 Cor.13:12). Just imagine! The "pure in heart" endure in the faith "as already seeing Him who is invisible" (Heb.11:27).

> **"For now <u>we see</u> through a glass, darkly; but then face to face: now I know in part; but then shall I know even as also I am known" (1 Cor.13:12).**

   b. Eternally, the pure in heart shall see God face to face. They shall "see Him as He is" and behold "His face in righteousness."

> **"Beloved, now are we the sons of God, and it doth not yet appear what we shall be: but we know that, when he shall appear, we shall be like him; for we shall see him as he is" (1 Jn.3:2).**

QUESTIONS:
1. Look carefully and honestly into your own life. What kinds of things keep you from having a pure heart?
2. What can you do to continually ensure that your heart is pure?
3. In what ways does having a pure heart make you a better witness for Christ?

3. THE PEACEMAKERS: SHALL BE CALLED THE CHILDREN OF GOD (v.9).

Peacemakers bring men together; they make peace between men and God; they solve disputes and erase divisions; they reconcile differences and eliminate strife; they silence tongues and build right relationships.

1. Who is the peacemaker?
   a. The person who strives to make peace with God (Ro.5:1; Eph.2:14-17). He conquers the inner struggle, settles the inner tension, handles the inner pressure. He takes the struggle within his heart between good and evil; he strives for the good and conquers the bad.

"Therefore being justified by faith, we have peace with God through our Lord Jesus Christ" (Ro.5:1).

b. The person who strives at every opportunity to make peace *within* others. He seeks and leads others to make their peace with God--to conquer their inner struggle, to settle their inner tension, to handle their inner pressure.

"Let us therefore follow after the things which make for peace, and things wherewith one may edify another" (Ro.14:19).

c. The person who strives at every opportunity to make peace *between* others. He works to solve disputes and erase divisions, to reconcile differences and eliminate strife, to silence tongues and build relationships.

"Let nothing be done through strife or vainglory; but in lowliness of mind let each esteem other better than themselves" (Ph.2:3).

2. The peacemaker is the person who has made peace *with* God (Ro.5:1), and knows the peace *of* God.

3. Peacemakers love peace, but they do not passively accept trouble. There are those who claim to love peace, yet they remove themselves from all trouble. They ignore and flee problems and threatening situations, often evading issues. They make no attempt to bring peace between others. The peacemaker (of whom Christ speaks) faces the trouble no matter how dangerous, and works to bring a true peace no matter the struggle.

4. The world has its troublemakers. Practically every organization has its troublemakers, including the church. Wherever the troublemaker is, there is criticism, grumbling, and murmuring; and, too often, a division within the body--a division that is sometimes minor, sometimes major; sometimes just distasteful, sometimes outright bitter. The peacemaker cannot stand such. He goes forth to settle the matter, solve the problem, handle the differences, and reconcile the parties.

5. The gospel of Christ is to be spread by peaceful means, not by forceful means. There are many kinds of force.

   a. There is verbal force through loudness, a dominating conversation, improper sales tactics, threats, bigotry, and abuse.
   b. There is physical force through facial expressions, body motions, an overpowering presence, and attacks.

QUESTIONS:
1. Sometimes a peacemaker gets caught in the crossfire and gets hurt. Does this mean he should cease from his efforts?
2. Are there times when you should not attempt to be a peacemaker? Why or why not?
3. When is it most difficult to act as a peacemaker? What can you do to be a better peacemaker in the future?

6. The picture of adoption, of being called a child of God, is a beautiful picture of what God does for the Christian believer. In the ancient world, the family was based on a Roman law called "patria potestas," the father's power. The law gave the father absolute authority over his children so long as the father lived. He could work, enslave, sell, and if he wished, he could pronounce the death penalty. Regardless of the child's adult age, the father held all power over personal and property rights.

Therefore, adoption was a serious matter. Yet, it was a common practice to ensure that a family would not become extinct by having no male children. And when a child was adopted, three legal steps were taken.

a. The adopted son was adopted permanently. He could not be adopted today and disinherited tomorrow. He became a son of the father--forever. He was eternally secure as a son.

b. The adopted son immediately had all the rights of a legitimate son in the new family.

c. The adopted son completely lost all rights in his old family. The adopted son was looked upon as a new person--so new that old debts and obligations connected with his former family were canceled and abolished as if they never existed.

The Bible says several things about the believer's adoption as a son of God.

⇒ The believer's adoption establishes a new relationship with God--forever. He is eternally secure as a child of God. But the new relationship is established only when a person comes to Christ through faith (Gal.3:26; 4:4-5).

⇒ The believer's adoption establishes a new relationship with God as father. The believer has all the rights and privileges of a genuine son of God (Ro.8:16-17; 1 Jn. 3:1-2).

⇒ The believer's adoption establishes a new dynamic experience with God as father, a moment by moment access into His very presence (Ro.8:14, 16; Gal.4:6).

⇒ The believer's adoption gives him a very special relationship with other children of God--a family relationship that binds him with others in an unparalleled spiritual union.

⇒ The believer's adoption makes him a new person. The believer has been taken out from under the authority and power of the world and its sin. The believer is *placed as a son* into the family and authority of God. The old life with all of its debts and obligations are canceled and wiped out (2 Cor.5:17; Gal.3:23-27; 2 Pt.1:4).

⇒ The believer's adoption is to be fully realized in the future at the return of Jesus Christ (Ro.8:19; Eph.1:14; 1 Th.4:14-17; 1 Jn.3:2).

⇒ The believer's adoption and its joy will be shared by all creation on a cosmic scale (Ro.8:21). There is to be a new heavens and earth (2 Pt.3:12-14; Rev.21:1-7).

QUESTIONS:
1. How could you explain your relationship as an adopted child of God to an unbeliever? Explain it simply and briefly?
2. The believer who has been adopted by God has an abundance of special blessings. What are some of the benefits you appreciate the most? What are some of the benefits you think of most often? What are some of the benefits you tend to forget?

4. THE PERSECUTED: SHALL BE GIVEN THE KINGDOM OF HEAVEN (v.10-12).

To be *persecuted* is to endure suffering for Christ; to be mocked, ridiculed, criticized, ostracized; to be treated with hostility; to be martyred. Note several significant points.

1. There are three major kinds of persecution mentioned by Christ in this passage:
   a. Being reviled: verbally abused, insulted, scolded, mocked (cruel mockings, Heb.11:36).
   b. Being persecuted: hurt, ostracized, attacked, tortured, martyred, and treated hostilely.
   c. Having *all manner* of evil spoken against you: slandered, cursed, and lied about (cp. Ps.35:11; Acts 17:6-7).
2. Who are the persecuted?
   a. The person who lives and speaks for righteousness and is reacted against.
   b. The person who lives and speaks for Christ and is reviled, persecuted, and spoken against.
3. Persecution is a paradox. It reveals that the true nature of the world is evil. Think about it: the person who lives and speaks for righteousness is opposed and persecuted. The person

who cares and works for the true love, justice, and salvation of the world is actually fought against. How deceived the world and its humanity is, rushing onward in madness for nothing but to return to dust, to seek life only for some seventy years (if nothing happens before then)!

4. Believers are forewarned: they shall suffer persecution.

a. Believers shall suffer persecution because they are not of this world. They are *called out* of the world. They are in the world, but they are not of the world. They are separated from the behavior of the world. Therefore, the world reacts against them.

"If ye were of the world, the world would love his own: but because ye are not of the world, but I have chosen you out of the world, therefore the world hateth you" (Jn.15:19).

b. They shall suffer persecution because believers strip away the world's *cloak of sin.* They live and demonstrate a life of righteousness. They do not compromise with the world and its sinful behavior. They live pure and godly lives, having nothing to do with the sinful pleasures of a corruptible world. Such living exposes the sins of people.

"If the world hate you, ye know that it hated me before it hated you....If I had not come and spoken unto them, they had not had sin: but now they have no cloke for their sin" (Jn.15:18, 22).

c. They shall suffer persecution because the world does not know God nor Christ. The ungodly of the world want no God other than themselves and their own imaginations. They want to do just what they want--to fulfill their own desires, not what God wishes and demands. However, the godly believer dedicates his life to God, to His worship and service. The ungodly want no part of God; therefore, they oppose those who talk about God and man's duty to honor and worship God.

"But all these things will they do unto you for my name's sake, because they know not him that sent me" (Jn.15:21).

d. They shall suffer persecution because the world is deceived in its concept and belief of God. The world conceives God to be the One who fulfills their earthly desires and lusts (Jn.16:2-3). Man's idea of God is that of a *Supreme Grandfather.* They think that God protects, provides, and gives no matter what a person's behavior is, just so the behavior is not too far out; that God will accept and work all things out in the final analysis. However, the true believer teaches against this. God is love, but He is also just and demands righteousness. The world rebels against this concept of God.

"Remember the word that I said unto you, The servant is not greater than his lord. If they have persecuted me, they will also persecute you; if they have kept my saying, they will keep yours also" (Jn.15:20).
"Marvel not, my brethren, if the world hate you" (1 Jn.3:13).

5. Persecutions can erupt from the most devilish imaginations of men. The sufferings of the early Christians were just what Peter says, "fiery." Most of us have seen pictures of believers being fed to wild lions and burned at the stake. But these were mild deaths compared to what some believers suffered. Some had boiling lead poured over their bodies; others had fiery red branding irons put to the private parts of their bodies; others were wrapped in the bloody skins of wild game and chased in a hunt by man and dogs; others were soaked with flammable oil and set aflame; others had their limbs torn apart from their bodies one by one,

both by machine and animals; others were subjected to the most devilish imaginations in torture chambers; and so the list goes on and on. (See Foxes Book of Martyrs for a complete discussion of the persecution of believers down through the centuries.)

William Barclay points out that there were essentially five slanders made against the church in the early days of its history.[1]

    a. Christian believers were thought to be cannibals. There were two reasons for this slander. (1) The teaching that one had to eat the flesh of Christ and drink His blood in order to have life (Jn.6:51f). (2) The practice of the Lord's Supper and its words, "This is my body and this is my blood" (Mt.26:26; Mk.14:22; Lk.22:19; 1 Cor. 11:24).

    b. The church was also charged with breaking up homes and tampering with family relationships. This was because some members of families became believers and others did not (Mt.10:34-39).

    c. The church was charged with heresy.

      ⇒ Judaism, the religion of the Jews, charged the Christians with heresy because the believers refused to put tradition before God and people, and they refused to obey the rules and regulations as prescribed by the traditional beliefs.

      ⇒ Other people charged believers with heresy because they refused to pay homage to Caesar and to worship the gods and goddesses of society.

    d. The church was charged with lust and immorality. This was because they practiced the *Agape* or the *Love Feast*. This was simply a fellowship meal in which Christian brotherhood was shared and experienced. But because it was called "The Love Feast" and such a close bond was seen between Christians, their behavior was twisted to be immoral.

    e. The church and its believers were charged with being revolutionary and with insurrection. They were thought to be traitors for three primary reasons.

    1) Christians preached Jesus Christ the Lord who is to return and establish His kingdom right here upon earth.

    2) Christians also preached the destruction of the world by fire.

    3) Christians refused to worship Caesar, the symbol of Roman government. This was the major reason for the official persecution of Christians by the government.

Rome had conquered the world with its vast number of peoples and their different cultures, politics, beliefs, philosophies, and languages. How could one government pull and hold all the diverse people of the world together as one nation and one people?

Rome needed a symbol, an object, something that could be held up before the people that would naturally demand their loyalty. As Rome began to conquer the world, the leaders began to notice something. The conquered people eventually became settled and thankful for the peace, prosperity, and civilization that Rome brought to the world. They were glad for a one-world government. And in the eyes of the people, that government was centered in the emperor. The emperor was therefore set up as the one unifying principle around which the vast empire was built and held together. A law was passed which demanded that every citizen go once a year and burn a dab of incense to the idol of Caesar and say, "Caesar is Lord." The worshipper was then given a certificate showing that he was loyal to the empire. He was free to worship as he wished for the rest of the year.

Christians were just unable to bow and worship and say "Caesar is Lord." Therefore, in the eyes of the government they were lawbreakers and disloyal to Rome. They were hunted down and charged with being revolutionaries and insurrectionists. The result was, of course, just what Peter says, "fiery persecution."

---

[1]   William Barclay. *The Gospel of Matthew*, p.108-109.

6. What is to be the believer's attitude toward persecution?
   a. It is *not* to be retaliation, pride, spiritual superiority.
   b. It *is* to be joy and gladness (Mt.5:12; 2 Cor.12:10; 1 Pt.4:12-13).
7. The persecuted are promised great rewards.
   a. The Kingdom of Heaven--now.
      ⇒ Believers experience a special honor (Acts 5:41).
      ⇒ Believers experience a special consolation (2 Cor.1:5).
      ⇒ Believers are given a very special closeness, a glow of the Lord's presence.
      ⇒ Believers become a greater witness for Christ (2 Cor.1:4-6).
   b. The Kingdom of Heaven--eternally (Heb.11:35f; 1 Pt.4:12-13).

ILLUSTRATION:

The persecuted believer must never put his trust in himself or in the power of others to save him. God has a great purpose in persecution, a purpose that is often hidden in His infinite wisdom and power.

> *"In the year 1662 there lived a godly preacher named Henry Havers. Christians were being severely persecuted at that time, and this earnest man too was being hunted from place to place by soldiers who were sent out to take him prisoner. He preached in the country one day to a number of eager listeners who had waited for hours to hear the simple message of free salvation. Suddenly an alarm was given that a party of officers were on their way to arrest him. There was not time to mount his horse and escape, so he ran into an old house nearby and hid in a narrow passageway. No sooner had he squatted down in the darkness than a spider began to weave a web across the opening. Presently voices were heard and a soldier approached the place where he lay. After a quick glance the officer exclaimed, 'It's no use looking for him in there. See the web across the opening? He couldn't have gotten in there without breaking it!' So off they went, leaving the preacher in a refuge that God had made safe through the work of a lowly spider. When all was quiet, the man of God crept from his hiding place. Looking at the feeble thing that had acted as a shield to guard him, he exclaimed, 'It is better to trust in the Lord than to put confidence in princes' (Ps.118:9)."[2]*

When persecution comes your way, in whom will you put your trust?

QUESTIONS:

1. Think of your own life. How severe has your persecution been when compared to those who have been tortured and martyred? How would you have stood up to such persecution? Are you confident that the Lord is still in control when you are suffering some form of opposition? How can you be sure?
2. How prominent is slander against the church today? How can you and do you respond to such slander?
3. What was the foundational conflict that the early Church had with Rome? How does that danger exist in the world today?

SUMMARY:

Can God trust you to make a difference for Him in the world today? God is looking for men, women, boys and girls whose lives are marked with the traits of mercy, purity, peace,

---

[2] *INFOsearch Sermon Illustrations* (Arlington, TX: The Computer Assistant, 1-888-868-9029, 1986-1996).

and the willingness to suffer--no matter the cost--for the cause of Jesus Christ. The person who makes the Beatitudes a part of his life will receive the great benefits promised.

1. The merciful: shall obtain mercy.
2. The pure in heart: shall see God .
3. The peacemakers: shall be called the children of God.
4. The persecuted: shall be given the Kingdom of Heaven .

PERSONAL JOURNAL NOTES:
(Reflection & Response)

1. The most important thing that I learned from this lesson was:

2. The thing that I need to work on the most is:

3. I can apply this lesson to my life by:

4. Closing Prayer of Commitment: (put your commitment down on paper).

	C. The True Disciple (Part II): The Salt of the Earth-- Serving God, 5:13 (Mk.9:50; cp. Lk.14:34-35; Col.4:6)
1. The disciples' character: Salt 2. The disciples' place to salt (to minister): The earth 3. The disciples' mission: To salt the earth 4. Their danger: Becoming useless & destructive	13 Ye are the salt of the earth: but if the salt have lost his savour, wherewith shall it be salted? it is thenceforth good for nothing, but to be cast out, and to be trodden under foot of men.

Section IV
THE TEACHINGS OF THE MESSIAH TO HIS DISCIPLES:
THE GREAT SERMON ON THE MOUNT
Matthew 5:1-7:29

Study 3: THE TRUE DISCIPLE (PART II): THE SALT OF THE EARTH-- SERVING GOD

Text: Matthew 5:13

Aim: To flavor the world with the presence of Christ in your life.

Memory Verse:
> "Ye are the salt of the earth: but if the salt have lost his savour, wherewith shall it be salted? it is thenceforth good for nothing, but to be cast out, and to be trodden under foot of men" (Matthew 5:13).

INTRODUCTION:
If you could take a peek at God's Recipe Book and allow your imagination to wander a little, what would you see? Perhaps one page would have a recipe called *"Mankind Casserole a la Salvation."* As you look at the ingredients, you begin to take stock of what is in your pantry.

INGREDIENTS
⇒ A world that is mixed up
⇒ People who need the Savior
⇒ A cup of the oil of the Holy Spirit
⇒ A measure of grace and faith
⇒ One generous helping of the salt of the earth

BAKING INSTRUCTIONS
Mix all of this into the pan of the gospel and serve with the Bread of Life. Serves "whosoever will."

When the gospel is prepared and shared with the world, it is important to include all of the ingredients and carefully follow all the instructions. If anything is left out, the recipe flops. Note that we cannot provide the power to save anybody. We cannot produce the Holy Spirit. We cannot manufacture grace and faith. What can we add? As the salt of the earth, we can distribute God's Word to the world, flavoring mankind with His goodness and mercy.

There is so much in this little parable, but the main thrust is *distinctiveness*. Salt is distinctively different from the thing upon which it is put. By nature and by purpose it is different. So are believers. They are distinctively different by nature and by purpose. *By nature* believers are a new creation, born of God (2 Cor.5:17; 1 Pt.1:23); *by purpose* believers are to penetrate and change the very taste of the earth. They are like salt.

OUTLINE:
1. The disciples' character: salt (v.13).
2. The disciples' place to salt (to minister): the earth (v.13).
3. The disciples' mission: to salt the earth (v.13).
4. Their danger: becoming useless and destructive (v.13).

1. THE DISCIPLES' CHARACTER: SALT (v.13).

Believers are *called and designed* (made) to be the salt of the earth. Several things can be said about salt that point out just what Jesus means.

1. Salt is *distinctive*. It is totally different from the food or object upon which it is put. The power of salt lies in this difference. Believers, just as salt, are to be different from the world. The power of their lives and their testimony lies in their being different and distinctive. They are to be "unspotted from the world" (Jas.1:27).

> **"And be not conformed to this world: but be ye transformed by the renewing of your mind, that ye may prove what is that good, and acceptable, and perfect, will of God" (Ro.12:2).**

2. Salt *preserves*. It keeps things from going bad and decaying. It cleanses and disinfects. Believers, just as salt, are to cleanse and preserve the world. They are to disinfect the world and keep the germs of the world from causing things to go bad. They are to save the world from corruption.

> **"Seeing ye have purified your souls in obeying the truth through the Spirit unto unfeigned love of the brethren, see that ye love one another with a pure heart fervently: being born again, not of corruptible seed, but of incorruptible, by the word of God, which liveth and abideth for ever. For all flesh is as grass, and all the glory of man as the flower of grass. The grass withereth, and the flower thereof falleth away: but the word of the Lord endureth for ever. And this is the word which by the gospel is preached unto you" (1 Pt.1:22-25).**

3. Salt *penetrates*. It inserts a new quality, substance, and life. It changes that upon which it is put. Believers are likewise to penetrate the world and insert a new life into it.

> **"Therefore if any man be in Christ, he is a new creature: old things are passed away; behold, all things are become new" (2 Cor. 5:17).**

4. Salt *flavors*. It influences the taste of things. It takes a bland, tasteless food and makes it enjoyable. Believers are to so flavor and influence the world for Christ. They are to take

the unappetizing and tasteless things of the world and salt them, making them appealing and inviting to the world.

> **"But the fruit of the Spirit is love, joy, peace, longsuffering, gentleness, goodness, faith, meekness, temperance: against such there is no law" (Gal.5:22-23).**

5. Salt is *quiet*. It is visible, but it works silently, making no noise whatsoever during its work. Believers, the salt of the earth, are to work quietly and discreetly.

> **"Let it [your behavior] be the hidden man of the heart, in that which is not corruptible, even the ornament of a meek and quiet spirit, which is in the sight of God of great price" (1 Pt.3:4).**

6. Salt *spreads*. Its flavor spreads all about. A sprinkle of salt has a widespread effect. A believer's *salt* spreads far and wide.

> **"For we cannot but speak the things which we have seen and heard" (Acts 4:20).**

7. Salt is *irrepressible*. Once applied, it cannot be stopped. A believer's *salt*, his testimony, is irrepressible; it cannot be stopped.

> **"For as the rain cometh down, and the snow from heaven, and returneth not thither, but watereth the earth, and maketh it bring forth and bud, that it may give seed to the sower, and bread to the eater: so shall my word be that goeth forth out of my mouth: it shall not return unto me void, but it shall accomplish that which I please, and it shall prosper in the thing whereto I sent it" (Is.55:10-11).**

ILLUSTRATION:

The believer must move freely within society and liberally salt the earth as he goes. Many unbelievers become uncomfortable when they realize that they are dealing with a Christian. It is important to be yourself, no matter how you are perceived. Author Rebecca Manley Pippert shares a humorous story and the challenge to salt the earth.

> *"I am often put in a religious box when people discover what my profession is. [a conference speaker and consultant in evangelism] Because I travel a great deal, I have a clergy card which sometimes enables me to travel at reduced rates. The only problem is that occasionally ticket agents won't believe that I am authorized to use it! A young female just isn't what they have in mind when they see a clergy card. More than once I've been asked, 'Okay, honey, now where did you rip this off?'*
>
> *"Once when I was flying from San Francisco to Portland I arrived at the counter and was greeted by an exceedingly friendly male ticket agent.*
>
> *"'Well, hel-lo-o-o there!' he said.*
>
> *"'Ah...I'd like to pick up my ticket to Portland please.'*
>
> *"'Gee, I'm sorry. You won't be able to fly there tonight.'*
>
> *"'Why? Is the flight canceled?'*
>
> *"'No, it's because you're going out with me tonight.'*
>
> *"'What?'*
>
> *"'Listen, I know this great restaurant with a hot band. You'll never regret it.'*
>
> *"'Oh, I'm sorry, I really must get to Portland. Do you have my ticket?'*
>
> *"'Aw, what's the rush? I'll pick you up at eight...'*
>
> *"'Look, I really must go to Portland,' I said.*

"'Well, okay. Too bad though. Hey, I can't find your ticket.'
"He paused, then said, 'Looks like it's a date then!'
"'Oh, I forgot to tell you, it's a...special ticket,' I said.
"'Oh, is it youth fare?'
"'No, um, well, it's...ah, clergy,' I whispered, leaning over the counter.
"He froze. 'What did you say?'
"'It's clergy.'
"'CLERGY!?!' he shouted, as the entire airport looked our way. His face went absolutely pale, as he was horrified by only one thought, 'Oh, no. I flirted with a nun!'

"When he disappeared behind the counter, I could hear him whisper to the other ticket agent only a few feet away, 'Hey George, get a load of that girl up there. She's clergy.' Suddenly another man rose from behind the counter, smiled and nodded and disappeared again. I never have felt so religious in my entire life. As I stood there trying to look as secular as possible, my ticket agent reappeared and stood back several feet behind the desk. Looking shaken and sounding like a tape recording he said, 'Good afternoon. We certainly hope there have been no inconveniences. And on behalf of Hughes Airwest, we'd like to wish you a very safe and pleasant flight...Sister Manley.'

"As humorous as this incident was, I think it shows how difficult it is to maintain our authenticity before the world. The challenge is to not allow ourselves to become more or less than human."[1]

QUESTIONS:
1. Of these seven qualities of salt, which one best describes your character?
   ...distinctive   ...flavors   ...spreads
   ...preserves   ...quiet   ...irrepressible
   ...penetrates
   Which of these qualities do you most need to develop?
2. Is it possible to become too *salty*? What are the signs and dangers of this happening?
3. What person whom you know displays and lives out the true character of salt in his life?

2. THE DISCIPLES' PLACE TO SALT (TO MINISTER): THE EARTH (v.13).

The world is the place where believers are to move about and salt (live and minister). Why? Because the world is (1) unappetizing and tasteless, (2) decaying and rotting, (3) corrupting and foul.

APPLICATION 1:
Too many believers live as though they are already in heaven: safe and secure from all harm. They do not pay enough attention to this earth: its needs, its decay, its corruption. While on this earth, believers are called to salt and flavor the earth not heaven.

APPLICATION 2:
There is a sense in which the church is the salt factory and the world is the marketplace for the salt. Too much salt is being stored and locked up at the church. There is

---

[1]   Rebecca Manley Pippert. *Out of the Salt Shaker and Into the World: Evangelism as a Way of Life.* (Downers Grove, IL: InterVarsity Press, 1979), p.125-126.

not enough salt being sent out into the marketplace. The result? The world is not being salted and flavored for Christ enough.

> **"Therefore said he unto them, The harvest truly is great, but the labourers are few: pray ye therefore the Lord of the harvest, that he would send forth labourers into his harvest" (Lk.10:2).**

QUESTIONS:
1. How can the world be described as unappetizing and tasteless when so many people are hungering after it?
2. In what ways is your church successfully taking the salt of their witness out into the community?
3. What can you do personally to better salt and impact your community for Christ?

3. THE DISCIPLES' MISSION: TO SALT THE EARTH (v.13).

Note a critical point: believers are the salt of the earth not of heaven. They can do nothing to salt heaven. They cannot penetrate, flavor, or preserve heaven. Any relationship whatsoever they have with heaven is a gift from heaven, from God Himself. However, believers are the salt of the earth; they can penetrate, flavor, and preserve the earth. But two things are necessary *before a person can salt* the earth.
1. *Believers must have salt in themselves*. Believers cannot give what they do not have.

> **"Salt is good: but if the salt have lost his saltness, wherewith will ye season it? Have salt in yourselves, and have peace one with another" (Mk.9:50).**

2. *Believers must spread out into the world*: their salt is necessary and useful. There is no true salt other than the believers' salt. There are many substitutes but only one true salt. There is nothing else that can salt and impact the earth like the believer, nothing whatsoever. The task belongs to the believers of the world. The success of the mission rests upon the believers.

> **"Let your speech be always with grace, seasoned with salt, that ye may know how ye ought to answer every man" (Col.4:6).**

QUESTIONS:
1. How can you be sure you have what it takes to salt the earth? How can you guard against losing your 'saltiness'?
2. Some believers tend to cluster together in clumps of salt, concentrating on one location. Why is it so important for the church to spread out and salt the entire earth?

4. THEIR DANGER: BECOMING USELESS AND DESTRUCTIVE (v.13).

Salt does not lose its saltiness and flavor. However, in the time of Christ the salt of Palestine was gathered in such a manner that dirt and other impurities were often mixed with it. The salt was thus useless and good for nothing. In fact, it actually destroyed the fertility of the soil. Therefore, it was not only useless but destructive. Note two significant points.
1. This is a picture of the backslider, of a believer who allows the impurities of the world into his life. He loses his *saltiness*, his impact or testimony. Three things can be said about the backslider.
   a. He becomes useless just as the salt did.
   b. He is of no value. He may as well be cast out and trodden underfoot.

127

c. He actually destroys the fertility of some out in the world by becoming a stumbling block and by not being able to salt them.

"And Jesus said unto him, No man, having put his hand to the plow, and looking back, is fit for the kingdom of God" (Lk.9:62).

ILLUSTRATION:
A believer does not become a backslider all at once. The strong pull of sin leads a person down a dangerous path of deception.

"Barney had always been proud of his thick wavy hair, but then he began to lose it. Finally just one lone hair remained on top of his shiny dome. One morning Barney awoke, looked at his pillow, and was shocked to see that last hair lying there. Jumping out of bed, he ran downstairs, crying, 'Martha, Martha, I'm bald!'
"That's kind of like the Christian who begins dabbling in the things of the world. He gets deeper and deeper in sin, slowly sliding away from the Lord, without even knowing what is happening. It is not until he has had some startling experience--perhaps due to God's discipline--that he sees his true condition. When suddenly brought under the powerful searchlight of the Word of God, the deceived one is shocked to realize how subtly and deceitfully Satan has stripped away his spiritual power and discernment."

Sometimes a backslider is the last one to see how bad things have become. It takes constant attention to keep out the impurities of the world.

2. If the believer's salt loses its flavor, the believer will experience the judgment of God.
   a. He will be cast out.

   "Ye are the salt of the earth: but if the salt have lost his savour, wherewith shall it be salted? it is thenceforth good for nothing, but to be cast out, and to be trodden under foot of men" (Mt.5:13).

   b. He will be a castaway.

   "But I keep under my body, and bring it into subjection: lest that by any means, when I have preached to others, I myself should be a castaway" (1 Cor.9:27).

   c. He will experience loss when he appears before the judgment seat of Christ.

   "For we must all appear before the judgment seat of Christ; that every one may receive the things done in his body, according to that he hath done, whether it be good or bad" (2 Cor.5:10).

APPLICATION 1:
If salt loses *its* flavor, what is going to restore *its* flavor? There is nothing. Once the flavor, the saltiness, is gone from salt, it is gone. It can no longer salt the earth.

---

[2] *INFOsearch Sermon Illustrations* (Arlington, TX: The Computer Assistant, 1-888-868-9029, 1986-1996).

MATTHEW 5:13

APPLICATION 2:
There is no one other than Christ who can salt and save a person from decay. A person who professes to have salt and remains bland, tasteless, and corruptible either lets Christ salt him or else he is never salted.

A person who has not been salted and saved from decay is doomed to ruin. He is good for nothing but to be cast out (cp. Jn.3:16-18; Heb.9:27).

QUESTIONS:
1. How is it possible for a believer to lose his flavor, his impact for Christ? How can you avoid this danger?
2. Have you known someone who became useless and destructive to the cause of Christ? What lessons can you learn from the error of this person's ways?

SUMMARY:

How *salty* is your life today? God has called each one of us to salt the earth with the presence of Christ. The only way the earth will be salted is for every believer to do his or her part. The world is waiting for the salt that will change the very taste of earth.
1. The disciples' character: salt.
2. The disciples' place to salt (to minister): the earth.
3. The disciples' mission: to salt the earth.
4. Their danger: becoming useless and destructive.

PERSONAL JOURNAL NOTES:
(Reflection & Response)

1. The most important thing that I learned from this lesson was:

2. The thing that I need to work on the most is:

3. I can apply this lesson to my life by:

4. Closing Prayer of Commitment: (put your commitment down on paper).

| | D. The True Disciple (Part III): The Light of the World—Shining for God, 5:14-16 (Mk.4:21-23; Lk.8:16-18; 11:33) | 14 Neither do men light a candle, and put in under a bushel, but on a candlestick; and it giveth light unto all that are in the house. | 3. The disciples' unavoidable witness
a. Like a city on a hill
b. Like a candle set on a candlestick |
| 1. The disciples' character: Light
2. The disciples' place to shine: The world | 14 Ye are the light of the world. A city that is set on an hill cannot be hid. | 15 Let your light so shine before men, that they may see your good works, and glorify your Father which is in heaven. | 4. The disciples' purpose
a. To show forth good works
b. To stir men to glorify God |

Section IV
THE TEACHINGS OF THE MESSIAH TO HIS DISCIPLES:
THE GREAT SERMON ON THE MOUNT
Matthew 5:1-7:29

Study 4: THE TRUE DISCIPLE (PART III): THE LIGHT OF THE WORLD-- SHINING FOR GOD

Text: Matthew 5:14-16

Aim: To make one clear decision: To become a stronger light to the world--a far stronger light.

Memory Verse:
> "Let your light so shine before men, that they may see your good works, and glorify your Father which is in heaven" (Matthew 5:16).

INTRODUCTION:
How does your light make a difference in a dark world today? Picture a lonely mountain cabin that rests in the hallow of a cliff. The cabin is surrounded by high drifts of snow that have cut off any outside contact with the rest of civilization. The cold, bitter winds are bending trees that have stood at attention for years. The daylight is nearly gone and twilight has come with the quick-advancing shadows that overcome the remainder of the day. The scene pictured is a desolate one. It is a scene of great barrenness that is void of life. All of a sudden, a solitary lantern is lit inside the cabin and the glow of its light fills the windows. The warmth of the light confronts all the elements that are raging outside the cabin. All shines brightly within the cabin as long as there is light.

Scripture says: "God is light" (1 Jn.1:5). Jesus Christ said, "I am the light of the world" (Jn.8:12; 9:5). Here Jesus says, "Ye are the light of the world." What an enormous compliment! God is light; Christ is light; and the believer is said to be "the light of the world." The believer is what God and Christ are: light. No greater compliment could be paid the believer. But note: to be identified with God is an enormous responsibility as well as a compliment. Whatever light is and does, the believer is *to be and do*.
Four things are said about the believer as the light of the world.

OUTLINE:
1. The disciples' character: light (v.14).
2. The disciples' place to shine: the world (v.14).
3. The disciples' unavoidable witness (v.15).
4. The disciples' purpose (v.16).

1. THE DISCIPLES' CHARACTER IS LIGHT (v.14).

Christ said, "I am the Light of the world" (Jn.8:12; 9:5). Here He says the disciple is to be like Him--"the light of the world." The disciple is to undergo a radical transformation: he is to *become like* Christ more and more and *to reflect* the light of Christ (2 Cor.3:18; 4:6-7). Light is and does several things.

1. Light is *clear and pure*. It is clean, that is, good, right, true.

> "For ye were sometimes darkness, but now are ye light in the Lord: walk as the children of light: (For the fruit of the Spirit is in all goodness and righteousness and truth)" (Eph.5:8-9).

2. Light *penetrates*. By nature it cuts through and eliminates darkness.

> "Ye are all the children of light, and the children of the day: we are not of the night, nor of darkness" (1 Th.5:5).

3. Light *enlightens*. It enlarges a person's vision and knowledge of an area.

> "Then Jesus said unto them, Yet a little while is the light with you. Walk while ye have the light, lest darkness come upon you: for he that walketh in darkness knoweth not whither he goeth" (Jn.12:35).

4. Light *reveals*. It opens up the truth of an area, a whole new world, and it clears up the way to the truth and the life.

> "Jesus saith unto him, I am the way, the truth, and the life: no man cometh unto the Father, but by me" (Jn.14:6).

5. Light *guides*. It directs the way to go, leads along the right path.

> "I am come a light into the world, that whosoever believeth on me should not abide [walk] in darkness" (Jn.12:46).

6. Light *strips away the darkness*.

> "And this is the condemnation, that light is come into the world, and men loved darkness rather than light, because their deeds were evil. For every one that doeth evil hateth the light, neither cometh to the light, lest his deeds should be reproved" (Jn.3:19-20).

7. Light *clears up and diminishes the chaos*.

> "That ye may be blameless and harmless, the sons of God, without rebuke, in the midst of a crooked and perverse nation, among whom ye shine as lights in the world" (Ph.2:15).

8. Light *discriminates between the right way and the wrong way*.

> "Then spake Jesus again unto them, saying, I am the light of the world: he that followeth me shall not walk in darkness, but shall have the light of life" (Jn.8:12).

9. Light *warns*. It warns of dangers that lie ahead in a person's path.

> **"And have no fellowship with the unfruitful works of darkness, but rather reprove them. For it is a shame even to speak of those things which are done of them in secret. But all things that are reproved are made manifest by the light: for whatsoever doth make manifest is light. Wherefore he saith, Awake thou that sleepest, and arise from the dead, and Christ shall give thee light" (Eph.5:11-14).**

10. Light *protects*. It protects a person from the dangers of darkness, from stumbling, falling, and injuring himself.

> **"The night is far spent, the day is at hand: let us therefore cast off the works of darkness, and let us put on the armour of light" (Ro.13:12).**

APPLICATION:

Believers are *now* the light of the world. Jesus said, "As long as I am in the world, I am the light of the world" (Jn.9:5). But Jesus is no longer in the world, not bodily. His light is now in the lives of believers. Believers are *reflections* of Him and His light; therefore the believer's light is to be pure. The believer is to walk in light, that is, in purity.

> **"For ye were sometimes darkness, but now are ye light in the Lord: walk as children of light" (Eph.5:8).**

QUESTIONS:
1. Light does at least ten different things. Which one of these can you most identify with? Are there other characteristics of light not addressed here? (For example, warmth, security.)
2. How can you compare these characteristics of light to a believer's life? What is the only way for a person to become the light of the world?

2. THE DISCIPLES' PLACE TO SHINE: THE WORLD (v.14).

The world is the place where believers are to move about and reflect their light (live and minister). Why? The world is...
- unclear
- in trouble
- stumbling
- groping
- falling
- in danger
- unseeing
- unaware
- in chaos
- in darkness

Note that the light *is* in the world; the city is in the world, and the candlestick is in the home. The same is true of believers: believers occupy some place in the world. Wherever that place is, they are to let their lights shine.

APPLICATION:

Note the statement: "You are *the* light!" Not just "You are light": the implication is that without the light of believers, the world has no other light. Therefore, the light is to be placed where its influence can be *best used and felt*. What a lesson for believers in their life and work and play! Every community, city, state, and nation--the whole world--is to be illuminated by the light of believers.

"For so hath the Lord commanded us, saying, I have set thee to be a light of the Gentiles, that thou shouldest be for salvation unto the ends of the earth" (Acts 13:47).

ILLUSTRATION:

The brightest light is useless unless it can be seen. There are far too many believers who keep their light from those who need it the most--people in the dark.

> *"Benjamin Franklin wanted to interest the people in Philadelphia in street lighting. He did not call a town meeting nor try to persuade the people by talking about it. He acted upon what he considered a good idea. He hung a beautiful lantern on a long bracket in front of his house. He kept the glass polished and carefully trimmed and lit the wick every evening at the approach of dusk. The lamp helped the people see the pavement ahead; made them feel more secure at night. Others began placing lights in front of their houses. Soon Philadelphia recognized the need for street lights.*
> *"Be the one today to light up your neighborhood with the light of life. Let it shine. Let your light shine TODAY!"*[1]

Is your light spreading to others--or are you keeping it all to yourself?

QUESTIONS:
1. Where do you need to reflect your light the most?
   Where I work
   Where I live
   Where I shop
   Where I go to church
2. What can you do to shine brighter in the dark places of the world?

3. THE DISCIPLES' UNAVOIDABLE WITNESS (v.14-15).

Two things are said about the city: it sits on a hill and it cannot be hid. Two things are said about the candle: it is put on a candlestick, and it gives light to all that are in the house. Note that the disciples' light is in the world, on a hill, and in the house.

APPLICATION:
Several lessons can be learned from this parable.
1) Believers shine as lights in the world. They are like cities and like candles sitting in a dark world.
2) Light has different strengths. It can be strong or weak, bright or dim. In fact, it can be so dim and provide so little light that a person can stumble and fall.
3) Some places in the world are brightly lit; others are dimly lit. Some cities have many bright lights, other cities have few bright lights. Some homes have strong lights; other homes have weak lights. Every city, every home, and every business-- every place on this earth that has the witness of a Christian believer--has some light, either weak or strong.
4) A light can become so weak it is of no use.
5) A light should not be lit to be hid. It should be lit to be seen and to give light. Therefore, a light should impact all who look upon it.

---

[1]   Ted Kyle & John Todd. *A Treasury of Bible Illustrations*, p.385-386.

"For God, who commanded the light to shine out of darkness, hath shined in our hearts, to give the light of the knowledge of the glory of God in the face of Jesus Christ" (2 Cor.4:6).

4. THE DISCIPLES' PURPOSE (v.16).

The believer has light. The light is already within him. He is the light of God upon earth. Note the exact words spoken by Christ: "Let your light so shine." The believer can refuse to *let* his light shine. He can turn it off, refuse to turn it on, shade it, darken it, turn it away, direct its beam in another direction.

Note the two purposes for *letting* our light shine.

1. Believers are to let their light shine in order to show forth good works. The command "Let your light so shine" means *let your good works be seen*. The believer is to show good works to the world, but he must be careful how he does his works before others (Jas.3:13).

> **"Charge them that are rich in this world, that they be not high-minded, nor trust in uncertain riches, but in the living God, who giveth us richly all things to enjoy; that they do good, that they be rich in good works, ready to distribute, willing to communicate; laying up in store for themselves a good foundation against the time to come, that they may lay hold of eternal life" (1 Tim.6:17-19).**

2. Believers are to let their light shine in order to stir men to glorify God. The glory of God is to be the primary aim of all believers (1 Pet.4:11; 5:11). The very way God is glorified is by the light, the good works of believers shining before men. Note two things.
   a. God is glorified when believers get out into the darkness where men are.
   b. The good works of believers are to be done out in darkness, not within cloistered walls with other lights.

> **"Herein is my Father glorified, that ye bear much fruit; so shall ye be my disciples" (Jn.15:8).**

APPLICATION:
There are several significant lessons in this point.
1) Light has one purpose: to shine *before men*. Light is not seen unless it is placed *before men*. If there are no people, there are no eyes to see the light. A believer must not seclude himself from others.
2) Other lights do not need light. It is the people in darkness who need light. Believers: "Let your light so shine before men"--before men out in darkness! Believers are not to be secluded in the church, moving only among other lights. The more light that is put out in the darkness, the more the darkness is eliminated.
3) Believers are not the only ones who are to glorify God. They are to go out and cause those in darkness to glorify Him.

MATTHEW 5:14-16

QUESTIONS:

1. How much control do you have concerning the amount of light you shine forth?
2. Why has God given you light? In what ways can you be a better steward of the light God has given?
3. Think about your community for a moment. Where is your light needed the most today? If you could shine your light upon this place for a few days, what kinds of things could happen?

SUMMARY:

What difference can one little light make in such a dark world? Without the light that believers shine in the world, darkness would consume everything. God has given every believer the capacity to shine on the darkness and melt it away. The great pastor and writer Charles Swindoll states this truth so well:

"The late Peter Marshall used to love to tell the story of The Keeper of the Spring, a quiet forest dweller who lived high above an Austrian village along the eastern slopes of the Alps. The old gentleman had been hired many years ago by a young town council to clear away the debris from the pools of water up in the mountain crevices that fed the lovely stream flowing through their town. With faithful, silent regularity, he patrolled the hills, removed the leaves and branches, and wiped away the silt that would otherwise choke and contaminate the fresh flow of water. By and by, the village became a popular attraction for vacationers. Graceful swans floated along the crystal clear stream, the millwheels of various businesses located near the water turned day and night, farmlands were naturally irrigated, and the view from restaurants was picturesque beyond description.

"Years passed. One evening the town council met for its semiannual meeting. As they reviewed the budget, one man's eye caught the salary figure being paid the obscure keeper of the spring. Said the keeper of the purse, 'Who is the old man? Why do we keep him on year after year? No one ever sees him. For all we know the strange ranger of the hills is doing us no good. He isn't necessary any longer!' By a unanimous vote, they dispensed with the old man's services.

"For several weeks nothing changed. By early autumn the trees began to shed their leaves. Small branches snapped off and fell into the pools, hindering the rushing flowing water. One afternoon someone noticed a slight yellowish-brown tint in the stream. A couple of days later the water was much darker. Within another week, a slimy film covered sections of the water along the banks and a foul odor was soon detected. The millwheels moved slower, some finally ground to a halt. Swans left, as did the tourists. Clammy fingers of disease and sickness reached deeply into the village.

"Quickly, the embarrassed council called a special meeting. Realizing their gross error in judgment, they hired back the old keeper of the spring...and within a few weeks the veritable river of life began to clear up. The wheels started to turn, and new life returned to the hamlet in the Alps once again.

"Fanciful though it may be, the story is more than an idle tale. It carries with it a vivid, relevant analogy directly related to the times in which we live. What the keeper of the springs meant to the village, Christian servants mean to our world. The preserving, taste-giving bite of salt mixed with the illuminating, hope-giving ray of light may seem feeble and needless, but God help any society that attempts to exist without them!

You see, the village without the keeper of the spring is a perfect representation of the world system without salt and light."[2]

1. The disciples' character: light.
2. The disciples' place to shine: the world.
3. The disciples' unavoidable witness.
4. The disciples' purpose.

PERSONAL JOURNAL NOTES:
(Reflection & Response)

1. The most important thing that I learned from this lesson was:

2. The thing that I need to work on the most is:

3. I can apply this lesson to my life by:

4. Closing Prayer of Commitment: (put your commitment down on paper).

---

[2] Charles Swindoll. *Improving Your Serve.* (Dallas, TX: Word Publishing, 1981), p. 127-128.

	E. The Law & Jesus: Breaking the Law of God, 5:17-20	these least commandments, and shall teach men so, he shall be called the least in the kingdom of heaven: but whosoever shall do and teach them, the same shall be called great in the kingdom of heaven.	order to be great in the Kingdom of Heaven
1. A person must know that Christ came to fulfill the law	17 Think not that I am come to destroy the law, or the prophets: I am not come to destroy, but to fulfil.		a. If a person disobeys & influences others, he is ranked least
a. The law is not to be destroyed	18 For verily I say unto you, Till heaven and earth pass, one jot or one tittle shall in no wise pass from the law, till all be fulfilled.		b. If a person obeys & influences others, he is ranked great
b. The law is perpetual--more sure than heaven & earth		20 For I say unto you, That except your righteousness shall exceed the righteousness of the scribes and Pharisees, ye shall in no case enter into the kingdom of heaven.	3. A person must have more righteousness than a religionist to enter the Kingdom of Heaven
2. A person must do & teach the law in	19 Whosoever therefore shall break one of		

Section IV
THE TEACHINGS OF THE MESSIAH TO HIS DISCIPLES:
THE GREAT SERMON ON THE MOUNT
Matthew 5:1-7:29

Study 5: THE LAW AND JESUS: BREAKING THE LAW OF GOD

Text: Matthew 5:17-20

Aim: To gain a fresh understanding of your relationship to the law of God.

Memory Verse:
> "For I say unto you, That except your righteousness shall exceed the righteousness of the scribes and Pharisees, ye shall in no case enter into the kingdom of heaven" (Matthew 5:20).

INTRODUCTION:
What would you do if money came raining down upon you? This very thing happened to a poor neighborhood. On the highway above the slum, an armored truck wrecked and turned over. The collision caused its rear door to open and spill out hundreds of thousands of dollars. As the money floated to the ground below, the people acted like human vacuum cleaners. No bill or coin was left behind. The streets were clean. Not a trace of the unexpected treasure was found by the police as they responded to the accident.

After the confusion had died down the owner of the lost money asked the people to return what they had collected. A few people brought back a few dollars, but the majority of the people who had taken the money refused to give up their "blessing." In fact, several people who were quoted by the media said that "God caused the truck to wreck and that the money was a gift from Him." These people had no problem with seeing God as a good God who provides for His people. But they were blind concerning God's law against stealing and greed.

This Scripture (Mt.5:17-48) is of critical importance. It is God's Son explaining the law of God. Jesus Christ had often been accused of destroying and minimizing the law of God. Many have felt that the thrust of Jesus was love and forgiveness and the afterthought was law and justice. As a result, many have felt less obligated to follow God's law, feeling that if they kept the law of God in the back of their mind, they had the Christian liberty to interpret behavior as they saw fit (within some reason).

Christ pulls no punches and comes straight to the point: "Think not that I am come to destroy the law...." (v.17), "whosoever therefore shall break one of these least commandments...." (v.19), "except your righteousness shall exceed the righteousness of the Scribes and Pharisees...." (v.20).

1. *Christ confirmed God's law*, all the Scripture of the Old Testament. Christ said He was not destroying *the law or the prophets*. The term "the law and the prophets" was a reference to the whole Old Testament. What Christ said was that He, as God's Son, came to fulfill the law; and His teaching was just as binding as the Old Testament law.

2. *Christ illustrated God's laws*, explaining the broad principles which were and still are to be applied to everyday life. He took a few practical laws and showed how a person was to take the broad principle and apply it to his own daily behavior.

3. *Christ condemned the oral or Scribal Law* (condemned it rather strongly.) When Jesus Christ and the other New Testament writers condemned the law, it always referred to the oral or Scribal Law, not to God's Law.

OUTLINE:

1. A person must know that Christ came to fulfill the law (v.17-18).

2. A person must do and teach the law in order to be great in the Kingdom of Heaven (v.19).

3. A person must have more righteousness than a religionist to enter the Kingdom of Heaven (v.20).

1. A PERSON MUST KNOW THAT CHRIST CAME TO FULFILL THE LAW (v.17-18).

Jesus said He was neither contradicting nor destroying the Old Testament Scriptures nor was He standing against them. He was fulfilling them, completing them, bringing out what was implied. He was showing what the real meaning of the Old Testament Scripture is, its full meaning--all that God intended the Scripture to say. As God's Son, He is the revelation of the truth. He is to reveal the true and complete meaning of the Scriptures.

There are several ways in which Jesus Christ fulfilled the law.

1. *Before Christ, the law described how God wanted man to live*. The law was the ideal, the words that told man what he was to do. But Christ fulfilled and completed the law; that is, God gave man more than just mere words to describe how He wants man to live. He gave man the Life, the Person who perfectly pictures and demonstrates the law before the world's very eyes. Jesus Christ is the Picture, the Living Example, the Pattern, the Demonstration of life as it is to be lived. He is the Perfect Picture of God's will, the Ideal Man, the Representative Man, the Pattern for all men.

> "And the Word was made flesh, and dwelt among us, (and we beheld his glory, the glory as of the only begotten of the Father,) full of grace and truth" (Jn.1:14).

2. *Before Christ, the law was only words and rules*. It could only inject the idea of behavior into the mind of a person. It had no spirit, no life, no power to enable a person to do the law. But Christ fulfilled and completed the law. He was *Spirit and Life*, so He was able to put spirit and life into the words and rules of the law. He was able to live the life described by the words and rules. As such, He was able to inject both the idea and the power to behave

into a person's mind and life. It is now His life that sets the standard and the rule for the believer; it is His Spirit and life that give the believer power to obey.

> "For I through the law am dead to the law, that I might live unto God. I am crucified with Christ: nevertheless I live; yet not I, but Christ liveth in me: and the life which I now live in the flesh I live by the faith of the Son of God, who loved me, and gave himself for me" (Gal.2:19-20).

3. *Before Christ, the law stated only the rule and the principle of behavior.* It did not explain the rule nor the spirit behind the rule. Neither did the law give the full meaning of the rule. The law always had to have an interpreter. But Christ fulfilled and completed the law. He explained the rule and the spirit behind the rule. He interpreted the law. He gave the law its real and full meaning.

> "But before faith came, we were kept under the law, shut up unto the faith which should afterwards be revealed. Wherefore the law was our schoolmaster to bring us unto Christ, that we might be justified by faith" (Gal.3:23-24.)

4. *Before Christ, the law demanded perfect righteousness;* it demanded a perfect life. But man failed at certain points. Man just could not obey the law perfectly; he fell short of perfect righteousness. But Christ fulfilled and completed the law. He kept the law in *every detail.* He secured the *perfect righteousness* demanded by the law. He fulfilled all the requirements, all the types, and all the ceremonies of the law--perfectly. As such, He became the Perfect Man, the Ideal Man, the Representative Man for all men. As the Ideal Man, He simply embraced all men; He embodied the righteousness that man must now have.

> "For he hath made him to be sin for us, who knew no sin; that we might be made the righteousness of God in him" (2 Cor.5:21).

5. *Before Christ, the law demanded punishment for disobedience.* If a man broke the law, he was to be punished. But Christ fulfilled and completed the law. In fact, He went to the farthest point possible in fulfilling the law. He paid the maximum price and showed the ultimate love. He bore the punishment of the law for every man's disobedience; He took the punishment of the law upon Himself. As the Ideal Man, He not only embodies the righteousness that must cover all men, He also frees all men from the penalty of the law. And He makes them sons of God. (Cp. Ro.8:15-17; Gal.3:13-14; 4:1-7.)

QUESTIONS:
1. How can you respond to the person who says that none of the Old Testament Law applies to the modern Christian believer?
2. Christ came to fulfill the law--all of it. What *practical* impact did Christ have upon the law?
3. If Christ had not come, what effect would the law have upon you now?

APPLICATION 1:
Several other passages need to be looked at for a complete understanding of Christ and the law and the believer. (See Ro.7:4; 7:14-25; 8:2-4.) Christ condemned sin in the flesh by three acts.
1) *Christ pointed to sin and condemned it as being evil.* The very fact that He never sinned points out that sin is contrary to God and to God's nature. Christ rejected sin, and by rejecting it He showed that it was evil, that it was not to be touched.

2) *Christ secured righteousness for all men.* When He came into the world, He came with the same flesh that all men are born with--the same flesh with all its desires, passions, and potential for evil. However He never sinned, not once. Therefore, He secured righteousness; that is, He was perfectly righteous.

> **"Which of you convinceth me of sin? And if I say the truth, why do ye not believe me?" (Jn.8:46).**
> **"For we have not a high priest which cannot be touched with the feeling of our infirmities; but was in all points tempted like as we are, yet without sin" (Heb.4:15).**

3) *Christ allowed the law of sin and death to be enacted upon Himself* instead of upon the sinner. Man has sinned, so the natural consequence is corruption and death. However, Christ allowed God to use Him in the flesh to satisfy two great needs of man. First, He allowed God to accept His *Ideal righteousness* for the unrighteousness of man. Second, He allowed God to lay man's sin and death upon Himself. He allowed God to let Him bear the law of sin and death for man and to experience hell for man. He allowed God to let Him condemn sin and death "in His own body upon the tree" (1 Pt.2:24). He was the perfect, ideal Man. Therefore, He could bear all the violations of the law and all the experiences of death for *all* men. God so designed, and God bore the awful price of having to condemn sin and death in the death of His very own Son. For the believer, sin and its power have been made powerless. Death has been conquered (1 Cor.15:1-58, esp. vs.54-57). And he who had the power of death has been destroyed, that is, Satan.

> **"For when we were yet without strength, in due time Christ died for the ungodly" (Ro.5:6).**
> **"But God commendeth his love toward us, in that, while we were yet sinners, Christ died for us" (Ro.5:8).**

APPLICATION 2:

Christ here speaks to two different people: 1) the strict religionist or legalist, and 2) the carnal or loose religionist.

Man is not released from the duty and responsibility of the law. But he is released from the penalty and condemnation of the law. Christ strengthened the law by obeying it perfectly and setting the example for man--but He fulfilled it by bearing the punishment Himself.

APPLICATION 3:

Christ considered His own coming to be significant--one of the pivotal points of history. The following words show this (cp. v.17-18).

⇒ "I am come...."
⇒ "I am come...to fulfill."
⇒ "I say unto you, until heaven and earth pass...."
⇒ "Till all be fulfilled."

He speaks as a person whose entrance into the world held great meaning for the world. This fact says something of extreme importance to man: "Hear Him. Listen to Christ." What He says is binding. It is *as* binding, if not *more* binding, than the law itself.

> **"For they being ignorant of God's righteousness, and going about to establish their own righteousness, have not submitted themselves**

unto the righteousness of God. For Christ is the end of the law for righteousness to every one that believeth" (Ro.10:3-4).

QUESTIONS:
1. What are some rules and regulations that men have added to the Scriptures?
2. How can you know whether you or someone else is interpreting Scripture too strictly or too loosely?

A CLOSER LOOK # 1

(5:17) **Law**: the law referred to four different writings to the Jews.
1. It referred to *the Ten Commandments*.
2. It referred to *the first five books* of the Bible, that is the Pentateuch (Genesis, Exodus, Leviticus, Numbers, Deuteronomy).
3. It referred to *the law and the prophets*, that is, all the Scripture of the Old Testament.
4. It referred to *the oral or the Scribal Law*.

God's law, given in the Old Testament, was not enough for the Jews. They reasoned that if the law was really God's Word, then it must include every rule and regulation for conduct. Therefore, they took the great principles of the law and reduced them to thousands upon thousands of rules and regulations. These rules and regulations became the oral or Scribal Law.

There were two groups who gave their lives to the teaching and keeping of the law.
1. The Scribes: they were the writers and teachers of the law.
2. The Pharisees: they were the strict followers of the law.

---

2. A PERSON MUST DO AND TEACH THE LAW IN ORDER TO BE GREAT IN THE KINGDOM OF HEAVEN (v.19).

Breaking and *doing* the law carries with it the idea of continuous action. No person is perfectly obedient all of the time. Every person fails sometime (Ro.3:23; Jas.3:2; 1 Jn.1:8, 10). But any person who continues to break a commandment, even if it is the least commandment, shall be called the least in the Kingdom of Heaven. And the person who continues to obey the commandments shall be called great in the Kingdom of Heaven. A person cannot break a commandment and ask forgiveness, then go out and break another commandment and ask forgiveness over and over. Such a person cannot expect God to think he is serious about the commandments of God. No man would think he is serious--why should God? The person only deceives himself. Note two significant points.
1. Three persons teach the law to others.
   a. The *keeper* and the *breaker* of the law. A person teaches by what he does. Others see and observe and learn from what he does. If a person breaks a law, no matter how small a law, he teaches that the law is not important--not worthy enough to be kept. Likewise if a person keeps a law, now matter how small a law, he teaches that the law is worthy of being kept.
   b. The *instructor* of the law. This refers to the teachers of the law and of religion. Each instructor either adheres to or rejects the law. Each instructor teaches his students the truth or else deceives his students into following human reasoning. Such behavior is consciously or unconsciously teaching men to *void the law*.
2. Christ warned all who break the law and teach others to break the law, even if they break only the least commandment: they shall be called the least in the Kingdom of Heaven. Note: there are four persons who are severely warned.
   a. The worldly or carnal: the person who continues to break the commandments of God.

b. The teacher or instructor: the person who teaches that the commandments of God are a farce. The person who says there is no such thing as God's law; there are only the commandments of men.

c. The person who teaches and encourages others to sin and to disobey the commandments of God--even if the commandment is one of the least. Nothing is more contemptible and nothing will be judged more severely. This is one of the most serious offenses among men.

> **"It were better for him that a millstone were hanged about his neck, and he cast into the sea, than that he should offend one of these little ones" (Lk.17:2).**

d. The mocker or persecutor: the person who rebels, mocks, and curses *God's law* and its strictness (and the God and the followers of it).

> **"And every one that heareth these sayings of mine, and doeth them not, shall be likened unto a foolish man, which built his house upon the sand: and the rain descended, and the floods came, and the winds blew, and beat upon that house; and it fell: and great was the fall of it" (Mt.7:26-27).**

APPLICATION 1:

Four significant lessons are seen in this point.

1) *All the commandments of God are important*, but some are less important than others.
2) *Breaking a commandment of God and continuing to break it is serious*, even if it is one of *the least* commandments. Such behavior teaches men that the commandment is not important. The result: a person shall be called least in the Kingdom of Heaven.
3) *When a commandment is broken, a person is to ask forgiveness and repent*. He is not to continue breaking the commandment and asking forgiveness over and over. Continuous disobedience teaches that the commandments of God are not really all that important. It is that person who will be judged severely.
4) *The obedient person can expect great reward.*
   - ⇒ He shall be called great in heaven.
   - ⇒ He is loved in a special way by both God and Christ (Jn.14:10, 14).
   - ⇒ He receives very special manifestations of Christ's presence.

APPLICATION 2:

Who fails to do the law? Who breaks the law?

1) The person who *neglects* the law--just fails to do it.
2) The person who *disobeys* the law--does what it says not to do.
3) The person who *does not know* the law--cannot do it because he just does not know it.
4) The person who *confines* the law, that is, limits and weakens the law by making it say less than what it really says. Many make the law apply only to what they want because it allows them to do their own thing and to live as they wish.

APPLICATION 3:

A person may neglect the law for several reasons.

- ⇒ He is deceived about the law's importance. Someone has misled him about its importance.
- ⇒ He is too preoccupied with worldly affairs to place much importance in the law.
- ⇒ He is reacting against some strict teaching in his past; therefore, he now neglects the law.
- ⇒ He has not been taught the seriousness of keeping God's law.
- ⇒ He fears the restrictions the law will place upon his life and behavior. He does not want to live as the law says, so he neglects it.

APPLICATION 4:

The law of God is often broken for two tragic reasons.
1) Some have never heard about God's law. Believers have failed to take the message of the law to the world.
2) Some do not have the law impressed upon their minds enough to worry about keeping it. Believers have not stressed the message with enough conviction and power to show its importance.

ILLUSTRATION:

There can be no compromise with the Word of God. Either all of it is true and must be obeyed or none of it can be accepted. God has entrusted His Law and its eternal, absolute truth to people. It is a tragedy that some professing Christians have fumbled the truth and caused innocent people to stumble. Author Chuck Colson shares a story that perfectly illustrates this point.

> "Several years ago a newly appointed Anglican bishop, David Jenkins, created a ruckus in England when he questioned the virgin birth of Christ. Jenkins evidently enjoyed the furor; in a second pronouncement he dismissed Christ's resurrection as a 'conjuring trick with bones.' That colorful phrase was widely reported by an amused secular press.
>
> "A few days later a dramatic event turned the story into front page news: Yorkminster, the beautiful cathedral belonging to the diocese of Jenkins' archbishop, was struck by a mysterious bolt of lightning that knocked its 13th-century oak ceiling beams to the flagstone floor.
>
> "A flood of articles ensued, most provocatively headlined, 'Coincidence or the Wrath of God?' But the story soon faded. Just as well, I thought. It was, after all, merely the prattle of a heretical bishop, sensationalized by the media. (It was not all that startling either, considering the views of Jenkins' colleagues: a poll had just revealed that of the 31 Anglican bishops in England, 19 said that to be a Christian one need only believe that Jesus was God's supreme moral agent. Only 11 bishops said that one must accept Jesus as fully God and fully man!)
>
> "But Jenkins' blasphemous statement did not just blow over, as I discovered during a subsequent visit to Sri Lanka. When I asked Desmond Goonasekera, an Anglican rector, about the growth of the Christian church in his country, he shook his head. 'We're losing badly to the Muslims,' he said. 'It all began with the Jenkins business.'
>
> "He explained that aggressive Muslims were visiting Christian communities and using Bishop Jenkins' quote as authoritative proof that Christians need no longer believe in Christ's resurrection. Since Muslims and Christians now see Jesus as merely a prophet, they argued, why not worship together in the mosque? 'They are killing us with our bishop's own words,' Goonasekera concluded.
>
> "What I had dismissed as one man's heresy had become a stumbling-block to Christian faith halfway around the world--a sobering reminder of the grave consequences of trifling with the truth."[1]

If you neglect God's Word, who are you putting at risk?

---

[1] Charles Colson. *The God of Stones and Spiders*. (Wheaton, IL: Crossway Books, 1990), p. 128-129.

QUESTIONS:
1. Christ has warned all people against breaking the law. What are some consequences a person faces if he habitually breaks God's commandments?
2. What conclusion can you reach when a person is in an endless cycle of breaking the same commandment again and again?
3. As you observe the society in which you live, what parts of God's law are ignored the most, are most abused?
4. What are some of the great benefits that come to the person who keeps God's commandments?
5. What are some of the reasons people give for neglecting God's law? Do you ever struggle with any of these excuses? If yes, what is the key to overcoming these struggles?

3. A PERSON MUST HAVE MORE RIGHTEOUSNESS THAN A RELIGIONIST TO ENTER THE KINGDOM OF HEAVEN (v.20).

Note three facts.

1. Righteousness is necessary to enter heaven. If a person abides in Jesus Christ, he lives a righteous life. The fruit that he bears and the things that he treasures in life are the supreme and final proof that he knows God.

> "For the wrath of God is revealed from heaven against all ungodliness and unrighteousness of men, who hold the truth in unrighteousness" (Ro.1:18).
> "As it is written, There is none righteous, no, not one....For all have sinned, and come short of the glory of God" (Ro.3:10, 23).

2. The religionists (the Pharisees and the Scribes) had some righteousness. They just did not have enough. They were, in fact, strict religionists. They worked at obeying thousands and thousands of rules and regulations, governing everything ranging from dress and social behavior to ministry and work. However, they lacked the one essential: loving God so much that they would deny themselves and seek their righteousness in His Son, Jesus Christ.

> "Therefore by the deeds of the law there shall no flesh be justified in his sight: for by the law is the knowledge of sin. But now the righteousness of God without the law is manifested, being witnessed by the law and the prophets; even the righteousness of God which is by faith of Jesus Christ unto all and upon all them that believe: for there is no difference" (Ro.3:20-22).

3. The point is shattering: a person must have more righteousness than a strict religionist to enter heaven. Many persons are religious, but few are strict religionists. What did Christ mean? Who can enter heaven if a strict religionist cannot?

> "To him who worketh not, but believeth on Him that justifieth the ungodly, his faith is counted for righteousness" (Ro.4:5).

APPLICATION:
There are four facts in this verse that must be heeded. They should stir everyone of us, stir us to search our hearts and make sure we are approaching God as we should be.

1) Many religionists make the same fatal mistake that the Pharisees and Scribes made. They seek acceptance with God...
- by giving God a formal worship instead of giving God a confession of unworthiness, a confession of their need for Him in a personal way.
- by giving God good works instead of giving God their hearts.
- by giving God a clean and moral body instead of giving God a confession of their need for spiritual help.
- by giving God only a part of their lives instead of giving God their all.

2) Many make the fatal mistake the religionists made, but to a lesser degree. They worship and do good...
- to be respectable in the community
- to seek the acceptance of God
- to have the fellowship of others
- because they were forced by their parents to do good
- to feel comfortable within their own consciences
- to secure the approval of family and friends
- because they were taught to do good

3) Some feel they must do good to be acceptable to God. Their motive in life is to work and work at doing good in order to secure God's acceptance. They have never learned the truth: they cannot do enough good to be perfectly acceptable to God. They must trust His love--that He loves them so much He will take their trust and count it as righteousness.
⇒ Many worship and do just enough good to satisfy their consciences. They do just enough good to make them feel comfortable and acceptable to God. But they miss the whole point. What God is after--the only thing that makes a person acceptable to God--is the giving of his total being over to God (day and night).
- in unworthiness and confession: that he has need for God in his life now and forever
- in trust and love: that he trusts and loves God because God has given His own Son and promised to accept him in His righteousness
- in thankfulness and appreciation: because God has accepted and assured abundant life now and eternally
- in adoration and praise: because God is God (Elohim) and has revealed His glorious love in Christ who has redeemed him eternally
- in worship and service: because the love of Christ constrains him

ILLUSTRATION:

There will be a great many religious people who will get to judgment day and be surprised at their destination: hell, not heaven. When your life on earth is over, what will you get out of it?

"A young man asked his minister to officiate at his brother's funeral. 'Let me see,' said the minister. 'Your brother was thirty-two years old?' 'Yes.' 'He worked hard for twenty years, didn't he?' 'Yes.' 'Well, what did he get out of it?' 'He left eighty acres of fine land, money in the bank, and thousands of dollars in insurance.' 'Yes, that's what you get out of it; but what did he get out of it?' 'Oh, we are going to buy him an expensive oak casket!'"[2]

The most important decision a person can make is to settle, once and for all, his relationship with Jesus Christ. When your life on earth is over, what will people say

---

[2] Spiros Zodhiates, Th.D. *Illustrations of Bible Truths*, p.189.

about you and the righteousness of Jesus Christ? Note that nothing was ever said about the young man ever trusting Christ and His righteousness.

QUESTIONS:
1. Just how much righteousness do you need in order to go to heaven?
2. In what ways do people try to accumulate righteousness? Why are these efforts, without Christ, doomed to failure in the end?
3. Why is religion *not* the answer to eternal life? What is the only way to guarantee eternal life?

SUMMARY:

What is your relationship with God's law? Are you one who tends to pick and choose what you like and disregard that which is not appealing to your sinful nature? The person who really wants a relationship with God must embrace these important facts:
1. A person must know that Christ came to fulfill the law.
2. A person must do and teach the law in order to be great in the Kingdom of Heaven .
3. A person must have more righteousness than a religionist to enter the Kingdom of Heaven.

PERSONAL JOURNAL NOTES:
(Reflection & Response)

1. The most important thing that I learned from this lesson was:

2. The thing that I need to work on the most is:

3. I can apply this lesson to my life by:

4. Closing Prayer of Commitment: (put your commitment down on paper).

	F. The Real Meaning of Murder, 5:21-26	memberest that thy brother hath ought against thee;	
1. The law	21 Ye have heard that it was said by them of old time, Thou shalt not kill; and whosoever shall kill shall be in danger of the judgment:	24 Leave there thy gift before the altar, and go thy way; first be reconciled to thy brother, and then come and offer thy gift.	a. The urgency: Must precede worship b. The time: While some openness exists
2. The real meaning: Anger	22 But I say unto you, That whosoever is angry with his brother without a cause shall be in danger of the judgment: and whosoever shall say to his brother, Raca, shall be in danger of the council: but whosoever shall say, Thou fool, shall be in danger of hell fire.	25 Agree with thine adversary quickly, whiles thou art in the way with him; lest at any time the adversary deliver thee to the judge, and the judge deliver thee to the officer, and thou be cast into prison.	6. The danger or damage of holding anger a. Earthly judgment b. Divine judgment symbolized
3. The growth of anger a. A brooding anger b. A contemptuous anger c. An accusing, cursing anger 4. The judgment of anger 5. The answer to anger: Reconciliation	23 Therefore if thou bring thy gift to the altar, and there re-	26 Verily I say unto thee, Thou shalt by no means come out thence, till thou hast paid the uttermost farthing.	7. The terrible end of anger: Judgment is sure

Section IV
THE TEACHINGS OF THE MESSIAH TO HIS DISCIPLES:
THE GREAT SERMON ON THE MOUNT
Matthew 5:1-7:29

Study 6:   THE REAL MEANING OF MURDER

Text: Matthew 5:21-26

Aim: To recognize and renounce every form of murder in your heart.

Memory Verse:
>**"Therefore if thou bring thy gift to the altar, and there rememberest that thy brother hath ought against thee; Leave there thy gift before the altar, and go thy way; first be reconciled to thy brother, and then come and offer thy gift" (Matthew 5:23-24).**

INTRODUCTION:
Some years ago on a dark night, a young mother pushed her car into a lake. Inside were her two precious babies strapped into their car seats. She then left them there to drown. For a period of weeks, the young woman told a story about a man stealing her car and taking her children. Her sad tale captured the sympathy of a nation. But after the truth of her treachery finally came out, the same people who had cried with her became enraged and demanded quick justice and revenge.

There are many things that go through our minds when we hear about a murder. Depending upon our relationship to the victim, we may become...

- repulsed
- sorrowful
- vindictive
- angry
- fearful
- hurt
- outraged
- mortified
- humiliated
- confused
- hardened
- ashamed

These are all very valid emotions. Murder should upset us and make us angry. But another question we should consider is this: Do I become as upset at *other* kinds of murder? What kinds of anger comes out of my own heart?

⇒ Do I ever become upset? Do I ever allow hatred to enter my own heart? Do I ever wish for someone else to be dead?

⇒ Do I become angry and bitter against someone when things do not go my way?

⇒ If looks could kill, how many people would I have murdered in my lifetime?

Civilized societies have always considered murder to be a serious crime worthy of judgment. But anger is a different matter. Few have ever thought of anger as being on the same level as murder, much less worthy of serious judgment. However, Christ says that anger "without a cause" is the same as murder and shall receive the same judgment from God.

Note the words "brother" and "whosoever" (v.22, 23, 24). Christ is saying that every human being is a brother under God's creation. Therefore, His words apply universally to every human being.

OUTLINE:
1. The law: do not kill (v.21).
2. The real meaning: anger (v.22).
3. The growth of anger (v.22).
4. The judgment of anger (v.22).
5. The answer to anger: reconciliation (v.23-24).
6. The danger or damage of holding anger (v.25).
7. The terrible end of anger: judgment is sure (v.26).

IT IS IMPORTANT TO UNDERSTAND THIS: the words **"Ye have heard"** and **"It hath been said"** are found in every paragraph or subject of these verses (5:21-48). Christ is referring not only to the Ten Commandments, but also to the Scribal Law of the Jewish teachers. He is directing the listeners' attention to what they had heard from their teachers, that is, to their interpretation of the law. Very simply put, Christ is giving the real meaning of certain laws, just what God originally intended the law to say.

1. THE LAW: DO NOT KILL (v.21).

The law against murder is the sixth commandment (Ex.20:13; Dt.5:17). Note that God's law is given to protect life. Life is to be respected and cherished. No life is to be taken, not one's own life nor the life of anyone else.

> **"Thou shalt not kill"** (Ex.20:13).
> **"But let none of you suffer as a <u>murderer</u>, or as a thief, or as an evildoer, or as a busybody in other men's matters"** (1 Pt.4:15).

QUESTIONS:
1. The law is clear: DO NOT KILL. Yet the sanctity of life is under attack on all fronts today. What can you do to be a defender of life?
2. Why does God place such a high value upon life? What events have led the world to cheapen life?

2. THE REAL MEANING: ANGER (v.22).

Note what Christ is saying: He is saying that man has a problem. Man misreads God's law. Man interprets God's law to say what he wishes it to say. He applies it only to the outward act, in this case to the act of murder. He fails to look inside--within himself--to the cause of the outward act.

Murder is deeper than just an outward act. It is an inward act: anger, bitterness, enmity. Murder is born from within, from an uncontrolled spirit, from an unregulated urge, from an inner anger. Anger itself is the real sin, the sin that breaks the law of God. Anger is...

- bitterness & enmity
- indignation & wrath
- striking out against a person
- slandering and destroying a person's image (who is created in God's image)
- a hatred of oneself
- rage & fury
- an uncontrolled spirit
- desiring a person's hurt
- envying & killing a person's happiness

APPLICATION:
Note three facts.
1) Jesus speaks to those who know the law. The person who *knows* the law (the Word) needs this message as much as anyone.
2) God's law (Word) existed from the beginning ("of old time"). It will never be annulled or done away with. It is always to govern man. Man is always to heed it.
3) Striking out at a person is clearly forbidden, but so are the bad *feelings* against a person. Anger--any bad feelings whatsoever against a person--is sin, serious sin.

QUESTIONS:
1. Murder is much more than an outward act. It is an inward act that spews forth anger, bitterness, and hatred. How can you make yourself more conscious of the sinfulness of anger?
2. What damage has someone's uncontrolled anger done against you? How did it make you feel?
3. Do you have any ill feelings toward another person? What does God's Word tell you to do with these feelings?

3. THE GROWTH OF ANGER (v.22).

The growth of anger is dangerous. Unresolved anger will fester. It can become uncontrollable and give birth to murder. There are three steps in the growth of anger given here.

1. *The anger that broods*, that is selfish. It harbors malice; it will not forget; it lingers; it broods; it wills revenge and sometimes seeks revenge.

2. *The anger that holds contempt* (raca). It despises; it ridicules; it arrogantly exalts self and calls another person empty and useless. This is an anger that is full of malice. It despises and scorns (raca). It arises from pride--a proud wrath (Pr.21:24). Such feelings or anger walk over and trample a person. It says that whatever ill comes upon a person is deserved.

3. *The anger that curses*. It seeks to destroy a man and his reputation morally, intellectually, and spiritually.

There is a justified anger. In fact, the believer must be an angry person in some things: angry with those who sin and do wrong, angry with those who are unjust and selfish in their behavior. However, a justified anger is always disciplined and controlled; it is always limited to those who do wrong either against God or against others. The distinguishing mark between justified and unjustified anger is that a justified anger is never selfish; it is never shown because of what has happened to oneself. It is an anger that is purposeful. The believer knows that he is angry for a legitimate reason, and he seeks to correct the situation in the most peaceful way possible.

> **"Be ye angry, and sin not: let not the sun go down upon your wrath" (Eph.4:26).**
> **"If it be possible, as much as lieth in you, live peaceably with all men" (Ro.12:18).**

APPLICATION:

Anger can be cast against anyone. Too often hurt feelings exist between those who are supposed to be the closest: husband and wife, parent and child, neighbor and friend, employer and employee. The Lord is clear about the matter: we must never allow anger to take hold of us without just cause.

> **"But now ye also put off all these; anger, wrath, malice, blasphemy, filthy communication out of your mouth" (Col.3:8).**

There are many reasons why people get angry and develop feelings against others:
⇒ To seek revenge and to hurt
⇒ To show ego or authority
⇒ To reveal passion or secure some end
⇒ To show hurt, resentment, or bitterness
⇒ To express disagreement or displeasure
⇒ To correct a wrong (a justified anger)
⇒ To give warning

ILLUSTRATION:

The anger that destroys another person is just like a fuse attached to a stick of dynamite. Once the fuse is burnt, a terrific blast will kill or maim anyone close to the explosion.

> *"Anger is hazardous to your health In a study conducted by the Gallup Organization and reported in 1994, Philadelphia ranked first among U.S. cites on what was called the 'hostility index.' The hostility index was based on a nine-question scale that asked people how they felt about such things as loud rock music, supermarket checkout lines, and traffic jams. Other cites on the hostility top five were New York, Cleveland, Chicago, and Detroit. At the bottom of the hostility index were Des Moines, Minneapolis, Denver, Seattle, and Honolulu.*
> *"Medical experts looking at the results felt it was no coincidence that the cities that rated high on the hostility index also had higher death rates. Commenting on the study, Dr. Redford Williams of Duke University Medical School said, 'Anger kills. There is a strong correlation between hostility and death rates, The angrier people are and the more cynical they are, the shorter their life span.'"*[1]

What does this say about *your* community?

QUESTIONS:
1. Why is unresolved anger such a dangerous thing for anyone? For the believer?
2. What would be a legitimate cause for justified anger? How can you act on it in a godly way?

---

[1] Craig B. Larson. *Contemporary Illustrations for Preachers, Teachers, and Writers*. (Grand Rapids, MI: Baker Books, 1996), p.17.

4. THE JUDGMENT OF ANGER (v.22).

It is a serious matter to hold feelings against another person--a very, very serious matter. There is (1) the *danger of judgment,* (2) the *danger of having to come before earthy courts*, and (3) the *danger of hell fire*. Violence is to be judged--not only before the councils of the world, but before the councils of God.

The teaching of Jesus should always be remembered. Remembrance is critical in determining a person's fate. Hell is a definite place, a real place that is specifically located. It was originally prepared for the devil and his angels. But all men who choose to follow self and evil, rejecting God, shall also be sent to hell eternally.

> **"And now also the axe is laid unto the root of the trees: therefore every tree which bringeth not forth good fruit is hewn down, and cast into the fire" (Mt.3:10).**

QUESTIONS:
1. Do you take seriously God's threat of judgment against anger? If not, why not?
2. What dangers await the person who continues to hold feelings against another person?
3. When and how can you teach others about the very real danger of anger?

5. THE ANSWER TO ANGER: RECONCILIATION (v.23-24).

Christ had two surprising things to say about this point.

1. The urgency of reconciliation. Reconciliation is always to precede worship. Even when we are entering the church to worship, if there is a problem with a brother, we are to turn around from worship and go to our brother seeking reconciliation. There are four reasons why reconciliation is more important than worship.

    a. Reconciliation with God is one of the major purposes for worship. A person worships in order to seek reconciliation and fellowship with God and His people. Therefore, God does not accept the worship of a person who holds malice against Him or against any of His people. Statements of the fact make the point perfectly clear.

        ⇒ A break with another person means a break with God.
        ⇒ Unforgiveness toward another person means unforgiveness by God.
        ⇒ Not being right with another person means not being right with God.
        ⇒ Broken fellowship with another person means broken fellowship with God.
        ⇒ Bad feelings toward another person mean unacceptance by God.
        ⇒ Anger against another person means rejection by God.

        A person cannot just hope or expect to be right with God if he is not right with his brother (1 Jn.4:20-21). He must forgive and be reconciled if he expects to be forgiven and reconciled to God.

> **"Forgive us, as we forgive our debtors" (Mt.6:12; Lk.11:4).**
> **"If ye forgive men their trespasses, your heavenly father will also forgive you...." (Mt.6:14-15; Mk.11:25-26).**

    b. A person is to worship, for worship is essential to life and eternity. But worship is unacceptable to God unless a person is reconciled with all his brothers.
    c. Bad feelings between believers hinder worship. Worship is meaningless unless a person is right with his brother. Reconciliation must always precede worship.

d. Worship is a time for a person to reflect and to examine his heart and life to see if there is "any wicked way" within him (Ps.139:24). It is essential that he search his heart. Worship is not acceptable if bad or wicked feelings against others are within the human heart.

ILLUSTRATION:
Christianity is the only faith where a man can start all over again, forgiven and restored. At one time or another, all of us have wished we could retrieve hurtful words we have spoken before the damage was done. Unfortunately, words that have left the mouth cannot be swallowed. The only way to get a fresh start in any relationship is to make things right with God. How? By first getting right with the person whom you have hurt or who has hurt you. Greg Laurie writes:

> *"I once read about a man whose name had been mistaken[ly] printed in the obituary column of his local newspaper. Can you imagine waking up one morning and reading that you were no longer among the living? To be sure, it would be a little disconcerting. This man did what any of us would do in the same situation: He went down to the newspaper office and demanded to see the editor.*
> *"'This is terrible,' he told the newspaper boss. 'Because of your error, I am going to face embarrassment. And I will probably lose business. How could you do this to me?'*
> *"'Sir, I'm sorry,' said the editor. 'It was a mistake. It was certainly not intentional.' But the man would not be consoled. He continued to rant and rave about the injustice of it all. 'Look, cheer up, buddy,' the editor finally said. 'Tomorrow I'll put your name in the birth column, and you can have a fresh start in life.'*
> *"All of us have done things we regret. Wouldn't it be great if starting over were that easy? The Bible teaches that we CAN start over: We CAN have our slates wiped clean."[2]*

APPLICATION 1:
How deceitful the human heart is!
1) Some persons try to worship while there are bad feelings between themselves and other persons (Mt.5:23-24).
2) Some persons try to pray with wrath in their heart (1 Tim.2:8; Is.1:15).
3) Some persons say "I love God" while they hate their brother (1 Jn.4:20).

And each person thinks he is acceptable to God!

APPLICATION 2:
Some persons say they stay away from worship because they have something against a brother. The point of Christ is clear: get right with your brother and *get in worship*. One sin heaped upon another is twice as dangerous and shall bring forth double judgment.

2. The time for reconciliation is while some openness still exists between the two parties. Reconciliation should be attempted immediately...
- while a person is still in a brother's presence: "While thou art in the way with him" (v.25)
- before the sun goes down on a person's wrath

> **"Be ye angry, and sin not: let not the sun go down upon your wrath" (Eph.4:26).**

---

2 Greg Laurie. *Life. Any Questions?* (Dallas, TX: Word Publishing, 1995), p. 149-150.

- because a person cannot truly worship with barriers existing in the heart
- because a person cannot offer acceptable prayers with barriers existing in his heart
- because a person *could die* before reconciliation takes place and be forced to face judgment with some unconfessed sin

> **"Forbearing one another, and forgiving one another, if any man have a quarrel against any: even as Christ forgave you, so also do ye" (Col.3:13).**

QUESTIONS:
1. Jesus said that reconciliation is always to precede worship. Have you ever tried to worship God with ill feelings in your heart toward a brother? How did it affect your worship?
2. As long as you don't *act* on your anger, is it acceptable not to worry about reconciliation? Why or why not?

6. THE DANGER OR DAMAGE OF HOLDING ANGER (v.25).

The danger is twofold.
    1. *There is an earthly danger.* Barriers can lead to serious action ranging from legal suits to imprisonment. Such action is tragic to God and among God's people. It is even forbidden among true Christian brothers (see 1 Cor.6:1-8). The damage of anger is manyfold:
    ⇒ It leads to increased barriers and bitterness.
    ⇒ It hurts families.
    ⇒ It is costly.
    ⇒ It damages the name of Christ and one's own testimony.
    ⇒ It says to unbelievers that Christianity is a sham--no better than any other belief.
    ⇒ It takes advantage of another person--always.
    ⇒ It can cause an injustice to be done.
    ⇒ It can cause a weak brother to turn away--forever.
    ⇒ It can cause fights, wars, suffering, and death.
    2. *There is an eternal danger.* Life on this earth does not last forever, and the day of final judgment is coming. A person's judgment for holding a grudge against a brother will be severe.

QUESTIONS:
1. What kind of testimony do you bear when you hold or express anger against another person--without seeking reconciliation?
2. Search your heart honestly today. Is there any anger you have against a person that needs to be resolved? If so, what can you do to begin the process of reconciliation?

7. THE TERRIBLE END OF ANGER: JUDGMENT IS SURE (v.26).

Christ reemphasizes three strong points.
    1. *Judgment is sure.* "The uttermost farthing" (the last cent) must be paid.
    2. *There will be no escape.* "Thou shall <u>by no means</u> come out." There will be nothing and no one to deliver a person from the judgment (2 Cor.5:10).

> **"Ye serpents, ye generation of vipers, how can ye escape the damnation of hell?" (Mt.23:33).**

"And thinkest thou this, O man, that judgest them which do such things, and doest the same, that thou shalt escape the judgment of God?" (Ro.2:3).

3. *Reconciliation should be sought quickly*: right now--before judgment, for Christ has borne all punishment for every believer (v.25).

"But now in Christ Jesus ye who sometimes were far off are made nigh by the blood of Christ. For he is our peace, who hath made both one, and hath broken down the middle wall of partition between us....and that he might reconcile both unto God in one body by the cross, having slain the enmity thereby" (Eph.2:13-14, 16).

QUESTIONS:
1. When judgment day comes, what options does the person have who has not resolve his anger with a brother?
2. If you were to stand before Christ today, would there be enough evidence to convict you of murder in your heart?
3. Christ has done everything necessary for the believer to gain reconciliation with God. Have you done all *you* can to accept it?

SUMMARY:

Everyone gets angry, but what a person does with that anger is the difference between life and death. We often find ourselves on the receiving end of the evil actions of others. If you have been abused or destroyed because of the angry words of another person, have you forgiven that person? If you have abused or destroyed another person by your visible anger or in the privacy of your heart, have you taken the first step toward reconciliation? The person who knows the real meaning of murder will be able to live life to its fullest.
1. The law: do not kill.
2. The real meaning: anger.
3. The growth of anger.
4. The judgment of anger.
5. The answer to anger: reconciliation.
6. The danger or damage of holding anger.
7. The terrible end of anger: judgment is sure.

PERSONAL JOURNAL NOTES:
(Reflection & Response)

1. The most important thing that I learned from this lesson was:

2. The thing that I need to work on the most is:

3. I can apply this lesson to my life by:

4. Closing Prayer of Commitment: (put your commitment down on paper).

	G. The Real Meaning of Adultery & Immorality, 5:27-30 (cp.Mt.19:3-11; Mk.10:2-12; cp.Lk.16:18; 1 Cor. 7:1-16)	eye offend thee, pluck it out, and cast it from thee: for it is profitable for thee that one of thy members should perish, and not that thy whole body should be cast into hell.	culprits: The eyes and hands
1. The law	27 Ye have heard that it was said by them of old time, Thou shalt not commit adultery:		**4. The danger** a. Offending or stumbling b. Being condemned to hell
2. The real meaning a. A deliberate look b. A desire: lust, passion c. An act of adultery	28 But I say unto you, That whosoever looketh on a woman to lust after her hath committed adultery with her already in his heart.	30 And if thy right hand offend thee, cut it off, and cast it from thee: for it is profitable for thee that one of thy members should perish, and not that thy whole body should be cast into	**5. The answer** a. Surgery: Cut out the offending body member b. Death: Let the offending body member perish c. Repentance: Turn from being cast
3. The two guilty	29 And if thy right	hell.	into hell

Section IV
THE TEACHINGS OF THE MESSIAH TO HIS DISCIPLES:
THE GREAT SERMON ON THE MOUNT
Matthew 5:1-7:29

Study 7: **THE REAL MEANING OF ADULTERY AND IMMORALITY**

Text: Matthew 5:27-30

Aim: To make one firm resolution: To keep yourself sexually pure and unstained.

Memory Verse:
> **"But I say unto you, That whosoever looketh on a woman to lust after her hath committed adultery with her" (Matthew 5:28).**

INTRODUCTION:
How much confidence do you put in a person who cheats? If you have any common sense, none at all. Look at the obvious facts:
⇒ A cheater is not honest--this person will lie to you.
⇒ A cheater is not ethical--this person will steal from you.
⇒ A cheater is really not to be trusted in anything--this person will ultimately deceive you and others.

It has been said that if a man will lie to and cheat on his wife by committing adultery, then he will also lie to and cheat you too. The person who lives a life marked by adultery starts a combustible chain reaction that can destroy everyone and everything around him. Who would even dream about causing such pain? An adulterer does.

Immorality and adultery cause great destruction, hurt, and pain--both within and without a person. There are at least three reasons why a person commits an immoral act.
1. The ego: the sense of conquering, taking, capturing, controlling, knowing, seeing, experiencing, enjoying, and on and on--a person's ego is boosted and inflated.
2. The inner need for attention and sharing.
3. The raw lust of the flesh.

Immorality is so common that it is often thought to be excusable and acceptable if it is agreed to by the other partner, and if other lives are not directly affected.

Man has always tended to glorify the body and the flesh: exposing the body, dressing the body for sexual attraction, looking at and observing the body and its movements--all are often acceptable practices of society. Inward desire (lust) and the act of sexual pleasure itself are often thought to be so much a part of nature and normal life that to restrict them is considered straight-laced and prudish, even abnormal.

Christ is strong, insistent in His demand for purity--so strong that He insists on radical surgery rather than allowing the hand or eye to sin. "An immoral eye and hand will carry the whole body into hell," Christ says, "so pluck out the eye; cut off the hand." But what do we say? "He doesn't mean this literally." And we use this attitude as a way to water down the sharpness and the strictness of His point. However, we ignore and neglect His words to our doom. This is His very point. We may...

- fantasize and lust as a result of reading immoral magazines and books
- lustfully look at the movements of a person walking (and call it recognizing beauty)
- dress to sexually attract
- take pleasure in the stimulation and sensation of sex outside of marriage

But Christ clearly warns: lustful looking, touching, and adulterous behavior will cause the whole body to be cast into hell. The matter is so serious that radical surgery is called for. No diluting, no evading, no explaining of His words and what He means can change the severe judgment that awaits the immoral person.

OUTLINE:
1. The law (v.27).
2. The real meaning (v.28).
3. The two guilty culprits: the eyes and hands (v.29).
4. The danger (v.29).
5. The answer (v.29-30).

1. THE LAW (v.27).

The law against immorality, against committing adultery, is the seventh commandment (Ex.20:14; Dt.5:18). Note that God's law is given for three reasons.

1. To assure the respect and protection of all families and neighbors. God will take vengeance upon those who destroy families through adultery.

> **"Thou shalt not commit adultery" (Ex.20:14; cp. Dt.5:18).**
> **"For this is the will of God, even your sanctification, that ye should abstain from fornication: that every one of you should know how to possess his vessel in sanctification and honour; not in the lust of concupiscence [desire, lewdness], even as the Gentiles which know not God: that no man go beyond and defraud his brother [neighbor] in any matter: because that the <u>Lord is the avenger</u> of all such, as we also have forewarned you and testified" (1 Th.4:3-6).**

2. To protect a man from judgment, the judgment of perishing in hell (v.30).
3. To protect a man from sinning against his own body.

> **"Flee fornication. Every sin that a man doeth is without the body; but he that committeth fornication sinneth against his own body" (1 Cor.6:18).**

QUESTIONS:
1. Why does God speak so strongly against sexual immorality?
2. In what ways can the seventh commandment protect you? This is a very important question. What are your thoughts?

A CLOSER LOOK # 1

(5:27-30) **Adultery--Sex**: the Bible does not teach that sex is wrong. But the Bible does teach that sex can be used wrongly, and the wrong use of sex is sin. Sex has been given by God for at least three reasons.

1. Sex causes a person to be attracted to another person. Therefore, sexual attraction is one of the major tools that brings about marriage (Gen.2:18, 21-25).

2. Sex is a tool with which to love. Sex, properly rooted and expressed in God, is one of the deepest and richest involvements and expressions of love (Eph.5:28-32).

3. Sex creates life. God has given man the privilege of being a sub-creator of life--under Him (Gen.1:29).

QUESTIONS:
1. In the right context, sex is good for people. What does God say that context is?
2. God has a grand purpose for the use of sex. How has the world perverted God's purpose?
3. The secular media (movies, television, magazines) have glamorized illicit sex. What attracts a person to imitate this worldly, immoral lifestyle?

2. THE REAL MEANING (v.28).

Adultery is often said to be sexual unfaithfulness by a married person. This is true, but it is much more. Man's idea of adultery is shattered by Christ. Christ says adultery is not only the actual act, but adultery is committed by any one of five acts:
⇒ A deliberate look.
⇒ Passion within the heart: desiring and lusting.
⇒ The actual act of sex with someone other than one's own spouse.
⇒ Divorce relationships (Mt.5:32; 19:9-11; Mk.10:11-12; Lk.16:18).
⇒ Spiritual unfaithfulness toward God or apostasy (desertion) from God (Mt.12:39; 16:4; Mk.8:38; Jas.4:4; cp. Ezk.16:15f; 23:43f).

Simply stated, Christ says there is eye adultery, heart adultery (lust), and body adultery. This is a shattering revelation that strikes at the experience of every young person and adult. There is no question: many dream and imagine, and if they had the opportunity they would commit the act. All they lack is the opportunity and the 'courage' to sin (although it takes greater courage *not* to sin). (Cp. Jas.1:14-15.) The eyes can lead to lust by looking upon persons or pictures or stimulating objects. The eyes can be used sinfully in several ways.
⇒ To look and seek out another person in order to lust.
⇒ To let another person know that one is available.
⇒ To attract, suggest, and entice.
⇒ To gratify lust visually where an actual experience is not possible.

There are two other matters that need to be thought about at this point.
1. Suggestive communication. This can arise from:
   a. unclean talk such as jokes, foul words, and suggestive statements made in passing;
   b. luring talk that arises when sharing with the opposite sex. This tends to lead a person to let down his guard or to play loose with his conviction and moral commitment.

Such sharing often dallies with enticing phrases and suggestive propositions that arouse pleasure. Suggestive conversation can occur anywhere: at work, at school, at parties, over the phone, or just standing around talking.

2. Dress. This arises from exposing parts of the body, from following the latest fad in dress that might be designed to display or attract, or simply dressing to emphasize the body.

There is real danger in using one's eyes sinfully. Peter warns that a person can lose control: "Having eyes full of adultery...that cannot cease from sin" (2 Pet.2:14). A person can actually become enslaved and bound by sex.

The seriousness of adultery is seen by the drastic action suggested by Christ in vs. 29-30. Adultery is a work of the flesh that will not inherit the Kingdom of God (Gal.5:19-21). It is a serious sin, very serious. There is the possibility of the whole body being cast into hell (Mt.5:29-30). The believer can conquer the eyes and lust and can keep from committing adultery by doing a few simple things.

⇒ In relation to others...
   a. Stay away from places that *lend* themselves to suggestive lust.
   b. Stay away from persons who *might* be suggestive and enticing--no matter how enjoyable and pleasing.
   c. Refuse invitations to functions or socials that *might* lead to suggestive conversation or enticement.

⇒ In relation to self:
   a. Dress decently: dress to please the Lord (1 Tim.2:9).
   b. Behave at all times as a genuine Christian believer.
   c. Build a testimony by conversation and behavior as a Christian believer.

⇒ In relation to the eyes and mind.
   a. Make a covenant (a vow, a solemn promise) not to look at or think about immoral persons, places, or things--and then keep the covenant. Job said of himself: **"I made a covenant with mine eyes; why then should I think upon a maiden" (Job 31:1)**.
   b. Keep the eyes and mind upon things that are true, honest, just, pure, lovely, and of good report (Ph.4:8). Start immediately: begin to think upon the positive and the moral day by day. Keep the mind upon the positive for the rest of your life.
   c. Learn to captivate every thought (2 Cor.10:3-5, esp. v.5).
   d. Resist the first thought--turn the mind and body immediately to other matters. Get busy at something else without hesitating, and stay there--stay busy.

⇒ In the presence of others.
   a. Guard yourself at all times.
   b. Flee when suggestive statements are made: excuse yourself--show displeasure by statements or force if necessary. Get away immediately, not allowing the pleasing words to stimulate and gratify your flesh. The flesh revels in expressions of pleasure and appreciation over the way one looks, dresses, works, serves, performs, and on and on. A person must simply appreciate such and then move on--immediately. Lingering to enjoy and revel in appreciative remarks *will* lead to attraction. Everyone is human.

"For out of the heart proceed <u>evil thoughts</u>, murders, <u>adulteries</u>, <u>fornications</u>, thefts, false witness, blasphemies" (Mt.15:19).

ILLUSTRATION:
The world exalts a loose lifestyle and glorifies the people who go from bed to bed, from partner to partner. Real men and women live by an opposite set of standards.

"A number of years ago Phyllis George interviewed Dallas Cowboy superstar Roger Staubach. It is was a typical, dull sort of interview until Phyllis blindsided the quarterback with this question: 'Roger, how do you feel when you compare yourself

with Joe Namath, who is so sexually active and has a different woman on his arm every time we see him?'

"We've all seen Staubach keep his cool in pressure game situations, and the tension in the air this time was just as great. But once again, Staubach kept his cool.

'"Phyllis,' he said calmly, 'I'm sure I'm just as sexually active as Joe. The difference is that all of mine is with one woman.'

"Touchdown! Roger hit the end zone with that comeback. Real men don't commit adultery."[1]

QUESTIONS:

1. No believer is above the temptation of sexual immorality--of looking at and desiring the 'forbidden fruit.' What is *your* best defense from falling into the sin of immorality in this area?

2. How should you react when a married person or someone else flirts with you sexually?

_____tease him with a wink?

_____act in a way that will encourage him to flirt a little bit more?

_____ignore him?

_____call him down in public?

A CLOSER LOOK # 2

(5:28) **Lusts**: a strong desire, a yearning passion for. The word is used in a good sense three different times in Scripture (Lk.22:15; Ph.1:23; 1 Th.2:17). A man is to turn his strong desires *toward* righteousness and godliness; however, a man has to struggle to turn *away from* the desire to please himself. Man's natural tendency is the desire or lust to satisfy self before others, in particular when survival and comfort are at stake.

1. The very nature of man is lust, the lust of the flesh and of the mind (Eph.2:2-3). Sinful and evil lust show that men are *by nature...*

...the children of wrath

...the children of disobedience

...the children of the spirit who is the prince and power of the air, that is, the devil

> **"Wherein in time past ye walked according to the course of this world, according to the prince of the power of the air, the spirit that now worketh in the children of disobedience" (Eph. 2:2).**

2. The very nature of man and of the world is lust, a tendency both *to be* and *to get*.

> **"Love not the world, neither the things that are in the world. If any man love the world, the love of the Father is not in him. For all that is in the world, the lust of the flesh, and the lust of the eyes, and the pride of life, is not of the Father, but is of the world. And the world passeth away, and the lust thereof: but he that doeth the will of God abideth for ever" (1 Jn.2:15-17. Cp. Ro.13:14; Gal.5:16, 24; Col.3:5; 1 Th.4:5; 1 Tim.6:9; 2 Tim.3:6; 2 Tim.4:3; Tit.2:12; 3:3; 1 Pt.1:14; 2:11; 3:3; 4:2; 2 Pt.2:1, 8, 10, 18; Jude 18; Rev.18:14.)**

What a man discovers is that his cravings are never satisfied. There is something within his innermost being that craves for more and more; the lust does not diminish. Therefore, his only answer is to consciously and actively control the cravings.

---

[1] Gary Smalley & Bill McCartney. *What Makes a Man.* (Colorado Springs, CO: The Navigators\NavPress, 1992), p. 80-81.

"From whence *come* wars and fightings among you? *come they* not hence, *even* of your lusts that war in your members? Ye lust, and have not: ye kill, and desire to have, and cannot obtain: ye fight and war, yet ye have not, because ye ask not. Ye ask, and receive not, because ye ask amiss, that ye may consume *it* upon your lusts" (Jas.4:1-3).

Note that desire, lust, and a yearning passion are not always evil. In Jas.4:5 the Spirit "lusts to envy" (to control us; to fulfill us; to bear the fulness of God in us). In Lk.22:15 Christ desires (yearns) to eat the passover with the apostles. What is it that distinguishes a good desire from an evil desire? At least two major things.

⇒ *Motive*: if one desires the necessities of life, his desire is good. The necessities—food, clothing, shelter, love, care—are essential for the fulness of life. When a man seeks God for these things, God provides the necessities.

⇒ *Greed*: desiring food is good, but if one desires food to "consume it upon [his] lusts," that is, he desires more and more and more food, it is wrong passion. It becomes sinful, sensual pleasure. Desiring love is good, but if one desires love to *consume it upon his lusts*, that is, he desires more and more and more love, it is wrong passion (1 Th.4:5).

QUESTIONS:
1. Why is lust, whether sinful or legitimate, such a strong force in the lives of people?
2. What is your greatest struggle concerning lust? Is it sex...food...fame... money? Other?
3. Even innocent things or good things can be the object of our lusts. How can you distinguish between a normal desire and an unhealthy lust for things?
4. What is your greatest resource in keeping lust in check?

3. THE TWO GUILTY CULPRITS: THE EYES AND HANDS (v.29).

Why did Christ use the eyes and hands to illustrate His point? Probably because a man is moved primarily by thoughts that arise from sight, and a woman is moved primarily by touch. It is the eye and hand that are the culprits in adultery (cp. Mk.9:43-48).

QUESTIONS:
1. How disciplined and controlled are your eyes and hands?
2. Most people get into trouble when the eye roves and the hand gropes in the wrong places. How can you guard yourself from looking in the wrong places and touching the wrong things?

4. THE DANGER (v.29).
The danger is twofold.
1. Offending or stumbling. The word "offend" means to stumble; to be baited; to be lured; to be tripped up. The eyes and hands are stumbling blocks.
2. Being condemned to hell. The sin is serious, extremely serious. Unless the sin is dealt with, it will cause a person to be cast into hell.

"Know ye not that the unrighteous shall not inherit the kingdom of God? Be not deceived: neither fornicators, nor idolaters, nor adulterers, nor effeminate, nor abusers of themselves with mankind, nor thieves, nor covetous, nor drunkards, nor revilers, nor extortioners, shall inherit the kingdom of God" (1 Cor.6:9-10).

APPLICATION:

The sin of immorality ruins the body as well as the soul. This is a terrible fact, yet it is a fact that is seldom considered.

> **"Flee fornication. Every sin that a man doeth is without the body; but he that committeth fornication sinneth against his own body" (1 Cor.6:18).**

QUESTIONS:
1. What consequences are dealt to the person who habitually commits sexual immorality?
2. If the price to pay is so great, why do so many people ignore the coming judgment and commit adultery?

5. THE ANSWER (v.29-30).

The answer to solving the problem of adultery is threefold.

1. Surgery: cut out the offending body member. The lustful look and the lustful touch should be cut out of one's life--completely.

> **"The mouth of the just bringeth forth wisdom: but the froward [suggestive] tongue shall be cut out" (Pr.10:31).**
> **"For if ye live after the flesh, ye shall die: but if ye through the Spirit do mortify the deeds of the body, ye shall live" (Ro.8:13).**

2. Death: let the offending body members perish. What feels good and pleases the flesh is not always good. Self-denial is sometimes called for.

> **"Wherefore take unto you the whole armour of God, that ye may be able to withstand in the evil day, and having done all, to stand" (Eph.6:13).**
> **"My son, if sinners entice thee, consent thou not" (Pr.1:10).**

3. Repentance: turn from being cast into hell. Note an important fact: Christ does not *appeal* for a man to forsake adultery; He *warns* man of the consequences of adultery. Some sins have to be restrained by warning, not by appeal. A man has to be warned about the lust of the flesh. Adultery is a sin that feels so good and seems so natural that it can be easily rationalized. The warning given to adulterers is "thy whole body shall be cast into hell" (Mt.5:30).

APPLICATION 1:

The members of the body are not to be yielded to sin. The members of the body are to be *counted dead* with Christ.

> **"Likewise reckon ye also yourselves to be dead indeed unto sin, but alive unto God through Jesus Christ our Lord. Let not sin therefore reign in your mortal body, that ye should obey it in the lusts thereof. Neither yield ye your members as instruments of unrighteousness unto sin: but yield yourselves unto God, as those that are alive from the dead, and your members as instruments of righteousness unto God" (Ro.6:11-13).**

"Walk in the spirit, and ye shall not fulfill the lusts of the flesh" (Gal.5:16).

APPLICATION 2:
A man must repent, that is, *turn from* adultery to God.

"I tell you, Nay: but, except ye repent, ye shall all likewise perish" (Lk.13:3).
"Then Peter said unto them, Repent, and be baptized every one of you in the name of Jesus Christ for the remission of sins, and ye shall receive the gift of the Holy Ghost" (Acts 2:38).

ILLUSTRATION:
God has the answer for the person who struggles with the sin of immorality and adultery. It is to repent of a hardened heart and renew a right relationship with the Lord.

"Cardiologists are hunting for a way to clear arteries clogged by plaque. They've tried using lasers to burn through the plaque. They've experimented with rotating burrs to grind away the plague. They've even tried using rotating knives to cut away plaque. None of these methods have succeeded.

"At the annual meeting of the American Heart Association in 1993, researchers reported on another experimental device that would work like a tiny jackhammer inside the arteries. Writer Jon Van says the device is inserted into the coronary arteries via a tiny wire called a catheter. There it emits low-frequency, ultrasound energy, vibrating the jackhammer-like tip of the probe at 19,500 times a second, about one-thousandth of an inch back and forth each time. After the jackhammer has done its work, a balloon is inserted into the narrowed artery and expanded to open the artery.

"In twenty-nine test cases, the jackhammer seemed to accomplish something the other methods could not. It broke down the calcium and gristle in the hard plaque without harming the soft walls of the artery.

"Hardening of the arteries is the enemy of the heart. A dangerous hardness can also develop in our spiritual lives, a hardness that constricts the life-giving love of God in our lives. If your heart has been hardened, there is no better 'jackhammer' than to humble yourself before the Lord."[2]

Remember: preventative care is always a whole lot easier than the alternative-- radical heart surgery.

QUESTIONS:
1. Are modern day solutions to immorality and adultery any different than in Jesus' day? Should they be? Why or why not?
2. The sins of immorality and adultery are prevalent sins even in the church. What practical steps can the believer take to remove these sins from his life, from his church body?

---

[2] Craig B. Larson. *Contemporary Illustrations for Preachers, Teachers, and Writers*, p.98.

SUMMARY:

The sins of adultery and sexual immorality have done more to sap the strength of the family than any other sins. The result of the "great sexual revolution" of the 1960's has produced rotten fruit. Marriages have been shattered, children have been scarred, and a great number of lives have been soiled by sexual sin. Each believer has an important role to play in the effort to remain sexually pure. Every revolution begins in the heart of just one person. Will you be the one to start the next great sexual revolution for God?

1. The law.
2. The real meaning.
3. The two guilty culprits: the eyes and hands.
4. The danger.
5. The answer.

PERSONAL JOURNAL NOTES:
(Reflection & Response)

1. The most important thing that I learned from this lesson was:

2. The thing that I need to work on the most is:

3. I can apply this lesson to my life by:

4. Closing Prayer of Commitment: (put your commitment down on paper).

	H. The Real Meaning of Divorce, 5:31-32	32 But I say unto you, That whosoever shall put away his wife, saving for the cause of fornication, causeth her to commit adultery: and whosoever shall marry her that is divorced committeth adultery.	3. Exception: Fornication
			4. The guilty parties
			a. The instigator
			b. The divorced who remarries
1. The law	31 It hath been said, Whosoever shall put away his wife, let him give her a writing of divorcement:		
2. The real meaning: Divorce disallowed			c. The one who marries the divorced

Section IV
THE TEACHINGS OF THE MESSIAH TO HIS DISCIPLES:
THE GREAT SERMON ON THE MOUNT
Matthew 5:1-7:29

Study 8: THE REAL MEANING OF DIVORCE

Text: Matthew 5:31-32

Aim: To make a sacred covenant to advocate and uphold the sanctity of marriage.

Memory Verse:
"But I say unto you, That whosoever shall put away his wife, saving for the cause of fornication, causeth her to commit adultery: and whosoever shall marry her that is divorced committeth adultery" (Matthew 5:32).

INTRODUCTION:

We live in an age where marriage vows have the same staying power as a sand castle built on a beach before high tide. The institution of marriage is under a great attack as thousands of homes are being washed away into the sea of secular morals.

After the excitement of the wedding and honeymoon wear off, the "real person" comes out and looks for an easy way to stop all problems. Listen to some of the excuses:
⇒ I don't love him or her any more.
⇒ It's not worth the effort.
⇒ Everyone is doing it!
⇒ He has changed. He is not the same person I married.
⇒ It's my choice. I don't have to put up with it.
⇒ One person for a lifetime is old-fashioned. It's not reasonable to live together forever.

Instead of living by the sacred vow--the commitment to work it out for better or for worse--people are scrambling out of marriages, out of the frying pan and into the fire.

But what does God's Word have to say about divorce? Throughout history there have always been two schools of thought when interpreting the laws of society--the strict, conservative interpreters and the broad, liberal interpreters. In Jesus' day, the strict interpreters were known as the school of Shammai; the broad interpreters were known as the school of Hillel. In dealing with the subject of divorce, Shammai said the words "some uncleanness" found in Dt.24:1 allowed for divorce, but the words meant adultery and adultery only. Hillel said "some uncleanness" meant that anything that destroyed unity was a justified reason for divorce; that perfect unity had to be maintained in the marriage state. Such allowance had disintegrated into the position that anything displeasing to a man was reason enough for divorce. (See Mt.19:1-12.)

A person can easily see which school human nature and most societies followed. Divorce had become so common that society itself was threatened. All a man had to do to divorce his wife was to have a Rabbi write out a bill of divorcement and hand it to his wife in the presence of two witnesses. The divorce was immediate and final (Dt.24:1-4).

OUTLINE:
1. The law (v.31).
2. The real meaning: divorce disallowed (v.32).
3. Exception: fornication (v.32).
4. The guilty parties (v.32).

1. THE LAW (v.31).

The law against divorce was given for three reasons.
    1. To protect the family.

> **"But from the beginning of the creation God made them male and female. For this cause shall a man leave his father and mother, and cleave to his wife; and they twain shall be one flesh: so then they are no more twain, but one flesh. What therefore God hath joined together, let not man put asunder" (Mk.10:6-9).**

    2. To protect the land or nation, preventing national disintegration (cp. Dt.24:4;. Mt. 19:1-12.)

> **"By the blessing of the upright the city is exalted: but it is overthrown by the mouth of the wicked" (Pr.11:11).**

    3. To prevent a person from becoming an adulterer.

> **"And I say unto you, Whosoever shall put away his wife, except it be for fornication, and shall marry another, committeth adultery: and whoso marrieth her which is put away doth commit adultery" (Mt.19:9; cp. Lk.16:18).**

QUESTIONS:
1. Are the reasons for the law against divorce *more relevant* today than when they were written? Or *less relevant*?
2. How would the law against divorce change society if it were enforced today?

2. THE REAL MEANING: DIVORCE DISALLOWED (v.32).

The real meaning of the law is that divorce is disallowed. Enormous protection is seen in this pronouncement. There is protection of the family, including the wife, husband, and children. There is emotional, physical, mental, and spiritual protection--protection against a family being ripped apart and having to undergo all the strain and disruption that follow. Divorce is one of the most traumatic experiences of human life. For many it is the most traumatic experience.

Divorce *touches* so many. It *touches*...
- husband
- wife
- children
- parents
- friends
- employer & employees

Divorce *affects* each person it touches, affects them ever so deeply. It *affects*...
- mind
- spirit
- behavior
- joy
- control
- security
- hopes
- plans
- peace
- purpose
- faith
- emotions
- love
- possessions
- estates

Divorce drastically *changes* each person's life. It *changes*...
- personal life
- private life
- spiritual life
- home life
- parental life
- recreational life
- social life
- dream life

Because divorce affects human life so much, it is of critical concern to Christ. When anyone hurts, Christ hurts. And because divorce hurts so much and hurts so many, Christ sets out to correct man's corrupt concept of marriage and easy divorce.

APPLICATION 1:
Teaching, preaching, and living by strict principles takes enormous courage. Christ demonstrated enormous courage by going against the grain of society and demanding strictness in marriage.

APPLICATION 2:
There are at least four attitudes toward marriage, three of which are *loose attitudes* that often lead to divorce.
1) *A back-door marriage*: "If it works, OK; if it doesn't work, OK."
2) *A cheap, sensual marriage*: based upon some reason other than love, some reason such as attractiveness, sex, or finances. "If it feels good, do it."
3) An *adventuresome marriage*: the marriage is entered into for the experience and the adventure of being married. "It's the thing to do."
4) *A marriage of commitment*: the full conviction of both spouses that they should fulfill the solemn vows taken--a conviction before God.

There is only one basis for marriage that can absolutely prevent divorce: a true union, both a spiritual and physical union.

"**What therefore <u>God hath joined together</u>, let not man put asunder**" (Mk.10:9).
"**Wives, submit yourselves unto your own husbands, as unto the Lord....Husbands, love your wives, even as Christ also loved the church, and gave himself for it**" (Eph.5:22, 29).

QUESTIONS:
1. In today's society, almost every person has been touched by the tragedy of divorce. How has divorce affected you?
2. What is the world's attitude toward marriage and divorce? How has this perspective crept into the church?
3. Is there any way a marriage can be made "divorce proof"?

4. EXCEPTION: FORNICATION (v.32).

The exception for divorce is the sin of fornication being committed by one of the spouses. The great tragedy of fornication or adultery is that it breaks the union and attachment between husband and wife. The union and attachment and all that goes with it--faith, hope, love, trust, assurance, confidence, and strength--are broken. If the husband and wife are not believers, then the physical union and the mental union of the marriage are broken. If they are believers, then all three unions are broken: the physical, mental, *and spiritual.* Two facts should be noted in the brief words of Christ here and elsewhere in the gospels.

1. Christ does not stand with either the conservative or the liberal school discussed in the introduction. He does not mention either school or either position.
2. Christ says two things about divorce.
   a. Divorce is not the purpose of God. This is silent, but clearly understood.
   b. Divorce is allowed only if one of the spouses has committed adultery.

What Christ is trying to prevent is what history shows. Societies have tragically ignored the command of God. They have planted the seed of national disintegration, that is, broken homes. This brief statement on divorce shows the great need to protect men, women, children, and the home. It points to the immense value of all three.

ILLUSTRATION:

No matter how we try to hide our sin, we will eventually be found out. Even when we do good deeds, our hidden sins will rise to the surface.

> *"A newspaper reported an unusual incident at a fast-food restaurant. The manager had put the day's cash in a paper bag for deposit that night, but an attendant mistook it for an order and gave it to a couple at the drive-through window.*
> *"A short time later, when the man and woman opened the bag in a nearby park, they were shocked by its contents. They immediately drove back to return it.*
> *"The manager had reported a robbery, so police cars and a TV crew were on the scene. How relieved he was to get the money back! He said to the couple, 'You should be featured on the evening news for your honesty.' 'Oh, please, no publicity!' replied the man nervously. 'She's not my wife.'"*[1]

A CLOSER LOOK #1

(5:32) **Marriage--Divorce**: there are two exceptions pointed out in 1 Cor.7:12-16. Note: Paul says (1 Cor.7:12-16) that this particular issue was never discussed by the Lord; therefore, there are no direct commandments of the Lord to share. However, Paul would issue the commands, which he made clear was under the guidance of the Holy Spirit.

> **"But to the rest speak I, not the Lord: If any brother hath a wife that believeth not, and she be pleased to dwell with him, let him not put her away. And the woman which hath an husband that believeth not, and if he be pleased to dwell with her, let her not leave him. For the unbelieving husband is sanctified by the wife, and the unbelieving wife is sanctified by the husband: else were your children unclean; but now are they holy. But if the unbelieving depart, let him depart. A brother or a sister is not under bondage in such *cases:* but God hath called us to peace. For what knowest thou, O wife, whether thou shalt save *thy***

---

[1] *Our Daily Bread.* (Grand Rapids, MI: RBC Ministries), Volume 41, Numbers 3,4,5, p. July 11, 1996.

husband? or how knowest thou, O man, whether thou shalt save *thy* wife?" (1 Cor.7:12-16).

Apparently there were many mixed marriages in the Corinthian church. But note: they were not believers marrying unbelievers. They were heathen who had become believers. Scripture never sanctions a true Christian marrying an unbeliever, for marriage is *sacred* to God (1 Cor.7:39).

It seems that some in the church were saying this: once a person gave his life to Christ, he was not thereafter to live with an unbeliever. They were saying that the new believer was to divorce the unbelieving wife or husband.

What should a Christian who is married to an unbeliever do: stay married or divorce? Scripture gives three instructions.

1. Stay together. The believing spouse should stay, but *only* if the unbelieving spouse is willing. The reason is clearly seen.

  a. The believer will influence his or her spouse for Christ.

    ⇒ The word "sanctified" in 1 Cor.7:14 does not mean that the believer's faith saves the unbelieving spouse. Nowhere does Scripture teach that one person can believe and trust Christ *for* another person. A person is saved only by *personally believing* in Christ himself. Every person stands personally before God as an individual.

    ⇒ The word "sanctified" means that the marriage is set apart unto God. If the unbeliever is willing to remain with the believer, the marriage is not to be dissolved. Simply stated, God accepts the marriage of a mixed couple if the unbelieving spouse is willing to accept the fact that his wife or her husband is a Christian *who lives for the Lord*. The unbeliever must support his spouse in her loyalty to Christ and His church.

  b. The believer will influence the children.

    ⇒ Note what Paul says: if God did not accept the marriage, then the children would be illegitimate in God's eyes. However, since the unbeliever supports his Christian spouse, God accepts his support as "sanctification" of the marriage and family. Of course, this includes the children.

    ⇒ Note how the believer affects both the spouse and the children. The presence of the believer in the family touches the whole family for God, as long as the unbeliever lends his support to the Christian. The whole family is accepted by God as a legitimate family, a family set apart for Him and His cause.

2. Separate if the unbelieving spouse wishes. If the unbelieving spouse leaves the believer, the believer is to let him leave. The bond of marriage is broken.

  "A brother or sister is not under bondage in such cases" (1 Cor.7:15. Note that this seems to be saying that the believer is free to remarry.)

The point is that God has called us to *peace*. This probably refers to all that has been said thus far in this chapter. Peace is certainly the purpose of God in the believer's life: peace with God and peace with each other. If a husband or wife will not live in peace and support his or her spouse in carrying the gospel of peace to the world, the spouse is to continue living for God even if it means divorce. The glorious gospel of peace is God's message to the world!

3. The reason the believer is to cooperate with the unbelieving spouse is clear: the unbelieving spouse may be won to Christ by the believer.

"Likewise, ye wives, be in subjection to your own husbands; that, if any obey not the word, they also may without the word be won by the conversation [behavior] of the wives" (1 Pt.3:1).

"For though I be free from all men, yet have I made myself servant unto all, that I might gain the more" (1 Cor.9:19).

APPLICATION:

It should always be remembered that adultery is not the only sin that can break the union of a marriage. Faith, hope, love, trust, assurance, confidence, strength--all can be dashed upon the rocks of selfishness and unkindness.

QUESTIONS:
1. Why is God so opposed to divorce?
2. What are some practical reasons why a believer should not divorce an unbeliever? How far should the believer go in this effort?
3. Have you ever known an unbeliever to come to Christ through the influence of a Christian spouse?

4. THE GUILTY PARTIES (v.32).

Divorce does not just happen by accident. Divorce is the end result of a sinful heart that becomes hard. Each divorce has at least one guilty party.

A CLOSER LOOK # 2

(5:32) **Marriage, Essentials**: "All cannot receive this saying." (cp. Mt.19:11) What saying?

1. The saying that a man and wife are "to cleave to one another." They are to be (1) totally united together as *one flesh*: "Wherefore they are no more twain, but one flesh" (Matthew 19:5-6).

2. The saying that it is God and God alone who can *join together* a man and a wife (Mt.19:6).

These two things, cleaving and God Himself, are the two essentials for a true marriage. Many are living together who refuse *to cleave* and refuse to let God join them together. They are not willing to cleave, nor are they willing to let God make them as *one flesh*. They are not willing to let God join them together.

(Note: a man and a woman can only cleave and join themselves together physically. God is not needed for a purely physical union. If a married couple wishes more than a physical union, they must turn to God. He alone can *join together* a couple spiritually.)

A CLOSER LOOK #3

(5:32) **Cleave**: to join fast together; to glue together; to cement together; to be joined in the closest union possible; to be bound together; to be so totally united together that two become one. Therefore, in relation to marriage, to cleave means a spiritual union. It is a union higher and stronger than the union of parent and child. It is a union that means more than living together, more than having sex and bearing offspring. Animals do this. It is a union that can be wrought by God alone (Mt.19:11). It is a spiritual union that places man above the physical level of animals. It is a spiritual fulness, a spiritual sharing of life together: a dedication, a consecration, a completeness, a satisfaction that makes a person the exclusive possession of God and of the spouse. As said, such a cleaving or spiritual union is wrought by God alone. Both husband and wife must be willing and submissive for God to bring about such a cleaving in their lives. "Submitting yourselves one to another in the fear [trust] of God" (Eph.5:21).

There are three unions within a true marriage, that is, a marriage that *really cleaves* and is really *joined together* by God (Mt.19:6).

1. There is the *physical union*: the sharing of each other's body (1 Cor.7:2-5). But note: physical sharing cannot reach its ultimate fulness unless it is experienced while conscious of God's warm and tender mercies (Eph.5:25-33).

---

2. There is the *mental union*: the sharing of each other's life and dreams and hopes and the working together to realize those dreams and hopes. It is important to note that this union still deals only with the physical and material world.

3. There is the *spiritual union*: the sharing and melting and molding of each other's spirit. This can be brought about only by God. Therefore, there has to be a sharing together with God for there to be a *nourishing* and *nurturing* of the spirit.

Now here is the point: the greatest thing in the world is to know God personally and to be perfectly assured that we shall live now and eternally—to have life abundant with all the love, significance, meaning, and purpose humanly possible. But a man and a woman cannot experience abundant life of and by themselves. They can only nurture the mind and mesh themselves together mentally and physically. To be meshed together spiritually the couple must share God and His saving grace together. When a couple shares God together day by day, God works supernaturally within their spirits, *melting* their beings and *molding* them into what He calls *one flesh*. They actually become as *one person*. This is what is meant by "God hath joined together." The Greek word for "joined together" actually means to *yoke together*. It is God yoking, God joining, God binding the couple together into a spiritual union that causes them to become one person.

⇒ A couple who is spiritually united does two very practical things.

1. The couple "submits themselves one to the other in the fear of God" (Eph.5:21). They submit, yield, surrender, sacrifice, give themselves up to the other as they live day by day in the fear (trust) of God. Day by day they deliberately set out to nourish and cherish the other, even as the Lord nourishes and cherishes the church (Eph.5:29). They work to become part of each other—so deliberately that they seek to become part of each other's body, each other's flesh, each other's bones (Eph.5:30). They seek to be joined "as one flesh," no matter the surrender and sacrifice required. The meshing together is done by God. God takes such a deliberate purpose and behavior, such a melting of one's being, and molds it into the flesh of the other—so much so that the two actually become as one, not only physically and mentally but spiritually as well.

2. The couple shares the presence of God and His saving grace together. As a result, God gives them a spiritual assurance and strength which they share together throughout life. They share the knowledge and confidence...

- that God shall care for and look after them now and forever
- that God shall carry them through the devastating trials of life that confront every human being every so often
- that God shall bless them with all that is necessary as they walk through life together
- that God shall give them an abundant entrance into the everlasting kingdom of the Lord Jesus Christ—forever and ever

Again, the point is this: God takes such deliberate sharing of spiritual things and melts and molds the man and woman into *one flesh* spiritually—so much so that they actually become one. A man and a woman being spiritually united by God as one person is what cleaving means. Cleaving to one another in God's Spirit is true marriage—the glorious gift of God.

ILLUSTRATION:

We often fail to fully understand just how strong the marriage bond is when we are yielded to God. Those who are truly committed to Christ will experience the true meaning of cleaving together.

"Dr. Joseph Henry said that during the Second World War, two physics graduate students heard their professor say that someday a method would be devised for polishing glass that would replace steel as the flattest surface known to man. When this was done, he said, a revolution in technology would take place.

"After graduation, these two young physicists formed a partnership and set out to prove their professor's theory. They established a laboratory and went to work. Several years later, after a very complicated process, they had a great breakthrough. They produced such a flat surface that it could be used to measure objects within two-millionths of an inch--a great improvement over anything previously developed.

"When Dr. Henry visited their plant, one of the owners said to him, 'See these two squares of glass? They have been put through this new process, and I want to show you something.' Then he simply placed the two pieces together, handed them to Dr. Henry, and said, 'Now, take them apart.' After he pulled, pushed, twisted, turned and exerted all of his strength, Dr. Henry still could not budge them.

"The young physicist explained, 'Two surfaces are held together by a certain number of points of contact, but ordinarily there are so few they easily come apart. The points on these two pieces of glass, however, have been ground down until they are almost completely flat surfaces. They are held together by so many points of contact that it is almost impossible to get them apart.'

"If you let God rub down the rough edges in you and your spouse, nothing will be able to tear you apart."[2]

QUESTIONS:

1. Is sin necessarily the cause of all divorce? Can it be just 'a bad marriage' that causes divorce? Can divorce ever be 'the best thing'?
2. What are some examples of a husband and wife cleaving to each other?
3. Which of the three unions that take place in a Christian marriage (physical, mental, and spiritual) is hardest to maintain? Can you maintain one or two without the other? Why is the spiritual union so important?
4. If a person gets a divorce, what happens to the "one flesh" that had been joined together? Can it ever be "one flesh" again?

SUMMARY:

Are you prepared to take a stand for the promises made in a marriage? The world is crying out for people who really mean what they say. Regardless of your age or current marital status, as a Christian you must support the sanctity of marriage in all walks of life. Otherwise, divorce will continue to be the downfall of all society.

1. The law.
2. The real meaning: divorce disallowed.
3. Exception: fornication.
4. The guilty parties.

PERSONAL JOURNAL NOTES:
(Reflection & Response)

1. The most important thing that I learned from this lesson was:

2. The thing that I need to work on the most is:

3. I can apply this lesson to my life by:

4. Closing Prayer of Commitment: (put your commitment down on paper).

---

[2]   Ted Kyle & John Todd. *A Treasury of Bible Illustrations*, p.238-239.

	I. The Real Meaning of Oaths & Profanity, 5:33-37	35 Nor by the earth; for it is his footstool: neither by Jerusalem; for it is the city of the great King.	b. Because all power belongs to God
1. The law a. Do not swear falsely & deceivingly: Committing perjury b. Keep all oaths	33 Again, ye have heard that it hath been said by them of old time, Thou shalt not forswear thyself, but shalt perform unto the Lord thine oaths:	36 Neither shalt thou swear by thy head, because thou canst not make one hair white or black.	3. The ideal oath or guarantee
2. The real meaning: Do not swear a. Because all things are sacred	34 But I say unto you, Swear not at all; neither by heaven; for it is God's throne:	37 But let your communication be, Yea, yea; Nay, nay: for whatsoever is more than these cometh of evil.	a. One's word--character b. The reason: Swearing has its source in evil

Section IV
THE TEACHINGS OF THE MESSIAH TO HIS DISCIPLES:
THE GREAT SERMON ON THE MOUNT
Matthew 5:1-7:29

Study 9:   THE REAL MEANING OF OATHS AND PROFANITY

Text: Matthew 5:33-37

Aim: To stake your reputation upon the surety of your word.

Memory Verse:
> "But let your communication be, Yea, yea; Nay, nay: for whatsoever is more than these cometh of evil" (Matthew 5:37).

INTRODUCTION:
What kind of impact does profanity have upon others? Throughout society many ungodly words are spewed out regularly, staining the souls of innocent men, women, boys, and girls. We are surrounded...
- by famous movie and television celebrities who condone cursing as a part of their act
- by superstar athletes who proudly mix profanity with their exploits as they are interviewed by doting writers and announcers
- by fellow employees who use swearing as a status symbol, seeking to be seen as tough and wanting to be accepted by their peers
- by professing Christians who have been swept up in the tide of profanity, telling coarse jokes that should make any God-fearing person blush

Swearing is a symptom of a greater problem--the problem of man's sinful nature. How can the person who wants to serve Christ live in such a profane environment? This important section of Scripture puts a new light on the real meaning of oaths and profanity.
Christ said, "Swear not at all" (v.34). He was enlarging the law governing oaths to include all swearing and profanity (cp. Mt.5:17f; Jas.5:12). All conversation should be straight to the point and factual, not injected with oaths or profanity (Mt.5:34, 37). A person is to be righteous. His word and character are to be his guarantee, the only oath he needs.

MATTHEW 5:33-37

OUTLINE:
1. The law (v.33).
2. The real meaning: do not swear (v.34-36).
3. The ideal oath or guarantee (v.37).

IMPORTANT NOTE: there are at least six types of swearing.

1. There is *swearing by oaths*. Jesus was put upon His oath (Mt.26:63), and Paul swore by taking an oath (2 Cor.1:23; Gal.1:20). What then does Christ mean by saying, "Swear not at all"? Simply that a man's word should be trustworthy in his day to day speech, so trustworthy that no oath is ever necessary. His character should be his guarantee, the only guarantee he needs.

A second explanation is also possible. Men are evil, so untrustworthy in their day to day dealings, that worldly men require oaths. Thus, Paul and Christ were required to take oaths. However, as stated above, the believer's word and character should be his bond.

2. There is *habitual, frivolous swearing*. The unrighteous are said to have "mouths full of cursing and bitterness" (Ro.3:10, 14).

3. There is *hypocritical swearing*. There are some who "bless God" in one breath and turn around and "curse men" in the next breath. **"Out of the same mouth proceedeth blessing and cursing" (Jas.3:9-10).**

4. There is *silent, universal swearing*. Every man is charged with secretly cursing others within his heart. **"Thine own heart knoweth that thou thyself...hast cursed others" (Eccl.7:22).**

5. There is *evasive swearing*. Some do not use words that are foul, dirty, ugly, harsh, or binding. They would never use God's name in vain. Rather, they choose substitute words-- words that are commonly used in everyday conversation, words that would never be considered swearing. Others choose what are thought to be milder curse words. By evading harsh swearing, they feel their word is not so binding. They count themselves less guilty.

6. There is *ego swearing*. Many swear to boost their ego, their manliness around others. They feel an identity with the crowd by crossing over to the forbidden.

QUESTIONS:
1. Why is it so important for your word to be your bond? How faithful are you in keeping your word?
2. Why is profanity so prevalent today? How should a believer respond when he is confronted with foul speech at his place of work?
3. When are you most tempted to swear? How can you guard your mouth and your heart when the temptation to swear comes upon you?

1. THE LAW (v.33).

The law was based on the third commandment (Ex.20:7; Lev.19:12; Dt.23:23; cp. Num.30:2). The law had been interpreted to say, "Do not make false vows"; "Do not swear falsely"; "Do not swear to a lie." But the law was much too narrow. Man had interpreted it to his own liking which allowed him to swear and curse as much as he wished. Note two significant points about the law:
1. God gave the law to men for several reasons.
   a. To keep man from dishonoring God by falsely calling upon His name or by cursing Him.
   b. To keep man from perjuring himself, showing himself to be a liar and an unjust and unstable person.
   c. To keep man from treating others unjustly.

2. The law was given to govern several things.
   a. Lying and then swearing that one is telling the truth. This is perjury. How often men perjure themselves--stretching the truth, exaggerating, or lying outrightly--and then swear that they are telling the truth!
   b. Making a false vow to God. How many vows have been made to God and never kept!
   c. Making a false vow to another person, promising something and not doing it.
   d. Using God's name in vain. So many use God's name as a *slang* or *curse word*. This person will stand especially guilty before God (Ex.20:7).

Scripture says that it is better not to vow than to vow and not pay (Eccl.5:4-5). The reason is clearly understood: a vow makes a person a debtor. The person is in debt to fulfill his vow or promise.
   1. A vow to God puts the man in debt to God. To break a vow is an act of lying to God (Acts 5:4).
   2. A vow to man puts the man in debt to man. To break his vow is an act of injustice to man.

> **"If a man vow a vow unto the Lord, or swear an oath to bind his soul with a bond; he shall not break his word, he shall do according to all that proceedeth out of his mouth" (Num.30:2).**
>
> **"When thou shalt vow a vow unto the Lord thy God, thou shalt not slack to pay it: for the Lord thy God will surely require it of thee; and it would be sin in thee" (Dt.23:21).**

QUESTIONS:
1. Why did God give man the commandment not to lie or swear? How has the worldly man responded to God's commandment? Are believers exempt from abusing this law?
2. Why does God consider a vow to be such a serious commitment? Have you ever vowed to do something that you later regretted? Did you follow through? Or did you back out? What would you do differently next time?

2. THE REAL MEANING: DO NOT SWEAR (v.34-36).

Do not swear or curse by anything.
1. Swear not, because all things are sacred.
   a. Heaven is God's throne: the place where His glory is manifested (Is.66:1). To swear by heaven or to curse heaven is to swear by God and to curse God.
   b. The earth is God's footstool: the place He governs and looks over (Is.66:1; Ps.24:1). To swear by earth or to curse earth is to swear by God and to curse God.
   c. Jerusalem is the city of the great King (Ps.48:2; Ps.46:4). He cares deeply for Jerusalem. There is a sense in which God cares deeply for every city and place on earth. He cares about how a place is treated and how it is spoken about (cp. Mt.10:15; 11:24; Mk.6:11; Lk.10:12).
2. Swear not, because all power belongs to God. In reality, no man has any power to do anything; for example, he cannot change his stature. What power he has is given by God. In fact, the power man thinks he has can be taken away at any moment. Therefore, he really does not have the power to keep oaths. He can be disabled or snatched away at any moment. The recognition of this reality should cause a man to live so honestly and straightforwardly that his word alone is acceptable. Oaths and vows should not be necessary.

Note this: all power belongs to God; therefore, a man should stand in awe of God, not curse Him. But observe what it is that is usually cursed: God and the things of God, the very things that should not be cursed. This says much about the selfish, depraved nature of man. Cursing God is a terrible sin, so terrible that it is one of the ten commandments. A special judgment is even pronounced upon the curser (Ex.20:7). Cursing is meaningless, thoughtless, and irreverent.

> **"But the tongue can no man tame; it is an unruly evil, full of deadly poison. Therewith bless we God, even the Father; and therewith curse we men, which are made after the similitude [likeness] of God" (Jas.3:8-9).**

APPLICATION 1:
Cursing has no mask; it cannot be hidden. It is spoken and it is heard. The problem is that it is often considered acceptable conversation. People who curse and use foul words seldom think about the seriousness of profanity. It *is* a very serious offense. No matter how little the *cursing* is considered, God says He "will not hold him guiltless" (Ex.20:7). Cursing is a problem, for it reveals several things:

⇒ a graceless heart
⇒ a thoughtless mind
⇒ an inconsiderate or selfish spirit
⇒ a hardness or enmity toward God
⇒ a problem with self-image
⇒ an inadequate vocabulary
⇒ a lack of individuality and/or independence
⇒ a foolish regard for judgment and eternity

APPLICATION 2:
There are differences of opinion about legal oaths. Some believe they should never take an oath even for the sake of justice (for example, the Quakers). Others feel they can be called upon to swear for the sake of justice; but they should never swear of themselves, that is, take the initiative in verifying their word. (Cp. Gen.22:16; 26:31; 31:53; 47:31; 50:25; Ex.22:11; Num.5:9; Dt.6:13; Josh.9:15, 19; 1 Ki.8:31; 2 Ki.11:4; Ps.89:35; 95:11; Is.14:24; 62:8; Jer.12:16; 38:16; Ezk.17:13; Mk.6:23; Lk.1:73; Acts 23:21; Heb.3:11; 6:17.)

QUESTIONS:
1. What consequences await the person who consistently curses God?
2. What are the hidden symptoms of a person's heart who curses?
3. In western cultures, a person is forced to place his hand upon the Bible and swear to tell the truth before the judge. What does the Bible have to say about this practice?

ILLUSTRATION:
The person who "shares" his profanity with other people spreads a cancer that ruins the innocence of many souls.

> *"Josaih Wedgwood, maker of the famous Wedgwood pottery, one day showed a nobleman through the factory. A boy who was an employee of the factory accompanied them. The nobleman was profane and vulgar. At first the boy was shocked by the nobleman's irreverence. Then he became fascinated by his coarse jokes and laughed heartily. Mr. Wedgwood was distressed. At the conclusion of the tour, he showed the nobleman a vase of unique design. The man was charmed with its exquisite shape and rare beauty. As he reached for it, Mr. Wedgwood designedly let it fall to the floor. The nobleman uttered an angry oath! 'I wanted that vase for my collection,' he said, 'and you have ruined it by your carelessness!'*
> *"Mr. Wedgwood answered, 'Sir, there are other ruined things more precious than a vase, howsoever valuable, which can never be restored. You can never give back to that boy, who has just left us, the reverence for sacred things which his par-*

ents have tried to teach him for years! You have undone their labor in less than half an hour!'[1]

Have you ever undone someone's labor with your mouth? Or have you been the victim of someone else's carelessness?

A CLOSER LOOK # 1

(5:34) **Swearing**: there were two kinds of swearing to the Jews.

1. *Bound swearing.* These were oaths using God's name. When God's name was used, He was considered a partner; therefore, the oath could never be broken.

2. *Unbound swearing.* These were oaths which omitted God's name but used such sacred phrases as "by heaven," "by earth," "by Jerusalem," "by my head," or some other statement to emphasize one's intention or truthfulness. Such oaths were not necessarily binding because God was not considered to be a partner in the oath.

What man so often fails to see is that God is always present. He sees and is concerned with all that a man says and does, whether by word or action, by statement or oath, by swearing or profanity.

QUESTIONS:

1. God knows we are all imperfect. So why is God offended when a person uses profanity?
2. What goes through your mind when you hear profanity?

_____I've gotten used to it. It does not bother me anymore.

_____I try to laugh it off and quickly change the subject.

_____I ignore it and wish I had the courage to confront the person who is swearing.

3. People often speak before thinking. What does this tell you about man's heart?

3. THE IDEAL OATH OR GUARANTEE (v.37).

There is *only one* ideal oath and guarantee for man: his word. His word should arise from his character. It should be the only oath and guarantee he needs. He should not say more than, "Yes, I will...." or "No, I will not." His life should be so honest and straight that no one would ever question his word. When he speaks, everyone should know that it will be done. The reason is simply stated: swearing has its source in evil.

At least two things are meant here. First, man has to take oaths because the world is evil. Second, man swears because he is evil and knows that he is evil. Therefore, he swears to emphasize the truth in the point he makes. The need for oaths and man's need for swearing to the truth are clear evidence of man's depravity. Something that is often overlooked is this fact: swearing and cursing do not make a matter more believable; they really make a matter more suspicious. A person swears something because his character or the matter is questionable. What an indictment of depravity! Yet swearing and cursing are the acceptable habits of men.

> **"Ye are the salt of the earth: but if the salt have lost his savour, wherewith shall it be salted? it is thenceforth good for nothing, but to be cast out, and to be trodden under foot of men" (Mt.5:13).**

---

[1] *Good News Digest.* Walter B. Knight. *Knight's Treasury of 2,000 Illustrations.* (Grand Rapids, MI: Eerdmans Publishing Company, 1963), p.319.

"Let your speech be alway with grace, seasoned with salt, that ye may know how ye ought to answer every man" (Col.4:6).

APPLICATION 1:

Oaths are required for one reason: men know the deceitfulness of the human heart. The heart is deceitful above all things and desperately wicked (Jer.17:9). All men are liars (Ps.116:11). Just think about how often a person leads others on in order to get what he wants.

"The heart is deceitful above all things, and desperately wicked: who can know it?" (Jer.17:9).
"I said in my haste, All men are liars" (Ps.116:11).

APPLICATION 2:

Oaths would not be necessary in a perfect world. Everyone would be perfectly honest and righteous. A man's life would speak loudly and clearly. Whatever a man said would be absolutely dependable. Therefore, believers should work to change the world by changing the hearts of men.

ILLUSTRATION:

One of a person's most precious possessions is the bond of his word. A person can be dirt poor but morally rich if his word can be trusted. In the same way, a person who is a millionaire is morally bankrupt if his word is worthless.

"A young Christian businessman from Nashville was invited to speak at a local church. He chose for his text, 'Thou shalt not steal,' and he spoke unswervingly on the topic. The next morning he boarded a city bus for the ride to work. He handed a dollar bill to the driver and received some change, which he counted as he proceeded down the aisle of the bus. Before he reached his seat, he realized he had been given a dime too much. His first thought was that the transit company would never miss it. But deep inside he knew he should return it. So he went back to the driver and said, 'You gave me too much change, sir.' To the businessman's amazement, the driver replied, 'I know, a dime too much. I gave it to you on purpose. Then I watched you in my mirror as you counted your change. You see, I heard you speak yesterday, and if you had kept the dime, I would have had no confidence in what you said.'"[2]

QUESTIONS:

1. How would the people who know you best judge the quality of your word? What about strangers?
2. What is the key to having a character that will produce a good word?

SUMMARY:

The world in which we live is filled with profanity and swearing. Instead of blending in and becoming a part of the problem, God has called you to be a part of the solution. How can you make a difference in such a profane society? Will you become a person whose word is his bond?
1. The law.
2. The real meaning: do not swear.
3. The ideal oath or guarantee.

---

[2]   *INFOsearch Sermon Illustrations* (Arlington, TX: The Computer Assistant, 1-888-868-9029, 1986-1996).

MATTHEW 5:33-37

PERSONAL JOURNAL NOTES:
(Reflection & Response)

1. The most important thing that I learned from this lesson was:

2. The thing that I need to work on the most is:

3. I can apply this lesson to my life by:

4. Closing Prayer of Commitment: (put your commitment down on paper).

	J. The Real Meaning of the Law Governing Injury, 5:38-42 (Lk.6:29-30)	other also. 40 And if any man will sue thee at the law, and take away thy coat, let him have thy cloke also.	a. Endure physical injury b. Endure property injury
1. The law	38 Ye have heard that it hath been said, An eye for an eye, and a tooth for a tooth:		
2. The real meaning: Do not retaliate **3. The ideal behavior**	39 But I say unto you, That ye resist not evil: but whosoever shall smite thee on thy right cheek, turn to him the	41 And whosoever shall compel thee to go a mile, go with him twain. 42 Give to him that asketh thee, and from him that would borrow of thee turn not thou away.	c. Endure any forced burden **4. The great Christian ethic: Give**

Section IV
THE TEACHINGS OF THE MESSIAH TO HIS DISCIPLES:
THE GREAT SERMON ON THE MOUNT
Matthew 5:1-7:29

Study 10:   THE REAL MEANING OF THE LAW GOVERNING INJURY

Text: Matthew 5:38-42

Aim: To learn how to walk in forgiveness, turning the other cheek.

Memory Verse:
>"But I say unto you, That ye resist not evil: but whosoever shall smite thee on thy right cheek, turn to him the other also" (Matthew 5:39).

INTRODUCTION:

Have you ever been so angry with another person that you wanted to retaliate? It is very probable that everyone of us have been abused at some time and wanted to take the situation into our own hands--whether it be with an individual, a company, or even the government. Listen to some of the *unwritten rules* that govern much of the world:
⇒ If you hurt me I am going to hurt you even more.
⇒ If you steal from me I am going to steal from you.
⇒ If you take my promotion at work I am going to ruin your reputation.
⇒ If you gossip about me I am going to spread vicious lies about you.

The list could go on and on. Many people are used to carrying on day to day life with this kind of attitude. But no matter how much we have been offended, the Christian believer has been called to a higher standard of behavior. God has taken us out of the gutter of sin for a greater purpose--to set an example to those who are caught up in the plight of revenge. God has a much better way for His people to live. It is the way of forgiveness.

This law has been used and misused, excused and abused down through the centuries. Man has often used the law to treat others as he wished. But the life and example of Christ have given us the true interpretation of the law. He says that the Christian is not to render evil for evil; he is not to bear a grudge or seek revenge. He must go beyond and forgive. However, the Christian has the right to avoid and resist evil for security's sake.

OUTLINE:
1. The law (v.38).
2. The real meaning: do not retaliate (v.39).
3. The ideal behavior (v.39-41).
4. The great Christian ethic: give (v.42).

1. THE LAW (v.38).

This law is often thought to be justification for retaliation (cp. Ex.21:24; Lev.24:20; Dt.19:21). It has been misused and abused. However, God's purpose for the law was to show mercy and to limit vengeance. In antiquity men killed for the most minor offenses. For example, if a person was injured accidentally, a whole family or village was subject to be killed in retaliation. Thus this law was the beginning of mercy in a merciless society. It limited retaliation to an equivalent injury. Several facts show the merciful aspect of the law.

1. The law was not a command that had to be executed. It was a law that *allowed* a person some justice *if he wished*. He did not have to insist upon it.

2. The law was given to the courts to guide the judges in the execution of justice. It was not given to individuals to take vengeance on others.

3. The law could be satisfied with money or some other ransom or payment deemed just (Num.35:31). However, no ransom was to "be taken for the life of a murderer." The murderer was to pay with his life.

APPLICATION:

The law was given to control the irresponsible and unregulated passions of men: to control evil and to limit retaliation and revenge. The law was given as a restraint, as a deterrent (1) to the criminal or person who would do evil; and (2) to the victim, lest he inflict a more terrible vengeance than what the crime deserved.

"Eye for eye, tooth for tooth, hand for hand, foot for foot" (Ex.21:24).

ILLUSTRATION:

Man's depraved nature often defends itself and returns an evil attack with an even greater volley of revenge. We are often tested in life to see how we respond in the presence of those who are looking to us as godly examples.

"Many years ago, a father and his young son were out for a ride with the horse and buggy. It had been a very rainy week, and the roads were extremely muddy. They turned on to a road that had one set of deep ruts in the middle of it, which they began to follow. As they came closer to the middle of the mile stretch of road, they saw another horse and buggy coming toward them in the same set of deep ruts. Both buggies stopped horse to horse.

"The father quietly told the other man that he would have to back up. The man argued that the father and his son could back up just as easily as he could. They began to argue about it, and finally the father looked the other man in the eye and said, 'If you don't back up, I'm afraid I am going to do something I will regret!'

"The man looked at the father and began backing his horse and buggy down the road. The father and his son remained still, giving the man time to get out of their way. The son, who had been raised in a Christian tradition that taught that the use of force or violence was not right, was astonished. He turned to his father and asked, 'Dad, what were you going to do that you were going to regret?'

"His father answered, 'I was going to back up.'"[1]

It is always best to err on the side of restraint!

---

[1] Michael Hodgin. *1001 Humorous Illustrations for Public Speaking.* (Grand Rapids, MI: Zondervan, 1994), p. 248-249.

2. THE REAL MEANING: DO NOT RETALIATE (v.39).

Christ says this: the law really means that a person is not to retaliate, but it means even more.

1. Christ is saying "resist not evil," that is, do not seek evil for evil; do not bear a grudge or resent those who have mistreated you. Do not seek revenge or look for a chance to retaliate. But forgive; go out of your way to help those who do evil against you. Such an attitude is the only way to ever reach them for the Kingdom of Heaven (Mt.4:17; 5:3, 10, 19, 21.)

2. But Christ is not saying that we are *never* to resist evil. Christ Himself resisted evil. (1) He drove out the money changers from the temple (Mt.21:12; Mk.11:15), and (2) He resisted the punishment of the High Priest (Jn.18:22-23). Paul the apostle also resisted evil (cp. Acts 16:35f; 22:25; 23:3; 25:9-10).

The point is this: Jesus and Paul followed the new law, "resist not evil." They observed the spirit of the new law, but they were not enslaved by it. There are times when evil should be resisted.

APPLICATION:

A Christian is not to be a vindictive person. He is not to be known as a person who holds a grudge. Among other reasons, revenge consumes. It can *eat up* a person's inner being.

1) It can consume a person's mind--be the focus of all his thoughts. A person can be so intent upon revenge that he does nothing but think about retaliation.
2) It can consume a person's emotions--cause all kinds of emotional problems. A person can be so engrossed in revenge that he becomes...
   - self-centered (harbors how great a wrong has been done to him)
   - withdrawn
   - self-pitying
   - paranoid
   - destructive (strikes out at other persons and other things)

> **"But I say unto you, That ye resist not evil: but whosoever shall smite thee on thy right cheek, turn to him the other also" (Mt.5:39).**

> **"Not rendering evil for evil, or railing for railing: but contrariwise blessing; knowing that ye are thereunto called, that ye should inherit a blessing" (1 Pt.3:9).**

3. THE IDEAL BEHAVIOR (v.39-41).

Christ shared three very practical illustrations, teaching the Christian how to treat those who do him wrong.

1. Endure physical injury. It is the right cheek that is slapped. This says something that is often overlooked. The person who slaps with his right hand has to strike with the back of his hand in order to hit someone's right cheek. Hitting someone with the back of the hand has always been considered more of an insult than the palm of the hand. Throughout history it has been used to symbolize a challenge to duel. It showed contempt and bitterness. Christ is clearly making His point: the believer is not to retaliate against the most terrible insults or bitter contempt--not even against threats of bodily harm.

Turning the other cheek is difficult. It means a person does not challenge, resent, avenge, retaliate, or enter a legal action against an attacker; but he prepares for another slap and bears it patiently. He lets it pass and endures it. He forgives and trusts the matter to God. There is the knowledge that God will work all things out for good as the person goes about his life and service for God.

APPLICATION 1:

Many a person has had his cheek slapped. A "slap in the face" can come by punishment, insult, slight, criticism, rumor, abuse, threat, or physical attack (cp. 2 Cor.11:20). But submission is sometimes the way to overcome (Pr.25:21-22). The believer who endures shameful treatment shall reap eternal glory.

> **"And unto him that smiteth thee on the one cheek offer also the other; and him that taketh away thy cloak forbid not to take thy coat also" (Lk.6:29).**
>
> **"[Love] beareth all things, believeth all things, hopeth all things, endureth all things" (1 Cor.13:7).**

QUESTIONS:
1. Have you ever had to turn your other cheek when you were insulted? What emotions ran through your mind? How did you finally respond?
2. The only way a believer can turn his cheek when he has been confronted is to look to God for strength. How does God help the believer who calls upon Him?

2. Endure property injury. The coat referred to in verse 40 was the tunic, the inner garment. The cloak was the long robe-like outer garment. William Barclay says that Jewish law allowed a man's tunic to be given as a pledge, but the cloak could never be taken. The reason was simply that a man would have a number of tunics (underclothing), but he might have only one[2] (cp. Ex.22:26-27).

Christ's point strikes at the heart of the matter. A Christian is not to be consumed with fighting over property and disputing rights. He is *not to retaliate just because he has the right to retaliate*. The believer is to forget self and forget property and rights; he is to live for God and for the salvation of others.

APPLICATION 1:

Giving one's cloak, one's good coat, is difficult. It means that a believer does not defend, stand up for, nor dispute the taking of his property. He forgives, and then he gives to the person who is taking. He even gives his coat (tunic) if necessary. A believer does not get tied up and preoccupied with his rights and privileges in or out of court. He has time only to go about his own duties and responsibilities. He is to be tied up and intent on living life to the fullest for Christ, reaching out to a world lost and consumed with *disputes,* a world that *needs the peace* which only God can bring.

---

[2] William Barclay. *The Gospel of Matthew*, Vol.1, p.165.

APPLICATION 2:

The world is full of division and disputes, bitterness and hatred, quarrels and wars. It is a divided world because individuals are self-centered. The Christian must be a person of peace, a person who keeps his mind upon God not upon self. He must deny the world and the things of the world. Disputes paint a person as being divisive, as a person who is worldly-minded.

In addition, sometimes recovering or fighting for one's property costs more than giving it up and purchasing more.

APPLICATION 3:

When does a person fight for his rights? These are some factors to consider:
⇒ if damage is being done to himself
⇒ if damage is being done to his family
⇒ if truth is being compromised

> **"Agree with thine adversary quickly, whiles thou art in the way with him; lest at any time the adversary deliver thee to the judge, and the judge deliver thee to the officer, and thou be cast into prison" (Mt.5:25).**

> **"Go not forth hastily to strive, lest thou know not what to do in the end thereof, when thy neighbor hath put thee to shame" (Pr.25:8).**

QUESTIONS:
1. Think of your material possessions. Are any of them worth...
   • a physical fight?
   • an argument?
   • hard feelings?
   • loss of testimony?
   What would be the hardest material thing for you to give up? Why?
2. When *does* a person have a legitimate right to fight for his property?
3. When *should* a person have a legitimate right to fight for his property?

3. Endure any forced burden. In antiquity the citizens of a conquered country could be enlisted into *forced service* by the conquerors in any way deemed necessary. A citizen could be compelled to carry water, supplies, anything (cp. Simeon of Cyrene, Mt.27:32).

Christ is saying that if a believer is forced to go a mile, he should go twice as far. Again, rights--even the rights of liberty--are not to be the primary concern of the believer. The believer's primary concern is to be people and their burdens--reaching and relieving their burdens in obedience to God.

Going a second mile is difficult. It means a person does not become bitter and resentful, grumbling and griping, complaining and criticizing, self-pitying and begrudging. It means a person forgives, serves, and offers even more service. He sets his mind and heart on reaching out to the offender by helping more and more. Such action will be more likely to reach the offender for the Kingdom of Heaven. It will certainly help bring the Kingdom of Heaven closer to this earth.

APPLICATION:

Some persons go well beyond reason in insisting, compelling, and enforcing their will. Others even enslave. Such actions exist within families, friendships, businesses, nations--everywhere.

There are times, of course, when a person is not to submit to the will of another. There are definite commands governing morality and injustice in the Bible, as discussed earlier.

Nonetheless, the believer's major concern is to be people and their burdens (Gal.6:2). The believer is to bear the burdens of people, serving them and helping all he can. His purpose is to fulfill the law of Christ which is the law of love, and thereby to help bring the Kingdom of God to this earth through their conversion.

> "A new commandment I give unto you, That ye love one another; as I have loved you, that ye also love one another. By this shall all men know that ye are my disciples, if ye have love one to another" (Jn.13:34-35).
> "Bear ye one another's burdens, and so fulfil the law of Christ" (Gal.6:2).
> "Charity [love] suffereth long, and is kind; charity envieth not; charity vaunteth not itself, is not puffed up" (1 Cor.13:4).

QUESTIONS:
1. Has God ever required you to go a second mile for someone? What lessons did you learn from your experience?
2. How can you keep the concerns of others as your focus when being burdened by them in some way?

4. THE GREAT CHRISTIAN ETHIC: GIVE (v.42).

Christ is pointedly clear: a Christian is to help those who have need, and he is to readily help. Christ allows no excuse. The picture is simple: when someone asks, the Christian *gives* and does not *turn away*. However, the Bible does not say to give without discretion. "A good man showeth favor, and lendeth: he will guide his affairs with discretion" (Ps.112:5). Giving is *always* to be done with discretion (Ps.112:5). Two things should be looked at and studied to see if a person should or should not give

First, the effect upon the receiver must be studied. Will it encourage laziness and shiftlessness, idleness and license?

Second, the ability of a person to give must also be studied. The believer must realistically know his ability to give and how much God wants him to give. He must try to determine if the person requesting help has a real need. He must give and learn to give more and more-- ever learning to trust God. It is not by chance that people come to the believer for help. They are either aware of the believer's interest and compassion or are brought by God. When brought by God, they are brought both for the growth of the believer and for the benefit of the needful.

The point is this: the believer is to live in readiness--a readiness to give and to lend (cp. 2 Cor.8:11-15 esp. 11). He is not to live for this earth and world. He is to live for God and for heaven. His citizenship is in heaven: it is where he looks for his Savior (Ph.3:20). Any concern he has for this world and its possessions is to be only for meeting the necessities of life and for helping others. He is to exist for ministry, for helping and giving to those who have need. In fact, Scripture is clear. The believer is to work for two reasons: 1) to meet his own necessities, and 2) to secure the means to help those in need.

> "Let him that stole steal no more: but rather let him labour, working with his hands the thing which is good, that he may have to give to him that needeth" (Eph.4:28).

APPLICATION 1:
A cheerful giver is loved by God in a very special way.

"Every man according as he purposeth in his heart, so let him give; not grudgingly, or of necessity: for God <u>loveth</u> a cheerful giver. And God is able to make all grace abound toward you; that ye, always having all sufficiency in all things, may abound to every good work" (2 Cor.9:7-8).

Giving should be done on a personal basis. Jesus Christ is a Person and gave as a person. Therefore, He expects every believer to be personally involved in the lives of others just as He Himself is. Too many feel their obligation to give is over when they have given through official channels. But this is not the case with Christ. He demonstrated that the believer is to get personally involved in helping others.

APPLICATION 2:
Giving should be handled in such a way that the dignity of the receiver is restored. The humiliation experienced by the needful is often unbearable.

APPLICATION 3:
Lending can help the person who borrows. It can teach him (1) to trust God more, and (2) to learn how to be more industrious. The borrower has to *get to it* in order to pay back what is loaned.

APPLICATION 4:
It is better to be misled by a *professional beggar* than to miss helping a truly needful person.

"And the people asked him, saying, What shall we do then? He answereth and saith unto them, He that hath two coats, let him impart to him that hath none; and he that hath meat, let him do likewise" (Lk.3:10-11).
"Sell that ye have, and give alms; provide yourselves bags which wax not old, a treasure in the heavens that faileth not, where no thief approacheth, neither moth corrupteth" (Lk.12:33).
"If thine enemy be hungry, give him bread to eat; and if he be thirsty, give him water to drink" (Pr.25:21).

QUESTIONS:
1. What things should you personally consider before giving money or material goods to a person in need?
2. How can you stay aware of the needs of others?
3. Some people do not give because they are afraid of being deceived. Is this justifiable? How can you strike a good balance between generosity and caution?

SUMMARY:

What rule do you live by: the rule that says revenge is your right or the rule that chooses to forgive the person who has hurt you?

"If somebody killed your child, could you ever forgive him? By God's grace the raging desire for revenge might eventually die down within our hearts, but most of us would probably prefer never to see that person again nor to help him in any way.
"Yet that was not the reaction of Walter Everett, a Methodist pastor in Hartford, Connecticut. When Michael Carlucci was convicted of manslaughter for shooting Ev-

erett's son, the bereaved father set an example that challenges all of us who claim Christ as Savior.

"Walter said he forgave Michael because people 'won't be able to understand why Jesus came and what Jesus is all about unless we forgive.' Was that mere rhetoric? Not in the least! Michael became a believer while in jail, and when he was released and wanted to be married, Walter performed the ceremony.

"If we have experienced the wonder of God's forgiveness, we will forgive others as He has forgiven us through Christ (Mt.18:21-35; Eph.4:32). It may require an agonizing emotional struggle and fervent prayer on our part. And full restoration of the relationship may not occur. But with the empowerment of the Holy Spirit we can forgive-- because we are forgiven."[3]

To choose the way of forgiveness and go on with life is much easier said than done. But, thank God, it is God's way!
1. The law.
2. The real meaning: do not retaliate.
3. The ideal behavior.
4. The great Christian ethic: give.

PERSONAL JOURNAL NOTES:
(Reflection & Response)

1. The most important thing that I learned from this lesson was:

2. The thing that I need to work on the most is:

3. I can apply this lesson to my life by:

4. Closing Prayer of Commitment: (put your commitment down on paper).

---

[3]   *Our Daily Bread*, Volume 41, Numbers 3,4,5, p. July 17, 1996.

	K. The Real Meaning of Human Relationships, 5:43-48 (Lk.6:27-36)	ther which is in heaven: for he maketh his sun to rise on the evil and on the good, and sendeth rain on the just and on the unjust.	of God b. Makes you like God
1. The law	43 Ye have heard that it hath been said, Thou shalt love thy neighbour, and hate thine enemy.	unjust. 46 For if ye love them which love you, what reward have ye? do not even the publicans	c. Makes you distinctive from other men
2. The real meaning a. Love your enemies b. Bless those who curse you c. Do good to those who hate you d. Pray for persecutors	44 But I say unto you, Love your enemies, bless them that curse you, do good to them that hate you, and pray for them which despitefully use you, and persecute you;	the same? 47 And if ye salute your brethren only, what do ye more than others? do not even the publicans so? 48 Be ye therefore	4. The charge: Be perfect
3. The incentive a. Makes you a child	45 That ye may be the children of your Fa-	perfect, even as your Father which is in heaven is perfect.	

Section IV
THE TEACHINGS OF THE MESSIAH TO HIS DISCIPLES:
THE GREAT SERMON ON THE MOUNT
Matthew 5:1-7:29

Study 11:   THE REAL MEANING OF HUMAN RELATIONSHIPS

Text: Matthew 5:43-48

Aim: To strive for genuine growth in human relationships.

Memory Verse:
> "But I say unto you, Love your enemies, bless them that curse you, do good to them that hate you, and pray for them which despitefully use you, and persecute you" (Matthew 5:44).

INTRODUCTION:

We all have enemies in the world. Does that surprise you? Even the sweetest person has some rival or foe--if only because he or she is so sweet! What is an enemy? Webster's Dictionary defines it as someone who seeks the injury, overthrow, or failure of an opponent; who shows hostility or ill will. The world's solution to dealing with enemies is to strike back or retaliate. But one of the most challenging tasks for the Christian believer is to learn how to relate to each of this group of adversaries in a godly manner. Whereas our friends love us and appreciate us, wanting only what is best for us, our enemies are bent on one thing: our destruction. What are we to do with people who oppose or torment us? God's approach toward this topic might surprise you. As the great American President Abraham Lincoln once said, *"The best way to destroy your enemy is to make him your friend."*[1]

No subject is more important than the subject of human relationships. God is creating a family of believers who are to live together eternally. Therefore, He wants that family to

---

[1]   *INFOsearch Sermon Illustrations* (Arlington, TX: The Computer Assistant, 1-888-868-9029, 1986-1996).

live together as a family, loving each other and loving their neighbors as they should. God's family must never allow hate to enter their hearts. God's family is to treat no person as an enemy. Every person is to be loved as a true neighbor.

OUTLINE:
1. The law (v.43).
2. The real meaning (v.44).
3. The incentive (v.45-47).
4. The charge: be perfect (v.48).

1. THE LAW (v.43).

The law said, "Thou shalt love thy neighbor as thyself" (Lev.19:18). Israel made two fatal mistakes in interpreting this law.

1. They said "neighbor" meant only the people of their own community, religion, and nation. They did not include anyone else. In fact, they shut out and cut off everyone else.

2. They inferred they were to *hate their enemies*. God said, "Love thy neighbor"; therefore they reasoned and added, "Hate thine enemy." Human reason actually leads a person to think that he should oppose and hate his enemy. But such is just *deduced* or *inferred* from depraved human reason. It is the natural reasoning of man at work. It is not God's reasoning, and it is not what God knows to be best for the world: love, joy, peace.... (Gal.5:22-23).

APPLICATION:
Many people fall into the same mistake as Israel. They interpret "neighbors" to be only their friends and those who live close by. They never think of enemies nor of the world as a whole as their neighbors.

QUESTIONS:
1. Who does God say your neighbor is? Do you honestly think of all people as your neighbors?
2. Think for a moment about a neighbor in your present or past whom you did not care for or did not get along with. Can you or could you have done anything that would be an act of love toward this person?
3. The world demonstrates that a person is to hate his enemies. What did Christ demonstrate?

2. THE REAL MEANING (v.44).

The real meaning of the law "to love" involves four very practical acts (cp. 1 Cor.13:4-7).

1. Love your enemies. Believers are to love *all* men, even enemies. They are to respect and honor all men (1 Pt.2:17). Every human being has something that is commendable, even if it is nothing but the fact that he is a fellow human being with a soul to be reached for God. Note two facts.

   a. Loving our enemies is against human nature. The behavior of human nature is to react, strike back, hate, and wish hurt. At best human nature treats an enemy with a cold shoulder and keeps its distance. The root of human reaction against enemies is self and bitterness. (Self-preservation is not evil of itself. See A Closer Look # 1, Love-- Mt.5:44. The section on agape love points out that love is not complacent acceptance of wickedness and license.)

   b. But there is one thing a believer can have for his enemy: mercy or compassion. If he does not have compassion for those who hate him, he has gained nothing of the spirit of Christ (Lk.6:36).

A CLOSER LOOK # 1

(5:44) **Love**: when Christ said "Love your enemies," He could have used any one of four words. The Greek language is very descriptive and detailed in its expressions. Its words are precise and full of meaning. In speaking of love, the Greek language describes exactly what is meant. It separates the various types of love, and uses four different words for love. Thus, it is always important to know which word is used in the New Testament and what that word means.

1. There is "eros" love. This is love that arises from passion, infatuation, and sexual attraction. It is the love (passion) of a man for a woman. The word is never used in the New Testament.

2. There is "storge" love. This is love that arises from affection, a natural born affection, the affection of family love. It is the love and natural affection between parent and child.

3. There is "phileo" love. This is love that arises from affection also, but from a different kind. It is a deep, intense, and warm affection. It is an affection that fills a person's heart with warmth, tenderness, preciousness, and a deep consciousness of really loving and really being loved. It is the love of precious affection and feelings toward those who are very near and very dear to one's heart (Jn.21:15-17).

4. There is "agape" love. This is the love that wishes well. It is a love that demonstrates kindness, benevolence, and respect. It is the love of the mind, reason, and choice. It is a sacrificial love, that is, a love that cares, gives, and works for another person's good--no matter how the person may respond or treat one (Jn.21:15-17).

The word Christ uses in saying "Love your enemies" is agape: the love that must be willed. The Christian must use his mind and reason and deliberately choose to love his enemy.

Note four things:

1. The Christian's love for his enemy is different from the love he holds for his family. It would be impossible to love an enemy with affection. Christ knew this.

2. The Christian sacrifices himself, bears all in order to work for his enemy's good. Whether Christian minister or layman, the Christian chooses deliberately to love a world of antagonistic men for their own good (their salvation and hope of eternity).

3. The Christian's love (agape love) is not complacent acceptance of open wickedness and license. It is not sitting back and allowing a person to do as he pleases. It is not allowing selfishness and deception and a wallowing around in license. Agape love is putting a stop to sin and license as much as possible. It is restraint, control, discipline, and even punishment when it protects the offender from himself and protects those whom he hurts. Very simply pictured, it is a parent controlling a child for his own good and for the good of those who love him.

4. Agape love is God's love. A Christian can have agape love only as he allows God to love through him (Jn.21:15-17). The believer deliberately wills to love as God loves, and God empowers him to do so (Ro.5:5).

> **"Thou shalt love thy neighbor as thyself" (Mt.22:39).**
> **"Beloved, let us love one another: for love is of God; and every one that loveth is born of God, and knoweth God" (1 Jn.4:7).**

QUESTIONS:
1. Briefly describe which people in your life fit into these four kinds of love.
2. Where do you draw the line between compassion and complacency with an enemy?

2. Bless those who curse you. "To bless" means that a person has to speak. Christ is saying to speak softly to the curser (Pr.15:1). Use kind, friendly words. When face to face, be

courteous; when behind his back, commend his strengths. Do not render "railing for railing," that is, do not condemn or attack him in bitter or abusive language (1 Pt.3:9).

A fact that is often forgotten is this: if we react with sharp, harsh words, it will only stir up more anger and hate in the curser.

> **"Not rendering evil for evil, or railing for railing: but contrariwise blessing; knowing that ye are thereunto called, that ye should inherit a blessing" (1 Pt.3:9).**

A CLOSER LOOK # 2

(5:44) **Curser**: the *curser* has two major problems.

1. The *curser* has a weak self-image. He has to play *the big boy* or *the big man*. He feels the need to assert himself, to come across as strong and forceful, to fit in as *one of the boys or men*. It should be noted that society itself can take on a weak image; that is, a whole generation can reflect a weak self image. One of the first signs of a weak self image is the acceptance of cursing as a normal part of conversation. What an indictment against so many societies!

2. The *curser* either does not know the Lord or else is very immature and weak in the Lord. Thus, he desperately needs the blessing and the help of the believer.

---

3. Do good to those who hate you. "Doing good" goes beyond words. It does things for the person who hates. It reaches out to him through his family or friends, employment or business. It searches for ways to do good to him, realizing that he needs to be reached for God. If no immediate way is found, then the Christian patiently waits for the day when he will face one of the crises that comes to every human being (for example, sickness, accident, death). And then the believer goes and does good, ministering to him as Christ Himself ministered.

APPLICATION:

The greatest proof of love is "doing good to those who hate you."

> **"But I say unto you which hear, Love your enemies, do good to them which hate you" (Lk.6:27; cp. Lk.6:28).**
> **"Therefore if thine enemy hunger, feed him; if he thirst, give him drink: for in so doing thou shalt heap coals of fire on his head" (Ro.12:20).**
> **"See that none render evil for evil unto any man; but ever follow that which is good, both among yourselves, and to all men" (1 Th. 5:15).**

4. Pray for those who persecute you. Three things in particular need to be prayed about: (a) for God to forgive the persecutor (Lk.23:34; Acts 7:60), (b) for peace between yourself and the persecutor, and (c) for the persecutor's salvation or correction.

Prayer for the persecutor will greatly benefit the believer. It will keep the believer from becoming bitter, hostile, or reactionary.

> **"Then said Jesus, Father, forgive them; for they know not what they do. And they parted his raiment, and cast lots" (Lk.23:34).**

ILLUSTRATION:

It might be easy to sit back and convince yourself you could obey the above commands from the Lord. But the real proof of obedience comes when a real life opportunity arises.

> *"In August 1983, Russell Stendal was taken hostage into the jungle of Colombia, South America, by a band of guerrilla soldiers. For nearly 5 months he learned what it really means to love one's enemies. He wrote a letter home, saying, 'I am in danger only of losing my life; they are in danger in losing their souls.' Through kindness, Russell befriended his guards. One day the commander told him, 'We can't kill you face to face; we like you. So we will have to kill you in your sleep.' God enabled Russell to forgive, but for the next 10 days and nights he couldn't sleep. A submachine gun was repeatedly thrust in his face under his mosquito net, but the guards couldn't bring themselves to pull the trigger. On January 3, 1984, Russell was released. When he said goodbye, tears filled the eyes of some of his captors."*[2]

Are your prayers changing your enemy?

QUESTIONS:
1. What is a practical way you can love your enemies? What would happen if you did this? Would this person still be your enemy?
2. What does hatred do to a person who is a believer and tries to follow Christ?
3. How does God see your enemies? How does understanding God's view help you to relate to your enemies?
4. How is it possible to bless a person who curses you? What is the key to keep from being unforgiving and vengeful?
5. Take a close look at your prayer list. Are there any enemies on it? How would your prayer life change if all your enemies were included on your list?

3. THE INCENTIVE (v.45-47).

The incentive to love everyone as a true neighbor is threefold.

1. Love makes a person a child of God. Love is unmistakable proof that a person truly loves and knows God. A believer cannot hate another person--not a true believer. If a person says he loves God and hates some person, whether former friend or foe, he needs to search his heart. He lacks the genuineness demanded by God (1 Jn.4:19-21; 1 Jn.3:23; cp. Jn.13:33-34).

> **"But when the fulness of the time was come, God sent forth his Son, made of a woman, made under the law, to redeem them that were under the law, that we might receive the adoption of sons. And because ye are sons, God hath sent forth the Spirit of his Son into your hearts, crying, Abba, Father" (Gal.4:4-6).**

2. Love makes a person like God. God loves His enemies. He causes the sun to shine and the rain to fall on His enemies as well as on those who love Him. The Christian is to be just like God: he is to love his enemies. In loving his enemies, the Christian becomes more and more like God. He becomes godly.

> **"So God created man in his own image, in the image of God created he him; male and female created he them" (Gen.1:27).**
> **"But thou, O man of God, flee these things; and follow after righteousness, godliness, faith, love patience, meekness" (1 Tim. 6:11).**

---

[2] *INFOsearch Sermon Illustrations* (Arlington, TX: The Computer Assistant, 1-888-868-9029, 1986-1996).

APPLICATION 1:
Man was created "in the image, after the likeness of God" (Gen.1:27). Man's very purpose for being is to glorify God and to be like God (cp.Mt.5:48).

APPLICATION 2:
No man can look at God's nature and learn hatred. God's sunshine and rain bless all. There is no indication of favoritism in the sunshine and the rain. Therefore, the learning of reaction and hatred does not come from *without man*, but from *within man* (Mt.15:18-20; Mk.7:21; cp. Mt.12:34-35; Lk.6:45).

3. Love makes a person distinctive from other men. A believer must do more than others. He must go beyond what others do. Everyone loves his friends, so *doing more and going beyond* means that the believer will love his enemies. Everyone is friendly to those who salute him; therefore, doing more and going beyond means that the believer salutes his enemies.

APPLICATION 1:
Motives have to be watched. Too many people are nice and kind out of self-interest. They hope to gain something (a vote, money, inheritance, support) from those to whom they are friendly. The believer is to be different and distinctive. His motive must be to reach out to the unfriendly with a pure heart, even the enemies of Christ.

APPLICATION 2:
If people loved and cared only for those who loved them, think how divided the world would be. Someone has to reach out to bring all men together. All must be reached: the bitter, the cold-hearted, the withdrawn, the angry, the murderer, the attacker, the thief, the enemy, the curser, the hater, the spiteful, the persecutor.

APPLICATION 3:
It is the task of the believer to *do more and go beyond*. The believer is to reach all, for he knows the true love of God. God has *done more and gone beyond* by sending His Son into the world (Jn.3:16; cp. Eph.2:11-18). The believer knows this; therefore, it is his calling to *do more and go beyond* (2 Cor.5:18-20).

> **"Give to him that asketh thee, and from him that would borrow of thee turn not thou away" (Mt.5:42).**
> **"I have showed you all things, how that so labouring ye ought to support the weak, and to remember the words of the Lord Jesus, how he said, It is more blessed to give than to receive" (Acts 20:35).**
> **"Distributing to the necessity of saints; given to hospitality" (Ro.12:13).**

QUESTIONS:
1. What incentive has God given you to love everybody as a true neighbor?
2. It is difficult to love someone who does not love you in return. Who is the most unloving person you know? Do you think God's love can change this person's heart?
3. Who is the most loving person you know? How does this person relate to those who are enemies? What can you learn from this person's example?

4. THE CHARGE: BE PERFECT (v.48).

The idea of perfection referred to here is perfection of purpose. It has to do with an end, an aim, a goal, a purpose. It means fit, mature, fully grown at a particular stage of growth. For example, a fully grown child is a perfect child; he has reached his childhood and achieved the purpose of childhood. It does not mean perfection of character, that is, being without sin. It is fitness, maturity for task and purpose. It is full development, maturity of godliness.

The Bible reveals three stages of perfection.
1. Saving perfection. Christ's death has guaranteed forever the perfection or redemption of those set apart for God.

> **"For by one offering he hath perfected for ever them that are sanctified" (Heb.10:14).**

2. Progressive or maturing perfection. God reveals anything that is contrary to His purpose, and the believer is expected to clean it up (Ph.3:13-15, esp. 15). The believer's "perfect holiness" (2 Cor.7:1) is "now being made perfect" (Gal.3:3). As a member of the church, the believer is experiencing "the perfecting of the saints" (Eph.4:12; Col.4:12; Heb.13:21; Jas.1:4; 1 Jn.4:17-18).

> **"And he gave some, apostles; and some, prophets; and some, evangelists; and some, pastors and teachers; for the perfecting of the saints, for the work of the ministry, for the edifying of the body of Christ" (Eph.4:11-12).**

3. Redemptive or resurrected perfection. The believer's purpose and aim is to "attain unto the resurrection of the dead...[to be] perfect" (Ph.3:11-12).

> **"That I may know him, and the power of his resurrection, and the fellowship of his sufferings, being made conformable unto his death; if by any means I might attain unto the resurrection of the dead. Not as though I had already attained, either were already perfect: but I follow after, if that I may apprehend that for which also I am apprehended of Christ Jesus" (Ph.3:10-12).**

The Lord's point is this: the mature believer will do good and show kindness to all men, both good and bad men. He is *mature* in heart when he shows love to his enemies as well as to his friends. God Himself is the believer's example in this.

APPLICATION 1:
God is love, perfect love (1 Jn.4:8, 16). He loves all; therefore, He wants a world of love from creatures who will freely choose to love. He challenges everyone to be like Himself: to love all, even his enemies. If a person will work to mature in this challenge, he will be marching ever forward to be like his "Father who is in heaven" (cp. Ph.3:12-16).

APPLICATION 2:
No man will ever gain perfection, particularly in the area of human relationships. Just consider how short each person comes in relating to spouse, child, friend, fellow workers, and enemies. Yet he is to "follow after...forget the past...reach forth...press." He is to walk as he has learned to walk--more and more like Christ (Ph.3:12-16; 1 Pt.1:14-16).

> **"Be ye therefore perfect, even as your Father which is in heaven is perfect" (Mt.5:48).**

"Whom we preach, warning every man, and teaching every man in all wisdom; that we may present every man perfect in Christ Jesus" (Col.1:28).

"But the God of all grace, who hath called us unto his eternal glory by Christ Jesus, after that ye have suffered a while, make you perfect, stablish, strengthen, settle you" (1 Pt.5:10).

ILLUSTRATION:

How consistent is your love? It takes a special effort for a person to love his enemies as well as his friends. Often we are quick to misjudge others instead of seeing what God calls a work of art--people who are created in His very own image.

"An elderly man who was very nearsighted thought of himself as an expert in evaluating art. One day he visited a museum with some friends. He had forgotten his glasses and couldn't see the pictures clearly, but that did not stop him from airing his strong opinions. As soon as they walked into the gallery, he began critiquing the various paintings.

"Stopping before what he thought was a full-length portrait, he began to criticize it. With an air of superiority he began, 'The frame is altogether out of keeping with the picture. The man is too homely and shabbily dressed. In fact, it was a great mistake for the artist to select such a shoddy subject for his portrait.'

"The old fellow was babbling on and on when his wife finally managed to get to him and pull him aside. She whispered to him, 'My dear, you are looking in a mirror.'

"Our own faults, which we are slow to recognize, seem so big when we see them in others."[3]

QUESTIONS:
1. If you can never reach perfection, why should you keep trying? What does it really mean for you to be perfect in God's eyes?
2. Why are all three stages of perfection (saving, maturing, redemptive) necessary for the believer to experience? Where are you in your Christian walk?
3. With relation to your enemies, what can you do to walk in closer obedience to Christ? What should be the goal of every believer?

SUMMARY:

One of the great distinctions about Christianity is that we are to love our enemies. History has recorded through the centuries countless numbers of believers who have loved people who did not deserve their love. But we too fall into that category. We do not deserve to be loved, but Jesus Christ does love us. As our Savior and our perfect pattern in life, and because of His great and unconditional love, do you have any other choice but to love your enemies with a sacrificial love?
1. The law.
2. The real meaning: be perfect.
3. The incentive.
4. The charge: be perfect.

---

[3] *Our Daily Bread*, Volume 41, Number 12; Volume 42, Numbers 1,2, p. April 24.

MATTHEW 5:43-48

1. The most important thing that I learned from this lesson was:

2. The thing that I need to work on the most is:

3. I can apply this lesson to my life by:

4. Closing Prayer of Commitment: (put your commitment down on paper).

	CHAPTER 6	hypocrites do in the synagogues and in the streets, that they may have glory of men. Verily I say unto you, They have their reward.	b. Characteristic of hypocrites
	L. The Right Motive for Giving, 6:1-4		c. Reward: Recognition by men only
1. Alms--doing good & giving	Take heed that ye do not your alms before men, to be seen of them: otherwise ye have no reward of your Father which is in heaven.		
a. Warning: Do not seek recognition			**3. The right motive**
b. The reason: God will not reward		3 But when thou doest alms, let not thy left hand know what thy right hand doeth:	a. Giving unconsciously
			b. Giving quietly--privately--secretly
2. The wrong motive	2 Therefore when thou doest thine alms, do not sound a trumpet before thee, as the	4 That thine alms may be in secret: and thy Father which seeth in secret himself shall reward thee openly.	**4. The reasons**
a. Giving for recognition			a. Father sees in secret
			b. Father rewards openly

Section IV
THE TEACHINGS OF THE MESSIAH TO HIS DISCIPLES:
THE GREAT SERMON ON THE MOUNT
Matthew 5:1-7:29

Study 12:   THE RIGHT MOTIVE FOR GIVING

Text: Matthew 6:1-4

Aim: To make an honest pledge to Christ: To seek no recognition for doing good deeds and giving.

Memory Verse:
"Take heed that ye do not your alms [doing good and giving] before men, to be seen of them: otherwise ye have no reward of your Father which is in heaven" (Matthew 6:1).

INTRODUCTION:

Every person who gives has a motivation for doing so. The key to giving is to have the *right* motivation. What would you do if *you* won a sweepstakes? This amusing story records one man's motive.

> "The story goes that while Robert Smith was taking his afternoon walk as part of his therapy in recovering from a massive heart attack, the phone rang and his wife Delores answered. The call was from the Reader's Digest Association Sweepstakes in New York. They were calling to inform the Smith family that Robert had just won $1,500,000 and that in a few days the certified check would be arriving. Well, as you can imagine, Delores was absolutely ecstatic. Now all those dreams would come true!
>
> "But then she remembered, her husband was just getting over his heart attack, and the doctor had said no excitement over anything. Delores was afraid that if she told him they had just won such a large sum, he would have another heart attack and die. What should she do? After some thought, she decided to call their pastor and ask his advice because he had had some experience in breaking difficult news to families.
>
> "Delores called him and said, 'Pastor, I just got a call from The Reader's Digest Sweepstakes informing me that Bob has just won $1,500,000.'
>
> "'That's great,' said the pastor, 'but what's the problem?'
>
> "'Well, I'm afraid if I tell Bob, he'll get so excited that he will have another heart attack and drop dead. Can you help me?'

"'Well, Delores, I think I can. I'll be right over.'

"So in about an hour, Bob is back from his walk and he and Delores and Pastor Baldwin are in the den having a nice chat. The pastor leans toward Bob and says, 'Bob, I've got a problem and need your advice.'

"'Sure, Pastor, if I can help, I'll be glad to,' said Bob.

"The pastor takes a deep breath and goes on, 'It's a hypothetical situation regarding Christian stewardship. What would a person--take you, for instance--do if all of a sudden you found out you had won $1,500,000? What would you do with all that money?'

"'That's easy,' Bob replied. 'I'd start by giving $750,000 to the church.' Whereupon Pastor Baldwin had a massive heart attack and dropped dead!"[1]

What a man does matters greatly to God. God expects men to be kind and to do good in the world: to help others both through personal involvement and through giving generously and sacrificially.

But there is something else that God expects, something of critical importance: God expects a man to have *the right motive*. Just why a man does good and shows kindness matters greatly to God. Because of this, Christ warns us about right and wrong motives.

OUTLINE:
1. Alms--doing good and giving (v.1).
2. The wrong motive (v.2).
3. The right motive (v.3-4).
4. The reason (v.4).

1. ALMS--DOING GOOD AND GIVING TO OTHERS (v.1).

The word "alms" means righteous acts; giving in order to meet the needs of the poor. To the Jew, giving alms and righteousness meant the same thing. Giving alms was the greatest thing a Jew could do; it was the first act of religion. It was considered to be the very embodiment of righteousness, so much so that the two words began to be used synonymously. The Jews felt that giving alms merited and assured one of righteousness and salvation. Christ warned there is great danger in giving and doing alms. Take heed and guard yourself. Do not give for recognition or you will lose your reward.

APPLICATION:
There are two important lessons in this verse.
1) Man must guard and be alert to the deception of giving and doing good before men. A person's heart can be deceived. The sin creeps up on man; it is insidious and subtle. It will keep a person from receiving anything from God.
2) A person must give alms and do good. It is a duty of the Christian. In this passage alone Christ says four times, "Do alms."

QUESTIONS:
1. Why is it so dangerous to seek public recognition for doing good?
2. What good deeds have you done in the past that drew attention to yourself? Could you have handled, avoided, or diverted the attention elsewhere?
3. What does it really mean to "lose your reward"? If you are already saved, does it really matter? Why or why not?

---

[1] Robert Strand. *Moments for Pastors.* (New Leaf Press, 1994). As cited in *INFOsearch Sermon Illustrations* (Arlington, TX: The Computer Assistant, 1-888-868-9029, 1986-1996).

2. THE WRONG MOTIVE (v.2).

There is the wrong motive for doing good. Christ takes for granted that the believer gives and does good. What Christ strikes at is the motive of the human heart for giving and doing good.

1. Giving for recognition is the wrong motive for giving. Recognition is said to be sought by blowing one's own horn in two places: (1) in the synagogue before religious people, and (2) in the streets before the public.

APPLICATION 1:
There are several wrong motives for giving and doing good.
1) A person may give for recognition and prestige: to be praised by men during life and to be remembered by men in death. A person may desire the applause of men: their thanks and appreciation, honor and praise, esteem and glory.
2) A person may give for self-applause, self-satisfaction, and self-admiration: to feel comfortable with what he has done and to see himself at his very best. He may wish to boost his ego and to glory in himself.
3) A person may give out of obligation: to fulfill his sense of duty.
4) A person may give to secure the recognition of God: to feel that God is pleased and favors him because he has done good.

APPLICATION 2:
It is not always wrong to give alms when men see us. This cannot always be helped. It is wrong to give alms *so that* men may see us. The point is not that a person should hold back from doing good, but that he should guard how he gives and does good.

"But all their works they do for to be seen of men" (Mt.23:5).
"Beware of the scribes, which desire to walk in long robes, and
love greetings in the markets, and the highest seats in the synagogues,
and the chief rooms at feasts" (Lk.20:46).

2. Giving for recognition is characteristic of hypocrites. Giving out of the wrong motive is hypocritical. The word "hypocrite" means an actor who puts on a show, who plays a part on stage; a mask, a fake picture; appearing to be something one is not.
   a. It is "sounding a trumpet" *before oneself* (v.2): blowing one's own horn for self praise.
   b. It is "sounding a trumpet" *in the synagogue*: blowing one's own horn in the church and before the religious; it is seeking the praise of the religious (v.2).
   c. It is "sounding a trumpet" *in the streets*: blowing one's own horn before the public, seeking the praise of the public (v.2).

"And whosoever shall exalt himself shall be abased; and he that
shall humble himself shall be exalted" (Mt.23:12).
"He that exalteth his gate seeketh destruction" (Pr.17:19).

3. Giving for recognition is rewarded on this earth only. A person receives the recognition of men only. There are two rewards for a wrong motive: the recognition of men and temporary self-satisfaction. Note the words, "they have their reward." This is an accounting statement: it means just what it says--payment has been made in full. One has received his payment and reward; he has received all he will ever receive. There is to be no reward--no reward whatsoever--from God (see note--Mt.6:4).

APPLICATION 1:

The person who gives out of a wrong motive fails at several points.

1) He fails to give of himself. He gives money and he gives things, but calculates exactly what he can give in order to meet the need; but he never becomes personally involved. He never gives of himself.

2) He seldom puts the need or the needy person first. Satisfying his own motive and having his own need met is put first.

3) He is always hurt, disappointed, unhappy, and sometimes even angry if his giving is not recognized and praised.

4) He is never permanently satisfied with what has been done. Why? Because Christ and the genuine giving of self is the only permanent satisfaction for the human heart.

5) He has accepted the recognition that lasts only briefly. The prestige and honor, thanks and praise of men are only temporary.

   a) The man who gives in this life soon fades in the memory of men. His giving fades into the background. Men move on to other things.

   b) Once gone, the man who gave in this life knows nothing of the thoughts and words spoken in his behalf. He stands only before God, accountable to Him alone.

APPLICATION 2:

Three things can be said about the person who chooses man's reward over God's reward:

⇒ he has chosen the poorest reward

⇒ he has cheated himself

⇒ he can expect no more

What a terrible fate! To have no more reward than what this world offers. Imagine! No hope and no expectation of a better future--nothing beyond this world.

> **"For all flesh is as grass, and all the glory of man as the flower of grass. The grass withereth, and the flower thereof falleth away" (1 Pt. 1:24).**
> **"Nevertheless man being in honour abideth not: he is like the beasts that perish" (Ps.49:12).**

QUESTIONS:

1. What are some of the wrong motives for giving and doing good that you witness every day? Which one of these motives do you struggle with the most?

2. Have you ever been tempted to seek recognition? What is the best way you can guard your heart in this area?

3. People who give for the wrong motives miss out on so much of life. What kinds of things do these people lose?

3. THE RIGHT MOTIVE (v.3-4).

What is the right motive for doing good and for giving? "Let not thy left hand know what thy right doeth." What a descriptive way to say it!

1. Give unconsciously. Pay no attention to what you are giving and doing. Do it out of an inner compulsion to give and help, out of intense love, out of genuine concern. Keep your mind on the need, not on what you are doing and the benefits you may receive. Do not harbor such self-centered thoughts. Just love and care and be concerned as you give and do good.

MATTHEW 6:1-4

ILLUSTRATION:
There is a lot that can be said about the person who gives for the right reasons. The person who has the right motive is governed by the joy of giving, bringing pleasure to the lives of others. Dale Galloway tells the following story:

"Little Chad was a shy, quiet young fella. One day he came home and told his mother he'd like to make a valentine for everyone in his class. Her heart sank. She thought, 'I wish he wouldn't do that!' because she had watched the children when they walked home from school. Her Chad was always behind them. They laughed and hung on to each other and talked to each other, but Chad was never included. Nevertheless, she decided she would go along with her son. So she purchased the paper and glue and crayons. For three whole weeks, night after night, Chad painstakingly made 35 valentines.

"Valentine's Day dawned, and Chad was beside himself with excitement! He carefully stacked them up, put them in a bag, and bolted out the door. His mom decided to bake him his favorite cookies and serve them up warm with a cold glass of milk when he came home from school. She just knew he would be disappointed...maybe that would ease the pain a little. It hurt her to think that he wouldn't get many valentines--maybe none at all.

"That afternoon she had the cookies and milk on the table. When she heard the children outside, she looked out the window. Sure enough, here they came, laughing and having the best time. And, as always, there was Chad in the rear. He walked a little faster than usual. She fully expected him to burst into tears as soon as he got inside. His arms were empty, she noticed, and when the door opened she choked back her own tears. 'Mommy has some warm cookies and milk for you.'

"But he hardly heard her words. He just marched right on by, his face aglow, and all he could say was, 'Not a one...not a one.'

"Her heart sank, but then he added, 'I didn't forget a one, not a single one!'"[2]

2. Give secretly, quietly, privately. Do not let others know what you are giving and doing. Keep it quiet--say nothing. Keep a low profile; stay out of the center ring of applause; avoid recognition if possible. Fleeing recognition is critical. The other members of a person's body--his hand, that is, his family--must not even know.

What is so desperately needed is a realistic view of the world. The world is a place of pain and suffering and sin and death--a world that needs to be saved and brought somehow to a state of incorruption. When a person faces the real truth of the world, he forgets himself and sets out to meet the needs of the world through the power of Christ. There is just no time for becoming entangled in the affairs of this world and seeking the applause of men. There is only time to minister. Taking time to applaud one another means there is another need that is going to be unmet.

There is only one right motive for giving and doing alms: to help those in need.
- ⇒ A person knows and lives with an awareness of the misery, misfortune, and desperate plight of the world.
- ⇒ A person loves and cares so much that he *wishes* to help those who need help.
- ⇒ A person literally *throws himself* into meeting the needs of the world and helping all he can.

APPLICATION:
There are three forceful lessons in this point.
1) A person is to be immersed in God and in the needs of the world. There is no time for centering attention upon himself if he wishes his life to be focused on God and to be spent saving his world.

---

[2] Charles Swindoll. *Improving Your Serve*, p. 92-93.

2) There is only one way the needs of the world will be met: we must all get out into the world where the needs are. There is no time for the right hand to be explaining and receiving applause from the left hand.

3) The servant of God is to be obsessed with his call and ministry to the world. He does not become entangled with the affairs of this world and the applause of men (2 Tim.2:4). He quietly and diligently goes about pouring himself into helping others.

> **"Jesus said unto him, If thou wilt be perfect, go and sell that thou hast, and give to the poor, and thou shalt have treasure in heaven: and come and follow me" (Mt.19:21).**
>
> **"Now when Jesus heard these things, he said unto him, Yet lackest thou one thing: sell all that thou hast, and distribute unto the poor, and thou shalt have treasure in heaven: and come, follow me" (Lk.18:22).**
>
> **"She stretcheth out her hand to the poor; yea, she reacheth forth her hands to the needy" (Pr.31:20).**

QUESTIONS:
1. What does it really mean for your left hand not to know what your right hand is doing?
2. How much thought do you need before you respond to an opportunity to give to the Lord's work? What kinds of things go through your mind as you decide to give or not to give?
3. What is the only right motive for giving and doing acts of righteousness?
4. What can you do to become better informed of the needs around you? What will it take to get you involved?

4. THE REASONS (v.4).

There are two reasons for doing good quietly and secretly.

1. God sees in secret. God sees secret giving and secret alms or deeds. Nothing passes His attention. He knows the motive and the acts of every man, every single motive and every single act.

> **"Can any hide himself in secret places that I shall not see him? saith the Lord. Do not I fill heaven and earth? saith the Lord" (Jer.23:24).**

APPLICATION:
Note the words "Thy Father." If God is truly a person's Father, then the person must give and do good just as his Father dictates. *Anything less is disobedience and displeasing.*

2. God rewards openly. Note the words, "[God] Himself shall reward thee openly."
   a. It is God Himself who shall reward a person.
   b. It is to be an open reward--a reward seen by all. A person is to have a personal moment before God when he shall receive his reward. This is the picture painted by Christ (cp. Mt.10:32; 1 Cor.4:5; Heb.11:6).

APPLICATION:
The faithful person will be rewarded as a son not as a servant. *His Father*, not *his Master*, will reward him.

"For if I do this thing willingly, I have a reward: but if against my will, a dispensation of the gospel is committed unto me" (1 Cor.9:17).

"Therefore, my beloved brethren, be ye stedfast, unmoveable, always abounding in the work of the Lord, forasmuch as ye know that your labour is not in vain in the Lord" (1 Cor.15:58).

ILLUSTRATION:

When God hands out rewards to His children, it is important to be in the right place. We can do a lot of good things in this life but still find ourselves sadly disappointed in the rewards they bring.

Most people can relate to the irritation that comes from picking the wrong line to stand in--at the bank, the grocery store, or a lane of busy traffic. But Dan had it all figured out. Standing in a line outside the pearly gates of heaven, he recalled the events of his life on earth. Dan was a respected community leader who served on all the important committees. It was true. Dan had done a lot of good things for people, but he always did it with one thing in mind: "What will it do for me?" As Dan looked around he noticed another line moving more quickly. He thought to himself, "Maybe I should change lines. I want to pick up my reward and get on with eternity."

Frustrated, Dan summoned an attending angel and said, "Hey, buddy! I've been waiting in line forever. Is there any way to get to the front of the line? I want to get my reward."

The angel checked his clipboard for Dan's name, frowned, and said, "I'm sorry sir. This line is for the folks who are getting rewards. According to my records you received your reward on earth." Dan reacted with disbelief, "What do you mean I've already received my reward!?" "Look, it says right here," replied the angel: "ALL GOOD DEEDS PAID IN FULL WITH THE PRAISES OF MEN. But that is the line you need to be in sir. It is the line for people who did everything for the wrong reasons."

When you get to heaven, will there be any rewards for you? Get in the right line while you can!

QUESTIONS:
1. How can you be quiet while doing good?
2. How can you make it your nature to give for the right reasons?
3. What rewards have you missed out on because of your failure to give in secret? What could you have done differently?

SUMMARY:

There are few things in life that bring greater joy to the believer than being a channel of blessing. The right motive makes that gift or act of service much sweeter. On the other hand, the wrong motive poisons the gift and the giver. Each one of us must strive to have the right motives as we give to the work of the Lord. These four points remind us just how critical this is:
1. Alms--doing good and giving.
2. The wrong motive.
3. The right motive.
   a. Giving unconsciously
   b. Giving quietly--privately--secretly

4. The reason.
   a. Father sees in secret
   b. Father rewards openly

PERSONAL JOURNAL NOTES:
(Reflection & Response)

1. The most important thing that I learned from this lesson was:

2. The thing that I need to work on the most is:

3. I can apply this lesson to my life by:

4. Closing Prayer of Commitment: (put your commitment down on paper).

	M. The Right Motive for Prayer (Part I), 6:5-6	of men. Verily I say unto you, They have their reward.	ognition c. Reward: Man's esteem

1. The wrong motive: Praying to be seen by men
a. Place: In public
  1) Only in the synagogue
  2) Only in the streets
b. Reason: For rec-
	5 And when thou prayest, thou shalt not be as the hypocrites are: for they love to pray standing in the synagogues and in the corners of the streets, that they may be seen	6 But thou, when thou prayest, enter into thy closet, and when thou hast shut thy door, pray to thy Father which is in secret; and thy Father which seeth in secret shall reward thee openly.	**2. The right motive: Praying to be heard by God**
			a. Place: In one's own closet or private place
			b. Reason: God is in one's secret or private place
			c. Reward: Will receive open blessings

Section IV
THE TEACHINGS OF THE MESSIAH TO HIS DISCIPLES:
THE GREAT SERMON ON THE MOUNT
Matthew 5:1-7:29

Study 13:   THE RIGHT MOTIVE FOR PRAYER (PART I)

Text: Matthew 6:5-6

Aim: To evaluate your prayer life in terms of *sincerity* and *motive*.

Memory Verse:
> **"But thou, when thou prayest, enter into thy closet, and when thou hast shut thy door, pray to thy Father which is in secret; and thy Father which seeth in secret shall reward thee openly" (Matthew 6:6).**

INTRODUCTION:
Why do people pray? Some people pray...
- because they are in a fix and want God to bail them out
- because they want to be perceived by others as *religious* or *pious* or *spiritual*
- because they have tried everything else and failed
- because they really want to commune with God and get to know Him better

But why do you pray? Or more importantly, *how* do you pray? How you answer these questions will go a long way toward examining your motives for prayer.

This passage is speaking to *those who do pray*--people who take prayer seriously. Prayer is one of the greatest acts of the Christian believer. Talking to God, whether by thought or tongue, is the way a believer fellowships with God; and the one thing God desires is fellowship with man (Is.43:10). Thus, it is essential that we pray and pray often, sharing all day long.

However, that we *do* pray is not the concern of Christ in this point. His concern is *how* we pray. It is possible to pray amiss, with the wrong motive and in the wrong way. It is possible to pray and never be heard by God. It is possible to pray and to be speaking only to ourselves, to have our prayer go no higher than our own ears. Therefore, Christ sets out to teach us the right and wrong motives for praying.

OUTLINE:
1. The wrong motive: praying to be seen by men (v.5).
2. The right motive: praying to be heard by God (v.6).

1. THE WRONG MOTIVE: PRAYER IS TO BE SEEN BY MEN (v.5).

Two preliminary things need to be looked at before discussing this point.
1. Praying--even loving to pray--is not a sign that a person really knows God.
2. The fact that a person really knows God means that he does pray. No matter what a man may think in his mind, if he really knows God and really believes in God, he talks to God. There is nothing that could keep him from praying. He knows God personally--knows Him as his Father who loves and cares for him ever so deeply. Therefore, just as any child who truly loves his father, the believer talks, converses, and shares with his Father.

This says something to the person who prays primarily in public and prays little, if any, in private. He must search the genuineness of his heart and profession.

Christ says that a man who prays to be seen by men *loves to pray, but he is a hypocrite.*
1. The places where he *loves* to pray are *out in public*, in the synagogue (church), and in the streets (restaurants, and other public places).

APPLICATION:
Note five lessons.
1) Some love to pray publicly. They love representing the group and vocalizing their praise and needs to God. Some have become very charismatic and fluent at public prayer, yet they lack that essential love for private praying. Christ says, "hypocrite" (v.5).
2) Some pray only in public. They pray before their family (at meals and family prayers, usually with children); in church (when called upon); and in public (when eating in restaurants). They seldom, if ever, pray in private. How destitute is the prayer life of so many!
3) Prayer is to be offered to God both in church and in public. But public prayer is to be public, not private. Too often a person has his *personal devotions* when called upon to pray publicly. He has neglected his *private prayers* and his inner need has not been met. Thus when he begins to pray publicly, he slips into praying his own *private prayer* instead of representing the group.
4) Some hypocrites pray and pray much. On the other hand, there are some *religious people* who pray little if any. They can learn from the hypocrites.
5) Note the posture of the hypocrite in v.5. He stood praying. This is an acceptable posture for prayer (Mk.11:25); but the picture is that of pride, arrogance, and self-confidence. Kneeling is a picture of humility, reverence, and dependence upon God (Lk.22:41; Eph.3:14).

> **"Be of the same mind one toward another, Mind not high things, but condescend to men of low estate. Be not wise in your own conceits" (Ro.12:16).**

2. The man who prays only in public prays for only one reason: not because he loves to pray but because he loves recognition.

APPLICATION:
Note two lessons.
1) The sin is not failing to pray. The sin is praying *only* in church and in public. A person who prays publicly but seldom prays privately fools himself. Christ says real prayer (prayer to the Father) matters nothing to that person. He prays only for recognition--to be heard by men.

2) Praying publicly should be done. There is a great danger, however, in public prayer: having one's pride stroked. It is so easy to be praying publicly and have self-centered thoughts run across one's mind...

- that one is really praying a good prayer. Such prayer is nothing but waxing eloquent with words
- that one's prayer will surely be admired
- that one's prayer is really demonstrating a close walk with God (a deep spirituality)

> **"Ye hypocrites, well did Esaias prophesy of you, saying, this people draweth nigh unto me with their mouth, and honoureth me with their lips; but their heart is far from me" (Mt.15:7-8).**

3. The man who prays only in public receives his reward: public recognition. Three things need to be clearly seen about this man.
   a. He will experience good feelings and satisfying thoughts about his spiritual state and religious piety. He will possess a good self-image and some confidence in his standing with God. The esteem and praise of men and feeling good about what he has done give him a good self image. *But,* in this case it is a false self-image.
   b. He has cheated himself, really missed out on the most intimate presence and greatest future in the universe. He has lost his soul. He shall never hear, "Well done thou good and faithful servant" (Mt.25:21).
   c. He gets just what he deserves: public recognition. If he places so little value upon sharing with God Himself, he deserves no more than what man can give him--human recognition.

APPLICATION:
Man's esteem fails at several points.
1) Man's esteem is temporary. Everything passes--ever so quickly. Man soon forgets and moves on to other things.
2) Man's esteem becomes commonplace. Even the greatest skills that elicit praise become routine and commonplace to man when performed day by day. Soon man no longer acknowledges his uniqueness. Such abilities are merely expected and accepted; he no longer elicits praise and recognition.
3) Man's esteem is powerless. It cannot answer prayer; it can only recognize man's ability to put words together and to see man's expression, fervency, and emotion. Its power is limited to the things of this world, and that power is even limited and short lived. Man's esteem can do absolutely nothing about the spiritual needs of his heart.
4) Man's esteem is not to be the judge of his life--God is. No man is any greater than any other man; men are mere men. All men have the same need: to turn to God in prayer, praying for His acceptance and recognition. Therefore, the esteem of man *by men* is meaningless in light of judgment and eternity.

> **"For all flesh is as grass, and all the glory of man as the flower of grass. The grass withereth, and the flower thereof falleth away" (1 Pt. 1:24).**

ILLUSTRATION:
A praying hypocrite can only hide his true motives for a short time. A quick change in this person's circumstances will expose him for all to see.

> *"Finding himself desperately in need of money, a man went to the city zoo, hoping to get a job feeding the animals. Although no such opportunity was available, the manager, seeing the size and the strength of the applicant, suddenly got an*

idea. 'You know,' he said, 'there are few creatures who attract attention like a gorilla. Unfortunately, ours died yesterday. If we got you a special fur suit, would you be willing to imitate him for a few days?' The hungry man agreed to try. He was quite successful as he beat his chest, bellowed, and shook the bars of his cage--much to the amusement of visitors who said they had never seen a gorilla with such intelligence. One day, while swinging on his trapeze, he accidentally lost his grip and landed in the lion's den. The huge beast gave a ferocious roar. Backing away, the impostor realized he couldn't cry for assistance without revealing that he was a fake. He retreated, hoping to crawl back over the fence into his own cage. The lion, however, followed him. Finally in desperation he yelled, 'HELP!' Immediately the lion said in an undertone, 'Shut up, stupid! You'll get us both fired!'"[1]

What kind of costume do you wear when you pray?

QUESTIONS:
1. Some of the most eloquent prayers are not sincere prayers. Flowery language and the tone of a person's voice have no bearing on a prayer's effectiveness. What kind of prayer does a believer need to offer up to God?
2. What causes a person to seek recognition with his prayers? How can you guard yourself from such a temptation?
3. When you are asked to make a public prayer, what should you consider before you pray out loud?

A CLOSER LOOK # 1

(6:5-8) **Prayer**: there are dangers surrounding prayer, some negative factors that must be guarded against.

1. Prayer can become hypocritical (v.5). A person can pray for the wrong reasons, with the wrong motives.

2. Prayer can become habit-forming (v.5). Prayer is a wonderful experience, very rewarding emotionally and mentally and in having our needs met as God answers our prayer. We can begin to *love praying* and still be praying amiss.

3. Prayer can become connected with certain places (v.5). A believer has places that mean much to him in his prayer life, but he must guard against limiting God's presence only to those places, even if it is the church.

4. Prayer can become empty repetition (v.7). A person can take any phrase or form of prayer and make it a meaningful experience, or make it a formal and meaningless occasion. (Note how often the Lord's Prayer is repeated by rote memory with the mind focused elsewhere.)

5. Prayer can become too long (v.7). A believer can begin to feel he is heard because of "much speaking" (cp. Eccl.5:1-2).

6. Prayer can become self-glorifying (v.8). A person can begin to feel he must inform and convince God of his *great* need. When the answer comes (out of the mercy of God, despite praying amiss), the believer begins to *glory in his spirituality*--that he has what it takes to get things from God.

7. Prayer can become self-deceptive (v.7-8). A person can begin to think he is heard (1) because of "much speaking," and (2) because he convinces God of his need.

[1] *INFOsearch Sermon Illustrations* (Arlington, TX: The Computer Assistant, 1-888-868-9029, 1986-1996).

QUESTIONS:
1. Many people assume that as long as you pray, that is all that matters. Why is this not true?
2. Look at the above list again. Which of these descriptions is a pitfall in your prayer life? What do you need to do to strengthen yourself in this area?

A CLOSER LOOK # 2

(6:5-6) **Prayer**: note several things.
1. Christ says "When thou prayest." He is referring to personal prayer (cp. v.6).
2. Christ assumes that the believer does pray, and the idea conveyed is that the believer prays often.
3. Christ says there is a right way and a wrong way to pray. "When thou prayest, thou shalt not...." vs. "But thou, when thou prayest...."
4. Christ says that some "love to pray," and they are the very ones who commit this fault. They pray amiss, with the wrong motive.
5. Christ pictures two men praying. One man prays to men (v.5); the other man prays to the Father (v.6). The first man is a hypocrite; the second man is a true son of the Father.

QUESTIONS:
1. Christ assumes that the believer does pray. Is this a correct assumption concerning you? How much do you pray?
2. How can you know that your motives are pure when you are praying?

2. THE RIGHT MOTIVE: PRAYING TO BE HEARD BY GOD (v.6).

Three preliminary things need to be looked at in this point.
1. The willingness to take time to pray: "When thou prayest." There has to be the will to pray. The believer must take time to get alone and pray. Too few ever take time to pray, and even fewer spend more than a few minutes in prayer. Too many stay all wrapped up in the world and its day-to-day affairs, some of which are necessary, but how much more necessary is prayer!
2. A closet is a necessity. The believer must have a private place deliberately chosen for prayer.
3. A personal relationship with God: a *Father-son* relationship is absolutely essential. God is our *Father*; He is available as all fathers are to be available to their children. We are to go to Him, pray, share, commune and let Him shower us with His care and protection, meeting our every need (Ps.91:1).

Note: Christ says that a man who is genuine prays to be heard by God and not by men.
⇒ The place he chooses for prayer is in his private closet. Christ says: "Get alone"; "Enter your closet...shut your door." (Cp. 2 Ki.4:33; Is.26:20.)

    a. *Get alone*: unobserved--out of everyone's sight.
    b. *Get alone*: undisturbed--avoid interruptions and disturbances.
    c. *Get alone*: unheard--concentrate and meditate to allow God the freedom to work in your heart as He wishes.

       "On the morrow, as they went on their journey, and drew nigh unto the city, Peter went up upon the housetop to pray about the sixth hour" (Acts 10:9).

"And in the morning, rising up a great while before day, he went out, and departed into a solitary place, and there prayed" (Mk.1:35).
"And it came to pass in those days, that he went out into a mountain to pray, and continued all night in prayer to God" (Lk.6:12).

⇒ The reason the believer prays in his private closet is because God is in secret (see note--Mt.6:4). Note two significant facts.

a. God "is in secret"; therefore, a person can meet God only in *secret*. Even in the midst of a worshipping crowd, a person must concentrate and focus his attention upon God who is unseen. There must be a secret heart-to-heart meeting and communion if a person wishes to pray and truly share with God.

b. God "is in secret"; therefore, He is not interested in show but in substance. Show is before men. Substance is found in the secret, quiet, meditative place. Remember: everything that exists began with an idea, and the development of the idea came from *private and quiet thought and meditation*, not out in the public before people-- at least not often. The same is true of spiritual matters. Spiritual show takes place before people, but spiritual substances or qualities that really matter take place in secret. The believer pours out his heart and receives his greatest encouragement and strength in the secret place of the Most High, not in the public places of mere man.

APPLICATION:

Many pray on the run; few pray in secret. Why do so few have a quiet time, a daily worship and devotional time? Why do so few keep their daily appointment with God? This is one of the most difficult things in the world to understand in light of who God is, and in light of man's desperate plight and need. No man would ever fail to keep his appointment with the state leader of his nation.

1) Many say they do not have the time, so they do not take the time. But in all honesty, it takes only a little effort to get up a while earlier in the morning--if they are really all that pressed for time. All they need to do is to rearrange their schedule to allow for a quiet time just as they arrange for any other important meeting. However, few do this; therefore, they are without excuse. Many believers are faithful in meeting God daily. It is just a matter of discipline and priority.

2) Most have the time; they just do not take the time. They neglect getting alone with God consistently.

3) Many have not been taught the importance and benefit of a quiet time with God every day. This is a justified accusation against Christian parents, preachers, and teachers. So few have practiced and stressed what they have always heard about the importance of prayer. The silence of believers and their failure to reach the world in sound doctrine is unbelievable, especially after two thousand years.

4) Some have not yet learned to discipline themselves and to be consistent in their spiritual lives. There is no better area to learn discipline and consistency than in a daily quiet time. A person should just begin and do it. When a day is missed, a person should flee discouragement, "forgetting those things which are behind," and reach forth to a new day and begin again. Eventually, consistency and discipline will be learned, and the person's soul will be fed with the "unsearchable riches of Christ" (Eph.3:8, 20; cp. Ph.3:13).

1. Where is the best place for you to get alone with God and pray? What time of the day is best for you? If you have not established a time and a place, why not? And why not start now?
2. What is your relationship with your heavenly Father?
   - Distant and abstract
   - It comes and goes according to my mood and my needs
   - Close and personal
3. How can you pray publicly and secretly at the same time?

⇒ The reward of the genuine prayer warrior is open blessings. The praying believer will be rewarded in two very special ways.
   a. The strength and presence of God will be upon his life (Ezra 8:22; 1 Pt.5:6). God's presence is unmistakable. There is a difference between a person who walks in God's presence and a person who walks only in this world (Mt.6:25-34, esp.33). God rewards the praying believer with His presence and blessings. The believer's needs, material and spiritual, are met day by day.
   b. The believer's prayers will also be answered (Mt.21:22; Jn.16:24; 1 Jn.5:14-15). The answers to prayer are clearly seen by a thinking and honest observer. God has promised to answer the true prayer of a genuine believer. God takes care of the genuine believer with a very special care. Sometimes the answer is seen...

   - in a renewed strength

       "Now unto him that is able to do exceeding abundantly above all that we ask or think, according to the power that worketh in us" (Eph.3:20).

   - in a provision of some necessity

       "But seek ye first the kingdom of God, and his righteousness; and all these things shall be added unto you" (Mt.6:33).

   - in a conquest of some great temptation or trial

       "There hath no temptation taken you but such as is common to man: but God is faithful, who will not suffer you to be tempted above that ye are able; but will with the temptation also make a way to escape, that ye may be able to bear it" (1 Cor.10:13).

   - in a peace that passes all human understanding

       "Be careful for nothing; but in every thing by prayer and supplication with thanksgiving let your request be made known unto God. And the peace of God, which passeth all understanding, shall keep your hearts and minds through Christ Jesus" (Ph.4:6-7).

   - in a soundness of mind that is incomprehensible

       "For God hath not given us the spirit of fear; but of power, and of love, and of a sound mind" (2 Tim.1:7).

APPLICATION:

The praying believer, the believer who becomes a true intercessor, will be rewarded openly on that special day of redemption.

1) God "wonders that there [is] no man, and...no intercessor" (Is.59:16).
2) Christ, the Great Intercessor, "ever liveth to make intercession for them" (Heb.7:25).
3) The interceding believer shall stand openly in a very special relationship with Jesus, the Great Intercessor Himself, before God the Father.

> "And all things, whatsoever ye shall ask in prayer, believing, ye shall receive" (Mt.21:22).
> "And I say unto you, Ask, and it shall be given you; seek, and ye shall find; knock, and it shall be opened unto you" (Lk.11:9).
> "And whatsoever ye shall ask in my name, that will I do, that the Father may be glorified in the Son. If ye shall ask any thing in my name, I will do it" (Jn.14:13-14).
> "If ye abide in me, and my words abide in you, ye shall ask what ye will, and it shall be done unto you" (Jn.15:7).

QUESTIONS:

1. In what ways does God reward the believer who fervently prays in secret? Have you ever experienced any of these rewards?
2. How can you know that God answers your prayers?

A CLOSER LOOK # 3

(6:5-6) **Prayer**: believers are expected to pray. Prayer is God's appointed medium through which He acts for man. *Sharing and talking* together is the way all persons communicate, fellowship, and commune together. This is true both with men and God. Prayer requires our presence, sharing, and talking; and God wants to fellowship and commune with us. Few persons heed this fact; few persons take prayer seriously. Therefore, if we want the blessings of God upon our lives and ministries--if we want the work of God going forth in power and bearing fruit--we must pray and we must intercede in prayer.

> "Pray to thy Father" (Mt.6:6; cp. Mt.6:7).
> "After this manner pray ye" (Mt.6:9).
> "Pray ye the Lord of the harvest" (Mt.9:38; Lk.10:2).
> "Watch and pray that ye enter not into temptation" (Mt.26:41; Mk.13:33; 14:38; Lk.21:36; 22:40, 46).
> "Men ought always to pray, and not to faint" (Lk.18:1).
> "Praying always with all prayer and supplication in the Spirit, and watching thereunto with all perseverance and supplication for all saints" (Eph.6:18).
> "Pray without ceasing" (1 Th.5:17).
> "I will that men pray everywhere" (1 Tim.2:8).

QUESTIONS:

1. Based on the amount of praying you do, would you say the lines of communication with God are...
    - ...wide open
    - ...only slightly ajar?
    - ...passable?
    - ...closed up tight?
2. What would happen to your prayer list if you made an even greater commitment to prayer?

A CLOSER LOOK # 4

(6:6) **Prayer**: "Your Father is in secret...." *Secret* means three things.

1. Concentration: meditation, contemplation, thinking deeply upon God and sharing accordingly.

2. Apart from all: secluded, alone, private, out of view from all.

3. Unseen: invisible, yet there; believing and having faith that God is there; spiritual, but still hearing and responding. Every believer should have a secret, quiet place that is dear to his heart, dear because it is the place where he draws near God and God draws near him.

ILLUSTRATION:

What kinds of results do your prayers produce? Prayer is never a waste of time if we focus our thoughts and our prayers on the God of the universe.

> *Little Billy had a habit of straying from his parents whenever they visited a toy store. The sights and sounds were too much for him to resist and so down the isle he went. Late one afternoon, Billy took a quick left turn while his parents went straight ahead. Billy had a great time for a while, until he noticed the empty isles and the lights going down. As the lights dimmed, a sweet voice over the intercom said, "Shoppers, our store is now closing. Please bring all purchases to the front of the store."*
>
> *Billy started to look for his parents, but they were nowhere to be seen. Worry replaced his excitement. With tears in his eyes, Billy prayed sincerely, "God, my parents are lost. Please help them to be found." At that moment, a deep voice came over the intercom, "Billy your parents are waiting for you at the front of the store." "Thanks God!" Billy exclaimed, "for speaking so quickly."*

If your prayer is sincere, you too can be assured that God will hear and answer it. But God answers our prayers in many ways. Are you listening?

SUMMARY:

The prayer life of the believer must be driven by a pure motive, the desire to glorify God alone. Prayer is a potent tool in the believer's arsenal. Used properly, it is powerful and beneficial. The wrong use of prayer is also powerful but very destructive. Remember these key points:

1. The wrong motive: praying to be seen by men.
2. The right motive: praying to be heard by God.

PERSONAL JOURNAL NOTES:
(Reflection & Response)

1. The most important thing that I learned from this lesson was:

2. The thing that I need to work on the most is:

3. I can apply this lesson to my life by:

4. Closing Prayer of Commitment: (put your commitment down on paper).

	N. The Three Great Rules for Prayer, (Part II), 6:7-8
1. Rule 1: Do not use empty repetition	7 But when ye pray, use not vain repetitions, as the heathen do: for they think that they shall be heard for their much speaking.
2. Rule 2: Do not speak much	
3. Rule 3: Trust God a. He knows your needs b. He desires to hear your prayer	8 Be not ye therefore like unto them: for your Father knoweth what things ye have need of, before ye ask him.

Section IV
THE TEACHINGS OF THE MESSIAH TO HIS DISCIPLES:
THE GREAT SERMON ON THE MOUNT
Matthew 5:1-7:29

Study 14: **THE THREE GREAT RULES FOR PRAYER (PART II)**

Text: Matthew 6:7-8

Aim: To learn and then apply the basic rules of prayer: To learn how to pray more and more effectively (Part 1).

Memory Verse:
"But when ye pray, use not vain repetitions, as the heathen do: for they think that they shall be heard for their much speaking" (Matthew 6:7).

INTRODUCTION:
Think for a moment of your favorite sport. What would happen if everyone playing made up his own rules as he went along? Suppose your favorite game was basketball. How effective would the game be...
- if the shooter was tackled?
- if the backboard had no rim?
- if the other team kicked the ball instead of dribbling it?

The game would be a strange mixture of chaos and confusion. In short, the game would lose its focus. In much the same way, many believers toss aside the basic rules of prayer and do whatever they feel will impress God, or other people, the most.

Among the religious there is often a tendency toward long prayers, particularly in public. Too often people measure prayer by its fluency and length, thinking that length means devotion. **"Be not rash with thy mouth, and let not thine heart be hasty to utter anything before God; for God is in heaven, and thou upon earth; therefore let thy words be few"** (Eccl.5:2). Christ puts the matter very simply, yet strongly: "When ye pray," follow three great rules.

Among the religious there is often a tendency toward long prayers, particularly in public. Too often people measure prayer by its fluency and length, thinking that length means devotion. **"Be not rash with thy mouth, and let not thine heart be hasty to utter anything be-**

fore God; for God is in heaven, and thou upon earth; therefore let thy words be few" (Eccl.5:2). Christ puts the matter very simply, yet strongly: "When ye pray," follow three great rules.

OUTLINE:
1. Rule 1: do not use empty repetition (v.7).
2. Rule 2: do not speak much (v.7).
3. Rule 3: trust God (v.8).

1. RULE 1: DO NOT USE EMPTY REPETITION (v.7).

The first great rule of prayer is: do not use empty repetition. There are several things that lend themselves to empty repetition.

1. *Memorized prayer*: just saying the words of a form prayer, for example, the Lord's prayer. There is nothing wrong with praying a memorized prayer, but it should be prayed through and not just repeated with no thought behind the words.

2. *Written, well-worded prayers*: thinking that what we say is so expressive and so well worded it is bound to carry weight with God. The words may be descriptive and beautifully arranged, but the heart must be offering the prayer not the mind and ego. Such prayer is empty repetition.

3. *Ritual prayer*: saying the same prayer at the same time on the same occasion--over and over again. This can soon become empty repetition.

4. *Formal worship*: praying in the same way on a rigid schedule can lead to praying by habit (repeated practice) with little or no meaning to it.

5. *Thoughtless prayer*: speaking words while our minds are wandering. Being tired is no excuse. It is better not to pray than to pray insincerely.

6. *Religious words and phrases*: using certain words or phrases over and over in prayer (just because they are religious sounding). (Compare using such words over and over as *mercy, grace, I thank thee O God, in Jesus' name*.)

7. *Habitual references to God*: using empty repetition such as "Lord this," and "Lord that," and "Lord...," "Lord...," "Lord...." How little thought is really given to approaching Him whose name is "Wonderful, Counsellor, The Mighty God, The Everlasting Father, The Prince of Peace" (Is.9:6).

There are several things that will keep us from using empty repetition in prayer.
1. A genuine heart: really knowing God personally and having a moment by moment fellowship with Him all day long.
2. Thought and concentration: really focusing upon what we are saying.
3. Desire for fellowship with God: praying sincerely, really meaning it.
4. Preparation: preparing ourselves for prayer by first meditating in God's Word.

Note something of extreme importance in discussing "vain repetition." Christ does not say repetition in prayer is wrong. It is not wrong. What is wrong is vain, empty, meaningless, foolish repetition. Christ Himself used repetition in prayer (Mt.26:44); so did Daniel (Dan.9:18-19), and so did the Psalmist (Ps.136:1f).

APPLICATION:
Note six lessons.
1) There is one major problem with the praying of believers: they do not pray enough. They do not take enough time to pray and to pray in earnest.

There is one major problem *when believers do pray*: prayer is often vain, empty, thoughtless, meaningless, and repetitive. Too often a believer prays and does not concentrate. His mind wanders off somewhere else; he only mouths the words.

Such thoughtless and meaningless prayer is clearly seen in public prayer and in the powerlessness of believers today.

2) There is one sure way to prepare our hearts for prayer: meditating in God's Word.

"All Scripture is given by inspiration of God, and is profitable for doctrine, for reproof, for correction, for instruction in righteousness" (2 Tim.3:16).

It is in the Scripture that the believer learns about God, himself, and the world-- the nature and truth of all things. It is the Spirit of God who takes the Word of God and moves upon the believer's heart, revealing that for which the believer should pray. Therefore, the believer is stirred to pray for whatever the Word of God and the Spirit of God has shown him (Ro.8:26; cp. Jn.14:26; 16:13; 1 Cor.2:12-13).

3) Vain repetition in prayer, whether formal or thoughtless, is *dull*.
    ⇒ It discourages the sincere and the newly converted.
    ⇒ It cools the willing and the gifted.
    ⇒ It stifles the committed and the mature.
    ⇒ It turns away the seeking and the lost.

4) Vain repetition is tragic. Prayer should be one of the most meaningful experiences in life. God is certainly willing to meet the believer in a very special way--anytime, anyplace. So many hearts are just...

• barren	• dry	• desolate
• dull	• hard	• corroded
• complacent	• lethargic	• still

So much praying is merely going over and over the same things ranging from "bless Mom and Dad" to "give us a good day tomorrow."

5) Empty repetition turns God away and cuts the heart of the committed.

"Having a form of godliness [long prayers], but denying the power thereof: from such turn away" (2 Tim.3:5).
"Ye hypocrites, well did Esaias prophesy of you, saying, this people draweth nigh unto me with their mouth, and honoureth me with their lips; but their heart is far from me" (Mt.15:7-8).

QUESTIONS:
1. Do you ever fall into the habit of empty repetition when praying?
2. What is the logical consequence that happens to the person who prays in "vain repetition?"
3. Before you pray, what should you do to prepare your heart? What *do* you do?

2. RULE 2: DO NOT SPEAK MUCH (v.7).

The second great rule of prayer is an eye-opener: do not speak much. Too many think that length equals devotion; that is, the longer they pray the more God will listen to them, and the more spiritual they will become.

God does not hear a person's prayer because it is long, but because his heart is genuinely poured out to God. Length has nothing to do with devotion, but a sincere heart does.

Long prayers are not forbidden. What is forbidden is the idea that long prayers are automatically heard by God. Christ prayed all night (Lk.6:12). The early disciples prayed and fasted, seeking God for ten days and nights while waiting for the coming of the Holy Spirit (Acts 2:1f). A believer should sense the needs of the world so much that he is driven to seek

God and His intervention for long periods of time, and the seeking should be often (Eph. 6:18).

1. Why do some pray long prayers?
   ⇒ Some feel long prayers convince God. They feel God has to be moved, nudged, and stirred to hear and answer.
   ⇒ Some feel they need long prayers to explain the situation. They feel God needs to be informed and made to understand a particular situation and how it has affected them.
   ⇒ Some feel long prayers make them more spiritual, more mature, and more devoted.
   ⇒ Some feel long prayers are just demanded of believers. It is expected; it is the religious and godly thing to do.
   ⇒ Some feel long prayers show God their sincerity. They secure God's approval by long prayers.
   ⇒ Some feel long prayers impress people. They show people just how deeply spiritual they really are.

2. What are ways to prevent the sins that arise from long prayers?

   "Be not rash with thy mouth, and let not thine heart be hasty to utter anything before God: for God is in heaven, and thou upon earth: therefore let thy words be few" (Eccl.5:2).

   ⇒ "Be not rash with thy mouth." Control your mouth. Do not let your mouth rattle on and on without thought. It will often rush and hurry with every thought that crosses your mind.
   ⇒ Be not "hasty to utter anything before God": sit still; be quiet, without saying a word for awhile. Do not rush forward to speak.
   ⇒ Think about who God is. Picture a man: his mouth is quiet; he has been still for some time. He has been preparing, gaining control of his mind and thoughts so he can appear before the Sovereign Majesty of the universe. He focuses his thoughts upon God, the One who is in heaven far above the earth. He meditates upon God's sovereignty and majesty. God is the center of his thoughts (Ps.46:10).
   ⇒ "Let thy words be few." Speak, but make your words deliberate--just as deliberate as the words of any interviewer before a sovereign ruler. Request--just as any obedient son would request of a revered father. The person who approaches God like this speaks with respect and thought, with care and love. He speaks few words and straight to the point--all from a prepared heart and mind.

3. When should the believer spend a long time in prayer? There *are* special times when an extended prayer time is necessary. Some of the times are clearly seen in Scripture.
   ⇒ Sometimes a special pull to praise and adore God is felt within. When the believer feels this pull, he should get alone and spend a long time praising and worshipping God (cp. Acts 16:25).
   ⇒ Sometimes a special need arises. This may be the believer's own need or a friend's need. He should intercede until God gives the assurance that the need will be met (Eph.6:18; cp. Acts 12:1-5, esp. v.5).
   ⇒ Sometimes an unusual experience or event has taken place or is about to take place in the believer's life or ministry. He should get alone and share the event with God. And he should stay before God until the experience has taken place (courage, confidence, power, faith, love).
   ⇒ Sometimes a great trial or temptation is faced. A long session of prayer may be needed to gain strength and to keep the believer away from the trial or temptation.

⇒ Sometimes a matter needs to be worked through or a major decision needs to be made. Help and direction should be sought from God. God should be acknowledged in all the believer's ways. He should remain before God until the answer is given. (Cp. Acts 13:1-3, esp. 2.)

APPLICATION 1:

Prayer is a matter of the heart not a matter of words and length. Praying is sharing; it is sharing with God just like a person shares with any other person. Just as he shares thoughts, feelings, praise, and requests with others, so he shares with God.

APPLICATION 2:

Prayer is a personal relationship. Prayer is not speaking into thin air. God may be "in secret" (v.6); He may be invisible, but He is there. He is there more than any other person who may be in our presence. He is the One whom all men are to know and to whom all men are to be vitally related. Too often, the awareness and consciousness of His presence are allowed to fade, and we just go through our long prayer with a wandering mind leaping from thought to thought. Long prayers lend themselves to this danger. How insincere! How irreverent! How often the heart of God must be cut and hurt!

APPLICATION 3:

There are prayers of believers and prayers of the heathen. A distinction is made by Christ Himself. He says that both pray.
1) The heathen pray using vain repetition and speaking empty words.
2) The believer is vitally related to God; therefore, he prays to God who is his Father. He prays to God just as a son shares with his revered father.

"Woe unto you, scribes and Pharisees, hypocrites! for ye devour widows' houses, and for a pretense make long prayer: therefore ye shall receive the greater damnation" (Mt.23:14).

"All the labor of man is for his mouth, and yet the appetite is not filled" (Eccl.6:7).

ILLUSTRATION:

Have you ever listened to someone who prays in public, prays a long and beautiful prayer, only to wonder at the end, "What did he say?" Here is one absurd example that makes the point clear.

"One day in church, an attorney was heard to pray: 'We respectively request, and entreat, that due and adequate provisions be made this day and the date hereinafter subscribed, for the organizing of such methods and allocations and distribution as may be deemed necessary to properly assure the reception by and for said petitioner of such quantities of baked cereal grain products as shall, in the judgment of the aforementioned parishioners, constitute a sufficient supply thereof.'
"What ever happened to 'Give us this day our daily bread'?"[1]

QUESTIONS:
Do you ever feel...
...that short prayers are not as effective as long prayers?
...that you must pray the same length of time as someone else?
...that you may as well not pray if you can't spend a long time in prayer?
What is the root problem with all these feelings? How can you guard against this pitfall?

---

[1] *Holy Humor*. Compiled by Cal and Rose Samra. (Mastermedia Limited, 1996), p. 118. As cited in *INFOsearch Sermon Illustrations* (Arlington, TX: The Computer Assistant, 1-888-868-9029, 1986-1996).

3. RULE 3: TRUST GOD (v.8).

The third great rule of prayer is forceful: trust God.
1. God knows the believer's need even before the believer asks. Why then should the believer pray?

Prayer demonstrates our need for God and our dependence upon God. Prayer gives time for concentrated sharing and communion between the believer and God. It is not enough for man to carry a knowledge of God in his mind as he walks through life. Man needs to have times when he is in the presence of God and can concentrate his thoughts and fellowship upon God. He needs such time with God just as he needs such time with his family and friends. Man is not meant to live in isolation from people nor from God. He must have times when he is in the presence of both man and God and can concentrate his thoughts and attention upon both.

The believer, therefore, does not pray only to have his needs met, but to share, to fellowship, and to enrich his life with God.

APPLICATION 1:
God knows the believer's needs. The believer does not have to worry about God knowing or meeting his needs. The believer's concern should be living in the presence of God, taking enough time to share and to fellowship with God. The more he shares and fellowships with God, the more he will know God, learning to trust and depend upon God's care and promises.

APPLICATION 2:
God is the believer's Father. The believer is God's son. The believer can, therefore, *rest* in God and His promises. He does not have to strain and pray long in order for his Father to hear him. His Father already knows and cares. He is to get with His Father for long periods of time sharing and fellowshipping, learning and getting to know his Father intimately.

2. God desires to hear. God knows the believer's need even before the believer asks (cp. 2 Chron.16:9; Is.65:24). God desires to hear and answer the believer's prayer, to meet the believer's needs. God desires to work for the believer's deliverance and salvation (see Ro.8:23-27; 8:28-39. This is one of the great passages on assurance and confidence.)
3. God has ordained prayer as the medium through which He blesses and moves among men.

> **"Oh how great is thy goodness, which thou hast laid up for them that fear thee; which thou hast wrought for them that trust in thee before the sons of men!" (Ps.31:19).**
> **"Many sorrows shall be to the wicked: but he that trusteth in the Lord, mercy shall compass him about" (Ps.32:10).**

ILLUSTRATION:
The believer who does not beat around the bush, who gets to the heart of the matter and goes to God in prayer, is the one who will get results.

> *"A group of scientists and botanists were exploring remote regions of the Alps in search of new species of flowers. One day they noticed through binoculars a flower of such rarity and beauty that its value to science was incalculable. But it lay deep in a ravine with cliffs on both sides. To get to the flower someone had to be lowered over the cliff on a rope.*

"A curious young boy was watching nearby, and the scientists told him they would pay him well if he would agree to be lowered over the cliff to retrieve the flower below.

"The boy took one long look down the steep, dizzy depths and said, 'I'll be back in a minute.' A short time later he returned, followed by a gray-haired man. Approaching the botanist, the boy said, 'I'll go over that cliff and get that flower for you if this man holds the rope. He's my dad.'"[2]

God is the believer's Father. He is the One who matters most. He is the One to trust.

QUESTIONS:

1. Why is it sometimes so difficult to trust in God for answers instead of man?
2. If a person trusts God, really trusts in Him, what are the great benefits promised by God?
3. When you pray, how aware are you that God is *listening* to you? How can you build your faith in this area of Christian growth?

SUMMARY:

The rules of prayer are quite simple if you will only listen to what God has said. Long and flowery speeches are not what God has in mind for His people who pray. You can say a lot more, using less words, and get a whole lot more done when you remember these three basic rules of prayer.

1. Rule 1: do not use empty repetition.
2. Rule 2: do not speak much.
3. Rule 3: trust God.

PERSONAL JOURNAL NOTES:
(Reflection & Response)

1. The most important thing that I learned from this lesson was:

2. The thing that I need to work on the most is:

3. I can apply this lesson to my life by:

4. Closing Prayer of Commitment: (put your commitment down on paper).

---

[2]   *Our Daily Bread*, Volume 40, Number 12; Volume 41 Numbers 1,2, p. April 8, 1996.

	O. The Model Prayer (Part III), 6:9-13 (Lk.11:2-4)	in heaven. 11 Give us this day our daily bread.	b. For God's will c. For daily bread
1. There is surrender a. To our Father in heaven b. To God's holy name 2. There is request & plea a. For God's kingdom	9 After this manner therefore pray ye: Our Father which art in heaven, Hallowed be thy name. 10 Thy kingdom come. Thy will be done in earth, as it is	12 And forgive us our debts, as we forgive our debtors. 13 And lead us not into temptation, but deliver us from evil: For thine is the king-dom, and the power, and the glory, for ever. Amen.	d. For forgiveness e. For deliverance 3. There is praise & commitment

Section IV
THE TEACHINGS OF THE MESSIAH TO HIS DISCIPLES:
THE GREAT SERMON ON THE MOUNT
Matthew 5:1-7:29

Study 15:   THE MODEL PRAYER (PART III)

Text: Matthew 6:9-13

Aim: To learn and then apply the basic rules of prayer: To learn how to pray more and more effectively (Part 2).

Memory Verses:
"**After this manner therefore pray ye: Our Father which art in heaven, Hallowed be thy name. Thy kingdom come. Thy will be done in earth, as** *it is* **in heaven. Give us this day our daily bread. And for-give us our debts, as we forgive our debtors. And lead us not into temp-tation, but deliver us from evil: For thine is the kingdom, and the power, and the glory, for ever. Amen**" **(Matthew 6:9-13).**

INTRODUCTION:
For many people (including some believers), prayer is a watered-down ritual carried out with no conviction. Why is this? The further people get away from the Scriptures, the fur-ther people are removed from Biblical prayer and its power.
⇒ Many people pray selfishly.
⇒ Many people pray not wanting to offend.
⇒ Many people pray for their own will not God's will
⇒ Many people pray strictly according to their circumstances, not by the leading of the Holy Spirit.
⇒ Many people pray in a way that says nothing and means even less.

This humorous but frightfully modern rendition of the "Politically Correct Lord's Prayer" gives a striking example of just how far things can get out of hand.

"*Our universal chairperson in outer space, your identity enjoys the highest rating on a prioritized selectivity scale. May your sphere of influence take on reality parameters; may your mindset be implemented on this planet as in outer space.*
"*Allot to us at this point in time and on a per diem basis, a sufficient and balanced dietary food intake, and rationalize a disclaimer against out negative feedback as we rationalize the negative feedback of others.*

"And deprogram our negative potentialities, but desensitize the impact of the counterproductive force. For yours is the dominant sphere of influence, the ultimate capability and the highest qualitative analysis rating, at this point in time and extending beyond a limited time-frame. End of message."[1]

Jesus Christ has given us the Lord's Prayer as a pattern to keep us on track--even when the rest of the world goes off the deep end.

What is the Lord's prayer? Is it a prayer to be recited as it so often is--just by memory, or just as a form prayer?

Note the words "After this manner...pray ye." Note also Luke's account where the disciples asked Jesus to teach them to pray (Lk.11:1-2). The prayer was given to show the disciples *how to pray*, not the *words* they should pray. The context of what Christ had just taught shows this very clearly (cp. Mt.6:5-8).

OUTLINE:
1. There is surrender and acknowledgment (v.9).
2. There is request and plea (v.10-13).
3. There is praise and commitment (v.13).

1. THERE IS SURRENDER (v.9).

The believer's prayer is to be a surrender.
1. There is the surrender of the believer *to God and to God's family.*
   a. When a person genuinely says "Father," he is surrendering to God. He is...
      - denying humanism, self-sufficiency, and all other gods.
      - surrendering himself to the Father of the Lord Jesus Christ.
      - acknowledging the Father of the Lord Jesus Christ to be his own Father.
   b. When a person prays "<u>our</u> Father," a person is surrendering his independence and accepting God's family as his own. He is assuming his responsibility in the family of God.
2. There is the surrender of the believer to *heaven*, the spiritual world or dimension of being. The believer surrenders and sets his mind and heart upon the Kingdom of God and His righteousness. His whole being is surrendered and committed to seeking the things of the spiritual world.
3. There is the surrender of the believer to the *holy name of God*. The believer just bows in total and abject poverty, in nothingness before the holy name of God. He is swallowed up in the knowledge of the "hallowedness," the sovereignty and majesty of God's being. God is all and man is nothing! He is totally dependent upon God.
Note: when a person reaches this point of surrender, then he is ready to present his needs to God. He is ever so conscious that only God can meet his needs.

QUESTIONS:
1. Why is it necessary to surrender in order to get results?
2. Of all the things you have had to surrender to God in prayer, what was the most difficult and why?
3. Why do you think it is so hard for people to surrender to God?

---

[1]   Cal and Rose Samra. *More Holy Humor*, p.67-68.

A CLOSER LOOK # 1

(6:9-13) **Prayer**: What is prayer?

1. Prayer is sharing and fellowshipping with God (Mt.6:9). It is not enough for a person to have a knowledge of God as he walks through life. He needs to have times when he can get alone with God and concentrate his thoughts and attention upon God. He needs such times with God just as he needs such times with his family and friends. Man was not made to live in isolation from people nor from God. He must have times when he is in the presence of both man and God and can concentrate his thoughts and attention upon both.

2. Prayer is surrendering to God (Mt.6:9). The believer surrenders himself and his time to God. There is no such thing as prayer without a person and time. A person must submit himself to God before he wills to pray, and even then he must take the time to pray. A person who has surrendered himself to God and is surrendering or taking his time to talk with God is praying.

3. Prayer is requesting and pleading with God (Mt.6:10). It is demonstrating one's need and dependence upon God. It is pouring out one's heart in need and trusting God to meet one's need.

4. Prayer is acknowledging and praising God (Mt.6:9-10, 13). It is acknowledging God as the Sovereign and Majestic Lord to whom belongs the kingdom, the power, and the glory, forever.

A CLOSER LOOK # 2

(6:9) **God--Father**: God is addressed as "Our Father." Father denotes a family relationship and shows three things.

1. It shows that "God [who is]...in heaven" is the believer's Father. Thus, a relationship with the unseen heavenly world and the seen earthly world is established. God represents the unseen world and the believer represents the seen world. In the believer a whole new being is created (a new creature) and a whole new world is recognized and established: a world of the spirit and the physical, of the unseen and the seen, of heaven and earth (2 Cor.5:17; Eph.4:23-24; Col.4:10).

2. The word "Father" establishes a relationship between a believer and all other believers. All believers belong to the same family; they all have common interests, cares, and responsibilities within the family.

3. The word "Father" pinpoints God as the believer's source. God, as Father, is the Person who loves and provides and cares for the believer's needs, even as an earthly father looks after his child (Mt.6:25-34, esp.33; Lk.11:11-13; Ps.103:13; Mal.3:17; cp. Heb.2:18; 4:15-16).

APPLICATION 1:

"Our Father" is the first point to pray. The believer is to pray "after this manner."

⇒ "Father, thank you <u>for yourself</u>: that you are <u>our Father</u>...."
⇒ "Thank you for adopting us as children of God: that you have chosen us...."
⇒ "Thank you for 'the household of faith,' for the 'family of God'...."

APPLICATION 2:

The phrase "Our Father" says three things about prayer.

1) The believer is not always to pray alone. The word "our" shows this. Whereas Christ has just taught that a person should pray in private. He now says there are times when a person should pray with others. God is "our Father."

2) The believer is taught to whom to pray: to God and to Him alone.

3) The believer is taught to address God as "Father." He is taught what his relationship to God is to be, that of a child to a Father. There is one time in particular when the believer must approach God as Father: when returning to God and repenting of sin (cp. the prodigal son, Lk.15:18).

> **"If ye then, being evil, know how to give good gifts unto your children, how much more shall your Father which is in heaven give good things to them that ask him? " (Mt.7:11).**
> **"And if ye call on the Father, who without respect of persons judgeth according to every man's work, pass the time of your sojourning here in fear" (1 Pt.1:17).**

APPLICATION 3:

God is "<u>our</u> Father." God has no favorites: "God is no respecter of persons" (Acts 10:34).

1) God is "our Father" by creation; that is, He is the Father of all men everywhere because He is the Creator of all men (Gen.1:1; Mal.2:10; Is.64:8; Acts 27:28). It settles a person's relationship with himself. Every person fails and comes short, and sometimes he gets down on himself. He feels like a failure--hopeless, helpless, worthless, useless. "Our Father" says that such a person matters; he always matters to God. He can come to the Father and share his concerns.

2) God is "our Father" by re-creation (2 Cor.5:17) and adoption (Gal.4:5-6; cp. Eph.1:5). He is "our Father" to all who believe in the Lord Jesus Christ and the redemption that is in Him (Eph.2:19).

> **"For ye have not receive the spirit of bondage again to fear; but ye have received the Spirit of adoption, whereby we cry, Abba, Father" (Ro.8:15).**

QUESTIONS:

1. When you pray, do you talk to God as a Father? Or do you address Him as One who is far off, unapproachable, unreal?
2. What are some traits of your heavenly Father that draw you to confide and depend upon Him?
3. Do unbelievers have the privilege of calling God "Father"? Why or why not? How can you explain this to an unbeliever?

A CLOSER LOOK # 3

(6:9) **Heaven**: the word is plural in the Greek, heavens. The New Testament speaks of at least three heavens:

⇒ the atmosphere surrounding the earth (cp. Mt.6:26, "the birds of the heaven").
⇒ the outer space of heavenly bodies (cp. Mt.24:29; Rev.6:13).
⇒ the place above and beyond the physical dimension of being where God's presence is fully manifested. In modern language "the above and beyond" is another dimension of being entirely; it is *the spiritual world, another dimension of being*. It is a spiritual world where God's presence is fully manifested, and where Christ and His followers live awaiting the glorious day of redemption. That glorious day of redemption is the day when God shall take the imperfect heavens and earth (the physical dimension) and transform them into the new heavens and earth (the spiritual and eternal dimension).

APPLICATION 1:

"Our Father...in heaven" is the second point to be prayed. The believer is to pray "after this manner":

⇒ "Father, thank you for heaven: the hope, the anticipation of heaven...."
⇒ "Thank you that you are in heaven...."
⇒ "Thank you for your promise that we shall be where you are...." (Jn.17:24).

APPLICATION 2:

Note several lessons.

1) The believer must direct his prayers to heaven. God's throne is in heaven (Ps.103:19), and it is before the throne of God that Christ is appearing as the Advocate or Mediator for the believer.

"But he, being full of the Holy Ghost, looked up stedfastly into heaven, and saw the glory of God, and Jesus standing on the right hand of God, and said, Behold, I see the heavens opened, and the Son of man standing on the right hand of God" (Acts 7:55-56).

2) How should we approach God? The words "Our Father...in heaven" tell us.
   a) "Father" says that we can approach Him boldly to "find grace to help in time of need" (Heb.4:16).
   b) "In heaven" says that we are to approach respectfully, in reverence and fear and awe (Ps.111:9; cp. Eccl.5:2).
3) The heavens reveal the power and glory of God. Space shows His handiwork (Ps.19:1; 150:1). When connected together, the words "Our Father" and the words "in heaven" put two great things together: the love of God and the power of God. God through love has become "our Father," and "God in heaven" has shown His glorious power which is at the disposal of His child. The believer's Father has the power to do anything, even to hang the world in space (Eph.3:20; Ps.121:1-8).
4) The believer's true citizenship is in heaven (Ph.3:20). God is there; the Lord Jesus is also there (Heb.8:1; cp. Ps.103:19). Therefore, the longing of the mature believer's heart is to be in heaven where His Father and His Lord are. He directs his attention, prayers, energy, and life toward heaven.

"Notwithstanding in this rejoice not, that the spirits are subject unto you; but rather rejoice, because your names are written in heaven" (Lk.10:20).
"In my Father's house are many mansions: if it were not so, I would have told you. I go to prepare a place for you" (Jn.14:2).

5) God sees all from heaven (Ps.33:13-19).
   ⇒ He sees all the sons of men.
   ⇒ He looks upon all the inhabitants of the earth.
   ⇒ He considers all their works.

However, there is one thing in particular that God sees: the person who fears Him and hopes in His mercy. He sees this person in order to deliver his soul from death (Ps.33:18-19). This is one of the prime reasons the believer is to keep his eyes upon heaven.

QUESTIONS:

1. What is the significance of your Father being in heaven versus man-made gods being scattered all over the earth?

2. Does God's being in heaven diminish His presence on earth (Omnipresence)? Does His being in heaven place Him far off in outer space someplace, make Him unapproachable, far, far removed from us? Why or why not?

A CLOSER LOOK # 4

(6:9) **Hallowed be:** to be counted and treated as holy; to be counted and treated as different. Men are to count and treat the name of God differently, to set His name apart from all other names.

APPLICATION:

"Hallowed be thy name" is the third point to be prayed. The believer is to pray "after this manner":

⇒ "Father, hallowed is your name. Your name is holy, set apart, different from all other names. There is none but you...you and you alone. You are above, before, over all...."

Note several lessons.

1) God's name is holy, righteous, pure. Therefore, the believer's prayer is for God's name to be adored and honored by all men.

2) The first thing prayer should do is praise and glorify God. That is the point Christ is making in the words...
   - "Our Father...
   - which art in heaven...
   - hallowed be thy name."

God has done everything; He has made the world and given life to it. Man owes his very life to God. Therefore, the first thing man should do is praise God.

"Every good gift and every perfect gift is from above" (Jas.1:17).

3) The first purpose of man is to glorify God by his life: "Be ye holy; for I am holy" (1 Pt.1:15-16). Life includes speech; therefore, man should be praising God's holiness by word as well as by life. In fact, since the primary purpose of man is to be holy, then it follows that the first words spoken to God should be praising His holiness. All prayer should be centered around praising God for who He is--in all His holiness and fulness. His name is "hallowed," different, set apart form all other names. And thank God that His name is set apart, for imagine what life would be if His name should be no more than a man's name.

"If in this life only we have hope in Christ, we are of all men most miserable" (1 Cor.15:19).

4) God's glory is the very reason Christ came to earth (Jn.17:1-26, esp. vs.1, 4-6, 22-26). God says He shall be exalted in the earth even among the heathen (Ps.46:10; cp. Ps.2:1-5, esp. vs.4-5). How much man needs to fix his mind upon the holiness and glory of God's name!

"For thus saith the high and lofty One that inhabiteth eternity, whose name is Holy; I dwell in the high and holy place, with him also that is of a contrite and humble spirit, to revive the spirit of the humble, and to revive the heart of the contrite ones" (Is.57:15).

5) Men praise and honor each other. Men glorify men, even make idols of them. Some are more loyal to the names of the famous (athletes, stars, politicians) than they are to the name of God. They are more disturbed when the name of their idol is spoken of disrespectfully than when the name of God is cursed. How differently Scripture presents God's name: "Hallowed be thy name." God says that the man who curses His name is to be judged severely (Ex.20:7).

QUESTIONS:
1. Do you treat God's name as holy? Or do you sometimes carelessly and loosely use His name? What can you do to honor His name more fully, to keep His name from ever being defiled by your lips?
2. In what practical ways can you hollow God's name in your prayers?

2. THERE IS REQUEST AND PLEA (v.10-13).

The believer is to request and plea for several things.

1. "Thy kingdom come" is the first request to be prayed. The believer is to pray "after this manner":
⇒ "Father, let your kingdom come right here on this earth. Let Christ rule and reign in the hearts and the lives of all. Send Him, His kingdom, His sovereignty right now.

The Kingdom of God is to be the focus of the believer's requests, the very first thing for which he asks. There are three reasons for this.
   a. It is the very message that Jesus Christ and the early apostles preached and taught and prayed (Mt.3:2; 4:17; 5:3, 10, 19-20).
   b. It is the very thing for which God longs. He longs for the day when He will rule and reign in the hearts of all men, perfectly--the day when all men will willingly submit and serve Him--the day when all thoughts, all words, all behavior will be exactly what they should be.
   c. It is the very substance of the believer's life, or at least it should be. The believer should be living, loving, and existing for God and God alone. His whole focus and attention, energy and effort should be centered on the rule and reign of God on earth.

> **"And saying, Repent ye: for the kingdom of heaven is at hand" (Mt.3:2).**
> **"From that time Jesus began to preach, and to say, Repent: for the kingdom of heaven is at hand" (Mt.4:17).**

2. *"Thy kingdom come" is future*. It is a request for something that is not now existing on earth. It is a request for the rule and reign of God and of His kingdom. The believer is to pray "thy kingdom come."

> **"For I say unto you, That except your righteousness shall exceed the righteousness of the scribes and Pharisees, ye shall in no case enter into the kingdom of heaven" (Mt.5:20).**
> **"Even so, come Lord Jesus, come" (Rev.22:20).**

3. *God's kingdom is available*. God's kingdom is desperately needed on earth right now. So much just eats and gnaws away at man--so much rebellion, wickedness, evil, enmity, bitterness, hatred, murder, injustice, deprivation, and hunger. God's rule and reign are needed

now. The believer needs to see the urgency to pray and to pray consistently, "Thy kingdom come," and to live as if God's kingdom had already come.

QUESTIONS:
1. When you pray "Thy Kingdom come," for what are you really praying? Are you wishing for the world to come to an end? Now?
2. True believers long for God's Kingdom to come. Unbelievers do not. Why the difference?
3. Can believers on earth now play a role in bringing God's Kingdom to earth?

A CLOSER LOOK # 5

(6:10) **God, Will of**: "Thy will be done" says three critical things to God.

1. That we will work to please God in all we do. We will do our part to see that God's will is done on earth.

2. That God can do with us as He pleases. No matter what He chooses for us, we put ourselves at His disposal, for His use--even if it requires the sacrifice of all we are and have.

3. That we will not be displeased with what God does. We may not understand; it may not make sense; there may be question after question; but we know that God's will is best, and He will work all things out for good.

APPLICATION 1:

"Thy will be done in earth, as it is in heaven" is the second request to be prayed. The believer is to pray "after this manner":
⇒ "Father, your will be done: your will and your will alone. There is no will but your will. Let it be done right here on earth...."

APPLICATION 2:

There are four wills that struggle for man's obedience.
1) Man's own will (Ro.12:1-2; cp. Ro.7:15f; Gal.5:17).
2) Other men's wills (1 Pt.4:2).
3) Satan's will (Jn.8:44).
4) God's will (Eph.5:15-17, esp. vs.17; Ph.2:13; 1 Jn.2:17).

APPLICATION 3:

Note three significant lessons.
1) Many call God King, but they do not honor Him as a King. They do not do His will. Their profession is false, and tragically it creates an image of a false and meaningless King to the world.
2) We *must know God's will* if God's will is to be done. This requires study: "Study to show thyself approved unto God" (2 Tim.2:15). The only way God's will can be done is for us to study His Word and ask for the wisdom and strength to apply it to our lives (2 Tim.3:16).
3) We are to ask for God's will to be done *on earth*. The earth is the place where God's will is so desperately needed. It is the place...
   • where there is so much sin and corruption
   • where there is so much suffering and pain
   • where there is so much struggling and death
   • where the believer goes through trial after trial

"And Mary said, Behold the handmaid of the Lord; be it unto me according to thy word. And the angel departed from her" (Lk.1:38).

> **"I delight to do thy will, O my God: yea, thy law is within my heart" (Ps.40:8).**

4) "Thy will be done on earth as it is in heaven." The believer is praying for *heaven (heaven's rule) to come to earth*. He is making a commitment to make earth more like heaven.
   a) By yielding himself to God (Ro.6:13)
   b) By going and teaching all nations (Mt.28:19-20)

QUESTIONS:
1. Think of your prayer life. How much of it focuses upon God's will? How much upon your own will?
2. When is the desire to do God's will strongest in your life?
3. What is the only way a person can know God's will?
4. Does praying for God's will mean you will always know His will immediately or perfectly? How can you be assured of knowing what God is saying to you?

A CLOSER LOOK # 6
(6:11) **Bread**: bread is the basic necessity of life, the symbol of all that is necessary for survival and for a full life. There is much meaning in this simple request.

1. "Give us...our bread." The words *our* and *us* overcome selfishness and show concern for others. Any person who goes to bed hungry should be of concern to the believer.

2. "This day." This eliminates worry and anxiety about tomorrow and the distant future. It also teaches and helps us to trust God day by day. "The just shall live by faith...." day by day.

3. "Our daily bread." Every believer has a portion of daily bread which is his. He does not ask for someone else's bread but for his own. He seeks and works for his own bread; he does not think of stealing or of eating from another man's table (2 Th.3:10).

4. "Give us...bread." We ask for the necessities not the desserts of this world.

5. "Give us...bread." The believer confesses his inadequacy and dependency upon God. He is dependent upon God even for the basics of life.

6. "Give...this day our daily bread." This teaches the believer to come to God daily in prayer and trust Him to meet his needs.

APPLICATION 1:
"Give us this day our daily bread" is the third request to be prayed. The believer should pray "after this manner":
   ⇒ "Father give us our bread this day, spiritually as well as physically. Feed our souls and our bodies. Make this a glorious day in You. And, O God, the world is starving for You, and many are starving from hunger...."

APPLICATION 2:
God cares for man and his welfare.
1) He cares for man's physical well-being (Mt.6:11; Mt.6:25-34).

> **"Therefore take no thought, saying, What shall we eat? or, What shall we drink? or, Wherewithal shall we be clothed? (For after all these things do the Gentiles seek:) for your heavenly Father knoweth that ye have need of all these things. But seek ye first the kingdom of God, and his righteousness; and all these things shall be added unto you" (Mt.6:31-33).**

2) He cares for man's mental and emotional well-being.

> **"But the God of all grace, who hath called us unto his eternal glory by Christ Jesus, after that ye have suffered a while, make you perfect, stablish, strengthen, settle you" (1 Pt.5:10).**

3) He cares for man's spiritual well-being.

> **"Know ye not that ye are the temple of God, and that the Spirit of God dwelleth in you? If any man defile the temple of God, him shall God destroy; for the temple of God is holy, which temple ye are" (1 Cor.3:16-17).**

APPLICATION 3:
God cares for the human body. Several things show this.
1) He said to ask for the necessities of life *daily* (Mt.6:11).
2) He sent His only Son into the world in a human body.
3) He raised up Christ in His body, a resurrected body.
4) He promises to give a new resurrected body to the believer. The believer will dwell in "the resurrected body" forever.
5) He has chosen the believer's body to be "the temple of the Holy Spirit" (1 Cor. 6:19-20).

APPLICATION 4:
This simple request is a great lesson for both the rich and the poor.
1) The rich man feels self-sufficient, as though what he possesses came from his own hands. Therefore he thinks, "Who is the Lord?"
2) The poor man has nothing and is often forced to steal. Thus, he raises his fist in anger and curses God for his state of life.

> **"Give me neither poverty nor riches; feed me with food convenient [that I need] for me: lest I be full, and deny thee, and say, Who is the Lord? or lest I be poor, and steal, and take the name of my God in vain" (Pr.30:8-9).**

The believer is to trust God for the necessities of life and praise God for what he receives. He has learned, "In whatsoever state I am, therewith to be content" (Ph.4:11; cp. 4:12-13).

ILLUSTRATION:
God will take care of us, if we truly trust Him. No matter how great our needs, God faithfully proves Himself again and again.

> *"Shortly after World War II, a woman entered a grocery store and asked for enough food for a Christmas dinner for her children. When the owner inquired how much she could afford, she answered, 'My husband was killed in the war. Truthfully, I have nothing to offer but a little prayer.' The man, an unbeliever, was unmoved by the woman's need, and said sarcastically, 'Write your prayer on a piece of paper and you can have its weight in groceries.' To his surprise she plucked a folded note out of her pocket and handed it to him. 'I already did that during the night while I was watching over my sick child,' was her immediate reply. Without even reading it, he put it on one side of his old-fashioned scales. 'We'll see how much food this is worth,' he muttered. To his dismay, nothing happened when he put a loaf of bread on the other side. But he was even more upset when he added other items and still nothing happened. Finally he blurted out, 'Well, that's all it will*

hold anyway. Here's a bag. You'll have to put these things in yourself. I'm busy!' With a tearful 'Thank you,' the lady went happily on her way.

"The grocer later discovered that the scale was out of order. As the years passed, he often wondered if that was just a coincidence. 'Why did the woman have the prayer already written before he asked for it? Why did she come at exactly the time the mechanism was broken?' Whenever he looks at the slip of paper that bears her petition, he is amazed, for it reads, 'Please, dear Lord, give us this day our daily bread!'"[2]

QUESTIONS:
1. People who are financially secure--those who are not lacking in daily bread--what are they to pray for?
2. Many are hungry and doing without the necessities of life. Do they have reason to feel that God has failed them?
3. Think back over your life. In what ways has God provided for you?
4. What is the easiest thing to trust God for? What is the most difficult thing to trust God for?

A CLOSER LOOK # 7

(6:12) **Forgiveness, Spiritual**: the word "debts" means dues, duties, that which is owed, that which is legally due. In relation to sin, it means a failure to pay one's debts, one's dues; a failure to do one's duty, to keep one's responsibilities.

God has given man certain responsibilities, certain things to do and not to do. Every man has failed at some point to do what he should. Certainly no man would ever claim he has fulfilled his duty perfectly--without any failure, without any shortcoming. Sin is universal. Everyone fails in his duty at some point to some degree. Everyone needs to pray "forgive us our debts, as we forgive our debtors."

This prayer is asking God to do three things.
1. To forgive *the debt of sin*. A person has failed God in his duty; therefore, he needs God to forgive his debt.
2. To forgive *the debt of guilt or punishment*. A person who has failed to pay his debts is guilty; therefore, he is to pay the consequences; he is to be punished. This is the reason he must pray "Father, forgive my debts...."
3. To forgive *his debts just as he has forgiven* his debtors. This is asking God to forgive a person exactly as he forgives others. If a person forgives, God forgives. If a person does not forgive, God does not forgive. Therefore, any person who holds anything against another person is not forgiven his sins, no matter what he may think or has been told by another person. (Cp. Mt.6:14-15.)

APPLICATION 1:

"Forgive us our debts, as we forgive our debtors" is the fourth request to be prayed. The believer should pray "after this manner."
1) "Father, forgive me--have mercy upon me, the sinner, the nothing. O' God, You are all--have mercy...."
2) "Father, forgive others--all others. I hold nothing within. O' God, if there is anything within my heart against anyone, help me to forgive...."

---

[2] *INFOsearch Sermon Illustrations* (Arlington, TX: The Computer Assistant, 1-888-868-9029, 1986-1996).

APPLICATION 2:

In seeking forgiveness, we have a duty both to God and to man.

1) Our duty to God is to ask forgiveness when we fail to do His will.

"If we confess our sins, he is faithful and just to forgive us our sins, and to cleanse us from all unrighteousness" (1 Jn.1:9).

2) Our duty to man is to forgive his sins against us.

"Forbearing one another, and forgiving one another, if any man have a quarrel against any: even as Christ forgave you, so also do ye" (Col.3:13).

If we wish to be forgiven ourselves, both duties have to be performed. We must forgive those who sin against us (Mt.6:12), and we must ask forgiveness for our sins (1 Jn.1:9).

APPLICATION 3:

There are those who do us much evil. In this world many say and do all manner of evil against us. Bad news and evil purposes run wild, and it is not always *outside* the church, nor *outside* the family. Sometimes terrible evil is committed by word and act both within the church and within a person's family (Eph.4:30-32; cp. Mt.10:21; Mk.13:12-13). Christ says we must not react nor be harsh toward those who sin severely against us, but we must forgive. We must forgive if we wish to be forgiven.

⇒ Some smite us (Mt.5:39).
⇒ Some compel us against our will (Mt.5:41).
⇒ Some hate us (Mt.5:44).
⇒ Some sue us (Mt.5:40).
⇒ Some persecute us (Mt.5:44)
⇒ Some curse us (Mt.5:44)
⇒ Some despitefully use us (Mt.5:44).
⇒ Some spread rumors about us (Mt.5:11).

APPLICATION 4:

There are four things a believer must do when sinned against.

1) *The believer must understand* (Pr.11:12; 15:21; 17:27-28; cp. Eph.1:8). There is always a reason why a person sins against a believer. Too often we forget this.
   a) A person may be mistreated by someone who is close to him. He may be withdrawn from, neglected, or ignored. Therefore, he may react against a believer, and the reaction may range from self-pity to bitterness and hostility.
   b) A person may be tired, aggravated, or worried. Therefore, he may become too direct or cutting or harsh toward the believer.
   c) A person may be of a shy nature or sense inferiority; therefore, he may act unfriendly and unconcerned toward the believer.
   d) A person may have rumor and gossip and wild imaginations shared with him, especially by a person who has been hurt; he may be lied to and misinformed. Therefore, he may act suspicious and have nothing to do with the believer.
   e) A person may have a great need for attention and for emotional support. Therefore the person may imagine, exaggerate, blame, or accuse a believer in order to rally the support of friends and to gain the attention needed.
2) *The believer must forbear* (Eph.4:2; Col.3:13).
3) *The believer must forgive* (Eph.4:31-32).
4) *The believer must forget*, that is, not harbor the wrong done to him (Ph.3:13; cp. 2 Cor.10:5).

APPLICATION 5:
Note four additional lessons that need to be noted.
1) An unforgiving spirit causes pain, hurt, and tragedy--both to self and others. It can ruin lives, especially the lives of those closest and dearest to self.
2) We can curse ourselves by praying the Lord's prayer. We are in trouble when praying the Lord's prayer if we are angry and do not forgive those who sin against us: "Father...forgive us...as we forgive our debtors." We pronounce the very same judgment upon ourselves that we hold for others.
3) Forgiveness is conditional. The reason is simply explained. We have sinned against God, and others have sinned against us. If we want God to forgive us, we must forgive those who have sinned against us. How can we expect God to forgive us if we do not forgive those who have sinned against us? We can expect no better treatment than we give.
4) Forgiving others is evidence that God has forgiven our sins.

QUESTIONS:
1. Does God really expect you to forget some great wrong or evil a person has done to you? How is this possible?
2. Think for a moment: To whom do you need to grant forgiveness before you go to bed tonight? Why is it unhealthy for you to keep forgiveness from others?
3. When someone sins against you, what are you to immediately do?

A CLOSER LOOK # 8
(6:13) **Temptation--Deliverance**: God does not lead a man to sin; He tempts no man (Jas.1:13). What Christ is saying is two things.
1. Pray--pray that God will keep you from the awful pull of temptation. The believer is to have a sense of his personal weakness against temptation.
2. Pray--pray that God will deliver you from evil. The Greek says "from the evil one," that is, Satan. The request is for God to rescue, preserve, and guard us. He, the evil one, is so deceptive and powerful; he is as powerful as a roaring lion (1 Pt.5:8).
The plea and the cry is for God to deliver us from (1) temptation, and (2) from the evil one. (Cp. Ro.8:31; 1 Jn.4:4; cp. 1 Cor.10:13.)

APPLICATION 1:
"Lead us not into temptation, but deliver us from the evil one" is the fifth request to be prayed. The believer should pray "after this manner":
⇒ "Father, lead us not into temptation. Temptation comes so often; its pull is so strong. We get in the way so much. We seek our own way and react at every turn. O' God do not leave us to ourselves....
⇒ "And, dear Father, deliver us from the evil one. He is the master of deceit and paints such a beautiful picture. If you leave us to ourselves, we will fall. And, O' God, he is capable of being 'a roaring lion' seeking to devour us. Deliver us--rescue us--preserve us--guard us...."

APPLICATION 2:
Once we have been forgiven our sins (v.12), we must ask God to keep us from sinning again. Two things are essential to keep us from sin: (1) deliverance from temptation, and (2) deliverance from "the evil one."

This request is a necessity for every believer. Why? For two reasons. (1) All believers are tempted and tempted often, not by strange things, but by things that are common to all. Temptations do come and will come to all--the same temptations (1 Cor.10:13.) (2) No believer stands above falling.

"Wherefore let him that thinketh he standeth take heed lest he fall" (1 Cor.10:12).

APPLICATION 3:
Temptation is to be prayed against for two reasons.
1) Because sin causes God great hurt and pain (Ps.15:4).
2) Because sin causes great trouble, guilt, and grief for both oneself and others (Lk.19:41-44; cp. Mt.23:37; Lk.13:34).

APPLICATION 4:
The believer must have help in overcoming "the evil one." The *evil one* attacks (1) by deception (2 Cor.11:3, 14-15; Rev.12:9), and (2) by direct assault, seeking to devour (1 Pt.5:8). In dealing with "the evil one," the believer needs to remember:
⇒ "Greater is He that is in you, than he that is in the world" (1 Jn.4:4).
⇒ "If God be for us, who can be against us?" (Ro.8:31; cp. Ro.8:31-39).

"There hath no temptation taken you but such as is common to man: but God is faithful, who will not suffer you to be tempted above that ye are able; but will with the temptation also make a way to escape, that ye may be able to bear it" (1 Cor.10:13).
"Blessed is the man that endureth temptation: for when he is tried, he shall receive the crown of life, which the Lord hath promised to them that love him" (Jas.1:12).

QUESTIONS:
1. What does it mean when you pray for God not to lead you into temptation? Is there another source that would be more helpful to keep you from sinning?
2. What temptation do you struggle with the most? How can you guard against falling into the same sin over and over? Can you let your guard down once you have overcome a particular sin?
3. How does Satan gain an advantage in your life? Will he ever give up?

3. THERE IS PRAISE AND COMMITMENT (v.13).

These words, "For thine is the kingdom, and the power, and the glory, for ever. Amen" are referred to as the doxology. They are not in the best and oldest manuscripts of the Greek. Many scholars believe the doxology was added at a later date to be used in public worship. However, there is a similar doxology by David (1 Chron.29:11). The point of the doxology is to stress that everything belongs to God.
1. He is *the Source* of the kingdom and the power and the glory.
2. He is *the Possessor* of the kingdom and the power and the glory.
3. He is *the Recipient* of the kingdom and the power and the glory.

The believer belongs to the kingdom and the power and the glory of God.
1. The believer belongs to God's kingdom: God has accepted the believer into the Kingdom of God and promises to transport him into the kingdom and its glory either at death or at the Lord's return.
2. The believer belongs to God's power: God has delivered him from sin and death and continues to deliver him daily.

3. The believer belongs to God's glory: God has done all for the believer that "in the ages to come He [God] might show the exceeding riches of His grace in His kindness toward us through Christ Jesus" (Eph.2:7).

APPLICATION 1:

"Thine is the kingdom, and the power, and the glory, forever. Amen" is the third major point to pray.
1) "Father, yours is the kingdom, the right to rule and reign...."
2) "Yours is the power, the only power that can really rule and govern...."
3) "Yours is the glory. O' God, all glory belongs to you...."

APPLICATION 2:

Note three significant points.
1) "Thine is the kingdom" says two things.
   a) The right to rule and reign throughout the universe is God's. It belongs to no one else.
   b) The only perfect and eternal government is God's. Only God's government can bring utopia: love, joy, peace, and the very best of life.

> **"God that made the world and all things therein, seeing that he is Lord of heaven and earth, dwelleth not in temples made with hands; neither is worshipped with men's hands, as though he needed any thing, seeing he giveth to all life, and breath, and all things" (Acts 17:24-25).**
> **"The LORD reigneth, he is clothed with majesty; the LORD is clothed with strength, wherewith he hath girded himself: the world also is stablished, that it cannot be moved" (Ps.93:1).**

2) "Thine is the power" says two things.
   a) God alone has the power to create and sustain perfect government. He alone has the power to support and bring perfect government to man and his earth.
   b) God alone has the power to change men so they can escape death and live forever within a perfect government. He alone has the power to stir men to live in love, joy, and peace and to serve completely and unselfishly so that all may have the very best.
3) "Thine is the glory" says that God alone deserves all the honor and praise and glory. For what? For all. He is all in all.

APPLICATION 3:

The one subject that is to dominate prayer is *praise for God*. The fact that the Lord's prayer begins with praise (surrender, v.9) and ends with praise (v.13^b) shows this.
⇒ God does not *need* praise. He has the praise of multitudes of angels, but He *deserves* our praise.
⇒ God created us with the ability to praise Him. He must *want* our praise.
⇒ A genuine believer is always praising God's name before all.

QUESTIONS:
1. In truth, everything belongs to God. What in your life has not been completely given over to Him?
2. Do you give God the praise He deserves? In what additional and practical ways can you praise God?

A CLOSER LOOK # 9

(6:13) **Amen**: so be it; it is and shall be so. When spoken by God, "Amen" means it is and shall be so, unequivocally. When spoken by man it is a petition meaning, "Let it be." Here in the Lord's Prayer, the word *Amen* is a word of commitment. When a man prays the Lord's prayer and closes by saying "Amen" (let it be), he is committing himself to do his part for the things which have been prayed.

ILLUSTRATION:

It has been said that we should pray as if it all depended upon God and to work as if everything depended upon us. This is the great mystery and blessing of prayer--that God would invite us to be a part of His Kingdom and fellow-workers with Him. God has already done His part. Now, our part is as simple as breathing.

> "In the 1994 Winter Olympics, held in Norway, twenty-three-year-old Tommy Moe of the United States won the gold on the men's downhill. It was 'a beautifully controlled run,' said William Oscar Johnson in *Sports Illustrated*, 'on which he held tucks and thrust his hands forward in perfect form at places where others had stood up and flailed their arms.'
>
> "After his victory, Tommy Moe explained his thought processes. 'I kept it simple,' he said, 'focused on skiing, not on winning, not on where I'd place. I remembered to breathe--sometimes I don't.'
>
> "The winner of the gold medal in the Olympics had to remember the most basic of basics: breathing! He kept it simple.
>
> "Likewise as we seek to have a strong walk with God, it doesn't take a rocket scientist to know where we win or lose. Spiritual strength depends on the basics. We need to make sure we're breathing the things of the Spirit."[3]

It doesn't get much simpler: pray...pray...pray...keep it simple and from the heart.

QUESTIONS:

1. If you pray for God to "let it be," are you asking for your will instead of His? How can you distinguish?
2. God expects you to come boldly before His throne in prayer. Are you accomplishing all you can or is much being left undone because of your lack of prayer?

SUMMARY:

God has given you the pattern and the mold that will help you learn how to pray effectively--that is, the Lord's Prayer. The believer who wants to grow in his prayer life makes the commitment to pattern his life according to these great principles:

1. There is surrender and acknowledgment.
2. There is request and plea.
3. There is praise and commitment.

---

3 *"The Son Finally Rises."* Sports Illustrated (21 February 1994), p. 20-28. As cited in Craig B. Larson's *Contemporary Illustrations for Preachers, Teachers, and Writers,* p.49.

MATTHEW 6:9-13

PERSONAL JOURNAL NOTES:
(Reflection & Response)

1. The most important thing that I learned from this lesson was:

2. The thing that I need to work on the most is:

3. I can apply this lesson to my life by:

4. Closing Prayer of Commitment: (put your commitment down on paper).

	P. The Basic Principle of Prayer (Part IV): Forgiveness 6:14-15 (Mk.11:25-26)
1. The promise: Forgive others & be forgiven	14 For if ye forgive men their trespasses, your heavenly Father will also forgive you:
2. The warning: Refuse to forgive others & be unforgiven	15 But if ye forgive not men their trespasses, neither will your Father forgive your trespasses.

Section IV
THE TEACHINGS OF THE MESSIAH TO HIS DISCIPLES:
THE GREAT SERMON ON THE MOUNT
Matthew 5:1-7:29

Study 16: THE BASIC PRINCIPLE OF PRAYER (PART IV): FORGIVENESS

Text: Matthew 6:14-15

Aim: To live in a spirit and attitude of forgiveness.

Memory Verse:
> "For if ye forgive men their trespasses, your heavenly Father will also forgive you" (Matthew 6:14).

INTRODUCTION:

Throughout history, man has seen the evolution of great sources of power. In the 20th century, man has seen the creation of...

- hydroelectric dams that provide power to millions of homes and businesses
- the laser that can burn through solid steel
- the jet-fueled rocket that can lift a space ship into the blackness of other worlds
- the nuclear bomb that is powerful enough to destroy the earth

These are only a few examples of the power that rests in the hands of mankind. But as great as these sources of power are, there is an even greater source of power that is available to the Christian believer. When put to use, this power is the world's greatest hope. When this power is withheld and not shared with those in need, people are destroyed. What is this great power? It is the power of *forgiveness*. The challenge from God's Word is straight to the point and must be heeded by every believer: in order to be forgiven, we must be willing to forgive.

Note the first word, "for." This connects these verses to the Lord's Prayer. Immediately after closing the Lord's Prayer, Jesus explained why He had said that forgiveness is conditional (Mt.6:12). This was a necessary explanation for two reasons.

1. The very idea that a person must forgive others in order for God to forgive him was totally new. It was a shocking concept, an eye-opener. It had to be explained.

2. God knows that He cannot forgive an unforgiving heart. His nature of love and justice will not permit Him to indulge in sin and give license to the passions of a man's unforgiving

spirit. He can forgive only where the mercy and tenderness of forgiveness are found. Therefore, Christ had to teach the basic principle of prayer--forgiveness (Mt.18:21-35; Mk.11:25-26; Lk.6:37; 17:3-4; Eph.4:32).

OUTLINE:
1. The promise: forgive others and be forgiven (v.14).
2. The warning: refuse to forgive others and be unforgiven (v.15).

1. THE PROMISE: FORGIVE OTHERS AND BE FORGIVEN (v.14).

The word "trespass" means to stumble; to fall; to slip; to blunder; to deviate from righteousness and truth. Note three things.

1. Christ takes for granted that we know we need forgiveness. This is seen in His words, "your heavenly Father will also <u>forgive</u> you." We are sinners; we have transgressed God's law and we need forgiveness. Even the most mature among us fails to keep God's law perfectly. We all stumble, fall, blunder, and slip; and we do it much too often.

    a. We are seldom doing to the fullest degree what we should do. We come short.

    b. We are *always crossing over* from the path we should be following. We deviate over into *the forbidden* area. Thus, we desperately need forgiveness. God promises that He will forgive our trespasses if we will do one simple thing: forgive men their trespasses.

2. The greatest thing in all the world is to be forgiven our sins: to be absolved and released from all guilt and condemnation, to be accepted and restored by God and assured of seeing Christ face to face. Forgiveness of sins means that we are freed: set at liberty in this life to live abundantly, and set at liberty in the next life to live eternally in perfection.

3. The only way we can be forgiven our sins is to forgive others their trespasses. Christ makes the promise: "Forgive men their trespasses [and] your heavenly Father will also forgive you." Forgiving men their trespasses means several very practical things.

    ⇒ We are not judgmental or censorious.
    ⇒ We do not become bitter or hostile.
    ⇒ We do not plan to take revenge.
    ⇒ We do not hold hard feelings against another person.
    ⇒ We do not talk about, gossip, or join in rumor; on the contrary, we correct the rumor.
    ⇒ We do not rejoice in trouble and trials that fall upon another person.
    ⇒ We love and pray for the person.

APPLICATION:
Note two facts.
1) Bad feelings against another person is sin. It is holding sin within our heart. Forgiving a person who has done us evil is proof that we wish to have a clean heart. We really wish God to forgive us.
2) Forgiving men their trespasses does not refer only to the trespasses against us but all trespasses.

    "Blessed are the merciful: for they shall obtain mercy" (Mt.5:7).
    "And when ye stand praying, forgive, if ye have ought against any: that your Father also which is in heaven may forgive you your trespasses" (Mk.11:25).

ILLUSTRATION:

The teaching of Scripture is clear: the believer is not to hold a grudge against anyone. Christian forgiveness forgives the past, present, and future.

> *"A man who was telling his friend about an argument he'd had with his wife commented, 'Oh, how I hate it, every time we have an argument; she gets historical.'*
> *"The friend replied, 'You mean hysterical.'*
> *"'No,' he insisted. 'I mean historical. Every time we argue she drags up everything from the past and holds it against me!'"*[1]

QUESTIONS:
1. There is a perception in many societies that Christians are supposed to be perfect. Why is this not true? How can you explain a person's need for forgiveness to someone who cannot forgive others?
2. What does it mean practically for you to forgive someone who has sinned against you? Have you ever struggled with this?
3. Why is it so hard to let go of hurt feelings? What is God's solution to your hurt?

2. THE WARNING: REFUSE TO FORGIVE OTHERS AND BE UNFORGIVEN (v.15).

The believer who prays for forgiveness and holds feelings against another person is hypocritical. He is asking God to do something he himself is unwilling to do. He is asking God to forgive his trespasses when he himself is unwilling to forgive the trespasses of others. Bad feelings against a person are clear proof that a person is not right with God.

1. Bad feelings show that a person does not know the true nature of man nor of God. He does not know the true exalted perfection of God nor the real depth of man's sinful nature--how far short he is of perfect righteousness.

2. Bad feelings show that a person walks and lives in self-righteousness (that is, that he thinks he is acceptable to God by deeds of righteousness). He feels better than others and judges himself able to talk about and look askance at the sins of others.

3. Bad feelings show that a person has not taken the steps he must take in order to be forgiven his own sins.

4. Bad feelings show that a person is living by the standards of society and not by God's Word. God's Word is clear: "there is none that doeth good, no, not one" (Ro.3:12; cp. Mt.19:17). Therefore, we are to help and love one another, to care for and restore one another when we stumble, slip, fall, blunder, and deviate.

> **"There is none righteous, no, not one" (Ro.3:10; cp. Ro.3:9-19).**
> **"All have sinned and come short of the glory of God" (Ro.3:23).**

Christ is explicitly clear in His warning about forgiving others.

> **"Be ye therefore merciful, as your Father also is merciful. Judge not, and ye shall not be judged: condemn not, and ye shall not be condemned: forgive, and ye shall be forgiven" (Lk.6:36-37).**

The warning is severe when the opposite statement is seen: "Judge, and ye shall be judged: condemn, and ye shall be condemned: be unforgiving and ye shall be unforgiven" (cp. Lk.6:36-37).

---

[1] Michael P. Green. *Illustrations for Biblical Preaching*, p.153.

APPLICATION 1:

Note three significant lessons in this point.

1) The man who holds bad feelings against others has not looked at himself and his own sins. He does not know himself, not his real self, not the inner selfishness and motives that plague the depravity of man.

2) Feelings against others cause inward disturbance. They eat away at a person's mind and emotions to varying degrees. Deep feelings against others can cause deep emotional and mental problems as well as serious physical problems.

3) Three things are necessary for God to hear our prayer for forgiveness of sins. (1) Lifting up holy hands, (2) being without wrath, and (3) not doubting.

"I will therefore that men pray every where, lifting up holy hands, without wrath and doubting" (1 Tim.2:8).

APPLICATION 2:

The answer to peace is Christ Jesus. "He is our peace"--the only possible peace between two persons. (Review the Scriptures below verse by verse in light of the following facts.)

1) He can make both one (Eph.2:14).
2) He can break down the wall between both (Eph.2:14).
3) He can abolish the enmity--in His own flesh (Eph.2:15).
4) He can make the two into one new man (Eph.2:15).
5) He can reconcile both to God--in one body--by the cross (Eph.2:15).
6) He can give peace to both and bring peace between both (Eph.2:17).
7) He can give both access to God the Father (Eph.2:18).

ILLUSTRATION:

Revenge is like a cancer that eats away at a person's emotions. Unchecked, revenge will consume a person. What is revenge's only cure? Forgiveness.

"Kevin Tunell will probably never forget what happened one Friday in 1982, when he was 17. As a result of his drunk driving, a young woman died. He was convicted of manslaughter. He had to serve a court sentence. He was mandated to spend one year campaigning against drunk driving--he did it for seven years. But the worst punishment was the payment he has to make to the victim's family. They sued him for $1.5 million, but Tunell only has to pay $936. The catch is he has to pay it a dollar at a time--one dollar every Friday--as a reminder of what he did.

"The problem is he keeps forgetting. Four times the family has taken him to court for not paying. He even had to spend 30 days in jail for failure to comply. Tunell insists that he isn't intentionally defying the court order; it's just that he is tormented by the constant reminders of the girl's death. He offered the family a box of checks covering the payments until the year 2001, one more year than is required, but they refused saying that what they want is not money, but penance.

"The question is whether 936 payments is really enough--not for Tunell to have to make, but for the family to receive. When they finally get the last one, will they be at peace? If you were in their place, how many payments would you require? In fact, we are all in that place. We've all been betrayed, hurt, or offended by someone. How much penance do we demand?"[2]

---

[2] Max Lucado. *In the Grip of Grace.* (Dallas, TX: Word Publishing, 1996), p.149-150.

A CLOSER LOOK # 1

(6:14-15) **Forgiveness**: there are several prerequisites to forgiveness. For a man to be forgiven, he must do several things.

1. He must confess his sins (1 Jn.1:9; cp. 1 Jn.1:8-10).

2. He must have faith in God: a belief that God will actually forgive (Heb.11:6).

3. He must repent (turn away from and forsake his sins) and turn to God in a renewed commitment.

4. He must forgive those who have wronged him (Mt.6:14-15). Hard feelings or anger against a person is sin. It is evidence that a person has not truly turned from his sins and that he is *not really* sincere in seeking forgiveness.

A CLOSER LOOK # 2

(6:14-15) **Forgiveness**: there are four different attitudes toward forgiveness.

1. The attitude of the agnostic or doubter. God may be; He may not be. Therefore forgiveness from God is immaterial. It does not matter. All that matters is for men to forgive each other and relate properly. Forgiveness from an invisible, personal God is a far-fetched idea.

2. The attitude of the guilt or conscience-stricken person. This is a person who knows little, if anything, about a personal God, yet he is deeply conscious of guilt and the need for forgiveness. He prays for forgiveness over and over, but he never comes to know forgiveness.

3. The attitude of the social religionist. This is a person who is sometimes mentally aware of the need for forgiveness; therefore, he makes an occasional confession. He feels forgiven, arises and goes about his affairs with no more thought about the matter. The problem with this is that it is a false forgiveness, a mental forgiveness. The person views God as a *pushover* who allows a person to live as he wishes as long as he occasionally confesses. He ignores and denies the righteousness and justice of a loving God.

4. The attitude of the mature believer. This is a believer who truly knows his own sinful self and his great need for God's forgiveness. Therefore, he lives in a spirit of confession and repentance, by which he comes to know God's forgiveness and the assurance of it.

MATTHEW 6:14-15

SUMMARY:

Within your very hands is the greatest power in the world. It is the power of forgiveness. Used in the right way, this power will become a tremendous blessing to many. Forgiveness withheld will be a weapon of destruction--beginning with you.
1. The promise: forgive others and be forgiven.
2. The warning: refuse to forgive others and be unforgiven.

PERSONAL JOURNAL NOTES:
(Reflection & Response)

1. The most important thing that I learned from this lesson was:

2. The thing that I need to work on the most is:

3. I can apply this lesson to my life by:

4. Closing Prayer of Commitment: (put your commitment down on paper).

1. The wrong way to fast	Q. The Right Motive for Fasting, 6:16-18	2. The right way to fast
a. Fasting as a hypocrite	16 Moreover when ye fast, be not, as the hypocrites, of a sad countenance: for they disfigure their faces, that they may appear unto men to fast. Verily I say unto you, They have their reward.	a. Fasting as a duty
b. Fasting for recognition	17 But thou, when thou fastest, anoint thine head, and wash thy face;	b. Fasting without notice
c. Reward: To receive only human recognition & esteem	18 That thou appear not unto men to fast, but unto thy Father which is in secret: and thy Father, which seeth in secret, shall reward thee openly.	c. Fasting to God alone
		d. Reward: God shall reward openly

Section IV
THE TEACHINGS OF THE MESSIAH TO HIS DISCIPLES:
THE GREAT SERMON ON THE MOUNT
Matthew 5:1-7:29

Study 17:   THE RIGHT MOTIVE FOR FASTING

Text: Matthew 6:16-18

Aim: To be sensitive to the leading of the Spirit in prayer and fasting.

Memory Verses:
>   "But thou, when thou fastest, anoint thine head, and wash thy face; That thou appear not unto men to fast, but unto thy Father which is in secret: and thy Father, which seeth in secret, shall reward thee openly" (Matthew 6:17-18).

INTRODUCTION:
The act of fasting is an exercise that can make a person look very spiritual. Whether praying or fasting, the question becomes, what is your real motivation?

>   *"One morning at the breakfast table a father asked the blessing as usual. Quoting Bible verses, he piously thanked the Lord for all His bountiful provisions. After he concluded, however, he grumbled loudly about the poor quality of the food and berated his wife for the way it was cooked. He seemed to be disgruntled with everything. Finally his young daughter interrupted him. 'Dad,' she began, 'do you think God heard what you said when you prayed?' 'Certainly,' he replied confidently. 'And did He also hear when you complained about the bacon and coffee just now?' 'Why, of course!' 'Then which did God believe?'"[1]*

When you do something 'for the Lord' or 'for someone else,' what is to be believed about you?

Fasting means to abstain from food for some religious or spiritual purpose. A study of the fasting practiced by Jesus and by the great leaders of the Bible reveals what God means by fasting. Very simply, fasting means being so consumed with a matter that it becomes more important than food. Therefore, the believer sets food aside *in order to concentrate on seeking God about the matter*. Biblical fasting means more than just abstaining from food; it

---

[1]   *INFOsearch Sermon Illustrations* (Arlington, TX: The Computer Assistant, 1-888-868-9029, 1986-1996).

means to abstain from food in order to concentrate upon God and His answer to a particular matter. Biblical fasting involves prayer, intense supplication before God. Note the words "when ye fast" (v.16, 17). Jesus assumed believers fasted; He expected them to fast. He fasted and He taught fasting (Mt.4:2); the early believers fasted (Mt.17:21; Lk.2:37; Acts 10:30; 13:3; 14:23; 1 Cor.7:5; 2 Cor.6:5; 11:27). Yet so few have continued such intense seeking of the Lord; so few truly fast.

The benefits of fasting are enormous, but there are also dangers. We can fast for the wrong reasons. This is the point of the present passage. Christ counsels us on the wrong and the right motives for fasting.

OUTLINE:
1. The wrong way to fast (v.16).
2. The right way to fast (v.17-18).

1. THE WRONG WAY TO FAST (v.16).

1. Fasting insincerely is wrong. Being hypocritical is a real danger when fasting. There are four reasons men fast, and all but one are false and hypocritical.
   a. Men fast to gain a sense of God's approval and of self-approval.
   b. Men fast to fulfill a religious act.
   c. Men fast to gain religious recognition.
   d. Men fast to genuinely meet God for some special purpose.

APPLICATION:
Fasting is not condemned by Christ. But fasting for any purpose other than to meet God is condemned: when you fast "appear...unto thy Father" (v.18).

"**Therefore when thou doest thine alms, do not sound a trumpet before thee, as the hypocrites do in the synagogues and in the streets, that they may have glory of men. Verily I say unto you, They have their reward**" (Mt.6:2).
"**For I desired mercy, and not sacrifice; and the knowledge of God more than burnt offerings**" (Hos.6:6).

2. Fasting for recognition is wrong. It poses several serious dangers that must be guarded against with all diligence.
   a. The danger of feeling super-spiritual. Few believers follow a true fast. Therefore when they really fast, they have to guard against a sense of super-spirituality and pride.
   b. The danger of over-confidence. The believer's confidence is to be in God not in self. After a genuine fast a believer usually feels spiritually confident, ready to go forth. He must go forth depending upon the strength of Christ and not upon his own energy and effort.
   c. The danger of sharing one's fasting experience. The believer has usually learned so much from being in God's presence that he is anxious to share it, especially with those closest to him. The best advice is to hush: share nothing, not even with one's dearest friend.
   d. The danger of changing one's appearance and the way one acts and behaves. Any change whatsoever from one's normal behavior and routine attracts attention and ruins the whole benefit of the fast. As Christ says, "they disfigure their face" (act super-spiritual) (v.16).

"**But all their works they do for to be seen of men**" (Mt.23:5).

"**Do ye look on things after the outward appearance?**" (2 Cor. 10:7).

3. Fasting the wrong way has its reward. A person will receive human recognition and esteem, but the recognition of men is all he will ever receive.

APPLICATION:
Some gain the control and discipline of their bodies through fasting, but they ruin themselves and their ministry through pride. They lose their reward.

"**For all flesh is as grass, and all the glory of man as the flower of grass. The grass withereth, and the flower thereof falleth away**" (1 Pt.1:24).

ILLUSTRATION:
The person who puts on a spiritual face that is not a true image of his heart will one day be exposed. When that day comes, he will have to face the music.

"The expression 'face the music' is said to have originated in Japan. According to the story, one man in the imperial orchestra couldn't play a note. Being a person of great influence and wealth, he had demanded the he be given a place in the group because he wanted to 'perform' before the emperor. The conductor agreed to let him sit in the second row of the orchestra, even though he couldn't read music. He was given a flute, and when a concert would begin, he'd raise his instrument, pucker his lips, and move his fingers. He would go through all the motions of playing but he never made a sound. This deception continued for 2 years.

"Then a new conductor took over. He told the orchestra that he wanted to audition each player personally. One by one they performed in his presence. Then came the flutist's turn. He was frantic with worry, so he pretended to be sick. However, the doctor who was ordered to examine him declared that he was perfectly well. The conductor insisted that the man appear and demonstrate his skill. Shamefacedly he had to confess that he was a fake. He was unable to 'face the music.'"[2]

If you are fasting for the wrong reasons, then you too will have to face the music.

QUESTIONS:
1. What are some inappropriate reasons for a person to fast?
2. What are the dangers of fasting for recognition?
3. If a person talks about his fasting, what logical conclusion can you draw about him?

2. THE RIGHT WAY TO FAST (v.17-18).

As stated in the introduction, fasting means being so consumed with a matter that it becomes more important than food. Therefore, the believer sets food aside *in order to concentrate on seeking* God about the matter. Biblical fasting means more than just abstaining from food; it means to abstain from food in order to concentrate upon God and His answer to a particular matter. Biblical fasting involves prayer, intense supplication before God.

1. Fasting is a duty. Every believer is expected to fast. Christ said "When ye fast." In other words, He expects us to fast.

---

[2] *INFOsearch Sermon Illustrations* (Arlington, TX: The Computer Assistant, 1-888-868-9029, 1986-1996).

⇒ Jesus Himself fasted.

"And when he had fasted forty days and forty nights, he was afterward an hungred" (Mt.4:2).

⇒ The apostles were to fast.

"Howbeit this kind goeth not out but by prayer and fasting" (Mt.17:21; cp. Mt.9:15; Mk.2:20; Lk.5:35).

⇒ Anna fasted.

"And she was a widow of about fourscore and four years, which departed not from the temple, but served God with fastings and prayers night and day" (Lk.2:37).

⇒ Cornelius fasted.

"And Cornelius said, Four days ago I was fasting until this hour; and at the ninth hour I prayed in my house, and, behold, a man stood before me in bright clothing" (Acts 10:30).

⇒ Church leaders fasted.

"As they ministered to the Lord, and fasted, the Holy Ghost said, Separate me Barnabas and Saul for the work whereunto I have called them" (Acts 13:2).
"And when they had ordained them elders in every church, and had prayed with fasting, they commended them to the Lord, on whom they believed" (Acts 14:23).

⇒ Husbands and wives are expected to fast.

"Defraud ye not [do not deprive] one the other, except it be with consent for a time, that ye may give yourselves to *fasting* and prayer; and come together again, that Satan tempt you not for your incontinency" (1 Cor.7:5).

⇒ Paul fasted often.

"In stripes, in imprisonments, in tumults, in labours, in watchings, in fastings; by pureness, by knowledge, by longsuffering, by kindness, by the Holy Ghost, by love unfeigned" (2 Cor.6:5).

2. Fasting is to be done without notice. The believer is to fast before God not before men. There is to be no change in appearance or behavior to indicate that he is fasting. Think about it. Why should there be? Why should anyone know that a person is seeking God in a very special way? The matter is God's affair not man's affair. It is between the person and God not the person and other people.

3. Fasting is to be to God alone. God is the object of the believer's fast. He needs to meet God in a very, very special way. In meeting God all alone, the believer is demonstrating his dependence upon God and His provision.

APPLICATION 1:

A religionist fasts before men. A genuine believer fasts before God.

APPLICATION 2:

God does not say when nor how often we should fast, but He does tell us how to fast. We must take every precaution to fast exactly as He says: before God, in secret, without any ostentation or show whatsoever. No one is to see or know.

ILLUSTRATION:

God will reward those who are willing to obey Him without reservation. The person who decides to fast and pray will see things that the natural man cannot understand.

> *"Dr. Diane Komp is a pediatric oncologist who teaches and practices at Yale University School of Medicine. She tells about attending a medical conference where physicians of different disciplines exchanged ideas on difficult tumor cases. The case at hand was that of a baby who had broken all the rules.*
> *"'Are you sure you had the right diagnosis?' asked the radiotherapist of the pathologist. 'I've never seen this particular tumor respond that way. You must be wrong.'*
> *"'No, I'm not wrong!' responded the somewhat indignant pathologist. 'I know that tumor when I see it.'*
> *"The radiotherapist, looking elsewhere for an explanation of the unexplainable, turned to the chemotherapist managing the case. 'That chemotherapy must have done the job.'*
> *"Don't look over here for the explanation. We only use a radio-sensitizing dose. Besides, the tumor was growing through the last course of different drugs. Are you sure it wasn't the radiation therapy that did the job?'*
> *"'No way. This tumor has never gone away like that before.' He turned half-joking to the radiologist who had interpreted the scans. 'Are you sure those are the right films?'*
> *"'Yes, they're the right x-rays! You can tell from the comparison to the old ones that it's the same child. Only the tumor is gone.'*
> *"'It doesn't make sense,' the radiotherapist kept repeating.*
> *"The minutes of that conference simply reflected the lack of a known medical explanation for the disappearance of the tumor. The medical records did not reflect other activities on her behalf. Teams from a local church fasted and prayed daily for Bethany, two by two. Many other family friends prayed for her tumor to go away."[3]*

Fasting will do things that no man can accomplish.

> **"And he said unto them, This kind can come forth by nothing, but by prayer and fasting" (Mk.9:29).**

4. Fasting the right way has its reward: God shall reward us openly. How much greater is His reward than the recognition of men! God's acceptance and eternal reward is enough for genuine believers.

> **"But when thou doest alms, let not thy left hand know what thy right hand doeth: that thine alms may be in secret: and thy Father which seeth in secret himself shall reward thee openly" (Mt.6:3-4).**

---

[3] Diane M. Komp, M.D. *A Child Shall Lead Them.* (Grand Rapids, MI: Zondervan Publishing, 1993). As cited in *INFOsearch Sermon Illustrations* (Arlington, TX: The Computer Assistant, 1-888-868-9029, 1986-1996).

"For we must **all** [publicly, before all believers] appear before the judgment seat of Christ; that every one may receive the things done in his body, according to that he hath done, whether it be good or bad" (2 Cor.5:10).

QUESTIONS:
1. Fasting is expected--not optional. Have you taken this as seriously as you should?
2. What is the Biblical basis for fasting? Why do you think fasting with the right motive is so powerful?

A CLOSER LOOK # 1

(6:17-18) **Fasting**: there are at least four times when the believer should fast.

1. There are times when the believer feels a special pull, an urge, a call within his heart to get alone with God. This is God's Spirit moving within his heart. When this happens, nothing--not food, not responsibility--should keep him from getting all alone with God. He should fast as soon as possible.

2. There are times when special needs arise. The needs may concern the believer's own life or the life of friends, society, the world, or some ministry or mission. Again, nothing should keep the believer from spending a very special time in God's presence when facing such dire needs.

3. There are times when the believer needs to humble his soul before God. At such times he learns not only humility but dependence upon God (Ps.35:13).

4. There are times when the believer needs a very special power from God. The Lord promised such power if the believer prayed and fasted (Mt.17:21; Mk.9:29).

QUESTIONS:
1. Have you ever felt led to pray and fast and brushed it aside because you were worried about your health or missing something 'more important'?
2. When you have special and urgent needs, how often do you think God wants you to fast and pray? Why?

A CLOSER LOOK # 2

(6:17-18) **Fasting**: Why are believers to fast? There are excellent benefits to fasting, and God wants His people to reap these benefits.

1. Fasting keeps the believer in the presence of God. He is fasting in order to seek God's presence for a very special purpose; he remains in God's presence until he feels God has or is going to meet his need.

2. Fasting humbles the believer's soul before God. It says that God is the most important thing in all the world to him (Ps.35:13).

3. Fasting teaches the believer dependence upon God. He is seeking God, and in so doing he is demonstrating his conviction that he is dependent upon God.

4. Fasting demonstrates to God (by action) a real seriousness. It shows by act that the matter being considered is a priority.

5. Fasting teaches the believer to control and discipline his life. He does without in order to gain a greater substance.

6. Fasting keeps the believer from being enslaved by habit. He lays aside all substances; in so doing, he breaks the hold of anything that might have him chained.

7. Fasting helps the believer to stay physically fit. It helps keep him from becoming overweight and soft.

QUESTIONS:
1. What benefits can you personally gain from fasting?
2. Have you ever been disobedient and refused to fast when God was leading in that direction? What would you do differently the next time?
3. Do you ever fast and pray? If not, why not?

SUMMARY:

When God calls you to fast and pray, are you prepared to follow Him? An experience of great spiritual power and blessing awaits the person who lends himself to this critically important ministry. Remember, there is...
1. The wrong way to fast.
2. The right way to fast.

PERSONAL JOURNAL NOTES:
(Reflection & Response)

1. The most important thing that I learned from this lesson was:

2. The thing that I need to work on the most is:

3. I can apply this lesson to my life by:

4. Closing Prayer of Commitment: (put your commitment down on paper).

	R. The Warning About Wealth & Materialism, 6:19-24	your heart be also. 22 The light of the body is the eye: if therefore thine eye be single, thy whole body shall be full of light.	a. A good heart: Like a good eye 1) Focuses & sees 2) Focuses on heaven (v.20)
1. A contrast: About two kinds of riches a. Earthly riches 1) Do not lay up 2) Are corruptible 3) Are insecure	19 Lay not up for yourselves treasures upon earth, where moth and rust doth corrupt, and where thieves break through and steal:	23 But if thine eye be evil, thy whole body shall be full of darkness. If therefore the light that is in thee be darkness, how great is that darkness!	b. A bad heart: Like a bad eye 1) Blind and dark 2) Focuses on the earth (v.19)
b. Heavenly riches 1) Lay up 2) Are incorruptible 3) Are secure	20 But lay up for yourselves treasures in heaven, where neither moth nor rust doth corrupt, and where thieves do not break through nor steal.	24 No man can serve two masters: for either he will hate the one, and love the other; or else he will hold to the one, and despise the	3. A choice: About two kinds of masters a. Either hate or love b. Either cleave or despise
2. A warning: About two kinds of hearts	21 For where your treasure is, there will	other. Ye cannot serve God and mammon.	c. The choice: Serve God or material things

Section IV
THE TEACHINGS OF THE MESSIAH TO HIS DISCIPLES:
THE GREAT SERMON ON THE MOUNT
Matthew 5:1-7:29

Study 18: THE WARNING ABOUT WEALTH AND MATERIALISM

Text: Matthew 6:19-24

Aim: To acknowledge who you are really serving in this life: To set in place a vigilant guard against materialism.

Memory Verse:
> "For where your treasure is, there will your heart be also" (Matthew 6:21).

INTRODUCTION:

Think about this hypothetical situation. War has come to your nation. For your own safety, the government has forced you to leave the comforts of home and move to a new place. There is no time to waste. You are allowed to take only a few material goods with you, in fact, you are allowed to take only what you can carry upon your back. What are you going to take with you? More importantly perhaps is what are you going to leave behind? What can you live without? Will you risk possible death and ride out the war in your home trying to save your material possessions, or will you forsake everything and flee with all your might? Do you own anything so valuable that you would risk your life to save it?

Or are you faced with the dilemma of being possessed by your material things instead of the other way around? Just as quickly as you accumulate things, do your financial commitments quickly overcome you? Is your pride and joy becoming a lethal noose around your neck?

The concern of Christ in this passage is money, possessions, and material things. His concern is that you guard against centering your life around houses, furnishings, cars, lands, buildings, stocks--all the things that make up security and wealth on this earth. The reason is simply understood: nothing on this earth is secure and lasting. It is aging, decaying, and wasting away. It is all corruptible and temporal. What Christ wants is for you to center your life around Him and heaven, for everything about Himself and heaven is life and security. It is all permanent and eternal. To stir your thinking, He gives a lesson on wealth and materialism.

OUTLINE:
    1. A contrast: about two kinds of riches (v.19-20).
    2. A warning: about two kinds of hearts (v.21-23).
    3. A choice: about two kinds of masters (v.24).

1. A CONTRAST: ABOUT TWO KINDS OF RICHES (v.19-20).

Christ gives a contrast about two kinds of riches.
    1. There are earthly riches. There are things on earth that men desire. Christ calls these earthly riches and treasures. Earthly riches would be such things as clothes, cars, jewelry, toys, houses, buildings, furnishings, pleasure, fame, power, profession, property, money--anything that dominates a person's life and holds it fast to this earth.
    A treasure is that which has value and is worth something to someone. Men take things and ascribe value to them: it may be stones (diamonds); or rocks and dust (gold); or money (paper and metal); or land (property); or wood, metal, chemical, and fabric (buildings); or influence (power); or the attention of people (fame).
    Christ says three things about earthly riches that are of critical importance to both the believer and the unbeliever.
        a. Do not lay up for yourselves earthly riches (material possessions). Christ says that a person is not to focus his life on earthly things, not to set his eyes, his mind, his energy, and his efforts on such passing treasures.

        APPLICATION:
        It is easier to covet earthly things than heavenly things for four reasons.
        1) They can usually be seen and handled.
        2) They are sought by most people, and other people influence us. A person is either worldly minded or heavenly minded (Ro.8:5-7).
        3) They are to varying degrees necessary for life.
        4) They are present, ever before us, and can be possessed right now.

        b. Earthly riches are corruptible. Something terrible happens to everything on earth. Everything ages, dies, deteriorates, and decays. Things are on the earth only for a brief time, and then they are no more. Everything has the seed of corruption within it.
        c. Earthly riches are insecure. The things on earth are insecure for three reasons.
            ⇒ They can be stolen or eaten up.
            ⇒ They do not last; they waste away.
            ⇒ A person cannot take a single thing with him when he passes from this world.

        "For we brought nothing into this world, and it is certain we can carry nothing out" (1 Tim.6:7).
        "For the love of money is the root of all evil: which while some coveted after, they have erred from the faith, and pierced themselves through with many sorrows" (1 Tim.6:10).

APPLICATION:

Note four striking lessons.

1) Wealth is sought, and it is sought by many. What is often forgotten is this: every bit of wealth is held by someone. Therefore, many are constantly figuring out how to get some of what someone else has. If someone *gets* it, another person *loses* it. Things of the world are very insecure.

2) A man can be snatched away from this earth as quickly as the twinkling of an eye. Everything for which he has worked so hard on this earth can be gone immediately (cp. Lk.12:16-21).

3) A man can lose much of what he has in this world and lose it quickly. He can lose it through financial difficulties, accident, marital problems, illness, death, and a myriad of other ways.

4) A person is a fool to seek an abundance of things--to grasp after more and more. Why? Because tonight or tomorrow or some day soon God will say, "Thou fool, this night thy soul shall be required of thee: then whose shall these things be, which thou hast provided? So is he that layeth up treasure for himself, and is not rich toward God" (Lk.12:20-21).

ILLUSTRATION:

God loves you enough to protect you from the dangers of earthly riches--if you let Him. Noted Bible teacher and writer Charles Stanley reminds us of this very truth.

"Dr. W. A. Criswell tells a story about a family he went to visit years ago when the oil business was booming. This particular family lived in an area where oil companies were buying the oil rights to people's property left and right. Throughout the area families were becoming wealthy overnight as oil was discovered on their property. When Dr. Criswell drove up to this particular family's property, he noticed a peculiar thing, however. There were no oil wells. On the land adjoining their property there were several wells pumping away, but not a single one on the property of the family he had come to visit.

"He was greeted at the door by a very dejected-looking woman whom he assumed correctly to be the lady of the house. Her husband came in, offered Dr. Criswell a seat, and told his 'sad' tale. 'Pastor,' he said, 'God has forgotten us. You see, about a year ago oil was found in this area. Engineers came in and assured everyone in our community that eventually we would be rich beyond our wildest dreams. Well, we saw this as the hand of God. A few weeks later crews came in and began digging around on property all over this area. Wells sprang up everywhere. We knew it was just a matter of time until they would begin digging on our property, but it never happened. Dr. Criswell, God overlooked us. They discovered oil on both sides of our property and even on the property behind us--but not a drop on our land. Our neighbors are selling their homes and moving in the city, and we are left out here alone.'

"A few years later, Dr. Criswell ran into that man. He was smiling from ear to ear. Dr. Criswell assumed they had finally found oil on his property. 'Quite the contrary,' the man replied. 'They never found any oil, and I'm glad of it.' This certainly took the pastor by surprise. 'The strangest thing happened,' the man went on. 'All our neighbors moved the city and bought big expensive houses and new cars. They sent their kids to the finest schools. Most of them joined country clubs, but before long that lifestyle began to take its toll. One by one their marriages started breaking up. Their kids rebelled. We don't know of any that are still attending church on a regular basis. Pastor, God did us a big favor by not putting any oil on our land. We are all still together and love each other like never before. We *thank Him every day for giving us what is important and protecting us from the things that aren't.'*[1]

2. There are heavenly riches. There are things in heaven that believers desire. Christ calls these heavenly riches. (See Eph.1:3.) Heavenly riches would be such things as...
- a blameless life
- becoming a true child of God
- the forgiveness of sins
- wisdom
- understanding the will of God (purpose, meaning, and significance in life)
- an enormous inheritance that is eternal
- a constant Comforter and Helper, the Holy Spirit of God Himself
- life that is abundant and overflowing (Jn.10:10)

Christ says three things about heavenly riches that are of critical importance to the believer and the unbeliever.

a. Lay up for yourselves heavenly riches. A person is foolish to seek and set his mind on perishable things. Why? Because he can seek and obtain that which gives all the meaning, purpose, and significance to life imaginable. To have meaning and purpose and significance in life is what life is all about.

Think about it. "A man's life consisteth not in the abundance of things which he possesseth" (Lk.12:15). How much meaning is there in something that passes and perishes? Even while a person seeks after something on this earth, there is an inner awareness that it will not last. There is an end to whatever meaning he finds in it. The earthly treasure may be a car, a job, a trip, a relationship, clothing, position, power, fame, or fortune. The fact is, no matter what the treasure is, it will end and pass away and be no more. A worldly man's meaning for living, his purpose and significance in life, is temporary, unfulfilling, and incomplete.

b. Heavenly riches are incorruptible. Corruption can be escaped (2 Pt.1:4). There is an "inheritance incorruptible, and undefiled, and that fadeth not away, <u>reserved in heaven for you</u>" (1 Pt.1:4). Everyone should lay claim and set his heart on *his* heavenly inheritance.

c. Heavenly riches are secure. Thieves cannot break through heaven; they cannot penetrate the spiritual dimension. No one nor anything can take away a person's heavenly riches. The love of God assures this (cp. Ro.8:32-39).

APPLICATION 1:

Christ does not stop a man from seeking treasure; contrariwise, He guides the man's search to real treasure. Heaven is worth more than all the wealth in the world.

"For what is a man profited, if he shall gain the whole world, and lose his own soul? or what shall a man give in exchange for his soul?" (Mt.16:26).

---

[1] Charles Stanley. *How to Handle Adversity.* (Nashville, TN: Oliver- Nelson Books, 1989), p. 53, 57.

APPLICATION 2:

A man must leave all to follow Christ or else he cannot be the Lord's disciple.

> **"So likewise, whosoever he be of you that forsaketh not all that he hath, he cannot be my disciple" (Lk.14:33).**

APPLICATION 3:

Christ says a man is to lay up treasures in heaven for himself, not lay up treasures on earth for his family. A pointed and disturbing message to many!

> **"But lay up for yourselves treasures in heaven, where neither moth nor rust doth corrupt, and where thieves do not break through nor steal" (Mt.6:20).**

QUESTIONS:

1. Jot down a list of heavenly riches that God has given to you. What would your life be like without these riches?
2. Heavenly riches are safe forever. How does this help detach you from a world that focuses upon material possessions?

A CLOSER LOOK # 1

(6:19) **Corruption--Incorruption**: there is a seed of corruption within the world--a principle or nature of corruption within everything on earth. Everything is imperfectly born and formed; it ages, dies, deteriorates, decays, and wastes away.

> **"Now this I say, brethren, that flesh and blood cannot inherit the kingdom of God; neither doth corruption inherit incorruption" (1 Cor. 15:50).**

There is also a seed of incorruption, a principle of incorruption, an eternal nature of incorruption in heaven (1 Pt.1:4, 23; cp. 1:18-23; 2 Pt.1:4; cp. 1 Cor.15:12-58).

> **"Blessed be the God and Father of our Lord Jesus Christ, which according to his abundant mercy hath begotten us again unto a lively hope by the resurrection of Jesus Christ from the dead, to an inheritance incorruptible, and undefiled, and that fadeth not away, reserved in heaven for you" (1 Pt.1:3-4).**

---

2. A WARNING: ABOUT TWO KINDS OF HEARTS (v.21-23).

Christ warns about two kinds of hearts.

1. There is the good heart. It is just like a good eye. Note that the eye is a gate that *gives entrance* to the mind of man. What man looks at is what he thinks about, and what he thinks about is what he actually becomes (cp. Pr.23:7). If a man focuses upon Jesus Christ, who is the Light of the world (Jn.8:12), then his mind and heart will be *full of light*. Therefore, the deeds of his body will be deeds of light. Singleness of the eye and heart means that a person sets his attention upon the Lord Jesus for the purpose of doing His will (cp. Acts 2:46; Eph.6:5; Col.3:22). An evil eye is one that focuses upon anything that is not of God.

A man's heart is precisely where his treasure is. If his treasure is on earth, his heart is on earth. If his treasure is in heaven, his heart is in heaven. The eye illustrates the truth. If a man's eye is *good and healthy*, then he is able to focus upon the treasure and grasp the truth. But if the eye is *unhealthy*, he is not able to focus upon the treasure. He is blind and in darkness. A *healthy heart* is like a healthy eye. It grasps the true treasure, the treasure in heaven.

But an *unhealthy heart* is like an unhealthy eye. It is in darkness, unable to see the treasure in heaven.

Note that the believer fixes his eyes upon heaven for two primary reasons.

    a. His citizenship is in heaven:

> **"For our conversation [citizenship] is in heaven; from whence also we look for the Savior, the Lord Jesus Christ: who shall change our vile body, that it may be fashioned like unto His glorious body" (Ph.3:20-21).**

    b. He seeks the treasures which are eternal:

> **"For the things which are seen are temporal; but the things which are not seen are eternal" (2 Cor.4:18).**

⇒ They are incorruptible (v.20).
⇒ They are secure (v.20).
⇒ They cause his "whole body to be full of light" (v.22).
⇒ They cause him to love and to serve God (v.24).
⇒ They consume his whole being in all the meaning and purpose and significance of life (v.24).
⇒ They draw him near to God (v.24).

> **"Blessed are the pure in heart: for they shall see God" (Mt.5:8).**
> **"But the natural man receiveth not the things of the Spirit of God: for they are foolishness unto him: neither can he know them, because they are spiritually discerned" (1 Cor.2:14).**

APPLICATION:

The believer has a clear-cut charge:

> **"Set your affection on things above, not in things on the earth" (Col.3:2).**
> **"Blessed be the God and Father of our Lord Jesus Christ, who hath blessed us with all <u>spiritual blessings</u> in heavenly places in Christ" (Eph.1:3).**

2. There is the bad heart. It is just like a bad eye. A bad eye is not able to focus upon the treasure, not able to focus upon the things of God. A bad eye is blind and in darkness. So it is with the heart. Christ says that a person is not to set his heart upon earthly treasures. Why? Such a person focuses his eyes (attention, mind, thoughts, energy, effort) on evil. What does Christ mean? Earthly things are evil because they are deceiving.

⇒ They are corruptible; they age, die, waste away, deteriorate, and decay.
⇒ They are insecure; they will be stolen or taken away or left behind.
⇒ They cause a person's heart to be full of darkness (v.23).
⇒ They will consume a person (v.24).
⇒ They cause a person to hate, despise, and reject God (v.24).
⇒ They alienate a person from God (v.24).

APPLICATION:

Several things happen to a man who sets his eye upon earthly things. The shadows of darkness set in upon him. He becomes deceived (cp. Mt.13:7, 22). He is deceived in that he becomes...

- covetous and consuming (to get more and more)
- complaining and grudging
- apprehensive and fearful (of losing it)
- hard and close-minded (to giving much) (cp. Jas.5:9)

"In whom the God of this world hath blinded the minds of them which believe not, lest the light of the glorious gospel of Christ, who is the image of God, should shine unto them" (2 Cor.4:4).

QUESTIONS:
1. Can a person's heart be both good and bad? What is the danger of letting 'just a little bit' of bad in with the good?
2. What things pull against your desire to have a good heart?
3. What causes a heart to be *bad*? Does everyone have a choice about the condition of his heart? Are some people 'doomed' or born with a bad heart?
4. What are the consequences of having a heart set upon earthly things?

3. A CHOICE: ABOUT TWO KINDS OF MASTERS (v.24).

Christ warns that a choice has to be made between two kinds of masters. There are two critical reasons why a choice has to be made.

1. A man hates one master and loves the other. When both masters call upon the man at the same time, he has to make a choice. He favors, serves, helps, and loves one; and while he is doing so, he is disfavoring, rejecting, and showing disrespect and hate for the other. A man cannot serve two masters.

2. A man either cleaves to or despises one of the masters. He has to choose which master to favor and serve. He has to cleave to one. In cleaving to one, he reveals disrespect and spite for the other. A man cannot serve two masters.

The choice is clear. A man either serves God or material things.
⇒ There are only two treasures: the earth and its treasures or God and His treasures, physical and material things or spiritual and eternal things.
⇒ Every man without exception has committed his life to one of two treasures: mammon or God. He is focusing his heart, eyes, mind, attention, thoughts, hands, and energy upon earthly things or upon heavenly things. He cannot "serve God and mammon."

APPLICATION 1:
So many look at wealth as a blessing of God, a sign that one is godly. But the Bible says differently.

"[Some] suppose that gain is godliness: from such withdraw thyself. But godliness with contentment is great gain. For we brought nothing into this world, and it is certain we can carry nothing out. And having food and raiment let us be therewith content. But they that will be rich fall into temptation and a snare, and into many foolish and hurtful lusts, which drown men in destruction and perdition. For the love of money is the root of all evil: which while some coveted after, they have erred from the faith, and pierced themselves through with many sorrows. But thou, O man of God, flee these things: and follow after righteousness, godliness, faith, love, patience, meekness" (1 Tim.6:5-11).

APPLICATION 2:
Mammon, earthly treasures, can be many things (see Mt.6:19-20).
1) Riches and wealth.

"Go to now, ye that say, To day or to morrow we will go into such a city, and continue there a year, and buy and sell, and get gain" (Jas.4:13).

2) Food, the filling of one's belly.

"Whose end is destruction, whose God is their belly, and whose glory is in their shame, who mind earthly things" (Ph.3:19).

3) An evil, lusting eye.

"But I say unto you, That whosoever looketh on a woman to lust after her hath committed adultery with her already in his heart" (Mt.5:28).

4) A lusting of the flesh.

"Love not the world, neither the things that are in the world. If any man love the world, the love of the Father is not in him. For all that is in the world, the lust of the flesh, and the lust of the eyes, and the pride of life, is not of the Father, but is of the world" (1 Jn.2:15-16).

5) Unproductive activity, relaxation, recreation, wasteful pastimes, sluggish feelings.

"Go to the ant, thou sluggard; consider her ways, and be wise: which having no guide, overseer, or ruler, provideth her meat in the summer, and gathereth her food in the harvest. How long wilt thou sleep, O sluggard? when wilt thou arise out of thy sleep? Yet a little sleep, a little slumber, a little folding of the hands to sleep: so shall thy poverty come as one that travelleth, and thy want as an armed man" (Pr.6:6-11).

APPLICATION 3:
God promises several great things to the man who serves Him.
1) All the necessities of life.

"But seek ye first the kingdom of God, and his righteousness; and all these things shall be added unto you" (Mt.6:33).

2) Freedom from anxiety.

"Be careful for nothing; but in every thing by prayer and supplication with thanksgiving let your requests be made known unto God. And the peace of God, which passeth all understanding, shall keep your hearts and minds through Christ Jesus" (Ph.4:6-7).

3) Joy and contentment.

"These things have I spoken unto you, that my joy might remain in you, and that your joy might be full" (Jn.15:11).

4) Abundant and eternal life.

"For God so loved the world, that he gave his only begotten Son, that whosoever believeth in him should not perish, but have everlasting life" (Jn.3:16).

ILLUSTRATION:

In the final analysis, every person is going to serve somebody. We will serve the person or thing that we love the most.

"*In 1893, Richard D. Armour was worth fifty million dollars. That's a lot of money today; it was much more back then. He had built his meat packing business from the ground up until he had fifteen thousand employees. Despite his enormous wealth, Armour arose at 5:00 each morning and drove to the plant. There he stayed, this mighty transformer of meat into money, until 6:00 in the evening, at which time he went home for dinner, followed by a 9:00 bedtime. 'I have no other interest in my life but my business,' he told an interviewer. 'I do not love the money. What I do love is the getting of it.'*

"*We serve what we love. Armour loved making money more than money itself. But he still had to serve somebody. In his case, he served the love of acquiring money. Now the question is this: what are you serving? We serve what we love. So perhaps the better question is this: What do you love? What is the primary attachment in your life? There is only one sane answer to that question in light of eternity.*"[2]

QUESTIONS:

1. Why is it impossible for a person to serve two masters?
2. Why would some persons consider material wealth to be a sign of godliness? On the other hand, is wealth necessarily a sign of ungodliness? What are true signs of godliness? Are these signs of godliness evident in your life?
3 Of all of the earthly treasures available, which one is the most tempting to you?
4. If you choose to trust and serve only Christ, what blessings are in store for you?

A CLOSER LOOK # 2

(6:24) **Wealth--Rich, The**: some rich persons did turn to Christ. They serve as excellent examples for the rich to follow in turning to God.

⇒ James and John (Mk.1:20; cp. Mk.10:36-37)
⇒ Matthew (Mt.9:9-13)
⇒ Zacchaeus (Lk.19:1-10)
⇒ Joseph of Arimathaea (Mt.27:57).
⇒ Nicodemus (Jn.20:39; cp. Jn.3:1f. He may or may not have been saved.)
⇒ Lydia (Acts 16:14-15)
⇒ Manaen, a foster brother of Herod, who was probably wealthy (Acts 13:1)
⇒ Some women who supported Jesus (Lk.8:2-3)

SUMMARY:

What things do you think about the most? Do you think about how much of the world's riches you can accumulate during your lifetime? Or is your mind fixed upon those things that will never fade away? Every person comes to a fork in the road at some point in life where he has to choose. One road is a well-beaten path that leads to earthly treasures that fade

---

2 Steve Farrar. *Better Homes and Jungles*. Portland, OR: Multnomah Press, 1991, p.86-87.

away. The other path is a road less traveled. It is the road that leads to heavenly treasures, the road of righteousness where the believer walks and places his complete trust in God. Are you trusting in God or are you trusting in goods?

> *"The first U.S. coin to bear the inscription 'In God We Trust' was a 2-cent piece minted in 1864. The idea for having a motto originated with a Pennsylvania minister who suggested it to Salmon Portland Chase, Secretary of the Treasury under Abraham Lincoln. Chase, a deeply God-fearing man, asked James Polloch, director of the Mint, to come up with appropriate words. In a letter to him, Chase wrote, 'No nation can be strong except in the strength of God, or safe except in His defense. The trust of our people in God should be declared on our national coins.' And so the motto 'In God We Trust' was born.*
>
> *"For millions of Americans, a more accurate motto might be, 'In goods we trust.' The material things money can buy have become such an important part of our lives that God is pushed into the background."*[3]

1. A contrast: about two kinds of riches.
2. A warning: about two kinds of hearts.
3. A choice: about two kinds of masters.

PERSONAL JOURNAL NOTES:
(Reflection & Response)

1. The most important thing that I learned from this lesson was:

2. The thing that I need to work on the most is:

3. I can apply this lesson to my life by:

4. Closing Prayer of Commitment: (put your commitment down on paper).

---

[3] *INFOsearch Sermon Illustrations* (Arlington, TX: The Computer Assistant, 1-888-868-9029, 1986-1996).

	S. The Counsel on Worry & Anxiety, 6:25-34
1. A counsel--do not worry about necessities a. About food & drink b. About body & clothing	25 Therefore I say unto you, Take no thought for your life, what ye shall eat, or what ye shall drink; nor yet for your body, what ye shall put on.
2. Do not worry about your life & body	Is not the life more than meat, and the body than raiment?
3. Do not worry about food & shelter a. Observe the birds	26 Behold the fowls of the air: for they sow not, neither do they reap, nor gather into barns; yet your heavenly Father feedeth them.
b. You are better than the birds	Are ye not much better than they?
4. Do not worry about your stature: Worry is pointless	27 Which of you by taking thought can add one cubit unto his stature?
5. Do not worry about clothing a. Consider the lilies	28 And why take ye thought for raiment? Consider the lilies of the field, how they grow;
1) They do not toil	they toil not, neither do they spin:
2) They are more adorned than Solomon	29 And yet I say unto you, That even Solomon in all his glory

was not arrayed like one of these.	
30 Wherefore, if God so clothe the grass of the field, which to day is, and to morrow is cast into the oven, shall he not much more clothe you, O ye of little faith?	b. Trust--believe: You of little faith
31 Therefore take no thought, saying, What shall we eat? or, What shall we drink? or, Wherewithal shall we be clothed?	**6. Do not worry: Do not be thinking & talking about food, drink, & clothing**
32 (For after all these things do the Gentiles seek:)	a. You are different from the heathen
for your heavenly Father knoweth that ye have need of all these things.	b. Your heavenly Father knows your needs
33 But seek ye first the kingdom of God, and his righteousness; and all these things shall be added unto you.	**7. Do not worry: Seek ye first the Kingdom of God & His righteousness**
34 Take therefore no thought for the morrow: for the morrow shall take thought for the things of itself. Sufficient unto the day is the evil thereof.	**8. Do not worry about tomorrow: Live one day at a time**

Section IV
THE TEACHINGS OF THE MESSIAH TO HIS DISCIPLES: THE GREAT SERMON ON THE MOUNT
Matthew 5:1-7:29

Study 19: THE COUNSEL ON WORRY AND ANXIETY

Text: Matthew 6:25-34

Aim: To make a strong commitment: To conquer worry and trust God's provision--more and more.

Memory Verse:

"But seek ye first the kingdom of God, and his righteousness; and all these things shall be added unto you" (Matthew 6:33).

MATTHEW 6:25-34

INTRODUCTION:

As the old saying goes: "Worry is like a rocking chair. You spend lot of energy going nowhere." A lot of people in our society spend a lot of energy worrying about things they have absolutely no control over:

⇒ what other people think of them
⇒ the rise and fall of the stock market
⇒ nuclear arms falling into the wrong hands
⇒ catching a disease for which there is no cure
⇒ getting old and having no one to care for them
⇒ the weather

People just worry about every possible circumstance. In fact, worry and anxiety can break down the human body. No wonder the major cause of sickness can be traced directly to an over-abundance of stress. God has a much better solution for the believer than to worry and fret. God's counsel for us is spelled out in eight practical commands. This counsel meets one of the greatest needs of men, the need to be delivered from worry and anxiety.

OUTLINE:

1. A counsel--do not worry about necessities (v.25).
2. Concentrate on your life and body: They are what is important (v.25).
3. Do not worry about food and shelter (v.26).
4. Do not worry about your stature (v.27).
5. Do not worry about clothing (v.28-30).
6. Do not worry: do not be thinking about food, drink, clothing (v.31-32).
7. Do not worry: seek ye first the kingdom of God and His righteousness (v.33).
8. Do not worry about tomorrow: live one day at a time (v.34).

1. A COUNSEL--DO NOT WORRY ABOUT NECESSITIES (v.25).

The believer is not to worry about necessities, about food and drink, about body and clothing. The words "take no thought" mean do not worry; do not be anxious; do not be overly concerned and caring (cp. Ph.4:6). The counsel is so needed it is given three times (v.25, 31, 34).

Jesus is not suggesting that a man not prepare for life, that he be lazy, shiftless, and thoughtless with a no-care attitude. God will not indulge license, that is, slothfulness and a lack of initiative, effort, and planning. A person has to look after his responsibilities (Pr.27:23; 2 Cor.11:28; Ph.2:20). He has to work in order to eat (2 Th.3:10). In fact, he is even to work extra in order to have enough to give to others (Eph.4:28). He must be diligent in looking after his affairs and profession, in helping and giving to others.

1. Jesus is talking about being *preoccupied* with the material possessions of life. Many fall into the trap of centering mind, thoughts, energy, and efforts on the necessities and luxuries of life. A believer is not to be wrapped up and entangled in the affairs of this world (2 Tim.2:4). He is not to be groping for more and more and hoarding more and more. He is *not* to "seek ye first" the things of the world, but he is to "seek ye first the kingdom of God and His righteousness"; then God will see to it that he receives all these necessities (Mt.6:33).

2. Jesus is talking about being so wrapped up in *securing* things that we become anxious, disturbed, and sleepless. Being focused upon the things of the world keeps a person from walking in the fulness and enjoyment of life. Worry and anxiety can cause serious health problems ranging from sleepless nights and headaches to ulcers, high blood pressure, and heart attacks.

3. Jesus is talking about being so consumed with *getting* that we think little of God. Fear of not having enough and spending all our time trying to *get* more and more causes disbelief,

a lack of trust in God and an increased dependence upon self. A person who works to gain more and more security never knows God. He never knows God's love and care. He never learns that God looks after those who truly trust him.

4. Jesus is talking about being so *entangled* with the affairs of this earth that we forget eternity. We just forget to take care of our lives and bodies beyond this life (Lk.12:20; cp. Ps.49:10-20; 2 Tim.2:4).

The charge is clear. We are not to worry. We are to be consumed with God and people not things. We are to seek God first, serving Him and our fellow man first. Then the necessities, and in some cases the luxuries, will be given to us (Mt.6:33).

APPLICATION 1:
There are two categories of food, drink, and clothing. There are...
- the necessary items
- the extravagant or luxury items that lead to self-indulgence

Living sumptuously and extravagantly, at ease and in luxury in the midst of a needy and starving world, is sin. It is a sin that condemns us to hell. The believer is not to be entangled in the affairs of material things (2 Tim.2:4).

APPLICATION 2:
Food, clothing, and shelter are necessities of life. It is not wrong to work for these, nor to make them secure for our future. But what is wrong is fourfold...
- ignoring and neglecting God while we work
- working day and night; then worrying about how to keep what we have and how to make more and more
- never being satisfied with the necessities; coveting to have more and more, to have bigger and better, to keep up with the next person
- neglecting the needs of others who have greater needs than we do

ILLUSTRATION:
People who spend all their time worrying about how to provide for their needs will find themselves bound to an early grave.

> "In a cemetery in England stands a grave marker with this inscription: SHE DIED FOR WANT OF THINGS. Alongside that stone is another which reads: HE DIED TRYING TO GIVE THEM TO HER.
> "In a laughable and yet tragic manner these epitaphs suggest the folly of living and working only for this world's goods."[1]

QUESTIONS:
1. Almost everyone at some point in life--as a child, a teen, or an adult--has experienced the feeling of not having enough of *something*. It might be an empty cupboard or an empty bank account or no job. With no apparent way of having that need met, how do you find the balance between trusting God for what you need *tomorrow* and what you actually have *today*?
2. What is the key to not allowing life's necessities to consume your every thought?
3. Every person has needs and wants. In your terms, what is the difference? How does the Bible define a need?

---

[1] *INFOsearch Sermon Illustrations* (Arlington, TX: The Computer Assistant, 1-888-868-9029, 1986-1996).

2. DO NOT WORRY ABOUT YOUR LIFE AND BODY (v.25).

The point is clear and striking: a person's life and body are of more value--much more value--than the food he eats and the clothes he puts on. Why then should a person allow these secondary things to consume and dominate his life? So many are controlled by the necessities and luxuries, the material things of the world.

A person can eat and wear only so much at one time. Enough is enough; more than enough is too much; too much means that a person is consuming it upon his lusts. His life is being dominated by, instead of dominating, the things of the world.

APPLICATION 1:
Note several significant lessons.
1) Do not worry: think about your life and body and learn to trust God for food and clothing. Concentrate your mind and effort upon your life and body not upon food and clothing.
2) The point is simple and clear. Life means more than just things, even more than food and clothing.

> **"Take heed, and beware of covetousness: for a man's life consisteth not in the abundance of the things which he possesseth" (Lk.12:15).**

3) Materialism (worldliness and possessions) can enslave a person to such a degree that it dominates his life. In order to get and possess more, spouses argue, men steal, employees crave, employers hoard, children pout, and nations war. Life--living and enjoying what God has given--is ignored and neglected in order to get and possess more and more.

> **"From whence come wars and fightings among you? come they not hence, even of your lusts that war in your members? Ye lust, and have not: ye kill, and desire to have, and cannot obtain: ye fight and war, yet ye have not, because ye ask not. Ye ask, and receive not, because ye ask amiss, that ye may consume it upon your lusts. Ye adulterers and adulteresses, know ye not that the friendship of the world is enmity with God? whosoever therefore will be a friend of the world is the enemy of God" (Jas.4:1-4).**

4) The basic problem of man is setting priorities and determining what is to be first in his life. The first priority of every man should be to take care of his life--eternally. Why should a man be concerned about a few short years when he has the opportunity to maintain life forever? Why seek the things that only sustain and adorn his physical body for a brief time and then fade away? Seeking the Kingdom of God and His righteousness should be the first priority of every man.

> **"And take heed to yourselves, lest at any time your hearts be overcharged with surfeiting, and drunkenness, and cares of this life, and so that day come upon you unawares" (Lk.21:34).**

APPLICATION 2:
A man will do anything to save his body if it is threatened. Therefore, two critical questions need to be asked.
1) Why does a man allow himself to become enslaved by possessions? If he does not have and possess, he is miserable--sometimes to the point of being physically sick. He is driven to seek and pursue and get. He is so enslaved that he misses out on real life.

2) Why does a man allow himself to become so enslaved to possessions that he neglects the eternal care of his life? He continually seeks and pursues things...
- ignoring and neglecting God
- failing to lay hold of eternal life

"And having food and raiment let us be therewith content. But they that will be rich fall into temptation and a snare, and into many foolish and hurtful lusts, which drown men in destruction and perdition. For the love of money is the root of all evil: which while some coveted after, they have erred from the faith, and pierced themselves through with many sorrows. But thou, O man of God, flee these things; and follow after righteousness, godliness, faith, love, patience, meekness. Fight the good fight of faith, <u>lay hold on eternal life</u>, whereunto thou art also called, and hast professed a good profession before many witnesses" (1 Tim.6:8-12).

QUESTIONS:
1. In our society, greater value is often placed on things than upon people. What can the believer do in order to impact his society with God's truth?
2. What are the basic dangers that arise from materialism? How can you guard yourself from these dangers?
3. Lusting for material possessions is much like craving illegal drugs. Both are sinful and harmful habits. What is the only way a person can be delivered from the destructive bondage of materialism?

3. DO NOT WORRY ABOUT FOOD AND SHELTER (v.26).

God gives food and shelter to the birds of the air. "Behold": look at them and study them. Use your eyes and learn from what you see around you. The providence of God takes care of the birds. Learn that God will likewise take care of the believer who really trusts Him. Note two points.
1. The believer is *better* than the birds.
   a. Man is a higher being, on a much higher level of creation than animals. He is more noble and excellent, a spiritual being made in the image of God and capable of a personal relationship with God.

   "Who teacheth us more than the beasts of the earth, and maketh us wiser than the fowls of heaven?" (Job 35:11).

   b. The believer is a child of God. God is *the Creator* of birds, but He is *the Father* of believers.

   "For ye have not received the spirit of bondage again to fear; but ye have received the Spirit of adoption, whereby we cry, Abba, Father. The Spirit itself beareth witness with our spirit, that we are the children" (Ro.8:15-16).

   c. The believer is an heir of God. He is to receive all that God possesses in that glorious day of redemption.

   "That being justified by his grace, we should be made heirs according to the hope of eternal life" (Tit.3:7).

2. Four things can be said about the person who is preoccupied with material things.
   a. He is covetous.

   "Let your conversation [behavior] be without covetousness; and be content with such things as ye have: for he hath said, I will never leave thee, nor forsake thee" (Heb.13:5).

   b. He is not as wise as the birds.

   "Yea, the stork in the heaven knoweth her appointed times; and the turtle and the crane and the swallow observe the time of their coming; but my people know not the judgment of the LORD" (Jer.8:7).

   c. He is a backslider who has forgotten what Christ said, "I will never leave you, nor forsake you" (Heb.13:5).
   d. He is not "seeking ye first the kingdom of God and His righteousness" (Mt.6:33).

APPLICATION 1:
Do not worry:
   ⇒ God knows every fowl on the earth. Watch the fowls of the air and learn to trust God for shelter and food. "I know all the fowls of the mountains," God says (Ps.50:11; cp. Job 38:41; Ps.147:9).
   ⇒ God knows every believer on the earth, even the most minute details about him (the number of hairs). God knows the needs of His followers. Therefore the believer need not fear. God will feed and shelter him if the believer will just seek Him first (Mt.6:33).

   A sparrow "shall not fall on the ground without your Father. But the very hairs of your head are all numbered. Fear ye not therefore, ye are of more value than many sparrows" (Mt.10:29-31).

APPLICATION 2:
   Nothing dampens a person's spirit and kills his testimony as much as being consumed with the cares of the world (worldliness) (1 Jn.2:15-16; cp. Ro.12:2). On the other hand, God will not indulge license, that is, laziness, slothfulness, a lack of planning, initiative, and effort. Jesus planned ahead (Jn.12:6) and preached industriousness (Lk.16:8, cp. 1-10). The Bible is clear about the duty of man to work, even to work extra in order to have enough to give to others (Eph.4:28).

QUESTIONS:
1. One of the world's biggest lies and paradoxes is equating the value of humans and animals. Why are *you* more important to God than a bird?
2. What are some character traits of a person who is preoccupied with material things?
3. God knows what we need a whole lot better than we do. Do you ever have a hard time trusting God to provide what you cannot provide for yourself?

4. DO NOT WORRY ABOUT YOUR STATURE: WORRY IS POINTLESS (v.27).

   The word "stature" means height, quality or status gained by growth, and sometimes it means age. The word "cubit" literally means measure of space or distance (approximately 18 inches), but it can also mean a measure of time or age (Jn.9:21). Therefore, the verse can read either "who can add one cubit to his stature" or *one minute to his life span.*

The point is striking. Worry is senseless--just as senseless as trying to add to one's stature or add a minute to one's life span (when it is time to die). No bodies are perfectly formed, not in this world. The world is corruptible and imperfect; but there is hope, a glorious hope in God--a hope that acknowledges that God loves and cares, that he has promised a new heavens and earth that will be perfect. In the perfect heavens and earth, all bodies will be perfectly formed. God shall "wipe away all tears" (Rev.21:4; cp. 1-7; 2 Pt.3:10-12; cp. 3-18). How does a person receive this hope?

> **"For whatsoever is <u>born of God</u> overcometh the world: and this is the victory that overcometh the world, even our faith. Who is he that overcometh the world, but he that believeth that Jesus is the Son of God?" (1 Jn.5:4-5).**

APPLICATION 1:

Do not worry: think about your stature and learn to trust God. Do not concentrate your mind and heart and effort on measuring up to the world's expectations. That is senseless. Concentrate and focus upon God and His righteousness. Such assures a perfect change in your life and body when you enter the next world.

APPLICATION 2:

Some things are senseless in this world, extremely senseless.

⇒ First, it is senseless for men to seek to add an inch to their stature, to *care* for their body in the here and now and *ignore* the hereafter. Think about it. All men are immortal; they are to exist forever. It is senseless to concentrate on a few short years upon earth.

⇒ Second, it is senseless for believers to seek to add an inch to their stature, to *worry* about their body in the here and now and *neglect* life hereafter. It is senseless for the believer to walk through life ignoring his Father and not trusting His care and love.

APPLICATION 3:

Some persons have physical handicaps or abnormal statures. How do they keep from being anxious and worrying?

1) There is a glorious hope for all.

> **"For our conversation [citizenship] is in heaven; from whence also we look for the Saviour, the Lord Jesus Christ: who shall change our vile body, that it may be fashioned like unto his glorious body, according to the working whereby he is able even to subdue all things unto himself" (Ph.3:20-21).**

2) There is the assuring promise of God to work all things out for good to those who truly love Him.

> **"And we know that all things work together for good to them that love God, to them who are the called according to his purpose" (Ro.8:28).**

3) There is the strong challenge to be content with one's condition or lot in life.

> **"Let every man abide in the same calling wherein he was called....Brethren, let every man, wherein he is called, therein abide with God" (1 Cor.7:20, 24).**

1. If worry is such a senseless thing to do, why do so many believers worry about things out of their control? How can you change this habit?
2. As you observe the focus of...
   - the fashion world
   - the entertainment world
   - the clothing industry
   - beauty and health consultants
   - and on and on
   ...what do people spend most of their time worrying about?
3. How much do you allow these things to affect you?

5. DO NOT WORRY ABOUT CLOTHING (v.28-30).

Consider the lilies, how they grow.

1. Lilies grow from a deep root. The roots are where they belong, in the soil to receive nourishment. The roots of believers are not to be in the material things of this earth. In order to receive their nourishment and fulfill their purpose on earth, believers are to put their roots where they belong, in God and His righteousness.

2. Lilies do not toil or spin at spinning wheels to adorn themselves with beauty. Their beauty comes naturally as they go about their purpose in the world. Believers are not to be consumed with toiling after material things in order to adorn themselves with the artificial and superficial coverings. They are to be laboring after God and His righteousness, letting their natural beauty shine forth, trusting God to provide "all these things" (Mt.6:33).

3. Lilies die from the weather. They drop to the ground, decay, pass out of existence, and are gone forever. Clothing fades, wears out, goes out of fashion, and is laid down. Clothing just ceases to exist, but not man. Unlike the lilies and his clothing, man is immortal; he exists forever. Therefore, he is to center his life on God and His righteousness, not on material clothing and physical beauty. God will provide necessary clothing to the person who diligently goes about life putting his priorities in order: seeking God and His righteousness first.

APPLICATION:
Note seven significant lessons.
1) Do not worry: consider the lilies and trust God for clothing.
2) Clothing is used for protection and covering and adornment. The human body needs to be...
   - protected from the weather
   - covered from being exposed to the public
   - adorned for attractiveness

   Yet, how foolish to place one's heart and fate in material clothing, especially when so many throughout the world have so little. A person's salvation is not found in clothing nor in any other material thing, but in seeking first the kingdom of God and His righteousness.
3) There are three concerns about clothing. (Sometimes the concern becomes so strong it turns into a literal fear.)
   a) The concern of popularity. A person fears not having the clothing necessary to make him popular. Sometimes the concern is so great that a person refuses to go to a particular function without the proper clothing.
   b) The concern of style and fashion. A person is concerned with the very latest in style and fashion. He cannot accept a single piece being outdated.
   c) The concern of acceptability. Most adults would fall into this category. Clothing is a matter that actually involves inward feelings. The concern over appearance

is really there. Time and effort are expended to stay in style, at least enough to be acceptable.

The point Christ is making is this: do not fret or worry; do not be anxious over clothing. But seek God first---center your thoughts and efforts upon God and His righteousness--and all these things (clothing) will be added unto you (Mt.6:33).

4) Many judge others by their clothes. How often someone has walked into a place (even into a church) and been looked at askance and thought to be out of place. How often people have felt uncomfortable in welcoming such a person lest they be associated with them. Why? Because the person was wearing old clothes, long out of fashion. The worldly too often worry about clothes, to the point that their judgment of others is affected by clothing. This is often true of youth and young adults.

5) The believer is to labor. He is to work his fingers to the bone seeking first the kingdom of God and His righteousness, and he is to trust God all the while to meet his needs. God, who adorns the non-working lily of the field, will certainly adorn the believer who is living and laboring for Him.

6) Man is as the lilies of the field: here today and gone tomorrow. There is so little time; he does not have time to become entangled with worldly affairs. He must be seeking first the kingdom of God and His righteousness (Mt.6:33).

7) It is folly to focus one's life and body on beauty and nice clothing:

"This...is their folly...they are laid in the grave; death shall feed on them...and their beauty shall consume in the grave" (Ps.49:13-14; cp. v.10-14. This is a descriptive passage covering this whole subject.)

"In like manner also, that women adorn themselves in modest apparel, with shamefacedness and sobriety; not with broided hair, or gold, or pearls, or costly array; but (which becometh women professing godliness) with good works" (1 Tim.2:9-10).

QUESTIONS:
1. Note the command of Scripture: consider the lilies. What lessons can you glean from...
   ...the beauty of the lilies?
   ...the growth of the lilies?
   ...the nourishment of the lilies?
   ...the death of the lilies?
2. What deductions can you make concerning God's love for you as you consider the lilies?
3. People spend a lot of money on clothes with the purpose of wearing the latest fashions. How concerned do you think God is with keeping you dressed in style?

A CLOSER LOOK # 1
(6:30) **Trust--Believe**: the words "O ye of little faith" can mean at least two things.

1. It can be a challenge to strengthen a person's faith. Christ could be saying, "Your faith is small right now. Believe, trust, strengthen, and enlarge your faith. God cares and will provide. You can trust Him. Just believe."

2. It can be a rebuke because a person's faith is terribly weak: "You are worrying, overly anxious; therefore, you are displeasing and disappointing God. God knows you need these things. Quit being distrustful and going through so much anxiety and so many sleepless nights. Turn from the world and trust God."

6. DO NOT WORRY: DO NOT BE THINKING AND TALKING ABOUT FOOD, DRINK, AND CLOTHING (v.31-32).

There are two reasons why such things are not to occupy our thoughts and conversation.

1. The believer is different from the heathen. "After all these things do the Gentiles [the heathen, the lost] seek." Do not be like them, for the genuine believer is to be different.

The lost are wrapped up in the world and in the things of the world. They know nothing else. All they know is seeking and securing all they can of what the world has to offer. They seek *the good life* that comes from possessions. Life to them is money, houses, furnishings, food, cars, televisions, toys, clothing, recreation, property--all the material things of the world that give comfort, pride, power, fame, and recognition.

There is a reason the Gentiles (the heathen, the lost) live this way. The Scripture states it clearly (Eph.2:12, 19).

- a. They are without Christ (Eph.2:12). They are unwilling to accept Christ as the Messiah, the Anointed One of God whom God sent into the world to save the world.
- b. They are aliens from God's people (Eph.2:12). They are not aware that God has a *family of genuine believers* on earth, a body of people who truly trust Him.
- c. They are strangers to the promises of God (Eph.2:12). They know little if anything about the promises of God and His care.
- d. They have no hope beyond this earth (Eph.2:12). They really know very little about a world beyond this life; therefore, they cling to this earth.
- e. They are without God in this world (Eph.2:12). They know nothing about His presence and care, His love and direction, His correction.

They are strangers and foreigners to the things of God and to the hope of God (v.19). Therefore, they know nothing except to seek the things of the earth--to secure whatever and however much their hearts desire.

2. The believer has a heavenly Father who knows his needs. The believer is different from the Gentiles (the lost) in that he has a heavenly Father and he lives for heaven. He does not live for the earth.

⇒ He knows Christ and he knows God's people.

⇒ He knows the promises of God and the glorious hope of eternal life.

⇒ He has God and His presence in this world.

⇒ He is *not* a stranger and foreigner to God but a fellow citizen with the saints of God's household.

Therefore, the believer is to seek "first the kingdom of God and His righteousness." He is to leave the cares of this world up to God as he diligently goes about his affairs upon earth. He makes his contribution to life as God has called him to do, and while so doing he knows that God will take care of all the necessities of life. The testimony of the mature believer is:

"I am poor and needy; yet the Lord thinketh upon me" (Ps.40:17).

APPLICATION:

The lost and unsaved of the world face two serious problems.

1) They do not personally know the only living and true God. They know little if anything of His day to day care. They are left to their own materialistic search for things, both necessities and luxuries. Tragically they have no assurance that all will be well.

2) They are strangers to the hope of an eternal world. Most men have some kind of hope in this world and in the things of this world, but the lost know little if anything about the eternal hope given by God in Christ. Therefore, their hope is seriously deficient. It is temporary, lasting only for a few short years. Their hope dies; it dies when they die. Therefore when worldly hope crumbles, they crumble.

⇒ What is the answer for the worldly (the unsaved, the lost)? The answer is given in the words "your heavenly Father." Make sure God is *your* heavenly Father, and get to know Him as *your* heavenly Father.

⇒ What is Christ saying to the believer? Do not be as the lost and unsaved of the world: a stranger to God and to the glorious hope of eternity. But live, actively live in the presence of God now and forever. He knows your needs. Trust Him and His care.

"**Seek ye first the kingdom of God and His righteousness and all these things shall be added unto you**" (Mt.6:33).

"**For what is a man profited, if he shall gain the whole world, and lose his own soul? or what shall a man give in exchange for his soul?**" (**Mt.16:26**).

QUESTIONS:
1. What causes a person to lust after material things?
2. When it comes to the things of the world, can the world tell a difference between your attitude and the attitude of the lost?
3. Can you distinguish or judge a person based solely upon his financial status? Why or why not?
4. The worldly person lusts after his own needs and wants. What makes you different in seeking to meet your needs?

7. DO NOT WORRY: SEEK YE FIRST THE KINGDOM OF GOD AND HIS RIGHTEOUSNESS (v.33).

The word "seek" means to go after; to strive; to pursue; to desire; to aim at; to search for; to endeavor to get. The believer's life is not to be preoccupied with material things, as necessary as some things are. The believer is first of all to be seeking the kingdom of God and His righteousness. He is to seek to become a citizen of God's kingdom, and he is to seek others, encouraging them to become citizens of God's kingdom. This is to be the first pursuit of his life.

APPLICATION 1:
There are two ways to go about taking care of yourself in this world.
1) Working and seeking in your own strength: depending only upon your own ability and energy alone; fighting and struggling to make it through life; fretting and worrying about succeeding.
2) Working and seeking in both God's strength and your own strength: trusting and acknowledging God while doing all you can; putting your hand to the plow and plowing; working hard and not looking back, and while working, trusting the results to God. God says He will see to it that such a trusting person will always have the necessities of life.

APPLICATION 2:
The believer whose work fails in the eyes of the world can know four sure things--if he has really put God first.
1) His failure is temporary. God will help and strengthen and even teach him through the trying times.
2) God will work all things out for good, for he loves God and has been called by God (Ro.8:28f).
3) God will see to it that the necessities of life are given to him.

4) God has much better things in store for him--eternally. The believer has been faithful in his work, so God will reward him as a faithful servant, even if his labor has failed in the eyes of the world.

    The believer who goes through a failure needs to remember just one thing: be faithful--continue to be faithful. In putting God first, God will lift the believer up now and eternally.

APPLICATION 3:

God made man a spiritual being. Therefore, the only way man can ever be satisfied is to seek spiritual things, God and His righteousness, first. This world and the things of this world will not satisfy. Man's major mistake is this: material things can only make a person *comfortable*. The things of the world can look good, taste good, and feel good; but this is all they can do. Think about it! They are external, *outside* man, and this is just the problem. The need that man senses within is not to be *externally comfortable* but to be *inwardly satisfied and spiritually satisfied*.
1) Material things cannot touch the inside of man. They can only make him comfortable outside.
2) Man really knows down deep within that all material things pass away, even himself. He subdues the knowledge, pushes it out of his thoughts, yet he knows it.

    "And I say unto you, Ask, and it shall be given you; seek, and ye shall find; knock, and it shall be opened unto you. For every one that asketh receiveth; and he that seeketh findeth; and to him that knocketh it shall be opened" (Lk.11:9-10).

    "But if from thence thou shalt seek the Lord thy God, thou shalt find him, if thou seek him with all thy heart and with all thy soul" (Dt.4:29).

QUESTIONS:
1. Do you face special challenges in seeking God's Kingdom first instead of your own needs? How do you go about meeting these challenges?
2. What is the key to seeking God *continuously*?
3. Material things are insufficient in meeting a person's spiritual needs. Why is this so? What example in your own life bears witness to this fact?

A CLOSER LOOK # 2

(6:33) **Kingdom of God--Kingdom of Heaven**: the Kingdom of Heaven evidently means the same thing as the Kingdom of God, eternal life, and salvation. The Kingdom of Heaven and the Kingdom of God are interchanged when Jesus says, "a rich man shall hardly enter into the Kingdom of Heaven" (Mt.19:23) or "Kingdom of God" (Mt.19:24). Eternal life (Mt.19:26) and salvation (Mt.19:25) belong to the very same concept. Eternity and salvation, the Kingdom of God and the Kingdom of Heaven, is the very subject being discussed in Mt.19:16-30. Having eternal life, being saved, or entering into the Kingdom of God or of Heaven is more difficult for a rich man than for a camel to go through the eye of a needle.

    The Kingdom of Heaven and of God is revealed in four different stages throughout history.

1. There is the spiritual kingdom that is at hand; it is present right now (Mt.4:17; Mt.12:28).
    a. The present kingdom refers to God's rule and reign and authority in the lives of believers.

    "The eyes of your understanding being enlightened; that ye may know what is the hope of his calling, and what the riches of the glory of

his inheritance in the saints, and what is the exceeding greatness of his power to us-ward who believe, according to the working of his mighty power, which he wrought in Christ, when he raised him from the dead, and set him at his own right hand in the heavenly places, far above all principality, and power, and might, and dominion, and every name that is named, not only in this world, but also in that which is to come: and hath put all things under his feet, and gave him to be the head over all things to the church, which is his body, the fulness of him that filleth all in all" (Eph. 1:18-23).

b. The present kingdom is offered to the world and to men in the person of Jesus Christ.

c. The present kingdom must be received as a little child.

"But when Jesus saw it, he was much displeased, and said unto them, Suffer the little children to come unto me, and forbid them not: for of such is the kingdom of God" (Mk.10:14-15).

d. The present kingdom is experienced only by the new birth.

"Jesus answered and said unto him, Verily, verily, I say unto thee, Except a man be born again, he cannot see the kingdom of God" (Jn.3:3).

e. The present kingdom is entered now and must be received now.

"Verily I say unto you, Whosoever shall not receive the kingdom of God as a little child, he shall not enter therein" (Mk.10:15).

f. The present kingdom is a spiritual, life-changing blessing.

"For the kingdom of God is not meat and drink; but righteousness, and peace, and joy in the Holy Ghost" (Ro.14:17).

g. The present kingdom is to be the first thing sought by believers.

"But seek ye first the kingdom of God, and his righteousness; and all these things shall be added unto you" (Mt.6:33).

2. There is the professing kingdom that is also in this present age. It refers to modern day Christianity in every generation. It pictures what the Kingdom of Heaven or professing Christianity is like, and what professing Christianity will be like between Christ's first coming and His return. This imperfect state is what is called "the mysteries of the kingdom of heaven" (Mt.13:1-52, esp. Mt.13:11).

"Another parable put he forth unto them, saying, The kingdom of heaven is likened unto a man which sowed good seed [good men] in his field: but while men slept, his enemy came and sowed tares [evil men] among the wheat, and went his way" (Mt.13:24-25).

3. There is the millennial kingdom that is future. It is the actual rule of Christ or the government of Christ that is to come to this earth for a thousand years.

a. The millennial kingdom is the kingdom predicted by Daniel.

   "And in the days of these kings shall the God of heaven set up a kingdom, which shall never be destroyed: and the kingdom shall not be left to other people, but it shall break in pieces and consume all these kingdoms, and it shall stand for ever" (Dan.2:44).

b. The millennial kingdom is the kingdom promised to David.

   "And when thy days be fulfilled, and thou shalt sleep with thy fathers, I will set up thy seed after thee, which shall proceed out of thy bowels, and I will establish his kingdom....And thine house and thy kingdom shall be established for ever before thee: thy throne shall be established for ever" (2 Sam.7:12, 16).

c. The millennial kingdom is the kingdom pictured by John.

   "And I saw thrones, and they sat upon them, and judgment was given unto them: and I saw the souls of them that were beheaded for the witness of Jesus, and for the word of God, and which had not worshipped the beast, neither his image, neither had received his mark upon their foreheads, or in their hands; and they lived and reigned with Christ a thousand years. But the rest of the dead lived not again until the thousand years were finished. This is the first resurrection. Blessed and holy is he that hath part in the first resurrection: on such the second death hath no power, but they shall be priests of God and of Christ, and shall reign with him a thousand years" (Rev. 20:4-6).

4. There is the perfect kingdom of the new heaven and earth that is future.
   a. The eternal kingdom is the rule and reign of God in a perfect universe for all eternity.

   "Let not your heart be troubled: ye believe in God, believe also in me. In my Father's house are many mansions: if it were not so, I would have told you. I go to prepare a place for you. And if I go and prepare a place for you, I will come again, and receive you unto myself; that where I am, there ye may be also" (Jn.14:1-3).

   b. The eternal kingdom is the perfect state of being for the believer in the future.

   "Now this I say, brethren, that flesh and blood cannot inherit the kingdom of God; neither doth corruption inherit incorruption" (1 Cor. 15:50).

   c. The eternal kingdom is an actual place into which believers are to enter sometime in the future.

   "And I say unto you, That many shall come from the east and west, and shall sit down with Abraham, and Isaac, and Jacob, in the kingdom of heaven" (Mt.8:11).

   d. The eternal kingdom is a gift of God that will be given in the future.

   "Fear not, little flock; for it is your Father's good pleasure to give you the kingdom" (Lk.12:32).

QUESTION:

Many believers think of eternity, of the Kingdom, only in terms of the future, after death. How can a more complete understanding of the Kingdom and eternity help you to become a better witness to the lost?

8. DO NOT WORRY ABOUT TOMORROW: LIVE ONE DAY AT A TIME (v.34).

The believer is not to be preoccupied with tomorrow and its affairs. He is to seek God's kingdom and His righteousness today, leaving tomorrow and its needs in God's hands. Christ is not forbidding a man to *take care of tomorrow*. He is striking at man's obsession with getting more and more, with ignoring and neglecting God and His righteousness.

APPLICATION:

There are at least five attitudes about the future.

1) *A no-care, worldly attitude.* A person eats, drinks, and is merry today, letting tomorrow take care of itself. The future is of little concern. It will take care of itself. Earthly pleasure, power, and fame are the major concerns of life. A person gets all he can now, while he can.
2) *A fretful, anxious attitude.* A person worries all the time, wondering if he is secure and if he will have enough to take care of himself and his family.
3) *A fearful, panicky attitude.* In the face of trial and failure, a person can barely function. Tragedy has hit: his job is lost, cutbacks have to be made, adjustments are needed. The strength and confidence to act and to continue on is lacking.
4) *A self-assured attitude.* A person has complete confidence in himself and his ability. He knows he can make out and take care of himself in this world, and he does it. But there is one thing this person fails to see and it is fatal: the confidence that he has in himself will end. He will die, and he will only have taken care of himself for a few short years. He will find out that self-confidence cannot bridge the great gulf between heaven and earth, time and eternity, God and man.
5) *A calm God-centered and trusting attitude.* A person goes about living and working ever so diligently and calmly, trusting God to take care of all. He does all he can about the necessities of life, both for himself and for others, but he seeks God and His righteousness first (Eph.4:28).

> "Therefore I say unto you, Take no thought for your life, what ye shall eat, or what ye shall drink; nor yet for your body, what ye shall put on. Is not the life more than meat, and the body than raiment?" (Mt.6:25).
> "Be careful for nothing; but in every thing by prayer and supplication with thanksgiving let your requests be made known unto God. And the peace of God, which passeth all understanding, shall keep your hearts and minds through Christ Jesus" (Ph.4:6-7).
> "Casting all your care upon him; for he careth for you" (1 Pt.5:7).

ILLUSTRATION:

A person who does not trust Christ will find it impossible not to worry about the future. The opposite is true for the committed believer. The person who trusts wholly in Christ has no need to worry about what is already in God's firm grip--the day we call tomorrow.

> *Jerry was not born with a silver spoon in his mouth, but he was determined his own kids would never do without anything. Blessed with the ability to make great sums of money, Jerry would never go back to the days of his own childhood where*

poverty caused his father to give up and walk out on the family. Jerry was a self-made man who controlled everything in his power. And one thing Jerry thought was in his power was the ability to guarantee his financial security.

But it was something out of his control that led to the greatest crisis of his life. The stock market fell right on his 'safe' stocks, and within a day his financial empire collapsed. Desperate for advice, Jerry called his friend Tom. Tom was a Christian businessman who had also taken his financial lumps in previous years, but kept his faith strong. "Tom, this is Jerry. I've lost everything! Before I do anything stupid, please tell me how you kept your sanity. What kept you from going off the deep end? How did you get through it?"

Tom thought a moment and then replied, "Jerry, none of us know the future. But what has kept me going is that I have a personal relationship with the One who holds the future in His hand...and my hand is in His."

QUESTIONS:
1. What is your attitude toward the future:
   Bleak?   Fearful?   Apathetic?
   No problem. *I* can handle anything that comes my way?
   God is in control (and I confess that I am not)?
2. Have you allowed your hand to rest in the hand of Jesus Christ? Or do you try to work out everything yourself? How can the believer's peace about the future be a strong testimony to an unbeliever?

SUMMARY:

How are you spending your time? Do you worry about everything or do you live your life in the assurance that God will take care of everything that concerns you? God has promised to take care of you and anyone who puts his faith in Christ. Three simple words stored in your heart will take you a long way in this life. *Do not worry!*
1. A counsel--do not worry about necessities.
2. Do not worry about your life and body.
3. Do not worry about food and shelter.
4. Do not worry about your stature.
5. Do not worry about clothing.
6. Do not worry: do not be thinking about food, drink, clothing.
7. Do not worry: seek ye first the kingdom of God and His righteousness.
8. Do not worry about tomorrow: live one day at a time.

PERSONAL JOURNAL NOTES:
(Reflection & Response)

1. The most important thing that I learned from this lesson was:

2. The thing that I need to work on the most is:

3. I can apply this lesson to my life by:

4. Closing Prayer of Commitment: (put your commitment down on paper).

	CHAPTER 7	own eye?	own faults
		4 Or how wilt thou	**4. The criticizer is de-**
	T. The Warning	say to thy brother, Let	**ceived about himself**
	About Judging	me pull out the mote	a. He speaks, but
	and Criticizing	out of thine eye; and,	unthoughtfully
	Others, 7:1-6	behold, a beam is in	b. He is not fit to
	(Lk.6:37-42)	thine own eye?	judge
		5 Thou hypocrite, first	**5. The criticizer is a**
		cast out the beam out	**hypocrite: He must**
1. Do not judge, do not	Judge not, that ye be	of thine own eye; and	**extract his own sin**
criticize	not judged.	then shalt thou see	**first**
2. The criticizer will be	2 For with what judg-	clearly to cast out the	
judged	ment ye judge, ye	mote out of thy	
a. For the same criti-	shall be judged: and	brother's eye.	
cism	with what measure ye	6 Give not that which	**6. The criticizer is un-**
b. With equal weight	mete, it shall be meas-	is holy unto the dogs,	**deserving serving of**
	ured to you again.	neither cast ye your	**the gospel**
3. The criticizer fails to	3 And why beholdest	pearls before swine,	a. He tramples the
examine himself	thou the mote that is	lest they trample them	gospel underfoot
a. He looks for faults	in thy brother's eye,	under their feet, and	b. He turns against &
in others	but considerest not the	turn again and rend	tears people apart
b. He overlooks his	beam that is in thine	you.	

Section IV
THE TEACHINGS OF THE MESSIAH TO HIS DISCIPLES:
THE GREAT SERMON ON THE MOUNT
Matthew 5:1-7:29

Study 20:   THE WARNING ABOUT JUDGING AND CRITICIZING OTHERS

Text: Matthew 7:1-6

Aim: To weed out the causes of a critical spirit in your life.

Memory Verse:
        "Judge not, that ye be not judged" (Matthew 7:1).

INTRODUCTION:
We live in a society that is set aflame with a spirit of criticism. A simple glance at your morning newspaper will show how widespread criticism has become:
   ⇒ The headlines are filled with politicians bent on destroying the reputation of their opponents.
   ⇒ The entertainment section features articles criticizing the work of artists, musicians, and actors.
   ⇒ The sports page spills over with commentary on any person or team on a losing streak.
   ⇒ Even the weather page can be critical if the weather is going to be less than perfect for the coming weekend.

This kind of criticism is not limited to the newspapers. Unfortunately, this same spirit has infiltrated the church. Far too many believers have gotten caught up in the frenzy to assassinate another person with critical words. No matter what is acceptable by the world's standards, Jesus Christ has a far different standard than the world. He declares a clear warning to the person who judges and criticizes others.

MATTHEW 7:1-6

OUTLINE:
1. Do not judge; do not criticize (v.1).
2. The criticizer will be judged (v.2).
3. The criticizer fails to examine himself (v.3).
4. The criticizer is deceived about himself (v.4).
5. The criticizer is a hypocrite (v.5).
6. The criticizer is undeserving of the gospel (v.6).

1. DO NOT JUDGE, DO NOT CRITICIZE (v.1).

The word "judge" means to criticize, condemn, censor. It is fault-finding; it is being picky. It is the habit of censorious and carping criticism. It is not the moral judgments that have to be made sometimes (cp.1 Cor.5:3-5, 12-13); not the specific occasions when value judgments have to be made; not the careful discrimination that is sometimes necessary (Mt.7:6). Note that the beam in the criticizer's eye is much larger than the speck in the eye of the one being judged (cp. Mt.2:1-3).

When a person has come short or done wrong and fallen, he is often judged, condemned, and censored. However, such judgment misses a critical point.

1. When a person has slipped, it is time for compassion not censoring. It is time for reaching out with one's hand and offering to pull the person to oneself, not to push him farther away. It is time to speak kindly of him, not negatively and destructively (Eph.30-32).

2. There is never a spirit of criticism in the humble and loving person. There is only a loving compassion for those who have come short (Gal.6:1-3).

There are several reasons why people tend to judge and criticize.
⇒ Criticism boosts our own self-image. Pointing out someone else's failure and tearing him down makes us seem a little bit better, at least in our own eyes. It adds to our own pride, ego, and self-image.
⇒ Criticism is simply enjoyed. There is a tendency in human nature to take pleasure in hearing and sharing bad news and shortcomings.
⇒ Criticism makes us feel that our own lives (morality and behavior) are better than the person who failed.
⇒ Criticism helps us justify the decisions we have made and the things we have done throughout our lives. We rationalize our decisions and acts by pointing out the failure of others.
⇒ Criticism points out to our friends how strong we are. Criticism gives good feelings because our *rigid beliefs* and *strong lives* are proven again. Proven how? By our brother's failure.
⇒ Criticism is an outlet for hurt and revenge. We feel *he deserves it*. Subconsciously, if not consciously, we think, "He hurt me so he deserves to hurt, too." So we criticize the person who failed.

There are several reasons why no person should ever criticize.

1. All the circumstances and all the facts are never known. What happened and why it happened are just not known. There are always many behind-the-scene facts. Children and parents, wife and husband, employer and employee, friend and friend--things happen when they are alone behind closed doors. And unfortunately there is something seldom remembered: when people emerge from the closed doors and enter the public, the one who does the talking does not always reveal the true facts. The spirit of talk to others is the spirit of self-justification. The spirit of silence is the spirit of caring and compassion. The spirit of silence is always the spirit which desires no hurt for others, at least no more pain than what has to be borne.

2. All people--religious as well as non-religious--come short, fail, and fall. And we all sin often (1 Jn.1:8, 10). No one is ever exempt from sin. When we criticize and judge, we have a problem: we forget that we are sinners. When we acknowledge our own true condition, we act with care and compassion toward all as they come short. They are failing now; we failed before. Our friend shall fail later. No one is ever exempt from sin. It is a continual cycle that is the downfall of mankind. The believer must always remember that his righteousness is Jesus Christ, and he is always dependent upon Christ's righteousness (2 Cor.5:21; Ph.3:8-16). He must always be seeking God's forgiveness and forgetting those things that are behind.... (1 Jn.1:9; Ph.3:13-14).

Now this does not mean that we have license to sin nor that our sin is excused. We are not to continue in sin, not by criticizing nor by doing any other evil. But we must acknowledge our weakness and remember that the person who really knows God is the person who is ever seeking God. "He that cometh to God must believe that He is, and that He is a rewarder of them that diligently seek Him" (Heb.11:6).

3. All there is to know about a person is never known. How then can we criticize? Think about childhood for a moment. Eighteen years is a long time. Day by day moves into a week, and week by week stretches into a month, and month by month lasts and lasts until a year has arrived. And year by year is a long, long time for a child to be molded into an adult. What kind of mother, what kind of father, what kind of friends did the *failing person* have to influence and mold him? What kind of genes and temperament has he inherited and developed: fiery, composed, inferior, strict, strong, lovable, shy? So much goes into influencing a human life that only God can know a person, know him well enough to judge him. Certainly we can never know one another well enough to pass judgment.

4. Judging others usurps God's authority. When a person criticizes another, he is saying that he is worthy and has the right to be *the Judge* over other lives. He is claiming the right to be God, which is ridiculous. Yet most lay claim to the right at one time or another, and some claim the right to exercise a judgmental spirit all the time.

Note what Scripture says, **"Who are thou that judgest another man's servant? To his own master [God] he standeth or falleth. Yea, he shall be holden up: for God is able to make him stand" (Ro.14:4; cp. Jas.4:11-12).**

ILLUSTRATION:

It is so easy to judge another person, especially if we think we have a little bit of expertise to urge us on.

> *"Children's television personality Fred Rogers (Mr. Rogers' Neighborhood) is also an ordained minister. He says, 'I remember so keenly one of the times I learned how individually the Spirit can work. It was years ago, and my wife and I were worshiping in a little church with friends of ours, another husband and wife. We were on vacation, and I was in the middle of my homiletics course at the time. During the sermon I kept ticking off every mistake I thought the preacher, who must have been 80 years old, was making. When this interminable sermon finally ended, I turned to my friend intending to say something critical about the sermon. I stopped myself when I saw the tears running down her face. She whispered to me, 'He said exactly what I needed to hear.'*
>
> *"That was really a [unique]...experience for me. I was judging and she was needing, and the Holy Spirit responded to need, not to judgment.'"*[1]

---

[1] *Christian Century*, Apr. 13, 1994, p.383. As cited in *INFOsearch Sermon Illustrations* (Arlington, TX: The Computer Assistant, 1-888-868-9029, 1986-1996).

QUESTIONS:

1. Have you ever judged someone or something too quickly and come to regret it later? At what point and time are you qualified to judge someone else?
2. Have you ever been falsely judged or accused? How did you feel? Did you learn from the experience?
3. What is the difference between fault-finding and making a moral judgment?

A CLOSER LOOK # 1

(7:1-6) **Criticism--Sins**: note the awful sins committed by the criticizer. Christ says the criticizer will stand in the day of judgment guilty of them all:

⇒ inconsistency, v.2
⇒ self-righteousness, v.3
⇒ spiritual blindness or self-deception, v.3
⇒ uncharitableness or lack of love, v.4
⇒ hypocrisy, v.5
⇒ abuse of the gospel, v.6

What Christ says is strong, so strong that He uses pictures to paint the truth about criticizers. Verse 6 is especially strong. Christ says three things.

1. Criticizers are unworthy of the gospel and the truth. They are subject to trample the gospel under foot and to turn and tear the messenger into pieces. When a believer criticizes, the very gospel he is supposed to represent is reflected in a distasteful light. In fact, the gospel is denied. The changed life of the believer is not seen. The criticizing brother shows himself to be no different than the world. Thus, he is unworthy of the gospel.

2. The preaching of the cross is foolishness to some. Some people are insensitive and censorious, cynical and prideful. Their minds are shut. They ridicule and despise. They are increasingly antagonistic. Every indication is that they are incapable of receiving the truth. Christ is saying the gospel is not to be shared with these lest they tear the believer to pieces.

3. The believer must follow God's Spirit in recognizing the differences between men. In dealing with men there is something that should always be remembered: we may not be able to talk about Christ with someone, but we can show Christ by our lives.

---

2. THE CRITICIZER WILL BE JUDGED (v.2).

Note three things.

1. The criticizer will be judged for the very same thing he criticizes. Whatever he criticizes, it is that for which he shall be condemned. And how frightening! His condemnation shall be by God Himself, not just by another person. Such a thought should cause us to care and love and to live a life of compassion.

2. The criticizer will be judged by one law only--the law of equal weight. The law can be stated several ways.

⇒ The law of equal judgment   ⇒ The law of equal weight
⇒ The law of equal measure   ⇒ The law of equal proportion
⇒ The law of equal retributions   ⇒ The law of equal retaliation
⇒ The law of reciprocal action   ⇒ The law of equal sin

3. Other passages of Scripture say the criticizer will actually receive the greater condemnation.

   a. He shall receive no mercy.

> **"For he shall have judgment without mercy, that hath showed no mercy; and mercy rejoiceth against judgment" (Jas.2:13).**

b. He shall be judged.

> **"For with what judgment ye judge, ye shall be judged: and with what measure ye mete, it shall be measured to you again" (Mt.7:2).**

c. He shall be condemned.

> **"My brethren, be not many masters [judges], knowing that we shall receive the greater condemnation" (Jas.3:1).**

d. He shall be unforgiven.

> **"Be ye therefore merciful, as your Father also is merciful. Judge not, and ye shall not be judged: condemn not, and ye shall not be condemned: forgive, and ye shall be forgiven" (Lk.6:36-37).**

APPLICATION 1:
The person who judges and criticizes can *expect* to be judged. He *will* be judged.

> **"Therefore thou art inexcusable, O man, whosoever thou art that judgest: for wherein thou judgest another, thou condemnest thyself; for thou that judgest doest the same things" (Ro.2:1; cp. v.2-16).**

APPLICATION 2:
God forgives the humble and repentant *sinner*, but He shall judge the judgmental and critical person. There is to be no mercy whatsoever for the person who shows no mercy (Jas.2:13).

APPLICATION 3:
There are two strong reasons for being compassionate and not being judgmental and critical.
1) "So speak ye, and so do, as they that shall be judged by the law of liberty. For He shall have judgment without mercy, that hath showed no mercy and mercy rejoiceth against judgment" (Jas.2:11-12).
2) "Grudge not one against another, brethren, lest ye be condemned: behold the judge standeth at the door" (Jas.5:9).

QUESTIONS:
1. A person will reap what he sows. In practical terms, what does this mean to the critical person? Can you think of a real instance of this happening?
2. Why is the judgment of God certain for the person who has a critical spirit?

3. THE CRITICIZER FAILS TO EXAMINE HIMSELF (v.3).

The criticizer is inconsistent in his judgment. The word "beholdest" has the idea of continuing to look. Too often we continue to look at the failures of others: we continue to gossip, criticize, and revel forever in the bad news.

When we judge and criticize, we reveal a very serious problem: we have a beam in our eye. We are blind to the truth of our own nature. We too fail, and we fail often.

> **"Let us search and try our ways, and turn again to the Lord" (Lam.3:40).**
> **"As it is written, There is none righteous, no, not one" (Ro.3:10).**

"For all have sinned, and come short of the glory of God"
(Ro.3:23).
"But let a man examine himself" (1 Cor.11:28).

4. THE CRITICIZER IS DECEIVED ABOUT HIMSELF (v.4).

1. The criticizer speaks unthoughtfully. He has not thought through what he is doing. If he was thinking, he would not criticize or judge. A thinking person knows that he is just as human and sinful as the next person. He has just as many motes in his eye as the next fellow. Therefore, he has no right to criticize. The person who judges is unthinking and deceived in particular points.
   a. Judging others is overlooking (ignoring, denying) our own sin.
   b. Judging others exalts us as gods. It usurps God's right. It says that we are worthy and have the right to sit upon the *throne* of judgment (Ro.14:4; Jas.4:11-12).
   c. Judging others pushes a brother farther down and tears him up. It does not embrace him in compassion nor pull and build him up.
   d. Judging others brings the greater condemnation (Jas.3:1-2).
   e. Judging itself becomes the beam in our eye when we judge others. There are degrees of sin. There are not small and large sins, but there are degrees of sin. No sin is small when it is committed against so great a God. All sin is great. But there are beams and specks, splinters and slabs, gnats and camels. Different sins carry different weight in their results. Nothing causes any more catastrophic rumblings than judging and criticizing a brother who has failed.
2. The criticizer is not fit to judge.
   a. He is as sinful as the next person, yet he is not considering his own sin. He feels free to be critical of those who come short and fail, yet he does not look at himself. He condemns others, yet he justifies himself. Note: God justifies neither the criticizer nor the sinner (2 Cor.5:10).
   b. The criticizer is the weaker of the two. It is the weak who judge and criticize the most. They have a great need to boost self over others in order to feel good about themselves.
   c. The criticizer does not examine himself. Self-examination hurts, so few of us do it. Yet God says, "If we would judge ourselves, we should not be judged" (1 Cor. 11:31).

"For if a man think himself to be something, when he is nothing, he deceiveth himself" (Gal.6:3).

APPLICATION:
Many protect their own conscience when judging and criticizing others. They deceive their conscience through several actions.
1) By trying to be sweet and nice, being soft spoken, using soft words.
2) By always giving some commendable strengths as well as passing along the failing.
3) By prefacing the criticism with a statement that they wish to make constructive judgment or constructive criticism.

QUESTIONS:
1. Do you know anyone good enough to sit in a position of judgment? What can keep you from being a critical person even in the smallest things?
2. Is there any justifiable reason to criticize someone else?

5. THE CRITICIZER IS A HYPOCRITE: HE MUST EXTRACT HIS OWN SIN FIRST (v.5).

When we judge and criticize, we are hypocrites.

1. We show ourselves to be full of strife and empty glory. We show that we are not *lowly of mind*, nor do we "esteem others better than ourselves" (Ph.2:3).

> "Let nothing be done through strife or vainglory; but in lowliness of mind let each esteem other better than themselves. Look not every man on his own things, but every man also on the things of others" (Ph.2:3-4).

2. We show that we fail to consider ourselves and to exhibit the spirit of meekness. We fail to bear a brother's burden.

> "Brethren, if a man be overtaken in a fault, ye which are spiritual, restore such an one in the spirit of meekness; considering thyself, lest thou also be tempted. Bear ye one another's burdens, and so fulfil the law of Christ" (Gal.6:1-2).

3. We show that we are polluted with bitterness, wrath, anger, clamor, evil speaking, and malice. We fail to be tenderhearted and forgiving. We forget that God for Christ's sake has forgiven us.

> "Let all bitterness, and wrath, and anger, and clamour, and evil speaking, be put away from you, with all malice: and be ye kind one to another, tenderhearted, forgiving one another, even as God for Christ's sake hath forgiven you" (Eph.4:31-32).

Many people suffer greatly because of the judgment and criticism of others. When a person has done wrong and failed or come short, it is time for compassion not censoring. It is time for reaching out and offering to pull the person up, not to push him down farther. It is time to speak kindly of him, not negatively and destructively. The hypocrite fails to do this.

The only hope for the hypocrite, that is, anyone who judges and criticizes, is the same as for any person who sins: "First cast out the beam out of thine eye" and turn to God.

> "Wash you, make you clean, put away the evil of your doings from before mine eyes; cease to do evil" (Is.1:16).
> "Wash thine heart from wickedness, that thou mayest be saved. How long shall thy vain thoughts lodge within thee?" (Jer.4:14).

APPLICATION:
When we judge and criticize, we are hypocritical. We too fail, and fail often; so to judge another person's failure is hypocritical. The point is that we have not only failed, we shall fail again. Thus our task is fourfold.

1) We are to know ourselves. We are as human as the next person and stand in just as much need of God's forgiveness. And we shall need God's forgiveness again and again as much as anyone else. We are all sinners saved by grace.
2) We are not to usurp God's position as judge. He and He alone is God. He alone has the right and ability to judge according to all the facts (Jas.4:11-12).
3) We are "first to cast out the beam out of [our] own eye." We are first to get rid of the sin in our own lives, the critical and judgmental spirit and whatever else is in us. Then we can see clearly to do what we should be doing: helping those who are failing.
4) We are to reach out in compassion and understanding to the person who has failed, not in judgment and criticism.

QUESTIONS:
1. If you could see inside the heart of a critical person, what would you see?
2. What is your responsibility if you are prone to have a critical spirit?

6. THE CRITICIZER IS UNDESERVING OF THE GOSPEL (v.6).

"Give not that which is holy unto the dogs, neither cast ye your pearls before the swine" (v.6).

What Christ was saying is very simply stated: we are not to be foolish and jeopardize ourselves. When we know that a person will not receive us or the instruction of the gospel, we are not to approach them. Very simply, there are some criticizers and scoffing sinners to whom we must not go. They will hurt us and abuse the glorious message of the gospel.

ILLUSTRATION:
One of the hardest things to do as a believer is to guard yourself from the effects of biting words, gossip, scoffing, and slander. The gospel is much too precious to waste it upon those who want nothing more than to pull you down into the muck and mire.

"Two good friends each bought a parrot. One of the birds did a lot of swearing, while the other was always repeating parts of Scripture he had heard. Both had acquired these habits before they belonged to their new owners. The gentleman who had the 'profane polly' was much annoyed by its frequent outbursts of four-letter words. He wondered how he could cure it. 'Ah,' he thought, 'if I move it into the cage with my buddy's Bible- quoting parrot, it will probably improve and may even begin to recite Scripture.' He talked it over with his friend, and they put the two birds together for several days. Did the swearing one learn from the other? Quite the contrary! The pious talker was soon using profanity."[2]

APPLICATION:
This was strong language used by Christ. He faced reality. There are some unbelievers so wicked and profane that they can be compared to dogs and swine. They are said to be unworthy of the gospel. Who are they?
⇒ the notorious sinner
⇒ the scoffers and scornful the
⇒ enraged and revilers
⇒ the hardened judgers and criticizers
⇒ the persecutors
⇒ the openly wicked and profane
⇒ the haters and despisers

[2] *INFOsearch Sermon Illustrations* (Arlington, TX: The Computer Assistant, 1-888-868-9029, 1986-1996).

MATTHEW 7:1-6

Can they be saved? Yes. "Whosoever shall call upon the name of the Lord <u>shall be</u> saved" (Ro.10:13). Any who turn and call upon the Lord shall be saved. But reality must be faced: there are some who have reached such a high level of evil they are unlikely to turn from their wickedness. They take their words and...

- wound
- scoff
- trample
- defy
- scorn
- revile
- rend
- rage

They take their minds and hands and power and...

- trample
- strike
- tear
- persecute
- beat
- kill
- torture

Not everyone does all of the above sins, but many people are guilty of some of them. They destroy the reputation and work of a person, if not his body. What a tragedy that so many believers are often caught up in the criticism and judgment of others. Believers are too often the very ones guilty of taking their words and hands to damage the reputation and work of others.

> "For this people's heart is waxed gross, and their ears are dull of hearing, and their eyes they have closed; lest at any time they should see with their eyes, and hear with their ears, and should understand with their heart, and should be converted, and I should heal them" (Mt.13:15).

QUESTIONS:
1. Scripture tells us to avoid the critical person (cp. 2 Tim.3:2-6). How can you tell when to stay away and draw the line with an individual?
2. What influence does a critical person have upon you? Whom do you need to avoid at all costs?
3. What hope does a critical person have if he refuses to repent?

SUMMARY:

Every day of your life is filled with people who are sinners, who make mistakes. And you are one of them! Remember God's mercy on you, and allow that compassion to carry over into every thought, word, and deed.
1. Do not judge; do not criticize.
2. The criticizer will be judged.
3. The criticizer fails to examine himself.
4. The criticizer is deceived about himself.
5. The criticizer is a hypocrite.
6. The criticizer is undeserving of the gospel.

PERSONAL JOURNAL NOTES:
(Reflection & Response)

1. The most important thing that I learned from this lesson was:

2. The thing that I need to work on the most is:

3. I can apply this lesson to my life by:

4. Closing Prayer of Commitment: (put your commitment down on paper).

	U. The Key to Prayer: Persevering in Prayer, 7:7-11	9 Or what man is there of you, whom if his son ask bread, will he give him a stone?	c. God cares much more than an earthly father cares (cp.11).
1. What is persevering prayer? a. Ask—until you receive b. Seek—until you find c. Knock—until it is opened 2. Why persevere in prayer? a. Prayer is conditional: Must ask—seek—knock b. Everyone is heard	7 Ask, and it shall be given you; seek, and ye shall find; knock, and it shall be opened unto you: 8 For every one that asketh receiveth; and he that seeketh findeth; and to him that knocketh it shall be opened.	10 Or if he ask a fish, will he give him a serpent? 10 If ye then, being evil, know how to give good gifts unto your children, how much more shall your Father which is in heaven give good things to them that ask him?	3. How does a person persevere in prayer? a. He must come to God as his Father b. He must come asking for good things

Section IV
THE TEACHINGS OF THE MESSIAH TO HIS DISCIPLES:
THE GREAT SERMON ON THE MOUNT
Matthew 5:1-7:29

Study 21:   THE KEY TO PRAYER: PERSEVERING IN PRAYER

Text: Matthew 7:7-11

Aim: To learn the basic steps to persevering prayer: To experience the power of persevering prayer.

Memory Verse:
"Ask, and it shall be given you; seek, and ye shall find; knock, and it shall be opened unto you" (Matthew 7:7).

INTRODUCTION:
One of the most important lessons a salesperson must learn is how to "close the deal." While it is important to know the product and the customer's needs, all is in vain if the salesperson fails to sell his product. This principle parallels the believer's relationship with prayer. Many of us spend a lot of energy telling God what we need from Him. And we know that God *has* everything we need. But the failure comes when we give up praying and do not "close the deal." How does a person *close the deal* in prayer?
⇒   By asking God until you receive.
⇒   By seeking God until you find what you need.
⇒   By knocking on the door until it is opened.

Heaven is filled with blessings that have yet to be claimed by God's people. God is simply waiting for the person who wants something badly enough to persevere. "Ask...seek... knock": the Lord commands and challenges us to *persevere* in prayer.

OUTLINE:
1. What is persevering prayer (v.7)?
2. Why persevere in prayer (v.8-10)?
3. How does a person persevere in prayer (v.11)?

MATTHEW 7:7-11

1. WHAT IS PERSEVERING PRAYER (v.7)?

Persevering prayer is asking, seeking, and knocking until the answer is received, found, or opened. It is being so obsessed with getting something that a person never gives up until God responds. The words ask, seek, and knock are in the present tense. A person is to keep on asking, keep on seeking, keep on knocking. He is to persist in prayer. The words *receive*, *find*, and *open* are also in the present tense (Mt.7:8). This shows that the answer to prayer is more than just a promise for the future. The person who perseveres in prayer possesses the answer now. Perhaps the thing has not yet happened, but by faith the believer knows that God has heard his prayer (cp. 1 Jn.5:14-15). (Cp. Eph.6:18.) Christ taught several important lessons about prayer.

1. True prayer is persevering prayer. God expects all of our prayers to be persevering. When we sense a real need to pray, we not only ask, but we seek and knock. We do not play around and glibly murmur a prayer. We pray, really pray.

2. Prayer is to be often. Christ commanded prayer. He pointedly said: "Ask...seek... knock." And, as pointed out above, He demanded that we pray often and pray with intensity.

3. The answers to our prayers are assured (v.9-10).
   a. God is not reluctant to give. He is not sitting back disinterested and unconcerned about our welfare. He is as a loving father is to his child--loving and caring. He will not refuse the request of His dear child.
   b. God will not mock our requests. He does not give grudgingly (Jas.1:5). He does not even hesitate to give. And what He gives is not of less quality than what an earthly father gives. God does not give ragged substitutes. He gives exactly, or better than, what we ask (v.11; Eph.3:20).

4. The thing wanted must be in God's will. It must not be asked from selfish desires and motives. God gives only what is good and wholesome for us (1 Jn.5:14-15; cp. Jas.1:17; 4:2-3).

5. True prayer, persevering prayer, acknowledges our dependence upon God. When we are genuinely in need, we come to God and ask and seek and knock. This has been the experience of all believers time and again.

The very fact that we are asking, seeking, and knocking demonstrates that we are truly dependent upon God. We are His children and He is our Father. Christ said that true prayer is prayer that really means business: it is sincere and genuine in its requests and it keeps on asking and asking until God answers.

ILLUSTRATION:
The believer who perseveres in prayer has to work at it, stay with it, and never quit. A life of prayer is cultivated by good habits that find their roots in *discipline*. It does not take long for grass to grow under our feet when we stop praying.

> *"In one region of Africa, the first converts to Christianity were very diligent about praying. In fact, the believers each had their own special place outside the village where they went to pray in solitude. The villagers reached these 'prayer rooms' by using their own private footpaths through the brush. When grass began to grow over one of these trails, it was evident that the person to whom it belonged was not praying very much.*
>
> *"Because these new Christians were concerned for each other's spiritual welfare, a unique custom sprang up. Whenever anyone noticed an overgrown 'prayer path,' he or she would go to the person and lovingly warn, 'Friend, there's grass on your path!'"*[1]

---

[1] *INFOsearch Sermon Illustrations* (Arlington, TX: The Computer Assistant, 1-888-868-9029, 1986-1996).

APPLICATION:

There is more to prayer than just asking. A person asks, then he seeks and knocks at the door of heaven until God grants the request. Note two things.

1) Seeking contains the idea that we seek to meet the request ourselves. This is especially true if the request can be met by human effort. There certainly is no idea of sluggishness or complacency in the tone of "ask...seek...knock." The thrust is action, a *get-to-it* attitude.

2) Knocking contains two ideas. First, we approach every door that we can until the right door opens. We certainly would not pound and pound away at the same door. We must move about knocking until the right door is opened. Second, we must continue knocking at the door of heaven. We must wrestle with God, not giving Him rest until He opens. Such action shows dependence upon Him. And coming to Him in fellowship and communication is bound to please Him, just as such communication pleases an earthly father.

"**Watch and pray**, that ye enter not into temptation: the spirit indeed is willing, but the flesh is weak" (Mt.26:41).

"And ye shall seek me, and find me, when ye shall search for me **with all your heart**" (Jer.29:13).

QUESTIONS:

1. Why do so many believers fail to persevere in prayer? What causes you to give up on prayer?
2. How is a person to know that he is really praying in God's will?
3. What is the ultimate purpose of prayer?

A CLOSER LOOK # 1

(7:7) **Persevering Prayer**: there is a difference between the words ask, seek, and knock.

1. The word "ask" says the following.
   a. We ask when there is a need or want.
   b. We ask when there is someone who has plenty and who can give what we need or want.
2. The word "seek" says the following.
   a. We seek when we need or want something of value.
   b. We seek when we ourselves are responsible for finding what we need or want.
3. The word "knock" says the following.
   a. We knock when we are shut out and need or want entrance.
   b. We knock when there is someone on the other side who can open to us.

QUESTIONS:

1. Which of these do you find easiest to do and why?
   _____ask?
   _____seek?
   _____knock?
2. When are you most confident that God will answer your prayer?

2. WHY PERSEVERE IN PRAYER (v.8-10)?

There are three reasons.

1. Prayer is conditional. Christ is pointed: if we ask, we receive. If we do not ask, we do not receive. If we seek, we find. If we do not seek, we do not find. If we knock, it is opened to us. If we do not knock, it is not opened to us.

"Ye have not because ye ask not" (Jas.4:3).

APPLICATION:

Failing to persevere in prayer shames God and ourselves. True prayer is persevering prayer. Our genuineness and sincerity are known by how much we persevere in prayer.
1) We show disrespect to the Giver when we ask and walk away before receiving what we ask.
2) We show our gross insincerity when we seek once or twice and stop.
3) We leave any resident questioning when we knock once or twice and walk away before he comes or has time to open.

2. Every believer is heard and every prayer is answered. It is not just the believers who are well-known--the leaders and official laborers--whom God hears and answers; He hears everyone who "asks and seeks and knocks."
3. God cares *much more* than an earthly father cares. God can be approached as Father. Above all others, He knows what a father should be. Whatever good is within earthly fathers has come from Him. He made fathers. He put within their hearts an *instinctive attachment and love and desire to nurture*. Therefore, we can expect Him to be personally attached to us and to love and nurture us (cp.Ps.103:13).

"And whatsoever ye shall ask in my name, that will I do, that the Father may be glorified in the Son. If ye shall ask any thing in my name, I will do it" (Jn.14:13-14).

QUESTIONS:
1. In what way is prayer conditional? How often do you meet the conditions?
2. What is the typical result when a person fails to persevere in prayer?
3. What benefits do you gain if you persevere in prayer?

A CLOSER LOOK # 2

(7:8) **Prayer**: Why does God not always answer our prayers immediately? Why is it necessary to ask and seek and knock and to keep on asking and seeking and knocking? Why do we need to ask at all when God knows our needs even before we ask?

There are at least four reasons .

1. Prayer teaches us to communicate and fellowship with God and to trust and seek God more and more. When God holds the giving back, we keep coming to talk and share with Him more and more. Just as a human father longs for our fellowship, our heavenly Father longs for our fellowship.

2. Prayer teaches us both patience and hope in God and His promises. When God does not give immediately, we patiently (enduringly) keep coming into His presence, waiting and hoping in what He has promised us (Mt.21:22; Jn.14:26; 1 Jn.5:14-15).

3. Prayer teaches us to love God as our Father more and more. Knowing that God is going to answer our prayer and having to wait on the answer causes us to draw closer and closer to God and His gifts. Then when the prayer is answered, our hearts are endeared to Him much more than before.

4. Prayer demonstrates how deeply we trust God and how much we love and depend upon Him. A person who really trusts God--who really knows he is going to receive what he has asked--will bring more and more concerns to God. He will come to God in prayer more and more. But the person who is not quite sure about receiving will only occasionally come, usually only in emergencies. God easily sees how much we love and trust Him by our prayer life.

1. What do you normally do when your prayers are not answered immediately?
2. Can you think of a time when your desire to pray was quenched because you did not see God acting fast enough? How did you resolve this?
3. Based on the amount of time you pray and your sincerity, how dependent are you upon God? Is it enough?

A CLOSER LOOK # 3

(7:8) **Prayer--Promise--Hope**: when we pray as Christ says, we have our request immediately. He assures us, yet the answer is not always in our hands immediately. What then does Christ mean? There are two ways we receive things whether dealing with men or God.

1. We receive things by promise and hope. If some reliable person promises something to us, we know beyond question the gift is ours. (Cp. monthly interest promised on money deposited in savings.) What we tend to forget is this: the promise is as much a fact as an immediate receipt is. The only difference between promise and receipt is time, and whether we are willing to patiently wait and demonstrate our belief in the Giver and the gift. If the Giver is reliable, then His promise is sure: the gift is ours. It will be handed to us when the time and conditions are right.

Now, note two simple but sure things.
   a. Promise and hope are as sure as receiving immediately if the Giver is reliable.
   b. Promise and hope are as sure as the Giver. If the Giver is reliable, the promised gift is coming at the appointed time.
2. We receive things by acceptance--just receiving the gift when it is handed to us.

> "And this is the confidence that we have in him, that, if we ask any thing according to his will, he heareth us: and if we know that he hear us, whatsoever we ask, we know that we have the petitions that we desired of him" (1 Jn.5:14-15).

QUESTIONS:
1. You can be totally confident of God's answer to prayer if you are faithful to ask. Can God be as confident in your faithfulness?
2. How confident are you in claiming the promises of God? In what way can your faith in God's promises grow?

---

3. HOW DOES A PERSON PERSEVERE IN PRAYER (v.11)?

1. The believer must come to God as his Father. Christ explicitly tells us how to come.
   a. We must come to God as "Our Father which is in heaven." The words "in heaven" acknowledge His sovereignty. God is able to do whatever we ask, and we are to expect Him to grant our requests.
   b. We must come to God as we come to an earthly father: freely and openly, communicating and fellowshipping. And we are to come often, not neglecting the love, respect, and trust due Him.

Note the words "how much more." Whatever earthly parents are, God is much more. He is much more as a Person and as a Father. He knows our every request and He has the knowledge, intelligence, wisdom, and power to grant them.

APPLICATION 1:
God has taken the initiative to create the family relationship with us. He has adopted us as His children. Therefore, we can come to Him in much more trust and confidence than we can to our earthly fathers.

"But when the fulness of the time was come, God sent forth his Son, made of a woman, made under the law, to redeem them that were under the law, that we might receive the adoption of sons. And because ye are sons, God hath sent forth the Spirit of his Son into your hearts, crying, Abba, Father" (Gal.4:4-6).

APPLICATION 2:
God is love (1 Jn.4:8, 16). He is so loving He compares His love and tenderness to that of a mother (Is.66:13).

2. The believer must come to God for good, wholesome things: beneficial, honorable, needful qualities.

APPLICATION:
Earthly fathers are human and sometimes carnal, and some fathers are even deliberately evil. Note three things about earthly fathers.
1) Earthly fathers sometimes make mistakes in what they give. They can and do give unacceptable and unsuitable things to their children--not deliberately but mistakenly. They are simply deceived by what the world calls acceptable and good. But God is not deceived. God gives only "good things," things which are truly wholesome and beneficial. If we ask for that which is wrong and harmful to us, God will quickly and pointedly say "No," or else He will give what is really needed.
2) Earthly fathers are sometimes ill-natured, cross, provoking, and wrong in their response to a child's request. But not God. He always understands and knows exactly how to respond and what and when to give.
3) Earthly fathers are sometimes evil and harmful, threatening and dangerous, forsaking and deserting. But not God. God knows exactly how to meet the need of the son or daughter who is forsaken or deserted (Ps.27:10).

"But seek ye first the kingdom of God, and his righteousness; and all these things shall be added unto you" (Mt.6:33).
"If ye then, being evil, know how to give good gifts unto your children: how much more shall your heavenly Father give the Holy Spirit to them that ask him?" (Lk.11:13).

ILLUSTRATION:
Our opinions about our heavenly Father are often twisted by experiences with our earthly fathers. This is unfortunate. Many people shun God because they feel He is indifferent and far away, unloving and uncaring. But God's Word is clear: believers are to come to Him as a loving heavenly Father and ask for whatever they need.

Tom was a new salesman for a chemical company. He trained in the company's lab for a year and then went on the road to make sales. Two months went by and Tom had sold nothing. He could not figure out what was wrong. He knew his product and he had a good sales delivery.

So Bill, Tom's sales manager, spent one day with him making calls. At the end of the day Bill said, "Tom you're missing only one thing, but it's the most important part of the sale. It's called 'closing the deal.' You're dancing all around the subject, but you're not asking for their order."

Bill's comment to Tom turned his career around. All Tom had to do was ask. In much the same way, believers know they have needs. And they know God can supply the need. But for one reason or another, many believers fail to ask and to keep on asking. Our heavenly Father wants to be asked to bless His children.

Have you asked God for what you need?

1. Many people do not have a good relationship with their earthly father. How can you help them understand God's nature and His relationship to believers?
2. Do you approach your heavenly Father with the proper respect?
3. Do you spend enough time with your heavenly Father to be comfortable in approaching Him?
4. God only has good things for His children. What *good things* do you need from God today?

SUMMARY:

How do you get your prayers answered? Christ declared the way: by asking, seeking, and knocking; that is, by persevering prayer. Bear in mind that prayer is more than just knowing what you *want* to receive from God. It is important that you receive what you *need*. What kind of track record do you have concerning persevering prayer? Remember: the key to persevering prayer can be described with three basic steps:

⇒ Ask
⇒ Seek
⇒ Knock

1. What is persevering prayer?
2. Why persevere in prayer?
3. How does a person persevere in prayer?

PERSONAL JOURNAL NOTES:
(Reflection & Response)

1. The most important thing that I learned from this lesson was:

2. The thing that I need to work on the most is:

3. I can apply this lesson to my life by:

4. Closing Prayer of Commitment: (put your commitment down on paper).

	V. The Summit of Ethics: The Golden Rule & Two Choices in Life, 7:12-14 (Lk.6:31; 13:23-24)	13 Enter ye in at the strait gate: for wide is the gate, and broad is the way, that leadeth to destruction, and many there be which go in thereat:	2. The two choices in life a. Two gates: Wide vs. narrow b. Two ways: Easy vs. hard c. Two ends: De- struction vs. life
1. The golden rule of life a. Demands true justice b. Includes real love c. Teaches the whole law	12 Therefore all things whatsoever ye would that men should do to you, do ye even so to them: for this is the law and the prophets.	14 Because strait is the gate, and narrow is the way, which leadeth unto life, and few there be that find it.	d. Two travelers: The wise vs. the unwise e. Two decisions: No effort vs. seeking to find

Section IV
THE TEACHINGS OF THE MESSIAH TO HIS DISCIPLES:
THE GREAT SERMON ON THE MOUNT
Matthew 5:1-7:29

Study 22: THE SUMMIT OF ETHICS: THE GOLDEN RULE AND TWO CHOICES IN LIFE

Text: Matthew 7:12-14

Aim: To make a most difficult choice in life: To live out the golden rule on a daily basis.

Memory Verse:
"Therefore all things whatsoever ye would that men should do to you, do ye even so to them: for this is the law" (Matthew 7:12).

INTRODUCTION:
Life presents us with many opportunities that demand clear-cut choices. There is the choice about...
⇒ what career to pursue
⇒ who to marry
⇒ whether to buy or rent a home

The list of possible choices is endless. Some choices are easy; some are difficult. But the fact remains the same: every person is forced to make choices and to live with the consequences. The key to a successful life is to consistently make the *right* choices.

This Scripture contains two of the most well known things Jesus ever said. They deal with two of the basic issues or choices of life. (1) There is the issue of righteousness. How can a person live righteously, that is, have a right relationship with his neighbor? (2) There is the issue of life. How can a person be sure he has life, real life?

OUTLINE:
1. The golden rule of life (v.12).
2. The two choices in life (v.13-14).

1. THE GOLDEN RULE OF LIFE (v.12).

The golden rule is probably the most well known thing Jesus ever said. It is the summit of ethics, behavior, righteousness, and godliness. It is a very practical statement of God's love; that is, God has done to us just as He wants us to do to Him. God has treated us as He wants us to treat Him (and everyone else).

292

The golden rule reveals the heart of God. It shows us exactly how God's heart longs for us to live and act. It is a simple statement revealing what love really is and what life in a perfect world is like. It tells believers that they are to live as the golden rule dictates while still on the earth before being transferred into the heavenly world or dimension.

There are four significant facts that set the golden rule apart from all other teachings and make it the summit of human behavior.

1. The golden rule is a one sentence statement that embraces all human behavior. The fact that all law and all love can be stated in one simple sentence is amazing. The simple statement of the golden rule includes all "the law and the prophets" (Mt.7:12).

2. The golden rule demands *true* law and justice. Note the wording: it is not negative and passive, yet it tells man how not to behave. It truly restrains man. For example, the golden rule is teaching a man not to lie, steal, cheat, or injure. And it is teaching much more.

3. The golden rule is concerned with true love and with positive, active behavior.
   a. It is more than not doing wrong (lying, stealing, cheating).
   b. It is more than just doing good (helping, caring, giving).
   c. It is looking, searching, and seeking for ways to do the good that you want others to do to you. It is seeking ways to treat others just as you want them to treat you.

4. The golden rule teaches the whole law. The whole law is contained in the words: "Thou shalt love thy neighbor as thyself" (Mt.22:39-40). Every human being would like to have all others treat them perfectly: to love and care for them to the ultimate degree and to express that love and care. The believer is to likewise love and care for others while still on earth. He is to give earth a taste of heaven before all things end. Men who are treated so supremely and get a taste of heaven are more likely to turn to God.

> **"Let love be without dissimulation [hypocrisy]. Abhor that which is evil; cleave to that which is good" (Ro.12:9).**

APPLICATION 1:
A one sentence *golden rule* has to do three things.
1) Demand true justice: insist that men be treated justly in all situations.
2) Include real love: insist that men actively do good and even go beyond and do more than good.
3) Teach the whole law: insist that men do all that the law teaches.

APPLICATION 2:
Three things are required of men.
1) To know what Christ taught.
2) To believe what Christ taught.
3) To do what Christ taught. It is not enough to know or to believe the golden rule. We must live it.

APPLICATION 3:
Two simple rules can revolutionize a person's life (or society itself).
1) Treating God as we want God to treat us.
2) Treating others as we want others to treat us.

APPLICATION 4:
In practice, the golden rule says several things.
1) We should not treat men the way they treat us: good for good, evil for evil.
2) We should not treat men the way they think they should be treated.
3) We should not treat men the way we think they should be treated.
4) But, we should treat men the way we want them to treat us.

APPLICATION 5:

Note several significant truths.

1) Our profession is empty unless we are *living out* the golden rule. The golden rule condemns us and shows us how far short we come.

2) How do we want men to treat us? The judgment as to how we wish to be treated is ours. We are totally responsible for our conclusion. Our conclusion is critical, for it is how we are to treat others. It is the basis of judgment upon ourselves. We will be judged for how we actually treat others.

3) The golden rule makes all men equal. How we wish to be treated is how we should treat others. And how others wish to be treated is how they should treat us. All people--the wealthy, famous, and powerful as well as the poor, unknown, and unimportant--all are to treat each other just as they would wish to be treated. If men would practice the golden rule, the ills of society would be solved: hunger, poverty, disease, and sin.

4) The golden rule would bring about a world of peace overnight if men would just commit themselves to it.

5) The course of wisdom is to live by the golden rule. It is the wisest thing that a man can do. Why? It assures many friends and the very best in life. Many will draw close to a person who treats them well all the time, and they will respond with like treatment, at least a good deal of the time. Realistically, not everyone will respond, but many will.

6) One way to practice the golden rule is to ask the simple question: "How would I want to be treated?" Then treat the other person that way.

7) The golden rule says very much the same thing as the second great law: "Thou shalt love thy neighbor as thyself" (Mt.22:39). Note that Christ says both the golden rule and the two great commandments contain all the law (Mt.7:12; cp. Mt.22:40). The laws of God and the laws of men would both be obeyed if we practiced the golden rule and the two great commandments.

ILLUSTRATION:

How we respond to people who need us will quickly show just how sincere we are about being a Christian. Every person wants to be treated decently, with fairness and respect.

> "A young man named Ross had an interesting experience while working as a waiter during his college days: 'I didn't know the couple who'd come into the restaurant. They were maybe in their mid-50s. Seemed like nice enough folks. I soon saw, though, that Kim, a new employee, was having a hard time with their order. She brought them the wrong entree, forgot their drinks, and was on the verge of tears because she believed the entree mix-up was their mistake, not hers.
>
> "I saw she was upset, so I went over to offer my assistance. Kim pulled me aside and asked if I'd please take over waiting that table. She just couldn't work with this couple. I agreed. After I assured the couple that their order was coming and quickly brought them their drinks, they thanked me warmly.
>
> "After their dinner arrived, I went to the manager and told him the story. I asked if we could give them their meals for free since there had been such a mix-up. The manager agreed. When I told the couple their dinners would be 'on the house,' they thanked me profusely. 'You've given us fine, fine service,' the man kept saying to me.
>
> "As they were getting their coats, I went to say good-bye and thanked them again for coming. The [man] was removing his coat from the coatrack, and as he did, I saw the name of our restaurant chain on the back of his jacket.

"'Oh, do you work for our chain?' I asked.
"'No,' the man responded, 'I'm the owner of the chain.'"[1]

Living by the golden rule keeps you on your toes!

QUESTIONS:
1. The golden rule must be lived out, not just talked about. Are you conscious of the golden rule as you relate to people with whom you work? With whom you go to church? Your family? Your neighbors? What do you need to do to follow the golden rule more consistently?
2. If the golden rule were adopted by the rulers of your nation, how would they govern differently?

2. THE TWO CHOICES IN LIFE (v.13-14).

The picture is not of a man standing at a crossroads, as some paint the scene. What man faces is a single gate not two gates. There are two gates, but man faces and sees only one. Man cannot see the narrow gate; it has to be searched for and found. (Note the words "find it," v.14.)

The charge is forceful: turn from the wide gate (worldliness); search for and find and enter the narrow gate.

1. There are two gates: one wide and one narrow. Every man stands before the wide gate. It is immediately before him, right before his face. It is the only gate that faces him; in fact, it is so close to him that no entrance is necessary. All he has to do is take a step and he has entered it.

The narrow gate is not seen. A person has to search for it in order to find it. It is both narrow and facing in the opposite direction from the wide gate. This means...

- it is not immediately or naturally seen
- it can be found only if one turns (repents) to find it
- it has to be sought
- it is difficult to enter when found (narrow)

The point is striking and forceful.
   a. The way to eternal life is very specific and very few will choose it (cp. Jer.21:8).
   b. There is no choice. There is only one way not many.
   c. The way is Jesus Christ. If a person wishes eternal life, he has to come to God through Jesus Christ (Jn.14:6; Acts 4:12).

APPLICATION 1:
The wide gate is the world. The narrow gate is the Kingdom of Heaven. The wide gate stands open. It is so wide that four things can be said about it.
1) There is not a single hindrance to entering the wide gate. Nothing keeps a person from entering it. It is as if a person naturally stands before its wide open doors.
2) Plenty of people can enter and are entering its wide doors at any given time. A person has plenty of company in entering the wide gate.
3) It appears to be the only gate to enter because...
   - there is so much growth around it
   - there are so many people entering it
   - there is so much activity going on
   The point is that a person does not even think of another gate, much less look for one.

---

[1] *Power for Living*, Jan 21, 1996, p. 8. As cited in *INFOsearch Sermon Illustrations* (Arlington, TX: The Computer Assistant, 1-888-868-9029, 1986-1996).

4) The wide gate is wide enough to include all: all philosophies and beliefs no matter how extreme, all appetites and passions, all liberties and licenses, all sin and selfishness. The gate is swung wide open so that any and all can enter.

> **"Now the works of the flesh are manifest, which are these; Adultery, fornication, uncleanness, lasciviousness, idolatry, witchcraft, hatred, variance, emulations, wrath, strife, seditions, heresies, envyings, murders, drunkenness, revellings, and such like: of the which I tell you before, as I have also told you in time past, that they which do such things shall not inherit the kingdom of God"** (Gal.5:19-21).

APPLICATION 2:

The narrow gate is so narrow it cannot be seen. This says several things.
1) We must turn from the wide gate: turn from following the crowd; turn from the pull of the activity and attractions around the gate.
2) We must search for the narrow gate and seek it out diligently.
3) We must enter immediately when we find the narrow gate. However, it is hard to enter, for it is very narrow.

APPLICATION 3:

How does a person enter the narrow gate (heaven)?
1) He must repent: turn from the wide gate, the crowd, the activity and attractions around the gate (the world).

> **"I tell you, Nay: but, except ye repent, ye shall all likewise perish"** (Lk.13:3).

2) He must confess that he does not know the narrow gate (heaven); the location (belief); the activity around it (righteousness, good works); and the attraction of it (hope, spiritual qualities, and real life), and that he needs help to find it.

> **"They are all gone out of the way, they are together become unprofitable; there is none that doeth good, no, not one"** (Ro.3:12).

3) He must be born again:

> **"Except a man be born again, he cannot see the kingdom of God...."** (Jn.3:3).

ILLUSTRATION:

We live in a society that offers a wide variety of choices. A popular ice-cream shop advertises more choices than a person could ever eat during one sitting. The majority of restaurants give their customers a menu offering so many tantalizing items it is difficult to select. But every now and then, you might find a diner that is a little more specific with its menu.

> *The weary traveler saw a sign on the road advertising a small southern diner with "the best tastin' food in the world." His hunger convinced him to find the diner and satisfy his hunger. As he drove along, he could just taste his favorite foods. "I think I'll order this...no, I'm more in the mood for that...then again, I may just see what's on special." Before he knew it, he was seated at a counter in the diner. A waitress came through the swinging door and approached him. "You want some-*

thin'?" she asked. "Well, what are my choices?" the man responded. Without missing a beat she said, "Yes or no."

As a person stands at the narrow gate, his choice is also yes or no. There are no additional selections on God's menu for salvation.

APPLICATION 4:
How does a person enter the narrow gate?
1) He must stoop and bow down: become as a little child (Mk.10:15; Lk.18:17).
2) He must strip down: put off the old man (Eph.4:23-24; Col.4:10).
3) He must struggle: struggle against the flesh (2 Cor.6:17; Gal 5:17).

QUESTIONS:
1. What dangers face the person who steps into the wide gate?
2. Once a person enters in the wide gate, is there any way he can continue his journey in it and be saved? Why or why not?
3. Once a person enters in the wide gate, is there any way he can change his mind and go back to the narrow gate? If so, how?
4. What is the only way that a person can enter the narrow gate?

2. There are two ways or two roads to life: one easy and one hard. *The broad and easy way* can be followed without thought. There is plenty of space to walk; there is plenty of space for the attractive things of the world to grow and entice a person; there is plenty of space for a person to wander about. It is difficult to wander off its path. The broad way is the way of the unthoughtful, the undisciplined, the lazy, the worldly, the ungodly, the materialistic, and the carnal.

The narrow and hard way requires commitment, determination, discipline, control, and self-denial. There is little space along its path. It is difficult to get through. A person has to stay alert at all times lest he wander out of the way off its path. The narrow way is the way of the thinking, the disciplined, the responsible, and the spiritual.

The two travellers may be contrasted as the thoughtless vs. the thinking, the undisciplined vs. the disciplined, the lazy vs. the responsible, the materialistic or carnal vs. the spiritual-minded.

APPLICATION 1:
The broad way is the easy way, the way of the world. The narrow way is the hard way, the way of heaven, the way of faith, hope, and righteousness. The broad way is very broad and ever so easy to travel.
1) It has very few hedges, restrictions, or stops to slow a person's journey down. A person can travel right along as he wishes with few prohibitions. He may stop as he is attracted or invited.
2) It offers many attractions along its way. There are attractions that stir the mind and the flesh, aesthetic values and sensual desires, cultural interests and pleasurable stimulators. There are many, many attractions that appeal to all the sensations of a person's nature.

> **"Whose ways are crooked, and they froward in their paths" (Pr.2:15).**
> **"...the way of transgressors is hard" (Pr.13:15).**

MATTHEW 7:12-14

APPLICATION 2:
The narrow way is very narrow, and it is hard and difficult to travel.
1) The way (road) is surrounded by a frightening, threatening, and swampy wilderness. Resistance is needed. The temptation to return to the broad way is sometimes strong. Self-denial and the will to struggle are needed to overcome the flesh and the fear.

> **"And he said to them all, If any man will come after me, let him deny himself, and take up his cross daily, and follow me" (Lk.9:23).**

2) The way (road) is unpaved, covered with gravel and rocks. It takes strong will, determination, and personal sacrifice to stick to the road (Ro.12:1-2). A person must endure hardness and sufferings.

> **"I beseech you therefore, brethren, by the mercies of God, that ye present your bodies a living sacrifice, holy, acceptable unto God, which is your reasonable service. And be not conformed to this world: but be ye transformed by the renewing of your mind, that ye may prove what is that good, and acceptable, and perfect, will of God" (Ro.12:1-2).**

ILLUSTRATION:
It was once said, "The narrow way would not be so narrow if more people walked on it!"

QUESTIONS:
1. How would you describe life on the broad road? Why is this such an attractive life for a person not walking with the Lord?
2. We live in a society that promotes "free love," "pro-choice," and "personal rights." How can the believer guard himself from having his own faith watered down?
3. Why is the narrow way such a difficult road for a person to trod?

3. There are two ends: death and life. The broad way ends in destruction and death. In fact, even as a person walks along the broad way, he is said "to be perishing [apoleian]."
The narrow way ends in life, that is, in "the fulness of life" and in "the highest ideal of life" (Jn.10:10.)

APPLICATION 1:
The broad way or road ends, but the traveler does not pay any attention to its end. The road appears to be so broad and long as he travels day by day that he figures he will know when he comes to the end. There is little chance he can miss it, so he thinks. But he overlooks one thing. The broad road has so many side attractions to draw and embrace the traveler's attention that he often runs upon the end without knowing it. He fails to see that the end is immediately ahead; therefore, he runs off the end without having prepared himself to face the abyss.

> **"For the wages of sin is death; but the gift of God is eternal life through Jesus Christ our Lord" (Ro.6:23).**

APPLICATION 2:
The narrow way does not end. It leads to a glorious world that is yet unseen, but it opens up an unbelievable life to the traveler.

> **"For God so loved the world, that he gave his only begotten Son, that whosoever believeth in him should not perish, but have everlasting life" (Jn.3:16).**

4. There are two travellers: the wise vs. the unwise. The unwise are *many*. They enter the wide gate, travel the broad and easy way, and end up perishing and experiencing destruction.

The wise are the *few*. The few search for, find, and enter the narrow gate. They travel the narrow and hard way and end up experiencing the fulness of life in its highest ideal.

APPLICATION 1:

Many travellers desire the crowd and the attractions of the broad way so much that they are willing to run the risk of wrecking among so much traffic.

APPLICATION 2:

Many travellers on the broad road figure this: since so many are traveling the broad road, they could not be wrong. All the *paths* taken within the broad way must end up at the same end. And they are right; the travellers of the broad way, no matter which *path* they take, do end up at the same end.

> **"No man can serve two masters: for either he will hate the one, and love the other; or else he will hold to the one, and despise the other. Ye cannot serve God and mammon" (Mt.6:24).**

5. There are two decisions: no effort vs. seeking to find. The wide gate requires no decision to enter. A person stands before it automatically by being in the world. Christ does not say a person has to enter it. To enter the gate requires no energy, no search, no commitment. A person is there, facing the gate already. All he has to do is to begin his journey in life and follow its broad and easy course.

The narrow gate requires a decision to enter. It requires (1) a personal decision, (2) a firm determination, and (3) a commitment of energy and effort to search out the entrance. And once the narrow gate has been found, an immediate and definite decision to enter is required: "Enter ye in" is the striking and clear decision that has to be made.

> **"Choose you this day whom ye will serve" (Josh.24:15).**

The wide gate is *the world* and the narrow gate is *heaven*. The broad way is the *way of the world*, and the narrow way is the *way of heaven*. The broad way leads to *destruction* (perishing) and the narrow way leads to *life*. Many are entering the wide gate and perishing. *Only a few* are entering the narrow gate and living.

APPLICATION 1:
Some seek the narrow gate and never enter it.

1) Some come upon it, but they decide it is too narrow for them. It requires too much effort, discipline, and self-denial to enter.
2) Some seek unthoughtfully. They carelessly walk right by it without ever seeing it.
3) Some seek half-heartedly. They still look back to the wide gate so as not to lose sight of it. They miss the narrow gate because of insincerity and lack of discipline.
4) Some seek and run across it, but they do not like what they see: the restraints, the discipline, the gravel and rocky covering. Therefore, they turn back to the wide gate.

APPLICATION 2:
The narrow gate is narrow and hard to find. But it is not shut. It is open to all who seek and find it. The invitation is out to whomever will enter it.

"Come unto me, all ye that labour and are heavy laden, and I will give you rest" (Mt.11:28).

QUESTIONS:
1. Why does it take no effort to enter the wide gate? Why does a person have to look for the narrow gate if it is to be entered? What does this tell you about God's holiness and man's sin?
2. Have you ever toyed with the idea of entering in the narrow gate and then backed off for selfish reasons? What brought you back again? Have you ever regretted walking on the narrow path?

SUMMARY:

A person's reputation is strongly based upon the choices he makes in life. God has given every believer the opportunity and ability to make the right choices. When you make a choice that affects your Christian witness, remember these two things:
1. The golden rule of life.
   a. Demands true justice
   b. Includes real love
   c. Teaches the whole law
2. The two choices in life.
   a. Two gates: Wide vs. narrow
   b. Two ways: Easy vs. hard
   c. Two ends: Destruction vs. life
   d. Two travelers: The wise vs. the unwise
   e. Two decisions: No effort vs. seeking to find

PERSONAL JOURNAL NOTES:
(Reflection & Response)

1. The most important thing that I learned from this lesson was:

2. The thing that I need to work on the most is:

3. I can apply this lesson to my life by:

4. Closing Prayer of Commitment: (put your commitment down on paper).

	W. The Warning About False Prophets, 7:15-20	tree bringeth forth good fruit; but a corrupt tree bringeth forth evil fruit.	not good but corrupt and evil
1. Their presence: Beware	15 Beware of false prophets, which come to you in sheep's clothing, but inwardly they are ravening wolves.	18 A good tree cannot bring forth evil fruit, neither can a corrupt tree bring forth good fruit.	5. Their hopeless cause: Cannot bear good fruit but only corrupt & evil fruit
2. Their chief trait a. Outwardly: As sheep b. Inwardly: Are wolves			
3. Their revealing mark: The fruit they gather	16 Ye shall know them by their fruits. Do men gather grapes of thorns, or figs of thistles?	19 Every tree that bringeth not forth good fruit is hewn down, and cast into the fire.	6. Their terrible future: Judgment
4. Their true nature: Is	17 Even so every good	20 Wherefore by their fruits ye shall know them.	7. Their fruit: Exposes them

Section IV
THE TEACHINGS OF THE MESSIAH TO HIS DISCIPLES:
THE GREAT SERMON ON THE MOUNT
Matthew 5:1-7:29

Study 23:   THE WARNING ABOUT FALSE PROPHETS

Text: Matthew 7:15-20

Aim: To recognize the symptoms of false teachers: To be on guard against their influence.

Memory Verse:
    "Wherefore by their fruits ye shall know them" (Matthew 7:20).

INTRODUCTION:
    When the Allies walked into the German concentration camps at the close of World War Two, the battle-hardened troops saw something that even a terrible war had not prepared them to face. As the prison gates were swung open and the prisoner's barracks were opened, the troops saw men, women, and children who looked like visitors from the other side of the grave. Lying on makeshift cots, those who were strong enough to raise their heads from the bed stared at their deliverers with starved bodies and sunken faces that looked dazed and lost. These poor, dear people were victims of a system that had gone mad. And the world swore, "Never forget; never again."
    But it has happened again. Today, in another generation, people are being put into spiritual prisons. The victims of spiritual abuse are dazed and lost. Led into spiritual chains by false teachers, the abused prisoner could be your neighbor, friend, or fellow-church member. In a very subtle way, false teachers have crept into society, even churches, and have taken captive innocent people who do not know any better. How great a threat is false teaching today? Author Mary Alice Chrnalogar says *"Abusive disciplers expect you to:*
    ⇒ *make considerable time in your schedule for them*
    ⇒ *call them frequently to get advice*
    ⇒ *meet with them often*
    ⇒ *share with or confess your sins to them, and to be 'transparent' to them in every area of your life*
    ⇒ *trust them with all your intimate secrets--even though they may have nothing to do with sin*

⇒ *discuss even your non-moral decisions with them*
⇒ *trust the advice your discipler gives you, and obey this discipler in every area of your life.*
"You may be led to believe that any violation of the discipler's rules can be a sin."[1]

The threat of false teachers is very real; there are wolves dressed in sheep's clothing waiting to pounce.

Note what Christ is talking about in this passage. He is talking about prophets, men who proclaim and teach the gospel. There are some who are false prophets, men who proclaim and teach a false gospel. Christ says seven things about false prophets. (Cp. Gal.1:6-9.)

OUTLINE:
1. Their presence: beware (v.15).
2. Their chief trait: they appear as sheep, but inwardly they are wolves (v.15).
3. Their revealing mark: the fruit they gather (v.16).
4. Their true nature: it is not good, but corrupt and evil (v.17).
5. Their hopeless cause: they cannot bear good fruit but only corrupt and evil fruit (v.18).
6. Their terrible future: judgment (v.19).
7. Their fruit: exposes them (v.20).

1. THEIR PRESENCE: BEWARE (v.15)!

False prophets are among us. Note two emphases.
1. Christ says: "Beware." The word means to take heed, guard, watch, keep yourself. The word is emphatic; the warning is clear and strong.
2. Christ warns us: one of the major things that keeps us from seeking the right gate and the right way (salvation and heaven) is false teachers.

> **"For the time will come when they will not endure sound doctrine; but after their own lusts shall they heap to themselves teachers, having itching ears; and they shall turn away their ears from the truth, and shall be turned unto fables" (2 Tim.4:3-4).**

ILLUSTRATION:
False teaching is dangerous, even deadly. What appears to be *safe* teaching will cause great destruction if it is not the true gospel.

> *"Some years ago a terrible railroad accident occurred, killing many people. A commuter train had stalled on the tracks just minutes before a fast freight was due to arrive. A conductor was quickly sent to flag down the approaching 'flier.' Being assured that all was well, the passengers relaxed. Suddenly, however, the speeding freight came bearing down upon them. The crash left a ghastly scene of horror. The engineer of the second train, who escaped death by jumping from the cab, was called into court to explain why he hadn't stopped. 'I saw a man waving a warning flag,' he said, 'but it was yellow, so I thought he just wanted me to slow down.' When the flag was examined, the mystery was explained. It had been red, but because of long exposure to the sun and weather it had become a dirty yellow. Dr. Harry Ironside commented on this incident: 'O the lives eternally wrecked by the 'yellow gospels' we are hearing today--the bloodless theories of [sinful and un-*

---

[1] Mary Alice Chrnalogar. *Twisted Scriptures*. (Chattanooga, TN: Control Techniques, Inc., 1997), p.11.

saved]... men that send their hearers to their doom instead of stopping them on their downward road!'"[2]

2. THEIR CHIEF TRAIT: THEY APPEAR AS SHEEP, BUT INWARDLY THEY ARE WOLVES (v.15).

1. Sheep's clothing: *outwardly* they appear as all ministers and sheep of God in profession, behavior, call, position, and message (2 Cor.11:12-15).
2. Ravening wolves: *inwardly*, false teachers are anything but sheep.
   a. Some false teachers are just like wolves in that they *may not be aware* that they are *not* what they should be. They go about doing what they know to do, not knowing that what they do is corrupt and evil (v.17). They appear as sheep, but consume all they can in order to fill whatever appetite--personal conviction or doctrine--they have.
   b. Some false teachers are just like wolves in that they are *out for self and personal gain*: ego, recognition, fame, prestige, position, livelihood, career, and comfort. They are concerned primarily with realizing their own motives and purposes, with pushing their own thoughts and formulas for succeeding in life.
   c. Some false teachers are just like wolves in that they *want a pack in which to move* and with which to identify. They want a following to acknowledge their lead in intelligence and creativity or knowledge and ability. They appear as sheep, but they howl their own formulas (false gospels), crying aloud: "This is the way, walk in it." When possible, they use all the media they can: screen, radio, journals, magazines, books, newspapers, pamphlets, and tracts.

APPLICATION 1:
False teachers are in sheep's clothing. They can easily deceive.
1) They appear as sheep or messengers of light (2 Cor.11:13-15). They appear harmless, innocent, and good. They start out as excellent examples of society, but they lack two things: a life and a testimony changed by the Word of God.

> **"For such are false apostles, deceitful workers, transforming themselves into the apostles of Christ. And no marvel; for Satan himself is transformed into an angel of light. Therefore it is no great thing if his ministers also be transformed as the ministers of righteousness; whose end shall be according to their works" (2 Cor.11:13-15).**

2) They secretly and deceivingly preach heresies (2 Pt.2:1-3; cp. Gal.1:6-10; 1 Cor.15:1-4). They proclaim justice, morality, righteousness, and good. They teach mental and emotional and physical strength--all the high ideals and commendable ideas of men. But they never preach the true gospel of the living Lord.

---

[2] *INFOsearch Sermon Illustrations* (Arlington, TX: The Computer Assistant, 1-888-868-9029, 1986-1996).

"But there were false prophets also among the people, even as there shall be false teachers among you, who privily [secretly] shall bring in damnable heresies, even denying the Lord that bought them, and bring upon themselves swift destruction" (2 Pt.2:1).

APPLICATION 2:
Inwardly false prophets are wolves, real wolves, knowingly or unknowingly.
1) They have not confessed the *Lord Jesus*: that God has raised Him from the dead.

"That if thou shalt confess with thy mouth the Lord Jesus, and shalt believe in thine heart that God hath raised him from the dead, thou shalt be saved. For with the heart man believeth unto righteousness; and with the mouth confession is made unto salvation" (Ro.10:9-10).

2) They have not "put off the old man" of the world.

"That ye put off concerning the former conversation the old man, which is corrupt according to the deceitful lusts" (Eph.4:22).

3) They have not been "renewed in the spirit of their mind" nor "put on the new man."

"And be renewed in the spirit of your mind; and that ye put on the new man, which after God is created in righteousness and true holiness" (Eph.4:23-24).

4) They have not been put into the ministry by God. (Note especially 1 Tim.1:12, the fact that God counts the men whom He chooses as *trustworthy*.)

"And I thank Christ Jesus our Lord, who hath enabled me, for that he counted me faithful, putting me into the ministry" (1 Tim.1:12).

APPLICATION 3:
A false prophet sometimes does not know he is false. He is *deceiving* because he is *being deceived*.

"But evil men and seducers shall wax worse and worse, deceiving, and being deceived" (2 Tim.3:13).

QUESTIONS:
1. A false teacher may display all the signs of being an expert, but he is totally off base in his understanding of the truth. How does a person fall into this error?
2. How can a false teacher not know that he is a false teacher?
3. Is it possible to be truly called to preach the gospel but not be called by God?

3. THEIR REVEALING MARK: THE FRUIT THEY GATHER (v.16).

How can we tell if a prophet is false? There is one revealing mark: the fruit he gathers. A false prophet is known by the fruit he feeds upon and the fruit he feeds to others. If he *feeds himself* on thorns and thistles and not on grapes and figs, that is one way to tell. If what he *feeds to others* is thorns and thistles instead of grapes and figs, that is another way to tell.

Thorns and thistles are false food, worldliness. Grapes and figs are true food. There is only one true food for the soul of man: the Lord Jesus Christ and His Word. (See Jn.6:30-36; 6:41-51). A prophet must feed upon the truth of the Lord and His Word, and he must feed the same food to others. Any other source of food for the human soul is false food: it is thorns and thistles (worldliness). If eaten or served to others, it will choke the life out of the soul (Mt.13:7. Cp. 1 Jn.2:15-16; 2 Cor.6:17-18; Ro.12:1-2.)

Note that Christ asks a question: "Do men gather grapes of thorns, or figs of thistles?" This can mean two things.
1. Does the prophet himself feed upon a worldly nourishment or a nourishment of Christ and His Word?
2. Does a person seek grapes and figs among thorns and thistles, among false prophets? A person knows false prophets by their fruits.

APPLICATION 1:
"Ye shall know them by their fruit."
1) "Try [test] the spirits," the prophets (1 Jn.4:1).
2) "Prove [examine] all things," the prophet's fruit (1 Th.5:21).

APPLICATION 2:
We cannot always tell a tree by its appearance (bark and leaves), but we can always tell it by its fruit. Fruit has to do with two things.
1) What a person bears in his own life.
2) What a person bears in the lives of others.

A prophet is to be measured by the fruit borne in his own life and the fruit borne by him in other lives.

QUESTIONS:
1. How can you determine whether or not a person is a false teacher without judging him?
2. What are some examples of false foods, thorns, and thistles? Have you ever been guilty of feeding on these things? How can you or did you stop?

4. THEIR TRUE NATURE: IS NOT GOOD BUT CORRUPT AND EVIL (v.17).

What is the true nature of a prophet? Note something critically important: a tree is not judged by a bad piece of fruit here and there but by the good fruit it bears. Every tree produces some bad fruit, yet the tree is not cast away. A tree is not rejected unless it *leans toward* bearing bad fruit. In testing and examining prophets we must observe not single acts here and there; but the tenor, the lean, the whole behavior of their lives. How important! Such considerations as the following are given in Scripture.
1. Their preaching and teaching. Are they "enemies of the cross of Christ"?

"For the preaching of the cross is to them that perish foolishness; but unto us which are saved it is the power of God" (1 Cor.1:18).
"For many walk, of whom I have told you often, and now tell you even weeping, that they are the enemies of the cross of Christ" (Ph.3:18).

2. Their minds. Do they usually keep their minds on carnal or on spiritual things?

"For they that are after the flesh do mind the things of the flesh; but they that are after the Spirit the things of the Spirit. For to be car-

nally minded is death; but to be spiritually minded is life and peace" (Ro.8:5).

3. Their appetite. Can it be said, "God is their belly"?

"Whose end is destruction, whose God is their belly, and whose glory is in their shame, who mind earthly things" (Ph.3:19).

4. Their day to day ethics or behavior. Is it their practice to live immorally, either vicariously (through what they look at, watch, read, talk, and joke about) or through what they do?

"Nay, ye do wrong, and defraud, and that your brethren. Know ye not that the unrighteous shall not inherit the kingdom of God? Be not deceived: neither fornicators, nor idolaters, nor adulterers, nor effeminate, nor abusers of themselves with mankind, nor thieves, nor covetous, nor drunkards, nor revilers, nor extortioners, shall inherit the kingdom of God" (1 Cor.6:8-10).

Now, how can Christ call a man corrupt who does good in the eyes of the world? How can Christ say the man's fruit, his good works, are evil? How can preaching strong character and moral justice, feeding and clothing, caring for and looking after the physical and emotional welfare of a person be wrong? It is not wrong. Christ is not saying social justice and welfare are wrong. What is evil is concentrating *only* upon social welfare. "Man shall not live by bread alone," not by the physical only, "but by every word that proceedeth out of the mouth of God" (Mt.4:4).

A prophet who only preaches and takes care of the physical and mental is corrupt in that he shortchanges and deceives people. He does not proclaim and minister the whole truth, but half truths. He preaches and teaches mental health in spiritual terms, but he lulls people to sleep spiritually. He leads them into thinking they are in good standing with God, but this is not the teaching of Scripture. They are not acceptable to God when only their physical and mental needs are ministered to, regardless of the spiritual terms used. They must have their spirits *made and kept* right with God. False prophets "are enemies of the cross of Christ" (Ph.3:18). Thus, Christ says they are corrupt and bear fruit of evil.

APPLICATION:
A false prophet's *true* nature is not good, no matter what he or others think and profess.

QUESTIONS:
1. It is important not to make wild accusations against a person, not just picking on an occasional character flaw, but instead looking at the whole nature of an individual. How do you know where to draw the line, when to speak up, and when to be quiet?
2. A false teacher can be a person who does good, who cares for people. But a false prophet is corrupt and the bearer of evil fruit. Somewhere there is a departure from the truth. How can you find it and recognize it?

5. THEIR HOPELESS CAUSE: THEY CANNOT BEAR GOOD FRUIT BUT ONLY CORRUPT AND EVIL FRUIT (v.18).

The results of his life and ministry are "evil," so says Christ. Why? His message at best is only half true. It is deceiving in that it leads a man into thinking he is acceptable to God when really he is not. Men believe what their prophets (ministers, pastors, and teachers) tell them and live before them. Thus, to share only part of the truth is evil and destructive.

What are some of the *evil fruits* (the evil gospel) proclaimed and taught by false prophets? Scripture covers the following.

1. There is the gospel which primarily stresses legalism and works, the efforts of man to do enough good to become acceptable to God.

> **"O foolish Galatians, who hath bewitched you, that ye should not obey the truth, before whose eyes Jesus Christ hath been evidently set forth, crucified among you? This only would I learn of you, Received ye the Spirit by the works of the law, or by the hearing of faith?...For as many as are of the works of the law are under the curse: for it is written, Cursed is every one that continueth not in all things which are written in the book of the law to do them. But that no man is justified by the law in the sight of God, it is evident: for, The just shall live by faith" (Gal.3:1-2, 10-11).**

2. There is the gospel which primarily stresses grace and faith and minimizes behavior. A person can be worldly as long as he takes care of his spirit at the appointed times of worship on Sunday (Ro.6:1f).

> **"What shall we say then? Shall we continue in sin, that grace may abound? God forbid. How shall we, that are dead to sin, live any longer therein?" (Ro.6:1-2).**

3. There is the gospel which primarily stresses negativism, rules and regulations to control every act of behavior: "Touch not, taste not."

> **"Touch not; taste not; handle not; which all are to perish with the using; after the commandments and doctrines of men? Which things have indeed a show of wisdom in will worship, and humility, and neglecting of the body [personal discipline]; not in any honour to the satisfying of the flesh" (Col.2:21-23).**

4. There is the gospel which primarily stresses physical and mental health in spiritual terms, as discussed in the previous point.

5. There is the gospel which primarily stresses formalism and ritual, externals and ceremonies--that a person is acceptable to God just as long as he is baptized and somewhat faithful to the church with its rituals and ordinances.

> **"For they being ignorant of God's righteousness, and going about to establish their own righteousness, have not submitted themselves unto the righteousness of God" (Ro.10:3).**

6. There is the gospel which primarily stresses separation and monasticism: a gospel that takes a person out of the world. Remember, the world is the place where believers are to move about and reflect their light (live and minister).

> **"I pray not that thou shouldest take them out of the world, but that thou shouldest keep them from the evil" (Jn.17:15).**

7. There is the gospel which primarily stresses the true spiritual needs of man, but ignores and neglects the physical needs.

> **"Then shall he say also unto them on the left hand, Depart from me, ye cursed, into everlasting fire, prepared for the devil and his an-**

gels: for I was an hungred, and ye gave me no meat: I was thirsty, and ye gave me no drink: I was a stranger, and ye took me not in: naked, and ye clothed me not: sick, and in prison, and ye visited me not" (Mt.25:41-43; cp. Mt.25:34-46).

APPLICATION:
Good fruit can never be expected or produced by a corrupt tree. Only evil fruit is reaped from a corrupt tree. A false prophet is lulling more and more persons into thinking they are acceptable and deepening their faith in a false gospel.

QUESTIONS:
1. One of the most dangerous things about a false teacher is the half-truths that they teach. Why is it so important for you to be grounded in the Word of God?
2. What are some popular teachings being pushed by false teachers? Why are so many people drawn to these teachings?

6. THEIR TERRIBLE FUTURE: JUDGMENT (v.19).

The terrible future of the false prophet is severe judgment (see A Closer Look # 1-- Mt.7:19). When a tree leans toward bearing bad fruit, it is...
- marked as corrupt
- cut down
- cast into the fire

Christ says the same fate is to be the destiny of the false prophets. The terrible judgment coming upon false prophets is given in several passages.

"Every branch in me that beareth not fruit he taken away: and every branch that beareth fruit, he purgeth it, that it may bring forth more fruit....If a man abide not in me, he is cast forth as a branch, and is withered; and men gather them, and cast them into the fire, and they are burned" (Jn.15:2, 6).

QUESTIONS:
1. Is the judgment that awaits the false prophet worth whatever benefits he may have reaped on earth (fame, wealth, a following)? With such a harsh judgment coming, why would anyone want to spread lies instead of the truth?
2. Is there hope for the false prophet to change while he is still on earth? Is so, how?

A CLOSER LOOK # 1
(7:19) **Judgment--Hell Fire**: note several facts about Hell or Geheena.
⇒ It is the same as the lake of fire (Rev.19:20; 20:10, 14-15).
⇒ It has to do with the second death (Rev.21:8; Jn.8:24).
⇒ It is a literal place called hell (5:29-30; 10:28; 23:15, 33; Lk.12:5).
⇒ It is everlasting fire (Mt.18:8).
⇒ It is hell fire (Mt.18:9; Jas.3:6).
⇒ It is unquenchable fire (Mk.9:43-49).

The teaching of Jesus should always be remembered. Remembrance is critical in determining a person's fate. Hell is a definite place, a real place that is specifically located. It was originally prepared for the devil and his angels. But all men who choose to follow self and evil and to reject God shall also be sent to hell eternally.

> "And now also the axe is laid unto the root of the trees: therefore every tree which bringeth not forth good fruit is hewn down, and cast into the fire" (Mt.3:10).
>
> "And fear not them which kill the body, but are not able to kill the soul: but rather fear him which is able to destroy both soul and body in hell" (Mt.10:28).

QUESTIONS:
1. Could false teachers really understand the reality of hell, the horror of hell, and still continue with their false teaching? What does this say to believers about witnessing to them?
2. Should you steer clear of false teachers or try to convince them of their eternal fate?

7. THEIR FRUIT: EXPOSES THEM (v.20).

A man's words expose five things about him.

1. The fruit borne by a man's words expose his true nature: what he is really like beneath the surface.

2. The fruit borne by a man's words expose what he is down deep within his heart: his motives, desires, ambitions, or lack of initiative.

3. The fruit borne by a man's words expose his true character: good or bad, kind or cruel.

4. The fruit borne by a man's words expose his mind, what he thinks: pure or impure thoughts, dirty or clean thoughts.

5. The fruit borne by a man's words expose his spirit, what he believes and pursues: the legitimate or illegitimate, the intelligent or ignorant, the true or false, the beneficial or wasteful.

> "Now the works of the flesh are manifest, which are *these;* Adultery, fornication, uncleanness, lasciviousness, Idolatry, witchcraft, hatred, variance, emulations, wrath, strife, seditions, heresies, Envyings, murders, drunkenness, revellings, and such like: of the which I tell you before, as I have also told *you* in time past, that they which do such things shall not inherit the kingdom of God" (Gal.5:19-21).

ILLUSTRATION:
A false teacher can hide within a fellowship of believers for years and never be exposed. Therefore, every church needs to do whatever is necessary to get rid of them.

> During the heat of the summer, it seemed every homeless insect and spider had found a place in Ron's house. When he would turn on the light in a dark room, the insects would make their way to the safety of cracks in the baseboard. Ron was at a loss for what to do. It seemed ordinary house sprays were ineffective. Finally, a friend recommended that he treat his house with a few bug bombs.
>
> That did the trick. After letting the insecticide work its way into every nook and cranny, the unwelcome pests rolled over and died. The darkness could protect them no more.
>
> The church faces much the same challenge that Ron faced. Unwelcome guests, false teachers, have found their way into many churches. The ordinary way of treating these intruders does not work. In fact, it multiplies them and increases their might. The only thing that will remove a false teacher from a church is to focus upon the purity of God's Word. Wherever God's Word is taught, it will find its way

into the nooks and crannies of a person's heart and exterminate the influence of the false teacher. And the darkness will protect the false teacher no more.

QUESTIONS:

1. What a person teaches will tell you a lot about his integrity. A person who bends God's Word to make his point should cause you to think carefully. Have you ever sat under the teaching of someone who stretched the truth?
2. False teachers can hide behind technical or deep theological words and discussions. What is your best defense against this technique?

SUMMARY:

Beware of false teachers! The warning that Christ gave can be made no clearer. It is the believer's responsibility to protect himself and others from the clutches of people who seek to pull others down with them. The world is filled with spiritual captives. Do not add to their number by letting a false teacher fool you too.

1. Their presence: beware.
2. Their chief trait: they appear as sheep, but inwardly they are wolves.
3. Their revealing mark: the fruit they gather.
4. Their true nature: it is not good, but corrupt and evil.
5. Their hopeless fruit: they cannot bear good fruit, but only corrupt and evil fruit.
6. Their terrible future: judgment.
7. Their fruit: exposes them.

PERSONAL JOURNAL NOTES:
(Reflection & Response)

1. The most important thing that I learned from this lesson was:

2. The thing that I need to work on the most is:

3. I can apply this lesson to my life by:

4. Closing Prayer of Commitment: (put your commitment down on paper).

MATTHEW 7:21-23

	X. The Warning About False Pretenses: Who Shall Enter the Kingdom of Heaven, 7:21-23 (Lk.13:26-27)	heaven. 22 Many will say to me in that day, Lord, Lord, have we not prophesied in thy name? and in thy name have cast out devils? and in thy name done many wonderful works?	2. The plea of false profession: Works a. Plea 1: Prophesied & cast out evil spirits b. Plea 2: Did great works c. Plea 3: Served in the Lord's name
1. The law of entrance a. A person must do more than profess b. A person must do God's will	21 Not every one that saith unto me, Lord, Lord, shall enter into the kingdom of heaven; but he that doeth the will of my Father which is in	23 And then will I profess unto them, I never knew you: depart from me, ye that work iniquity.	3. The rejection of false profession a. Bc. Christ never knew b. Bc. worked iniquity

Section IV
THE TEACHINGS OF THE MESSIAH TO HIS DISCIPLES:
THE GREAT SERMON ON THE MOUNT
Matthew 5:1-7:29

Study 24: **THE WARNING ABOUT FALSE PRETENSES: WHO SHALL ENTER THE KINGDOM OF HEAVEN**

Text: Matthew 7:21-23

Aim: To make absolutely certain that your status before God matches your profession.

Memory Verse:
"Not every one that saith unto me, Lord, Lord, shall enter into the kingdom of heaven; but he that doeth the will of my Father which is in heaven" (Matthew 7:21).

INTRODUCTION:
Years ago a book was written that listed all the people who claimed to be a part of a European royal family. Thousands of families were interviewed and researched, but of all those who claimed to be legitimate, only a small percentage of people had royal blood. The majority of the people had added royal titles to their names to impress others. Most of these people had assumed they were linked to the king because their parents and their grandparents had falsely claimed to be of royal blood. When the book was published, a lot of people were sorely disappointed not to be included in the royal number.

The disappointment that these 'fake nobles' experienced will be nothing compared to what millions will face who call themselves Christians. The Europeans lost their claim to nobility. The person who has no blood line that can be traced to the shed blood of Christ will lose more than prestige. This person will lose his soul for eternity.

Who will enter the kingdom of heaven? Will everyone who professes Christ enter? The Lord says, "No! There are some who profess my name only...." The *false professor* is a person who uses the Christian vocabulary, recites his prayers, attends services, participates in church functions, yet he does not know nor accept the Lord's Word. He does not obey the Lord's Word (Mt.7:18; Lk.6:46). He does not really know Christ--not personally. Therefore, Christ says he shall not enter the Kingdom of Heaven.

311

OUTLINE:
1. The law of entrance (v.21).
2. The plea of false profession: works (v.22).
3. The rejection of false profession (v.23).

1. THE LAW OF ENTRANCE (v.21).

A person cannot get into heaven by just professing that Jesus Christ is Lord. He can get into heaven only by doing the will of God. This is the law that governs the gate and entrance into heaven. Note two points.

1. A person must do more than profess Christ to enter heaven. There are two kinds of people who say "Lord, Lord," making a false profession. First, there are those who profess and do very little else. They do not hesitate to talk about their religion or church and to express confidence in it. They feel religion has its place in the lives of men and in the structure of society. They attend church, give and serve others as much as is needed in order to make them feel comfortable with themselves and acceptable to God. Some feel comfortable and acceptable attending a few services, giving a little and serving only when approached. Others need more, so they do more.

Second, there are those who profess and do a tremendous work for their religion and society. They are as sincere as can be; and they call Christ, "Lord, Lord" in all the areas of religious life, in...

• prayer	• confessions	• conversation
• witnessing	• rituals	• preaching
• teaching	• giving	• writing
• dress	• activities	• helping others
• ordinances	• appearance	• church or synagogue attendance

Yet this person, a person who calls Christ "Lord" and labors so diligently "in His name," is also rejected and shut out from heaven. Why?" There are three primary reasons.

    a. Profession alone is just words. Profession alone is the big "I." Note the words, "Have we not" done all these things, "many wonderful works" (v.22). They were wonderful works, but when we stand before God, the works we have done will count for nothing. In that day (Judgment Day), a genuine believer is not going to be professing what he has done. What he has done is nothing compared to what Christ has done. He is going to be worshipping Christ. This is the critical point: profession only shows just how inadequate our understanding of God and self really is. It shows just how focused we are upon our own ability and goodness.

        Just think and be honest: How can anyone ever stand before the Supreme Being and Intelligence of the Universe, before God Almighty, and claim anything? If such a *Person as God* is going to let any man enter heaven, it is going to be because He wills to accept the man, not because the man has done anything. Profession alone does not *understand* or else rejects the true nature of God and man--the true nature of God and man as revealed by the Bible and witnessed by history. History exposes the selfishness, greed, and evil of every nation and person of the world day by day.

    b. *Profession alone* does not do God's will. *Profession alone* is "a form of godliness, but denies the power thereof" (2 Tim.3:5). This simply means that a person goes through all the forms of religious life, yet he denies the power of godliness. What is godliness?

        "That <u>God was in Christ</u>, reconciling the world unto Himself... For He [God] hath made him [Christ] to be sin for us, who knew no sin; that we might be made the righteousness of God in him" (2 Cor.5:19, 21).

This is the crux of the matter: the only Lord that God knows is the Lord Jesus Christ whom He sent from heaven (Jn.3:16). God sent the Lord Jesus to die for our sins, to die so that through belief...
- we might be counted free of sin's penalty--the penalty *paid by Him*
- we might be justified, that is, counted perfectly righteous and acceptable to God *because of Him*

God sent the Lord Jesus to arise from the dead, to arise so that through belief...
- we might be counted as new men in *His resurrected life*
- we might be acceptable *in Him* to live eternally with God

Anyone who denies the power of godliness--the power of Christ's death and resurrection to impart forgiveness and life to him--will not enter heaven. All man's works and religion, no matter how good, are only a form of godliness.

c. *Profession alone* acknowledges and honors self, not Christ. Note something of critical importance. When Christ died *for us*, He was the One who had done all the good, all the work of salvation. We have done nothing. He was the One who died; therefore, He is the One who is to be honored and lifted up and praised. He is the Subject, the only Subject, of redemption.

This is the very thing God is after: the honor of His dear Son. It is the man who trusts Christ's death and resurrection who honors Christ. And it is that man who shall be allowed to enter heaven and that man alone.

> **"Not every one that saith unto me, Lord, Lord, shall enter into the kingdom of heaven; but he that doeth the will of my Father which is in heaven" (Mt.7:21).**
> **"He answered and said unto them, Well hath Esaias prophesied of you hypocrites, as it is written, This people honoureth me with their lips, but their heart is far from me" (Mk.7:6).**

2. A person must do God's will in order to enter heaven. Note: Christ is talking about people who *are* interested in heaven, who are saying "Lord, Lord." He is not talking about those who are not even interested in heaven. Heaven should be the final goal of every man. It should be the place every man seeks to enter. However, not everyone interested in heaven will enter heaven. The people who wish to enter heaven must do the will of Him who is in heaven, who controls the entrance into heaven. Who is that? The Father of the Lord Jesus Christ, not some other *god* or *prophet*. Now, what is the primary will of God?

> **"This is His commandment, that we should believe on the name of His Son Jesus Christ, and love one another, as He gave us commandment" (1 Jn.3:23).**

The person who does God's will is the person who *truly believes, obeys, and loves* God's Son.

> **"He that hath my commandments, and keepeth them, he it is that loveth me: and he that loveth me shall be loved of my Father, and I will love him, and will manifest myself to him" (Jn.14:21).**

APPLICATION 1:
What do we mean when we call Jesus "Lord"? Do we mean...
- that He was a great teacher?
- that He was a living example of what all good men should be?
- that He was a great martyr who shows all men how they should embrace a purpose?
- that He was a great man upon whom the Spirit of God rested in a special way?

Jesus Christ is all the above and so much more! He is the Son of God, our Master and Savior, and He is to be the future Judge of the world (Jn.5:22, 27). Note that the person who *professes only* calls upon Christ and even calls Him "Lord," but he is rejected by Christ.

APPLICATION 2:

In the deepest moments of our thoughts, we know that we need help in living, in particular if we are to escape death and live forever--help from Someone above and beyond ourselves. Why then do we have so much difficulty confessing our need?

Confession and obedience and honor are due God; it is not due man. We are the ones who have a desperate need for life. The person who confesses and obeys and honors God shall enter heaven eternally.

QUESTIONS:

1. The old saying is true: "Talk is cheap." Before you became a true believer in Christ, what empty words or professions did you make?
2. Church members are typically kept busy--especially if they are willing to volunteer. A lot of people equate their position before God to their *busyness* in the church. What is the relationship between a person's service and his salvation?
3. How can a person really know for sure that he is not just professing?

2. THE PLEA OF FALSE PROFESSION: WORKS (v.22).

There is all the difference in the world between a man who professes that his righteousness is due to Christ alone and the man who professes that his works please God and make him acceptable to God.

The first man believes that Christ died for his sins and rose again to give him life; he trusts God to *count him forgiven and righteous* "in Christ's death" and *alive* "in Christ's resurrection." This man works, yes, but he works because he loves Christ. Christ has done so much for him by counting him righteous and giving him eternal life that he surrenders his life in service to Christ.

The second man works also, but he works to become acceptable to God. He believes his works please God; therefore he thinks God accepts him because he does good and lives righteously. This man has a *formal* religion, resting his destiny upon his good works. His confidence is in his own goodness and ability. Thereby Christ is not honored; the man is honored.

Note the three great pleas of false profession in the Day of Judgment.

1. The great plea to the Lord Himself: "Lord, Lord." The problem is what a person really means by "Lord" (see Application 1 above).

Christ said to His own apostles "Ye call me Master (teacher) and Lord: and ye say well, for so I am" (Jn.13:13). He *is* Lord (Ph.2:5-11; cp. 2 Cor.5:21; Heb.1:1-3; 1 Pt.2:24; 3:18).

> **"[The gospel] concerning his Son Jesus Christ our Lord, which was made of the seed of David according to the flesh; and declared to be the Son of God with power, according to the spirit of holiness, by the resurrection from the dead" (Ro.1:3-4).**

2. The great plea of their profession: "Have we not...done many wonderful works?" The works are wonderful, a tremendous help to mankind. But two things are wrong with the profession of their lives: they rest in their works and they embrace only half of the gospel.

"Many will say to me in that day, Lord, Lord, have we not prophesied in thy name? and in thy name have cast out devils? and in thy name done many wonderful works? And then will I profess unto them, I never knew you: depart from me, ye that work iniquity" (Mt.7:22-23).

"Therefore by the deeds of the law there shall no flesh be justified in his sight: for by the law is the knowledge of sin" (Ro.3:20).

3. The great plea of confidence: "Lord, Lord, have we not [done these works] in thy name?" "Lord, You know...You know." But they are deceived. Confidence in self is not God's way. God's way is confidence in Christ and His righteousness.

"For they being ignorant of God's righteousness, and going about to establish their own righteousness, have not submitted themselves unto the righteousness of God" (Ro.10:3).

APPLICATION:
The pleas are strong pleas.
⇒ to preach, teach, predict, or bear witness in Christ's name is good
⇒ to cast out evil spirits or turn men from evil and the evil one is good
⇒ to do any one of many great works (listed in note Mt.7:21) is good
⇒ to do all "in the Lord's name," to profess to live and do all their works for Him, is good
⇒ to do honor to the name "Christian" and have a good reputation among men is good
⇒ to be dedicated to the church and be of service to mankind and society is good
⇒ to be a leader in the church and society is good

Society asks, "What is their lack? Where in the world do they come short?"

"This is His commandment, that we should believe on the name of His Son Jesus Christ, and love one another" (1 Jn.3:23).

God's will is a two-edged sword: it is not only *loving one another*, that is, preaching and teaching and doing many wonderful works. It is first, "that we should believe on the name of His Son Jesus Christ." To believe is not only believing in the wonderful works that He did, but believing in *who He is and all that He did* including the cross and the resurrection.

ILLUSTRATION:
A person can say all the right things, know all the correct answers, perform every religious ritual and still be lost. Our salvation is not based upon how good we are but upon how right we are with God.

"In one of his sermons, A. C. Dixon told of an incident that took place in Brooklyn, New York. A detective who had been looking for a local citizen finally tracked him down in a drugstore. As the man began to make his purchase, the officer laid his hand on the citizen's shoulder and said, 'You're under arrest; come with me!' Stunned, the man demanded, 'What did I do?' The detective calmly replied, 'You know what you did. You escaped from the Albany penitentiary several years ago. You went west, got married, and then came back here to live. We've been watching for you since you returned.' Quietly the man admitted, 'That's true, but I was sure you'd never find me. Before you take me in, could we stop by my house so I can talk to my family?' The officer agreed. When they got to his home, the man *looked at his wife and asked, 'Haven't I been a kind husband and a good father? Haven't I worked hard to make a living?' His wife answered, 'Of course you have, but why are you asking me these questions?' Her husband then proceeded to explain what had happened and that he was now under arrest. He apparently had hoped that his record as an exemplary husband and father would impress the officer. Even so, he was still an escaped criminal and he would have to return to prison. Though he was 'right' with his family, he was all wrong with the state of New York."*[1]

It will do you no good to be right with everyone but wrong with God. Are you right with God?

QUESTIONS:
1. If you spent your life doing good works with the right motives, not seeking recognition, would that be enough to gain entrance into heaven? Why are works just insufficient to make you acceptable to God?
2. Many, many people are expecting to get into heaven because of their works. How can you know if someone has this expectation? What is your obligation toward these people?

3. THE REJECTION OF FALSE PROFESSION (v.23).

The rejection of false profession is for two reasons.
1. False professors do not know Christ personally; they do not acknowledge His redemption and their need for His redemptive power. They never come to Him for personal salvation. Therefore, Christ never has the chance to know them. In the Day of Judgment, He is tragically forced to pronounce the truth: "I never knew you" (Mt.10:32; Jn.3:18 cp. 3:16-18).

> **"But he answered and said, Verily I say unto you, I know you not"**
> **(Mt.25:12).**

2. False professors only work iniquity. The word *iniquity* means lawlessness, wickedness. It is neglect of or opposition to the law of God; it is substituting the will of self in the place of God's will (1 Jn.3:4). It is looking to self or to the world instead of looking to God. It is following the course of self and the desires of self instead of following the course of God.

> **"And then will I profess unto them, I never knew you: depart from me,**
> **ye that work iniquity" (Mt.7:23).**

APPLICATION 1:
Judgment is to be public: before the many who are pleading, "Lord, Lord." The *many* will have to depart from God's presence--to go away and be cut off from Him, leaving the place where He is. No matter what man may think (in his small world and short life), Christ said the day is coming when He shall say to *many*: "Depart from me."

> **"But the children of the kingdom shall be cast out into outer darkness: there shall be weeping and gnashing of teeth" (Mt.8:12).**

---

[1] *INFOsearch Sermon Illustrations* (Arlington, TX: The Computer Assistant, 1-888-868-9029, 1986-1996).

APPLICATION 2:

Why are *many* to be cut off from Christ? How can anyone who does *good* in the eyes of men be called "a worker of iniquity"? Very simply, "man shall not live by bread [the physical] alone." To stress only the physical, mental, and moral strength of man, even if they are stressed in religious terms, is to miss the gospel.

But there is a message in the word "depart"--a message that can save us. "Let everyone that nameth the name of Christ depart from iniquity" (2 Tim.2:19). There is still time to come to Christ.

ILLUSTRATION:

The most important thing a person can do is make absolutely certain his relationship with God is right. The person who has made peace with God looks forward to getting to heaven, to being with the Lord and his whole family of believers. On the other hand, the person who is not known by Christ is on a lonely and terrifying journey that will end in death--eternal death--eternal separation from God, from loved ones, from any thing that is good or peaceful or comforting.

"Toward the close of World War II, a soldier, who had spent more than three years in the South Pacific, sat in a railway coach with a look of joyous anticipation on his face! The train was speeding toward Chicago. 'How fast are we traveling?' asked the soldier.... '...we are making about 105 miles an hour!' the porter answered. 'How far are we from Chicago?' asked the soldier. 'A little over a hundred miles, Sir.' 'We can't get there too quickly,' said the soldier as he took his duffel bag and bundles from the overhead rack. 'I'm going to be the first one off this train!'

"Why was he so eager to reach his destination? His father, mother, brothers, sisters, friends, and sweetheart were all waiting to welcome him!

"There was another serviceman in that same coach. His face looked like a blown-out lamp. He was a picture of gloom and dejection. He was in handcuffs and in [the] charge of military policemen. He was not eager to reach his destination, for only judgment and punishment for crime awaited him there. There would be no friends or loved ones to greet him.

"Do you look forward with joy to your home-going? Will you be received 'into [an] everlasting [home]...,' and be 'forever with the Lord,' and with loved ones in glory? Or do you look forward with fear to meeting the One whose love you spurned, and whose mercy and forgiveness you rejected?'"[2]

QUESTIONS:
1. Do you feel like you know God well enough? Can you ever know God too well? What is the key to having your relationship with Christ grow even more?
2. One of the greatest tragedies imaginable will be when a loved one or friend is rejected by Christ. Knowing that this day is coming, what impact should this have upon the intensity of your prayers?

SUMMARY:

There will be no one in heaven who gets there on the basis of what he says or the good works that he does. Every person who gets to heaven will be there because of the shed blood of Jesus Christ and His atoning work on the cross.
1. The law of entrance.
2. The plea of false profession: works.
3. The rejection of false profession.

---

2 Walter B. Knight. *Knight's Treasury of 2,000 Illustrations*, p.156-157.

MATTHEW 7:21-23

PERSONAL JOURNAL NOTES:
(Reflection & Response)

1. The most important thing that I learned from this lesson was:

2. The thing that I need to work on the most is:

3. I can apply this lesson to my life by:

4. Closing Prayer of Commitment: (put your commitment down on paper).

1. A wise builder: Hears the instructions & obeys them	Y. The Wise & Foolish Builder, 7:24-27 (Lk.6:47-49)	fell not: for it was founded upon a rock.	2. A foolish builder: Hears the instructions & does not obey them
a. He builds a house	24 Therefore whosoever heareth these sayings of mine, and doeth them, I will liken him unto a wise man, which built his house upon a rock:	26 And every one that heareth these sayings of mine, and doeth them not, shall be likened unto a foolish man, which built his house upon the sand:	a. He builds a house
b. He builds upon a rock			b. He builds upon the sand
c. He faces a storm	25 And the rain descended, and the floods came, and the winds blew, and beat upon that house; and it	27 And the rain descended, and the floods came, and the winds blew, and beat upon that house; and it fell: and great was the fall of it.	c. He faces a storm
d. He built wisely: The difference is the foundation			d. He built foolishly: Suffers great destruction—the difference is the foundation

Section IV
THE TEACHINGS OF THE MESSIAH TO HIS DISCIPLES:
THE GREAT SERMON ON THE MOUNT
Matthew 5:1-7:29

Study 25:   THE WISE AND FOOLISH BUILDER

Text: Matthew 7:24-27

Aim: To be sure--absolutely sure--that your life is built upon a solid foundation, a foundation that will stand the harshest storms of life.

Memory Verse:
> "Therefore whosoever heareth these sayings of mine, and doeth them, I will liken him unto a wise man, which built his house upon a rock" (Matthew 7:24).

INTRODUCTION:

One of the world's most famous landmarks is the Leaning Tower of Pisa. Construction on the tower began in 1174 but was halted when the builders noticed that the soft, marshy soil would not be able to support the foundation. As the years went by, other builders continued the work and eventually finished the tower before the end of the 14th century. Scientists report that the tower moves about one-twentieth of an inch a year. Observed by the natural eye, the 179 foot Leaning Tower of Pisa looks unchanged from day to day. But the scientific measurements do not lie. One day the priceless tower, because of its weak foundation, is going to fall. The spiritual application is clear. Unless our foundation is firm, solidly based, everything built upon it will eventually fall to ruin.

Jesus Christ knew the building trade. He was a carpenter by trade and profession. For that reason He knew houses. Several important matters about building a house need to be noted here.

1. Hearing instructions. This is critical, for a person must heed the instructions in order to know *how* to build the house.

    a. A person must hear and follow (obey) the instructions.

    b. A person must hear, then build upon what he hears, using the best materials and the safest methods for construction. Builders must always be "laying up in store for themselves a good foundation against the time to come...." (1 Tim. 6:19).

2. Selecting the foundation. This is also critical, for selecting the site and material determine the future of the house.

    a. A person must build upon a solid foundation. There is only one foundation upon which to build: the rock (1 Cor.3:11).

    b. A person must make sure of his call and choice to build (2 Pt.1:10).

    c. A person must know that building upon rock takes time and skill.

3. Counting the cost. This, too, is critical: it is brought out by Christ in another passage. Beginning and not finishing the house brings mockery and shame (Lk.14:28-30).

Several introductory applications are clearly seen in this picture of house building.

1. Every person has a house (a life) to build. How he builds his life determines his destiny, not just for this life but for eternity. How he builds his life makes all the difference...

- between success and failure
- between life and death
- between reward and loss
- between acceptance and rejection
- between standing and falling

2. There is only one Foundation for every life: Jesus Christ (1 Cor.3:11). He is the Rock upon which both individuals and churches are to build (Mt.16:18).

3. Everyone builds his life either upon this world or upon Christ (heaven itself). Jesus teaches there are two kinds of builders.

OUTLINE:

1. A wise builder: hears the instructions and obeys them (v.24-25).
2. A foolish builder: hears the instructions and does not obey them (v.26-27).

1. A WISE BUILDER: HEARS THE INSTRUCTIONS AND OBEYS THEM (v.24-25).

1. The wise builder builds a house.

    a. Every person has a house to build, a life to build. Once in the world we cannot escape the fact--we are building our lives. How we build our lives determines our eternal destiny.

    b. God's own Son instructs a man how to build. A man hears and follows (obeys) the instructions or hears and rejects (disobeys) the instructions and builds his own way.

    c. As Christ says, His *sayings*, instructions, and words are the materials which determine the structure and fate of our lives. Our lives and our destinies depend upon how we respond to the *sayings* of Christ.

APPLICATION:

    Every man is put into one of two classes by Christ. There is the class of men called "wise" and there is the class of men called "foolish." How we build our lives determines in which class we are placed.

    Note: both builders *hear* and receive the instructions. This means Christ is talking about people who...

- are in the church
- have Christian friends
- have Christian parents
- have a source of some Christian influence

2. The wise builder builds upon a rock.

    a. Christ is the only Rock, the only Foundation upon which we can build and structure our lives.

        "For other foundation can no man lay than that is laid, which is Jesus Christ" (1 Cor.3:11).

        "And are built upon the foundation of the apostles and prophets, Jesus Christ himself being the chief corner stone" (Eph.2:20).

b. The Lord is not a lifeless rock but "a living stone" (1 Pt.2:4). When we come to Him as "a living stone" we are "built up a spiritual house" (1 Pt.2:2-5). What does this mean?
⇒ We are to thirst after His Word; We are to "desire the sincere milk of the Word"
⇒ We grow through His Word
⇒ We taste that the Lord is gracious through His Word
⇒ We come to the Lord through His Word
⇒ We are built up through His Word

Our lives and destinies are determined by what we do with the Word, the *sayings* of the Lord Jesus.

"As newborn babes, desire the sincere milk of the word, that ye may grow thereby: if so be ye have tasted that the Lord is gracious. To whom coming, as unto a living stone, disallowed indeed of men, but chosen of God, and precious, ye also, as lively stones, are built up a spiritual house, an holy priesthood, to offer up spiritual sacrifices, acceptable to God by Jesus Christ" (1 Pt.2:2-5).

APPLICATION 1:
Building upon the rock takes time and commitment and energy. We have to deny ourselves, sacrifice, and apply ourselves ever so diligently.

APPLICATION 2:
The man who builds upon the Rock is wise: prudent and sensible (Pr.16:21). He knows several things.
1) Where he has come from (his instructions).
2) Why he is here (to build an excellent house).
3) Where he is going (the kind of house or life he should build). He sees the finished product by faith and hope.

3. The wise builder faces a storm. There have always been storms in life and there always will be. The wise man is not exempt from the storms just because he builds an excellent house. In fact, the major reason for building a solid house is to assure that he will be able to weather all storms. It rains "on the just and on the unjust" (Mt.5:45).

"That ye may be the children of your Father which is in heaven: for he maketh his sun to rise on the evil and on the good, and sendeth rain on the just and on the unjust" (Mt.5:45).

APPLICATION:
All kinds of rain and storms come. There are storms of...

• sin	• sickness	• tension	• temptation	• disappointment
• pain	• sorrow	• poverty	• mistreatment	• loneliness
• death	• neglect	• emotion	• accident	• suffering
• stress	• disease	• rejection	• handicaps	• misunderstanding
• loss	• pressure	• gossip	• complaint	
• abuse	• doubt	• failure	• hospitalization	

4. The wise builder built wisely: the difference is the foundation. One thing alone determines if a man is *truly wise*: the kind of foundation he lays in this life.

"Laying up in store for themselves a good foundation against the time to come, that they may lay hold on eternal life" (1 Tim. 6:19).

APPLICATION 1:

If a person builds his life upon Christ, he never falls, no matter the severity of the storm. This reason is clearly seen in the promises of God.

1) God accepts us in Christ (the beloved, Eph.1:6); He adopts us as His children.

"But when the fulness of the time was come, God sent forth his Son, made of a woman, made under the law, to redeem them that were under the law, that we might receive the adoption of sons. And because ye are sons, God hath sent forth the Spirit of his Son into your hearts, crying, Abba, Father" (Gal.4:4-6).

2) God promises to provide the necessities of life.

"Therefore take no thought, saying, What shall we eat? or, What shall we drink? or, Wherewithal shall we be clothed? (For after all these things do the Gentiles seek:) for your heavenly Father knoweth that ye have need of all these things. But seek ye first the kingdom of God, and his righteousness; and all these things shall be added unto you" (Mt.6:31-33; cp. Mt.6:25-34).

3) God promises to work all things out for good to those who build wisely.

"And we know that all things work together for good to them that love God, to them who are the called according to his purpose" (Ro.8:28).

4) God blesses those who **"hear the Word of God and keep it" (Lk.11:28).**
5) Christ promises joy to those who hear and receive the things He said.

"These things have I spoken unto you, that my joy might remain in you, and that your joy might be full" (Jn.15:11; cp. Jn.13:17).

6) The Lord promises to deliver the believer into His heavenly kingdom when the believer passes from this world into the next.

"And the Lord shall deliver me from every evil work, and will preserve me unto his heavenly kingdom: to whom be glory for ever and ever" (2 Tim.4:18).

APPLICATION 2:

"The wise in heart" shall receive more and more instructions from the Lord. His life shall be directed day by day through all the storms of life, even through eternity (Pr.10:8; Jn.16:13-15; Heb.13:5).

ILLUSTRATION:

When a person builds a house for you, you want to make sure he is using the best materials you can afford. You want the person who builds your house to obey the local building codes and not take short-cuts. Cheaper materials and short-cuts might save you money now but could cost you everything in the future.

"David Culver tells of watching a TV news report showing the destruction in southern Florida after Hurricane Andrew:
"In one scene, amid the devastation and debris stood one house on its foundation. The owner was cleaning up the yard when a reporter approached him.

> *"'Sir, why is your house the only one still standing?' the reporter asked. 'How did you manage to escape the severe damage of the hurricane?'*
>
> *"'I built this house myself,' the man replied. 'I built it according to the Florida state building code. When the code called for 2x6 roof trusses, I used 2x6 roof trusses. I was told that a house built according to code could withstand a hurricane. I did and it did! I suppose no one else around here followed the code.'*
>
> *"When the sun is shining and the skies are blue, building our lives on something other than the guidelines in God's Word can be tempting, but there's a hurricane coming--for everyone."*[1]

Will your spiritual house stand when the storms of life come your way?

QUESTIONS:
1. Every person has a life, a house, to build. Up to this point, how would you describe the house you are building:
    _____A shanty that shakes every time the wind blows
    _____A duplex: on one side I live for the Lord and on the other side I live for the world
    _____A single-family dwelling where Jesus Christ is the head of my home
2. In practical terms, what does it actually mean to build your house upon the Rock?
3. Think back over your life for a moment. What were some of the fiercest storms you have had to endure? What enabled you to survive these storms?
4. What are some the many benefits of building your life upon Christ?

2. A FOOLISH BUILDER: HEARS THE INSTRUCTIONS AND DOES NOT OBEY THEM (v.26-27).

1. The foolish builder builds a house, but note something of critical *importance and interest*.
    a. He hears the instructions of the Master Builder. This means he is in the church and he has some Christian influence from someplace. He receives the seed, the Word, through church, parents, radio, books, friends, tapes, or television (Mt.13:4).
    b. He is in a most dangerous position. He knows how to build, but he chooses not to build according to instructions. How foolish not to follow instructions when building a house!

    "He that trusteth in his riches shall fall: but the righteous shall flourish as a branch" (Pr.11:28).
    "He that trusteth in his own heart is a fool: but whoso walketh wisely, he shall be delivered" (Pr.28:26).

APPLICATION:
    The counsel is clear: "Hear counsel, and receive instruction, that thou mayest be wise in thy latter end" (Pr.19:20). There is no middle ground. Once we hear, we either build wisely (obey) or build foolishly (disobey).
    There are those who hear time and again, get up and go out, and still do not follow the instructions of the Master Builder.

2. The foolish builder builds upon sand. This is the depth of foolishness, as Christ well illustrates. Imagine a man building a house. He knows how to build it; he knows that he

---

[1] *Leadership Journal*. Wint.1993, p. 49. As cited in *INFOsearch Sermon Illustrations* (Arlington, TX: The Computer Assistant, 1-888-868-9029, 1986-1996).

should build it upon rock. But he goes out and builds it upon sand. The sand is anything other than Christ (1 Cor.3:11; cp. 1 Jn.2:15-16; 2 Cor.6:17-18).

⇒ There is the sand of the world, the material possessions and wealth of the world.
⇒ There is the sand of the flesh, the pleasures that stimulate and satisfy it.
⇒ There is the sand of fame and recognition and the pride of it.

Any honest and thinking person knows that sand cannot withstand serious storms either in this life or in the life to come. Therefore, any life built upon sand is doomed to collapse.

> "How shall we escape, if we neglect so great salvation; which at the first began to be spoken by the Lord, and was confirmed unto us by them that heard him" (Heb.2:3).

APPLICATION 1:
Tragedy! This man heard what the prophets and righteous men of old desired to hear (Mt.13:17; 1 Pt.1:10). What a privilege he had, but what an abuse of privilege--to receive the instructions (the grace of God) in vain (2 Cor.6:1). Week after week, year after year he heard, yet he never followed the instructions on how to build his life.

> "For verily I say unto you, That many prophets and righteous men have desired to see those things which ye see, and have not seen them; and to hear those things which ye hear, and have not heard them" (Mt.13:17).

APPLICATION 2:
The foolish builder is like the man who receives the seed "by the wayside." He is in church, under some proper (Christian) instruction about how to build his life. But he is *off to the side*. He deliberately puts himself there. And he refuses to receive the instruction (Word). He refuses to be stirred or warned, ignoring and neglecting the instructions and warnings.

APPLICATION 3:
Even religion can be sinking sand if a person thinks *being good* and *going good* is good enough!

> "Not every one that saith unto me, Lord, Lord, shall enter into the kingdom of heaven; but he that doeth the will of my Father which is in heaven. Many will say to me in that day, Lord, Lord, have we not prophesied in thy name? and in thy name have cast out devils? and in thy name done many wonderful works? And then will I profess unto them, I never knew you: depart from me, ye that work iniquity" (Mt.7:21-23).

APPLICATION 4:
Many hear, but few are willing to heed. There are many foolish builders and only a few wise builders. A hearer only deceives himself. The doer is the man who is to be blessed. He will withstand the storms of life and judgment.

> "Enter ye in at the strait gate: for wide is the gate, and broad is the way, that leadeth to destruction, and many there be which go in thereat: because strait is the gate, and narrow is the way, which leadeth unto life, and few there be that find it" (Mt.7:13-14).
>
> "But be ye doers of the word, and not hearers only, deceiving your own selves. For if any be a hearer of the word, and not a doer, he is like unto a man beholding his natural face in a glass: for he beholdeth himself, and goeth his way, and straightway forgetteth what manner of man he was. But whoso looketh into the perfect law of liberty, and

continueth therein, he being not a forgetful hearer, but a doer of the work, this man shall be blessed in his deed" (Jas.1:22-25).

APPLICATION 5:

There are many who profess loyalty and respect (even love) for the Master Builder, yet they go right on building their way, as they will.

"And they come unto thee as the people cometh, and they sit before thee as my people, and they hear thy words, but they will not do them: for with their mouth they show much love, but their heart goeth after their covetousness. And, lo, thou art unto them as a very lovely song of one that hath a pleasant voice, and can play well on an instrument: for they hear thy words, but they do them not" (Ezk.33:31-32).

3. The foolish builder faces a storm. The fact is clear and descriptive, easily pictured.
   a. "The rain descended." Pellets of rain or trials do fall upon men. No man stops them. Sometimes the rain or trials fall slowly and in small drops; sometimes they fall rapidly and in large drops. The house built upon the sand is eroded away by both the rains and the trials of life.
   b. "The floods came." Floods of trials do come against us. The floods cannot be stopped. The house built upon sand cannot stand. The sand is washed away by the floods of trials.
   c. "The winds blew." The winds of trial do blow against us and no man can stop them. The force ranges from small to great, and no matter how much they are dreaded or feared, they come with whatever force nature packs. Again, the house built upon the sand has its foundation blown away by the winds of trial.

APPLICATION:

Every man faces the rains and storms of life. They wait upon no man, prepared or not. A terrible storm is coming at death, and in the Great Day of Judgment, a storm against which no man can stand unless he is held up by Christ (Joel 2:31; Mt.24:51; 25:30, 46).

4. The foolish builder built foolishly: there was great destruction--the difference was the foundation. The house fell. If we do not follow the Lord's sayings, His instructions, we will see our house fall and collapse. The trials of this life and the great trial to come will beat upon our house and condemn it to destruction: "And great was the fall of it."

APPLICATION 1:

Every man's work shall be made manifest. Our work is to be tested in this life through many trials, and in the next life by Christ. Great will be "the fall" of our lives if they are not built upon Christ. The man who built his house upon sand *will have to face* Christ in that day (1 Cor.3:13). The man who builds on sand is without hope.

"What is the hope of the hypocrite...when God taketh away his soul?" (Job 27:8).
"The hypocrite's hope shall perish....he shall lean upon his house, but it shall not stand" (Job 8:13, 15).

APPLICATION 2:

When do we need a solid house the most? Isn't it when the winds begin to blow and the storms come? But note: when the storm begins, it is too late to build the house. How tragic: to build and then experience the collapse of our lives when the storms come!

Storms can come anytime, anywhere. They can come today: through accident, through death, through some other tragedy--whatever. The day is coming when it will be too late to build.

ILLUSTRATION:

Everyone who has suffered loss from a storm because of lack of preparation has the same excuse: I didn't think it would happen to me. Or as one person said, "It was just never convenient."

"A heavy rain had been falling as a man drove down a lonely road. As he rounded a curve, he saw an old farmer surveying the ruins of his barn. The driver stopped his car and asked what had happened. 'Roof fell in,' said the farmer. 'Leaked so long it finally just rotted through.' 'Why in the world didn't you fix it before it got that bad?' asked the stranger. 'Well, sir,' replied the farmer, 'it just seemed I never did get around to it. When the weather was good, there weren't no need for it, and when it rained, it was too wet to work on!'"

Don't wait for the storms to come before you prepare your life--it might be too late to repair!

QUESTIONS:

1. The foolish builder builds upon sand. What does this person place his trust in? Have you ever been guilty of doing the same?
2. What conclusion would you come to if the person who built your house ignored your instructions? How do you think God feels when people scorn His building plans?
3. When the storms of life come, what options does the person have who has built his house on sand? Is it too late to start over? Is there any hope at all?

SUMMARY:

What kind of life are you building? God has given every person a unique opportunity to build something that will last for eternity. God has given the plans and everything that is needed to build your life. The only thing God has not done is decide for you. Every person must decide for himself whether to listen and obey or go his own way. Which kind of builder are you?
1. A wise builder: hears the instructions and obeys them.
2. A foolish builder: hears the instructions and does not obey them.

PERSONAL JOURNAL NOTES:
(Reflection & Response)

1. The most important thing that I learned from this lesson was:

2. The thing that I need to work on the most is:

3. I can apply this lesson to my life by:

4. Closing Prayer of Commitment: (put your commitment down on paper).

---

2   *INFOsearch Sermon Illustrations* (Arlington, TX: The Computer Assistant, 1-888-868-9029, 1986-1996).

	Z. The Teaching of Jesus & Its Impact, 7:28-29
1. The impact: The people were amazed	28 And it came to pass, when Jesus had ended these sayings, the people were astonished at his doctrine:
2. The reason: Jesus taught with authority	29 For he taught them as one having authority, and not as the scribes.

Section IV
THE TEACHINGS OF THE MESSIAH TO HIS DISCIPLES:
THE GREAT SERMON ON THE MOUNT
Matthew 5:1-7:29

Study 26: **THE TEACHING OF JESUS AND ITS IMPACT**

Text: **Matthew 7:28-29**

Aim: To accept the authority of Christ as Supreme and understand why His teachings are so invaluable to man.

Memory Verse:
> "For he [Jesus] taught them as one having authority, and not as the scribes" (Matthew 7:28).

INTRODUCTION:
Do you remember who your favorite teachers were when you were in school? What made them your favorite teachers?
- ⇒ Was it *what* they taught?
- ⇒ Was it *how* they taught?
- ⇒ Was it how they *looked*?
- ⇒ Was it because they were *interesting*?
- ⇒ Was it because they were *easy to understand*?
- ⇒ Was it because they were *teaching your favorite subject*?

We owe a great debt of gratitude to people who invest so much time and energy and so much of themselves into our lives. But as great as our favorite teachers were, not one of them can compare with the greatest teacher of them all--our Lord Jesus Christ.

No one has ever taught like Jesus. In fact, He was such a strong teacher that many who deny His deity still commit their lives to the ministry of His teaching. Few deny the strength of His ability as a teacher and the strength of His ethics. In addition to these, there are those who believe that Jesus is truly the Son of God. To these, there is no one who compares to Jesus as a person or teacher.

OUTLINE:
1. The impact: the people were amazed (v.28).
2. The reason: Jesus taught with authority (v.29).

1. THE IMPACT: THE PEOPLE WERE AMAZED (v.28).

The impact of Jesus' teaching is forcibly stated, "The people were astonished," that is, amazed. Note several facts.

1. Jesus was compelled to preach and teach, no matter who the audience was. He reached out to everyone who would listen. His compulsion is a dynamic example for all believers.

> **"Even as the Son of man came not to be ministered unto, but to minister, and to give his life a ransom for many" (Mt.20:28).**

2. Multitudes of people were astonished. But note: those astonished were not the religionists, the wealthy, and the ruling class, but the common people. Too often the wealthy and those with position feel threatened by Christ. They fear that discipleship might cost them something. And it will, for Jesus Christ demands *all that a person is and has.*

> **"And fear not them which kill the body, but are not able to kill the soul: but rather fear him which is able to destroy both soul and body in hell" (Mt.10:28).**

3. All that is said about the people is that they were astonished. There is a big difference between being astonished and doing what Jesus says, between hearing and doing, between profession and true discipleship.

Astonishing the audience was not what Jesus was after. He had already conquered the threat of this enticement when tempted by Satan. What He was after was their lives, their commitment, a change of behavior. Being astonished just is not enough. We must follow Christ. There is nothing wrong with being amazed at the teaching of Christ; most people are. But the point and purpose of His teaching is obedience to God's will (Mt.7:21).

> **"Not every one that saith unto me, Lord, Lord, shall enter into the kingdom of heaven; but he that doeth the will of my Father which is in heaven. Many will say to me in that day, Lord, Lord, have we not prophesied in thy name? and in thy name have cast out devils? and in thy name done many wonderful works? And then will I profess unto them, I never knew you: depart from me, ye that work iniquity" (Mt.7:21-23).**

ILLUSTRATION:

Jesus Christ did not come to the world to impress anyone. His purpose for coming was to seek lost men and save them, exhorting them to obey God's will. But Christ's message will move any audience to amazement, especially when a person realizes what Christ has done for him.

> *"A valuable painting had been purchased by F. W. Boreham called 'The Chess Player.' It portrayed Satan playing the game with a young opponent, and the man's soul was at stake. The game had progressed to the point where it was the novice's turn, and there seemed to be no move he could make that would not mean defeat for him. Awful despair was on his face as he realized his soul was lost, and Satan was grinning as he anticipated victory. A champion player who had come to view the canvas studied the picture for a time and then called for a chessboard. Placing the pieces in exactly the same position as in the painting, he said, 'I'll take the young*

man's place.' He then made a move that showed how the devil's captive could have won and been set free. "[1]

Nothing could be more amazing than when Christ came to earth as a man, taught and showed us how to live, and then took our place when facing the toughest opponent of all--the cross. That is truly amazing!

QUESTIONS:
1. To you, what are some of the most astonishing things Christ has said and why?
2. Many people on earth speak amazing and astonishing things. Why are astonishing words not enough to prove who a person is? What is the difference with Jesus Christ?

2. THE REASON: JESUS TAUGHT WITH AUTHORITY (v.29).

The reason the people were amazed is that Jesus taught with authority. This probably means several things.
1. He spoke with a tone that sounded authoritative.
2. He spoke as the true Messiah, a Person who had the right to dictate laws, give commandments, and expect obedience.
3. He spoke in the power of the Holy Spirit. As He spoke, the Spirit of God moved in the hearts of those who believed Him to be the Messiah. When Christ teaches there is always an attraction, a draw, a pull to Him.

> **"And I, if I be lifted up from the earth, will draw all men unto me" (Jn.12:32).**

In contrast to Christ, the Scribes did not speak or teach with authority. This was most unusual, for they actually had as much authority backing them as any group of teachers in history. They not only had the Holy Scriptures, but they also had the oral tradition and the influence of their religion, as well as their personal commitment to it.
Their problem was twofold.
   a. They were always calling upon other authorities--always referring to the source of their statements. This tended to lose their audiences.
   b. They seldom elaborated or illustrated. This made their messages or lessons flat, dull, and uninteresting.

APPLICATION:
The major reason Jesus was able to speak with authority was that He was the Son of God. Everything He did was with the authority of God.

> **"And Jesus came and spake unto them, saying, All power is given unto me in heaven and in earth" (Mt.28:18).**

ILLUSTRATION:
Every believer needs to be able to speak with authority. There are far too many people who want to apologize for what they believe. David Halbrook, a staff member of Promise Keepers, relates this personal incident.

---

[1] *INFOsearch Sermon Illustrations* (Arlington, TX: The Computer Assistant, 1-888-868-9029, 1986-1996).

"The Flat Rock Cafe was empty when I arrived for a late dinner on the opening night of the Promise Keepers' conference at Boise State University. The cook behind the counter eyed my green staff shirt and ID badge. Serving up a plate, he asked in an offhand manner, 'So what's with all these guys here this weekend? What is Promise Keepers?'

"With practiced diplomacy, I began to explain that Promise Keepers is a Christ-centered ministry devoted to uniting men through vital relationships to become godly men. He interrupted, 'Why Christ? Why is it that all you Christians think that Jesus is the only way?' It was a startling question, yet I was excited by an unforeseen opportunity to share the gospel.

"I put my plate down and, in my warmest tone, began to explain why and how I came to my faith. What followed were several minutes of spirited debate, encompassing the spectrum of objections to Christ. Ultimately, nothing between us was settled. With some resignation, I encouraged him to keep searching and, with an open heart, asking God for the truth.

"At this a slight grin appeared on the cook's face. 'That's good', he replied. 'But the next time someone asks you about Buddha or Mohammed, tell them to examine who they said they were, and who Christ said He is. It'll bring them to an intellectual crisis.'

"I stood there stunned, until it hit me that this grinning cook was a Christian. 'You'd be surprised how many brothers and sisters have no explanation for their faith,' he explained. 'Iron sharpens iron, right?' As we stood laughing, it struck me how rare and special such encounters are. It heightened my awareness of the crucial role brothers have in honing one another's spiritual edges. Moreover, it reminded me of the importance of having a ready answer for the hope that is within us."[2]

QUESTIONS:
1. Why is it important for you as a Christian believer to speak with authority about your faith? How do you balance this with being meek and humble? Where does your authority come from?
2. If you do not speak of your relationship with Christ in a convincing and believable manner, how is your message received? Does this mean you have to memorize great portions of Scripture? What is the key to conveying the true gospel message?

A CLOSER LOOK # 1

(7:29) **Scribes**: the Scribes were a profession of men sometimes called lawyers. They were some of the most devoted and committed men to religion in all of history, and were of the sect known as the Pharisees. However, every Pharisee was not a Scribe. A Scribe was more of a scholar, more highly trained than the average Pharisee. They had two primary functions.

1. The Scribes copied the written law, the Old Testament Scriptures. In their copying function they were strict copiers, meticulously keeping count of every letter in every word. This exactness was necessary, for God Himself had given the written law to the Jewish nation. Therefore, the law was not only the very Word of God, it was the greatest thing in the life of the Jewish nation. It was considered the most precious possession in all the world; consequently, the Jewish nation was committed to the preservation of the law (Neh.8:1-8). A young Jew could enter no greater profession than the profession of Scribes.

---

2 *Men of Action*, Jan 1996, p. 2. As cited in *INFOsearch Sermon Illustrations* (Arlington, TX: The Computer Assistant, 1-888-868-9029, 1986-1996).

2. The Scribes studied, classified, and taught the moral law. This function brought about the Oral or Scribal Law that was so common in Jesus' day. It was the law of rules and regulations. There were, in fact, so many regulations that over fifty large volumes were required when they were finally put into writing. The great tragedy was that through the centuries, the Jews began to place the Oral law over the written law.

The Scribes felt that the law was God's final word. Everything God wanted man to do could be deduced from it; therefore, they drew out of the law every possible rule they could and insisted that life was to be lived in conformity to these rules. Rules were to be a way of life, the preoccupation of a man's thoughts. At first these rules and regulations were taught by word of mouth; however, in the third century after Christ they were put into certain writings.

The Halachoth: rules that were to govern the ritual of worship.

The Talmud: made up of two parts.
  ⇒ The Mishnah: sixty-three discussions of various subjects of the law.
  ⇒ Germara: the sacred legends of the people.

Midrashim: the commentaries on the writings.

Hagada: thoughts on the commentaries.

QUESTIONS:

1. The Scribes had a real respect for the written law--every word of it. In one sense, we can learn from them. But what caution do we need to take in studying God's law?
2. What is the difference between the written law and the oral law? What are the dangers of equating the two laws?

SUMMARY:

The greatest teacher in the world was Jesus Christ. His teaching bridges every period of time, every generation of man, and every society in the world. Although many people think they can do a better job than Christ did, no one can improve on Christ's teachings. But we can learn from His great example:
1. The impact: the people were amazed.
2. The reason: Jesus taught with authority.

PERSONAL JOURNAL NOTES:
(Reflection & Response)

1. The most important thing that I learned from this lesson was:

2. The thing that I need to work on the most is:

3. I can apply this lesson to my life by:

4. Closing Prayer of Commitment: (put your commitment down on paper).

OUTLINE & SUBJECT INDEX

MATTHEW, Volume 1

(Chapters 1-7)

OUTLINE & SUBJECT INDEX

MATTHEW, Volume 1

(Chapters 1-7)

REMEMBER: When you look up a subject and turn to the Scripture reference, you have not only the Scripture, you have <u>an outline and a discussion</u> (commentary) of the Scripture and subject.

This is one of the <u>GREAT VALUES</u> of the <u>Teacher's Outline & Study Bible</u>. Once you have all the volumes, you will have not only what all other Bible indexes give you, that is, a list of all the subjects and their Scripture references, <u>BUT</u> you will also have...

- An outline of <u>every</u> Scripture and subject in the Bible.
- A discussion (commentary) on every Scripture and subject.
- Every subject supported by other Scriptures or cross references.

<u>DISCOVER THE GREAT VALUE</u> for yourself. Quickly glance below to the very first subject of the Index of Second Timothy. It is:

<u>ADULTERY</u>
Acts of: four.   Mt.5:28

Turn to the reference. Glance at the Scripture and outline of the Scripture, then read the commentary. You will immediately see the GREAT VALUE of the INDEX of the <u>Teacher's Outline & Study Bible</u>.

OUTLINE AND SUBJECT INDEX

ADULTERY
Acts of: four. 5:28
Commandment against. Reasons for. 5:27
Culprits. Hands and eyes. 5:28
Discussed. 5:28
Duty of the **a.** To pluck out, cut off. 5:27-30
Grounds for divorce. 5:31-32
Is committed.
   By looking and desiring. 5:27-30
   By marrying a divorced person. 5:31-32
Kinds of **a.** Mental **a.** Desiring and lusting.
   5:27-30
Meaning. 5:28
Misconceptions. **A.** is excusable & acceptable.
   5:27-30
Penalty. Death by stoning. 1:19
Results. Breaks the union of marriage. 5:32

AGNOSTIC
Described. 6:14-15

ALMS
Meaning. 6:1

AMEN
Meaning. 6:13

ANDREW, THE APOSTLE
A fisherman. 4:18-19
One of the first disciples called by Jesus. 4:18-22

ANGELS
Appearances. To Joseph. 1:18-25
Function toward Christ. To announce His
   conception. 1:20-21

ANGER
Danger of. 5:25
Discussed. 5:21-26
Judgment of. 5:25
Justified **a.** 5:21-22
Kinds. 5:22
Meaning. 5:21-26; 5:21-22
Results of. 5:22; 5:25
View of. World's view of. 5:21-26

OUTLINE & SUBJECT INDEX

OUTLINE & SUBJECT INDEX

OUTLINE & SUBJECT INDEX

OUTLINE & SUBJECT INDEX

OUTLINE & SUBJECT INDEX

Described.
  As narrow gate. 7:13-14
  As two gates, roads. Five **d.** 7:13-14
  As wise & foolish builder. 7:24-27
  Two choices in **l.** 7:13-14
Discussed. More than things. 6:25
Essential - Duty.
  Not to worry about. 6:25
  To build wisely, not foolishly. 7:24-27
Foundation of - Privileges of. Wise vs. foolish.
  7:24-27
Golden rule of. 7:12
How to secure. Building **l.** 7:24-27
Kinds of. Wise vs. foolish. 7:24-27
Mystery to man. 1:23
Righteousness of. 7:12
Storms of. Calmed by Christ. 7:24-25; 7:26-27

LIGHT
Discussed. 5:14
Essential - Duty. To shine for God. 5:14-16
Symbolized. As believers. 5:14-16
What **l.** does. 5:14

LOVE
Discussed. 5:44
  Greek words for **l.** Four words. 5:44
  Essential - Duty. To love enemies. 5:44
  Kinds. Four **k.** 5:44
  Views of **l.** In Old Testament. 5:43

LUST
Concept of. Viewed as acceptable & natural.
  5:27-30
Enslaves. Grows & grows. 5:27-30
Immoral looking, dressing. 5:27-30
Prevention - cure. Discussed. 5:28; 5:30

MAN (See **JUDGMENT; LUST; SIN**; Related
Subjects)
Decision. Chooses between two lives. 7:13-14
Depravity. Shown by cursing. 5:33-37
Errors of - Misconceptions of.
  Seeks recognition. How. Failure of. 6:5
  Setting priorities. Basic priorities. 6:25
  Wrapped up in this world. Reasons. 6:31-32
Nature.
  Esteem. Fails. Several ways. 6:5
  Stature. Cannot be changed. 6:27
  Three things. 5:3
Needs of. (See **NEEDS**)
Response to Christ.
  Disturbed. Reasons. 2:3
  Evil. Some men extremely evil. 2:13-18

Seeking after Jesus. (See **SEEK - SEEKING**)
State of - Present. (See **MAN**, Depravity;
  Nature)
  Five fold **s.** 4:16
Value - worth. More important than birds. Three
  reasons. 6:26

MARRIAGE - MARRIED
Attitudes toward. Loose attitudes. 5:32
Basis. Only one **b.** 5:32
Jewish. Steps involved. Three. 1:18
Kinds of. Fourfold. 5:32
Union of. Weakened & broken by adultery.
  5:32

MASTER
Kinds of **m.** God & world. 6:24

MATERIALISM
Described.
  As a master. 6:24
  As evil. Reasons. 6:21-23
  As necessary & niceties or extravagant. 6:25
Discussed. 6:19-24
Duty.
  Not to be wrapped up in. 6:31-32
  To set mind on God, not on materialism.
    6:19-24
Error of. Four **e.** 6:26
Meaning. 6:19-20
Problems with - Dangers of.
  Are evil. Reasons. 6:21-23
  Are insecure. 6:19-20
  Passes away. 6:25-34
Results.
  Can enslave. 6:25
  Loss of life. Meaning, purpose. 6:19-20
Vs. God. 6:19-24
Warning against. 6:19-24

MEDITATE - MEDITATION
Essential. 3:1
  For preparation & temptation. 4:1
MEEK - MEEKNESS
Meaning. 5:5
Reward. Three **r.** 5:5

MERCY - MERCIFUL (See **GOD**, Mercy)
Meaning. 5:7
Of God. Symbolized. 1:3-6
Results. Seven **r.** 5:7
Women (four) who received **m.** 1:3

MESSAGE (See **PREACHING**)
Content. Summary of Jesus' **m.** 4:17

OUTLINE & SUBJECT INDEX

OUTLINE & SUBJECT INDEX

OBEY - OBEDIENCE
Described. Wise & foolish builders. 7:24-27
Duty. To o. because God expects obedience.
2:13-18
Example. Joseph, father of Jesus. 1:24-25
Reward for. Made great in the Kingdom of
Heaven. 5:19

OFFEND - OFFENDING
Meaning. 5:29

PAMPER
God does not p. 6:25-23

PARABLE
Listed.
Light of the world. Shining for God. 5:14-16
Salt. Serving God. 5:13
Wise and foolish builders. Life. 7:24-27

PASSIONS
Indulgence of. God does not indulge passions.
6:14-15

PEACE
Answer to. Christ. 6:15

PEACEMAKERS
Meaning. 5:9
Vs. Troublemakers. 5:9

PERFECT - PERFECTION
Discussed. 6:5-6

PERSECUTION - PERSECUTORS
Described. Doing evil against. 6:12
Kinds. 5:10-12
Meaning. 5:10-12; 7:7
Response to. Four things believers must do. 6:12
Results. Reveals evil nature of the world. 5:10-12
Why believers are p. Four reasons. 5:10-12

PERSEVERANCE - PERSISTENCE (See
STEDFASTNESS)
Duty to p. In prayer. Meaning. 7:7
Meaning. 7:7

POOR - POVERTY (See **NEED -
NECESSITIES**)
Facts.
Jesus was p. 2:19-23
Not a disgrace. 2:19-23

POOR IN SPIRIT
Meaning. 5:3

POWER - POWERFUL (See **JESUS CHRIST**,
Power)
Lack of - Problems. Tempted to seek. 4:3
Purpose.
To exercise p. over the whole man. 4:24
To heal. 4:24

PRAY - PRAYER - PRAYING
Answers - Answered.
Assured. 7:7-11
Clearly seen. 6:6
Two ways. 7:8
Discussed. 6:5-6; 6:7-8
Duty. Commanded. Several verses. 6:5-6
Essentials.
Forgiveness. 6:14-15
Three e. 6:6
For what. Discussed. 6:9-13
Hindrances to.
Empty repetition. 6:7-8
Hypocritical p. 6:5
Long p. 6:7
Today's problem twofold. 6:7
Unforgiving spirit. 6:14-15
Wrong motive. 6:5-6
How to pray.
Approach God as our Father. 7:11
Basic principle of. Forgiveness. 6:14-15
Discussed. 6:9-13
In secret, in one's closet. 6:6
Three great rules. 6:7-8
Persevering. 7:8-11
Meaning. Talking & sharing with God. 6:5-6
Model p. of Jesus. 6:9-13
Perseverance in. Meaning. 7:7
Purpose. To have one's needs met. 6:8
Results - Assurance.
Where to p. - Places.
Churches & streets. 6:5
Discussed. 6:5-6
Public. 6:5

PREACH - PREACHING
Mission.
Of believers. 4:17
Of Christ. 4:17

PROFANITY (See **CURSING**)

PROFESSION, FALSE - PROFESSION ONLY
Danger of religionists. 3:7-10
Described as. Big "I." 7:21
Discussed. 7:21-23
Two kinds of people. 7:21-23

OUTLINE & SUBJECT INDEX

OUTLINE & SUBJECT INDEX

ILLUSTRATION INDEX

MATTHEW, Volume 1

(Chapters 1-7)

ILLUSTRATION INDEX

ILLUSTRATION INDEX

353

ILLUSTRATION INDEX

ILLUSTRATION INDEX

ILLUSTRATION INDEX

ILLUSTRATION INDEX

PURPOSE STATEMENT

LEADERSHIP MINISTRIES WORLDWIDE

exists to equip ministers, teachers, and laymen in their
understanding, preaching, and teaching of God's Word
by publishing and distributing worldwide
The Preacher's Outline & Sermon Bible®
and related *Outline* Bible materials,
to reach & disciple men, women, boys, and girls for Jesus Christ.

•MISSION STATEMENT•

1. To make the Bible so understandable - its truth so clear and plain - that men
   and women everywhere, whether teacher or student, preacher or hearer,
   can grasp its Message and receive Jesus Christ as Savior; and...
2. To place the Bible in the hands of all who will preach and teach God's Holy
   Word, verse by verse, precept by precept, regardless of the individual's
   ability to purchase it.

The *Outline* Bible materials have been given to LMW for printing and especially
distribution worldwide at/below cost, by those who remain anonymous. One fact,
however, is as true today as it was in the time of Christ:

• The Gospel is free, but the cost of taking it is not •

LMW depends on the generous gifts of Believers with a heart for Him and a love and
burden for the lost. They help pay for the printing, translating, and placing *Outline*
Bible materials in the hands and hearts of those worldwide who will present God's
message with clarity, authority and understanding beyond their own.

LMW was incorporated in the state of Tennessee in July 1992 and received IRS 501(c) 3 nonprofit status in March 1994. LMW is an international, nondenominational mission organization.
All proceeds from USA sales, along with donations from donor partners, go 100% into under-
writing our translation and distribution projects of *Outline* Bible materials to preachers,
church & lay leaders, and Bible students around the world.

5/97 © 1997, Leadership Ministries Worldwide

PO Box 21310 - Chattanooga, TN 37424 • (423) 855-2181 • FAX (423) 855-8616
• E-Mail 74152.616@compuserve.com — Web site: http://www.outlinebible.org •

LEADERSHIP
MINISTRIES
WORLDWIDE

Sharing

The

OUTLINED

BIBLE

With the World!